THE ORIGIN OF MEDITATION

Meditation is to link self with the greater Self. Meditation has no origin and no beginning. It was and has been practiced for aeons.

THE ORIGIN OF MEDITATION

SNEH CHAKRABURTTY

ISBN: 978-81-7822-323-0 (Indian)
ISBN: 0-9730057-4-2 (Canadian)
First Edition: Delhi, 2009

Published by
New Age Books
A-44 Naraina Industrial Area Phase I
New Delhi-110028 (India)
Email: nab@vsnl.in
Website: www.newagebooksindia.com

Printed in India
at Shri Jainendra Press
A-45 Naraina Phase-I, New Delhi-110028

Dedicated to the Master Swami Chinmayananda

Appreciation is felt for my husband
Joti Chandra Chakraburtty and my friend Carolyn Gray
for suggestions during its writing.

Preface

Yoga is the constant union of body and soul, which the traditional body-conscious individual is unable to imagine or understand. Meditation is to link self with the greater Self. Meditation has no origin and no beginning. It was and has been practiced for aeons.

From even the earliest ages, many applicants of various spiritual and educational institutions have upheld the practice of devotion, worship and meditation on the One Supreme Spirit, *Brahman* or God. This has been the principal means to liberation, as well as possible bondage and sorrows of life and living. There therefore arose in that old period, many sects and subsets, seeking everlasting spiritual bliss.

Each of these sects and subsets had its distinctive feature, a religious philosophy, and a code of moral and spiritual self-discipline for fulfilling life and winning liberation or *moksha.* Each claimed devotion to the Source of all existence – the supreme Lord of the Universe. While each sect recognized the authority of the four *Vedas,* developing each denomination became more and more humanized. Over the centuries qualities of mercy, forgiveness, love and grace became steadily more and more practiced.

Devotees of *Shiva, Vishnu, Rama, Shakti, Durga* and *Kali* uniformly developed into devotional sects, which became increasingly popular. Each believed they were worshipping God in these many Names and Forms. With the arrival of the *Aryans,* their culture developed and expanded to spread all over *Bharat* or India. The society now became diverse and increasingly varied. Assimilation of new and existing schools of devotion continued. In all these changes, the ideals and spiritual values stipulated in the *Vedas* were deliberated on and heeded. Despite heated discussions, exponents of different ideas cooperated for the sake of unity, peace, progress of society and the perpetuation of the race itself.

Faith in the *Vedas* was the strong bond of alliance among all sections of the race. Sages with extraordinary intellectual talents and intuitive spiritualism flourished throughout these ages. They succeeded in spreading their influence into the hearts and minds of seekers at large, even if some of these were alien races from afar. The paths and practices were honored through cooperation and a responsibility for coexistence. They were given practical applications in day-to-day life. The understanding and annexation of knowledge or *gyana,* devotion or *bhakti,* service or *karma* and meditation or *yoga* made assimilation possible through faith.

Earnest seekers felt a need for an integration of all the paths. In this compulsion they felt their domestic and social responsibilities gratified. Their duty in life and accountability to the beliefs of Moral Consciousness could then become perfect. Their energies would become spiritualized through detachment from worldly affairs. These efforts could then consummate in realizing the Origin of Cosmic Awareness and Consciousness through love, devotion and meditation.

Existing literature explains that even from ancient times, many sages and saints made many serious attempts for a rational agreement of the various interpretations of the *Vedas. Krishna,* in the *Bhagavad Gita,* made the most successful attempt at combining the different viewpoints made by the different schools of thought. The truest representation of the spirit of the *Vedas* was made by this extraordinary personality, who was of an intense spiritual insight. He delivered to posterity the most comprehensive and practical philosophy and religion. In the history of religious evolution, *Krishna* gave India a unique place in the annals of spiritual culture. Even in his lifetime he was acclaimed and adored as an incarnation of God in a human form. Even then, this political leader and strategist was declared a hero. Students of the twenty-first century continue to regard him the most spiritually enlightened politician of all time.

It is believed *Krishna* taught *Arjuna* the message of *Bhagavad Gita* on the battlefields of *Kurukshetra,* just before the start of a horrible battle that was to follow. Within the shortest time frame, *Krishna* delivers a rational and the most practical synthesis of all forms of moral, social, emotional and spiritual disciplines. The discussion is about a spiritual outlook on human life and society, in all environments, as taught by the *Vedas.*

The celebrated sage and author of many epics, *Vyasa,* gave *Krishna's* discussion with *Arjuna* the widest publicity possible. *Krishna's* instruction in the *Bhagavad Gita* is the centerpiece in the *Mahabharata,* one of the most celebrated national epics of India. In the *Gita, Krishna* has succeeded in exposing the true essence of the *Vedas,* without doing injustice to any of their instruction. Every denomination, creed and school of thought is given thoughtful esteem and consideration. He has succeeded in raising ordinary domestic and social activity to a high spiritual level.

Krishna taught humankind to perform all action efficiently for the sake of duty in the service of the Cosmic Whole. By spiritualizing the entire human life, *Krishna* succeeded in reaching the common people, of all strata of rational society. Man has for many millenniums understood the message of the *Gita,* as the ideal instructions filled in the teachings of all the *Vedas.* Narrow interpretations of *Vedic* disclosures were given relevance in everyday life.

Krishna explained that *Yoga* of meditation should be the regulative principle of everybody's life. He asserted the practice of meditation is not only for the exceptional few who renounce all worldly connections, but for all, of all religious disciplines, whether in solitude or while performing the mundane. He proved that *Yoga* was essentially living a God-centric life, an existence governed by a moral and spiritual perspective, in all affairs of experiences.

With this enlightened idea of *Yoga, Krishna* succeeded in unifying all differences between all paths, by bringing out the inner significance and underlying spiritual unity of the two major disciplines. One asserting that Man is by nature self-conscious and able to self-determine, without a regulatory body – this school felt Man has every potential for nobler actions of permanent and intrinsic value. The second school prescribed rules and laws for men of different physical and intellectual talents - the aim, with this school, was to ensure progressive development towards higher planes of consciousness.

Krishna, however, pointed out that when God is worshipped as a deity, with offerings or *yagna* of the self or with material things, the gift goes to the same One Spirit, even if this happens indirectly. He urged all men and women to cultivate a divine outlook on everything and to feel the divine presence in every breath. For the sake of love and reverence for that One Spirit, *Krishna* said, perform action without care or apprehension for the fruits of such endeavors, which belong to and are determined by God. By cherishing such a cordial personal love, Man is able to look on the Spirit as the eternal father, mother, and brother, friend, Lord and the Soul itself.

Acknowledgments

Swami Tejomayananda of Chinmaya Mission Worldwide for permission to use material written and commented on by Swami Chinmayananda.

B K S Iyengar who personally wrote allowing me to use statements from his writings

Anil Metre and Vivek Pareek for their help in creating this text.

Characters

Ambalika:	One with the power of discrimination
Ambika:	One who doubts
Arjuna:	Pandu identified with the lumbar plexus or manipura chakra. Pure of mind and heart. Granted with a fiery need for perfection through repetitive activity [abhyas].
Bhaarat:	India
Bharata:	Ancestors of Kuru race.
Bheema:	One of formidable strength over elements and life force. Identified with thoracic plexus or the anahata chakra.
Bhishma:	Individuality and reflected Consciousness. Egoism and self-awareness easily become soul-awareness.
Devadatta:	Devotion.
Devavrata:	Santanu and Ganga's eighth son-later renamed Bhishma.
Dhrishtadyumna:	Self-control and leader among forces of spirituality.
Dhritarashtra:	Blind deluded mind.
Draupadi:	Energy of view. Wife of the five Pandus called Panchali.
Drona:	Past habits of materialism supporting present lifestyle and destiny.

Drupada:	Swift footed and concentrated.
Duryodhana:	Lust and want
Gandhari:	The blind king's wife and mother of 100 Kauravas. Self-serving mind.
Gandiva:	Arjuna's bow. Represents the upright spine while seated in meditation to overcome restlessness.
Ganga:	Goddess of the River Ganges who represents continuous creative force of Om. First wife of Santanu who threw seven sons into the Ganges. She merges with the river after the birth of her eighth son Devavrata who is renamed Bhishma. It is Om that is awarded with a guiding and governing intelligence.
Gangotri:	Mouth of the river Ganges.
Gunas:	Qualities of Nature [tamas is inertia or grossness or negative polarity; rajas is creativity or positive polarity; sattva is harmonization of the two.]
Karna:	Selfishness and unrighteousness.
Kauravas:	Ten sense tendencies multiplying to 100 offspring of wants.
Kripa:	Family priest of the Kuru dynasty. Emotion without discrimination.
Krishna:	Universal Intelligence and the indwelling Self.
Kunti:	Energy that attracts compassion, astuteness and prevents errors. Mother of Arjuna, and Bheema - the first three of the Pandavas.
Kuru:	Ancestors of both Kauravas and Pandavas.

Kurukshetra: Field of individualized self-awareness where righteous inclinations [soul-awareness] are in opposition with unrighteous inclinations. The field of dharmakshetra is in the brain. The field of Kurukshetra is the spinal cord. Dharmakshetra-Kurukshetra is the brain and spinal cord in the divine cave.

Madri: Pandu's second wife of pure intelligence. Mother of twins and last two Pandavas identified with the first two chakras -Nakula and Sahadev.

Mahabhisha: Celestial royal sage who displayed on earth as Santanu who later married Ganga.

Maya: Cosmic illusion innate in Nature.

Nakula: Identified with the second chakra [svadhisthana] the astral-causal spiritual center within the physical sacral plexus. Powers resistance to unrighteousness.

Panchajanya: Power of Krishna permeating Creation with Om.

Pandava: Five children of Pandu [Yudhishthira, Bheema, Arjuna, Nakula, and Sahadev].

Pandu: Pure intelligence.

Sahadev: First of the two Madri twins. Identified with the first astral-causal muladhara chakra within the physical coccygeal plexus harnessed for restraint of wants.

Sanjaya: Inner reflection and introspection.

Santanu: Pure Consciousness who weds Ganga [Om]. They give birth to eight sons of expressive consciousness. The first seven are subjective and merge with the life-giving power of Om. The eighth is Consciousness expressing as individuality or Bhishma.

Satyavati: Second wife of Santanu. She is Om and expresses primitive Nature. Her first son is born between Consciousness and Om and reveals as Chitrangada, the first mutation to grossness. He died soon after. Her second son is Vichitravirya displaying as the deluded self who thinks he is able to exist independently. He married Amba and Ambalika who were left childless and widowed.

Sikhandi: Is incarnation of Amba the third sister who wished to marry Bhishma and was refused. She swore she would be born a man just to kill Bhishma someday.

Sharira and koshas: Vedantic idea that creatures have three bodies [sharira] – waking, dreaming and dreamless deep-sleeping and five sheaths [koshas] – physical, physiological, intellectual and causal.

Subadhra: Krishna's only sister and Arjuna's second wife.

Vasus: Angelic celestials.

Vashishta: Preceptor of the Solar Dynasty.

Vedas: Four scriptural texts of Hinduism.

Vidura: Realized soul.

Vikarna:	Repulsion
Virata:	The spiritual eye pictured in the Kutastha between and behind the eyebrows
Yudhishthira:	Righteous one.
Yuga:	Cycle of Creation – each nearly a million years. Is divided into four yugas of: 12,000 years [Kal Yuga]; 24,000 years [Dwapara Yuga]; 36,000 years [Treta Yuga]; and 48,000 years [Satya Yuga]. According to Indian calendars we have been in Dwapara Yuga for the last 200 years.

Contents

1. Vyasa and Krishna

Vyasa, a great poet and seer, knew that Religion has to be a philosophy in action, as recognised by *Krishna,* on the battlefield of *Kurukshetra.* As the most senior contemporary of *Krishna,* who lived long after him to continue cultural work, *Vyasa* played a unique role in consolidating spiritual thought of India.

This eminent intellectual, philosopher, poet, preacher and great organiser compiled and synthesised all earlier moral and spiritual achievements of the *Aryan* society, assimilated all important cultural developments of the non-*Vedic* and even non-*Aryan* people with those of the *Vedic* society. *Vyasa* brought about harmony among exponents of the different paths because of inspiration earned from the life and teachings of *Krishna.* He laid down a solid philosophical foundation of all the views and lofty thoughts of the greatest saints and sages of all philosophical religious schools in the country. He thus brought about philosophy within the scope of understanding and appreciation of the common people. *Vyasa's* works held permanent values and gave the Hindu spiritual culture an everlasting shape.

Even in those days, nearly 6000 years ago, Man endured confusing tensions and the stresses of psychological maladjustment: This shattered mental equipoise led to, and still is, because of the loss of ability to act with true determination in life.

Nature, with her variety and physical Laws is an evolution of this Reality. She, through Cosmic Illusion or *Maya,* makes One appear as many. All these forms and intellects exist in seeming separation from Reality, the Creator.

The main theme of this story is that one should renounce

ego, blind wishes including ego prompted needs, all of which cause separation between man's soul and Spirit. It is about Creation and how man descends and then changes back to his own excellent nature. The infrastructure used to trace the historical journey of a seeker is recorded in the wisdom of the *Bhagavad Gita. Krishna* nurtured *Arjuna* on the battlefield of life, where, everyone makes important decisions about life and living.

Arjuna's bodily blind Uncle King *Dhritarashtra* was exposed to laws of righteous living from childhood, but the king chose a lifestyle of a materialist whose thirst for life was unquenchable. *Sanjaya,* a wise and learned counselor chosen by *Vyasa,* must report the nurturing of *Arjuna* on the battlefield. A gift of divine sight saw the goings-on on the terrain of *Kurukshetra. Vyasa* makes it possible for *Sanjaya* to describe the battle during its progression from beginning to the end. When *Dhritarashtra's* blind mind refused to understand *Krishna's* conversations with *Arjuna, Sanjaya* time and again repeated this historic conversation for *Dhritarashtra's* conscience, to dissect, rationalize and digest.

The story starts with a marriage between Matter and Spirit. In olden times, there lived a celebrated King *Santanu,* who emulated eternal tranquillity. *Santanu,* who was a descendent of the *Bharata* race that ruled *Hastinapur,* wedded *Ganga,* the daughter of the mighty *Himalayas* and goddess of the holy river *Ganga.* They had a son *Bhishma,* an expression of pure Consciousness, who was even more renowned than his father. After *Ganga's* death, *Santanu* married a fisherwoman, *Satyavati* who already had a son, *Vyasa,* the famous poet and sage.

Dhritarashtra and the high-spirited *Pandu* and *Vidura* were *Bhishma's* younger stepbrothers, fathered by *Vyasa. Dhritarashtra,* the older brother, was born blind and thus had to renounce his rights to the throne. *Pandu* therefore became king. *Vidura* was the wisest of the three *Vyasa* children.

Dhritarashtra the blind prince of *Hastinapur* married

Gandhari an intelligent princess from *Gandhar* in Afghanistan. She was not only devoted but subservient to her husband's deceptive ways. To make matters worse she devotedly swathed her fully awake eyes to match *Dhritarashtra's* unseeing eyes. She therefore never visually distinguished her husband's misdeeds! They had 100 sons, the *Kauravas.*

Pandu had two wives. *Kunti,* the first wife, was a resemblance of divine energy, attracting goodness. She was *Krishna's* favourite aunt and treated all with compassion and discrimination. She gave birth to three sons. The oldest *Yudhishtra* was the infinitely calm, just and righteous son. *Arjuna* was not only chaste but resolute of mind and heart – he was granted with passionate energy; and *Bheema,* the fierce one, had the power to control his own life-breath.

Madri, the second wife, was compassionate and of pious intellect. They brought into being: *Nakula,* known for his deep resistance to unrighteousness and *Sahadev,* who remained devoted to spiritual awareness.

The five children were collectively known as the *Pandus* or *Pandavas.* They were collectively mindful of their abilities and fame. After the death of *Pandu* and *Madri,* the selfless *Pandava* princes were educated in the company of their lively sense-inclined *Kaurava* cousins. Supervising them was the aristocratic but highly individualistic grandsire *Bhishma.* The rightful crown prince *Yudhishtra* was educated to be king because he was the oldest of the *Pandus.*

While under the patronage of their blind uncle *Dhritarashtra,* the *Pandus* endured the resentment of their one hundred cousins. *Dhritarashtra* was now ruling *Hastinapur* on behalf of his dead brother *Pandu,* until the oldest of the 105 princes, *Yudhishtra,* came of age for coronation.

Duryodhana, the eldest of the *Kauravas,* resented the *Pandavas* and *Yudhishtra's* birthright to the throne. With the help of his maternal uncle and his brothers he consistently tried to kill his five cousins. When *Yudhishtra* was proclaimed king, *Duryodhana,* the eldest of the one hundred evil brothers, could not accept this and persuaded his blind father to cheat the crown prince of his rightful sovereignty. *Gandhari,* the blind king's wife, counseled her husband against their son's evil manipulation, but the blind king would hear none of it.

Duryodhana premeditated ways to kill the *Pandavas.* While still children, the one hundred brothers poisoned *Bheema's* dessert. As adults, they set ablaze a palace to kill the *Pandus* and their mother *Kunti.* When their uncle *Vidura* understood the deceit and importance of a palace made in wax, his spies warned the five brothers and their mother to build an escape tunnel under the building. While *Kauravas* rejoiced, the *Pandu* family was secretly helped to escape from their burning house.

The five brothers roamed the forests instead of returning home. For over a decade, the *Kauravas* in *Hastinapur* believed the *Pandus* were dead, until they heard of an unusual marriage. A gifted and enterprising princess, *Draupadi,* married *Arjuna.* He won her in a combat possible only by an *Arjuna*-like warrior. *Kunti,* his mother, decreed the five *Pandus* share *Draupadi's* camaraderie. From then on she was called *Panchali,* the life force linked to the first five spiritual centers of the spinal cave.

Kunti was *Krishna's* paternal aunt. *Krishna's* maternal uncle wanted him dead. He therefore spent his childhood in *Gokul.* Although of imperial bloodline, *Krishna* was hiding with the rural farmers in the village. Even as a child he displayed his systematic thinking and intelligence. He spread happiness in the heart of the inhabitants through service, love, and concern for both young and old.

When *Krishna* came of age, he went to school with his older brother, away from the village. Meanwhile, *Kunti* married the *Pandus* who fathered five sons. *Krishna* befriended his gallant *Pandu* cousins. *Arjuna,* the youngest of *Kunti's* three children, was *Krishna's* favored cousin and companion.

The *Pandus,* now exposed, returned to *Hastinapur.* To pacify the Kauravas, the royal chain of command divided the Old Kingdom between the two groups of cousins, the *Pandus* and *Kauravas.* With the help of inhabitants and celestials, *Krishna* helped *Pandus* build a new beautiful city on a desolate inhospitable piece of rocky land. However, jealousy overcame *Duryodhana* and he unlawfully won *Yudhishtra's* kingdom, in a deceitful game of loaded dice. The elders from the *Kauravas* including the grandsire *Bhishma,* watched the deceit, seemingly favouring it.

Not satisfied with this deceitful victory, *Duryodhana* tried to insult *Draupadi* by stripping her openly in the court. *Krishna's* compassion disallowed anything humiliating to happen to this highborn woman. Fearing calamity from such an act by his sons *Dhritarashtra* appealed for her forgiveness. He begged *Draupadi* to ask whatever she wanted. With visible and public disdain for the elders of the royal family, she freed her five *Pandava* companions, and walked away.

Duryodhana again convinced his royal elders to invite the *Pandava* cousins to a game of dice. The reluctant *Yudhishtra.* felt pressured by his physically and morally blind king. *Dhritarashtra* ordered *Yudhishtra* to play. Finding no middle ground he played with the loaded dice. *Yudhishtra* lost again. The *Pandus* were once more banished from their newly built kingdom for 13 years. They were warned: if sighted during that period, they would be banished forever.

The *Pandus* spent the 13th year of their exile as servants to a wise King *Virat.* A suspicious death of a *Kuru* brother-in-law prompted the *Kauravas* to a reprisal attack on the *Virata's* kingdom. When attacked, the *Pandus* who had remained hidden for thirteen years came out of hiding to help King *Virat.* The *Kauravas* recognized the *Pandus.* The *Pandus* demanded a return of their kingdom.

The *Kauravas* refused despite many peaceful requests and petitions. War was therefore declared, and fought on the battlefields of *Kurukshetra*. The *Pandus'* who had a virtuous preference, fought on the side of *Dharmakshetra*. The unethical *Kauravas* fought on the opposite side but on the same battlefield of *Kurukshetra,* to resolve any allegation.

Since *Krishna* was related to both the *Kauravas* and the *Pandavas* he felt torn between friendship, duty and truth. The one hundred *Kauravas,* the individualistic *Bhishma,* their preceptor *Drona, Ashvathama,* and the family adviser *Kripa* were on one side with the *Kauravas. Krishna, Drupad, Drishtadyumna,* and *Sikhandi* were on the side of the *Pandus.* To be fair to both sides, *Krishna* gave his army to the *Kauravas* and agreed to remain with *Arjuna,* as his charioteer.

The armies assembled in readiness for war. The large army of the *Kauravas* led by the grandsire *Bhishma* stood opposite *Dhrishtadyumna* who led the *Pandavas. Arjuna,* enthusiastic to face his enemy, asked *Krishna* to drive the chariot to the front of the battlefield between the two forces so he could get a good look. But there, he saw not enemies but his relatives, teachers and friends. *Arjuna* suddenly lost both his eagerness and fortitude for war. He turned to *Krishna* and told him that neither did he wish to fight, nor did he want any kingdom, at the cost of spilling the blood of his loved ones. Hearing *Arjuna's* refusal to act or fight, *Krishna* gave *Arjuna* a message in the shortest time frame amid a terrible battle, about to happen.

Krishna is the central figure of the *Mahabharata* and the *Gita* occupies the central position in its discussion of all human problems. There is scarcely any important domestic, social, political, ethical, economic, religious or visionary problem, which is not introduced for discussion in the *Mahabharata.* The final solutions of all these problems are arrived at because of the spiritual outlook, as taught in the *Vedas.*

Krishna advised *Arjuna* on the vast and deep learning enshrined in all scriptures, irrespective of race, creed, sect, and position in life. *Krishna* spoke about duty, the active conquest of evil versus passive resistance, and knowledge of the self and of reality. The *Gita* contains a revival of all views of all philosophical and religious schools of that period.

The advice given to *Arjuna* is a universal guide, meant for the entire humanity, in all climes, for all times, irrespective of age, sex, caste or creed. It was applicable in the age of the *Puranas* in the *Dwapara Yuga* and is equally applicable in this *Yuga,* in any place, now and ever, to every individual young or old, man or woman.

2. Mahabharata

This story begins in *Hastinapur* in early *Bharat,* many thousands of years ago. There lived in this old land now called India, a King from the lunar dynasty called *Santanu,* who was ever self-possessed and whose personality was of blameless **Consciousness.**

One day, while walking along the banks of the River *Ganges,* King *Santanu* met with a graceful lovely Lady of the River – *Ganga.* Her persona was that of uncontaminated **Awareness**. It was natural that Consciousness and Awareness were attracted to each other.

King *Santanu* took one night to muster enough courage to approach *Ganga* for her hand in marriage. He was sure he would find her again on the banks of the mighty River. As he approached the Ganges, he noticed an unusual rising and falling vibration of Aum. He pursued this lyrical humming. After many miles of walking along the verdant banks of the river, he suddenly came across *Ganga.* She was the source of the humming. She resonated as if the whole pageant of earthly manifestation depended on the music she made.

Santanu surprised her with his presence. She seemed pleased to see him and stopped singing, but the refrain of the hum echoed around them. *Santanu* mustered his kingly courage to ask *Ganga* for her hand in marriage. Without hesitation, she agreed to be *Santanu's* wife, but demanded one condition.

"O King, I agree to become your wife and comply with all your dictates. But O monarch, you must not oppose or question my actions, be they agreeable or disagreeable. Also you will never speak to me harshly." She warned *Santanu* she would abandon him for the River *Ganga-Bhagirathi* if he ever questions her actions.

Santanu pledged he would forever endure, as witness, all of *Ganga's* actions. He would depend on her ability and wisdom, to look vigilantly at the affairs of their marriage. They lived together happily. *Santanu* remained immersed in *Ganga* and she in him. He left governing his kingdom to his trusted ministers. It was a long honeymoon.

Ganga gave birth to seven sons. Each time a son was born, *Ganga* would walk out of the regal birthing room and down a flight of stairs of the residential palace. In the presence of *Santanu* and his ministers she would lovingly carry the infant to the banks of the Ganges and toss him into the center of the flow. She drowned each inside the mighty currents of the Ganges. Each time *Ganga* drowned her infant sons, the King and his ministers heaved in despair, but none dared to question her actions.

With the birth of the eighth son, *Santanu* begged for the infant's life. He challenged *Ganga* to justify her actions. In response *Ganga* gently gave *Santanu* their last son. She named him God's gift of devotion, *Devavrata*. She then clarified why she had immersed their first seven sons in the immortal river, the *Ganges* that constantly roared the inviting vibration of Aum.

She sat down on the boulder and explained. "These seven sons embody both the cosmic and individualized physical creation of the Energy of *Shiva.*" *Ganga* explained they are the life force revealing the Creativity of *Brahma. Vishnu* sustained them in essence within Causal Creation, she said. The seventh son, she explained, represented the all-pervading Spirit of the Soul in the Cosmic Self.

Ganga explained these are subjective gods who rule Creation. In contrast, their eighth son *Devavrata* guards the objective expression of creation, through his own will. He would be a good son to his father, *Ganga* promised. He would serve the family and the Kingdom.

Santanu was by now both confused and curious. *Ganga* therefore decided to tell *Santanu* about their past incarnation. *Ganga* started by reminding him how they fell in love while in the Heavens, as *Mahabhisha* and *Ganga.*

"One day the celestials assembled to jointly worship *Brahma,* the Creator. Many royal sages and King *Mahabhisha* were present. I, *Ganga,* the queen of all rivers, also came to pay homage to the Grandsire. A sudden gust of wind displaced my white moon-like veil off my head and chest. When my body became exposed, the celestials respectfully and virtuously looked away until I could cover myself again. You royal sage *Mahabhisha,* disrespectfully continued to stare at me, at the Queen of Rivers. Your seductive attention was magnetic and I gazed back at you with shameless abandon."

"*Brahma* became angry with our insolent conduct amid his heavenly guests and cursed both of us, *Ganga* and *Mahabhisha,* to become mortals. On my way down to earth, I met other residents of heaven, the *Vasus,* also on their way towards earthly expression. They seemed disheartened with themselves. I dared to ask them because of their dejection."

"The heavenly *Vasus,* explained they had been cursed for an excusable fault. *Vashishta,* the distinguished sage, was engaged in his twilight adoration, and seated as he was, the *Vasus* could not see what he was doing. They crossed his path in ignorance and he cursed them in anger. He cursed the *Vasus'* rebirth as earthlings. *Vashishta* was after that unable to demystify what had been already uttered."

"Therefore these *Vasus* were born as our sons. Since they were unwilling to enter the womb of human females, they requested they be fathered by you, *Santanu* and in my womb. They begged death by drowning as soon as they were born. Their termination by drowning, therefore, was to rescue them from living on earth for any time."

"As soon as I promised to keep their word, the *Vasus* allowed us to have at least one fruit of our earthly marriage. The *Vasus* agreed to contribute one-eighth part of each of their respective energies and with these, we were given this one son, according to your desired ambition. But, this son will never marry on earth. Empowered with great energies of will, wisdom, intelligence, love and commitment to service for humanity, he shall remain forever childless."

"Therefore this our meeting, as *Santanu* and *Ganga* on earth, was unavoidable," she said.

After *Ganga's* departure, *Santanu* spent many years in ascetic penance at the source of the River Ganges in *Gangotri*. *Ganga* and *Santanu* who desired each other in heaven met on earth and *Ganga's* promise to the *Vasus* was unfolding. *Santanu* meanwhile realizes his meeting with *Ganga* was foreordained.

With permission, *Ganga* took *Devavrata* to heaven during his childhood and early formative years. She promised to return *Devavrata* once his private education in moral values, and martial arts is complete. *Ganga* promised this training will make their son a just ruler, who would prove his duty and devotion to country, family and humanity. Having said that, *Ganga* with her son in arms walked into the River Ganges and merged within its depths. The speechless *Santanu* was once more alone with unfulfilled hopes and reflections. Every day he walked along the banks of the Ganges, hoping *Ganga* would appear sooner or later.

When *Devavrata* was eighteen years old, he surpassed his father in all accomplishments. *Ganga* now told her son it was time for them to part and for him to return to his father, King *Santanu,* whom he had never met.

The well-known *Santanu* was the most adored of gods and royal sages. He was known for his wisdom, virtue, and truthfulness. Qualities of self-control, liberality, forgiveness, intelligence, modesty, patience, and superior energy coursed his royal blood.

Santanu was out walking when he beheld an unbelievable sight. The mighty Ganges, the holy *Bhagirathi,* had stopped flowing. Just upstream, a dam built from simple bamboo cane obstructed the mighty river's flow. He turned to call for the guards when he suddenly saw *Ganga* walking on the river's surface and towards him. With her flowing white *sari,* and an amused smile on her lips, she sauntered gracefully. By her side strolled a handsome youth. Tresses of black hair cascaded onto his broad shoulders. He was also dressed in white.

Santanu walked slowly towards the riverbank where mother and son had by now arrived. She introduced *Devavrata* to his father, *Santanu. Devavrata* bowed in reverence. *Santanu* quickly lifted his son and embraced him with thoughtful tenderness. He then asked his estranged wife and son to sit while he examined *Devavrata's* education.

With an arm around *Devavrata's* shoulders, *Ganga* said: "O tiger among men, this eighth son whom you had with me, know that this excellent child is familiar with weapons. Receive him now. I have nurtured him with care. He is gifted with exceptional intelligence. The enlightened sage *Vashishta* tutored him in the *Vedas* and their branches. He is skilled in all knowledge of weapons and is a mighty archer. He is like *Indra* the god of heaven, when in battle. Both gods and demons look on our son with favor. Whatever branch of knowledge that is known, this child knows it. O King of superior courage, take this, your own heroic son. I give him back to you."

Santanu decided to test his son's knowledge and asked:

"When life is destroyed with age, and worms eat the body. Where then does man live? Does he come back to life? I have never heard of any hell".

Devavrata replied: "After dissolving the body, man, according to his acts, reenters the womb of a mother and stays there in an indistinct form. He soon assumes a distinct and visible shape and appears in the world, and walks on its surface. This is that earth-hell where man falls, because he does not see nor understand how to dissolve his continued existence. He does not act towards his own emancipation from this earth-hell. As he falls sons, grandsons, and other relatives who withdraw his heart from acting for his liberation attack him."

Santanu was impressed and asked the next logical question: "After death, the body is burned and destroyed. Having been reduced to nothing after such devastation, by what principle is man enlivened?"

Devavrata said, "O lion among kings, the person that dies assumes a subtle form. He saves awareness of all his acts as in a dream. He enters some other form with a speed quicker than air itself. The chaste arrive at superior and the corrupt go to inferior forms of existence."

Santanu said: "How do men reach the superior regions from where there is no return to earthly existence? Is it by asceticism or by knowledge? How does man gradually arrive at suitable regions?"

Devavrata answered: "The wise say that for men there are seven gates through which admission is gained into Heaven. These include asceticism, compassion, and calmness of the mind, self-confidence, humility, being clear or uncomplicated, and thoughtfulness towards all creatures. The prudent also say that a person loses all these because of his egotism."

Santanu then asked *Devavrata* to elaborate further on the seven gates into Heaven.

Devavrata continued: "That man who having gained scholarship, and regards himself expert, and with his learning, destroys the reputation of others, will never gain the regions of happiness. The wise should never triumph at receiving honors, nor should he grieve at insults."

"To declare that 'I have given away so much, I have performed so many sacrifices, I have studied so much, I have obeyed these vows' – these statements arise from egotism. Vanity breeds fear especially if mixed with study, veneration and atonement before fire."

Santanu next posed several questions on issues needing

both compassion and harsh justice while ruling as king. *Devavrata's* answers were wise, thought provoking, well referenced, and just. *Ganga* watched this communication with amusement. Having ensured that father and son were now friends, *Ganga* asked to be excused. *Santanu* begged her to stay. *Ganga* reminded him of his promise to her, before she had agreed to marry him. She gently bid them farewell and elegantly strolled into the mist hovering over the Ganges waters.

Father and son returned to the palace. *Santanu* lavished his fondness, respect, friendship and devotion. He allowed *Devavrata* to practice all the arts and skills he had learned in Heaven. There was great rejoicing and the subjects of the Nation delighted in their beloved King's newfound happiness. Sharing and conscious admiration ruled *Santanu* and *Devavrata* relationship. It was common knowledge grooming was for future kingship. Deep devotion and selfless service to the father and Kingdom became *Devavrata's* hallmark. The country enjoyed peace and plenty.

When four years had passed, *Santanu* asked his charioteer, who over the years had become his trusted friend, to take him hunting on the other side of the River *Yamuna.* After a successful run in the forest, *Santanu* relaxed in the shade of a tree by the river. He saw a pile of lotus petals floating down the waters of the *Yamuna. Santanu* decided to follow the stream of petals and walked several miles on the riverbank. He suddenly came upon a radiantly beautiful woman rowing her boat, and making a ritual offering of lotus petals into the river. *Santanu* immediately fell in love with her. He secretly watched *Satyavati.* Her beauty expressed and embodied the spirit of primordial Nature. Her perfection echoed into the wholeness of purity.

Unknown to *Satyavati, Santanu* followed her to the home of her father, the area's fisher-king and asked for her hand in marriage. *Satyavati's* father agreed if she is made *Santanu's* principal wife and her yet unborn children inherit the throne. *Santanu* rejected the conditions of the marriage and returned home to his palace.

As days passed, the ministers and *Devavrata* became aware of *Santanu's* intense sadness. At last, *Devavrata* resolved to take action. Unknown to his father, he asked the charioteer to take him to the fisher-king. After much discussion, the fisher-king consented to the marriage, provided *Devavrata* would never marry and abdicate his rights to the throne.

Devavrata swore by the gods in Heaven that he would never claim the throne. He willed he would never marry nor have children. Because of these monumental vows, *Devavrata* was renamed *Bhishma* by the gods to distinguish him as a free spirit and fierce enemy.

Because of *Bhishma's* actions, *Santanu* married *Satyavati*. Her constitution was of primal nature. She bore two sons, *Chitrangada* and *Vichitravirya*. *Chitrangada* was born undeveloped and weak and died childless while being crowned king, *Vichitravirya,* was also physically fragile, and lived to marry off two sisters: *Ambika's* personality was underhanded and unreliable but *Ambalika* had an intelligent discriminative personality. *Vichitravirya* also died childless. *Satyavati* was dismayed. The dynasty could not be perpetuated without the help of her first child, born out of wedlock. She sent for *Vyasa* who lived as an ascetic in the forests.

Vyasa arrived at the palace and asked: "What are your commands, Mother?"

"Your brothers are both dead. *Vichitravirya* has left behind two wives, both childless. Beget virtuous children for him!" *Satyavati* said.

Vyasa consented and was introduced to his half brother's two widows and their servant. Each of them bore a son. *Ambika's* son, *Dhritarashtra* was born first. He was born blind. He inherited his mother's distrustful and treacherous mind. *Ambalika's* son *Pandu* was gifted with logical intelligence but a fragile appearance. The servant gave birth to the magnificent, devout and intelligent son, *Vidura.*

All matters of the state as well as the education of the descendants were decided by their Uncle and grandsire, *Bhishma*. In consultation with the stepmother *Satyavati,* the three children qualified to become princes. Under the tutelage of the best teachers of the land, the three brothers, who were also *Bhishma's* nephews, were educated. *Bhishma* ruled the kingdom until the two older princes came of age.

The blind prince, *Dhritarashtra* had one hundred sons with his wife *Gandhari*. She had convenient self-serving mental tendencies. Of their one hundred sons, four became famous for their disagreeable conduct. *Duryodhana* was known for his quarrelsome nature, his unquenchable wants, jealousy, pride and egotism. *Dushasana* was physically unable to sit still. *Vikarna* disliked and hated anyone who crossed his path. And *Chitrasena* was of irresolute mind and personality.

Pandu had two gifted wives, *Kunti* and *Madri*. *Kunti* gave birth to the first three *Pandava* brothers, and *Madri* gave birth to twins. *Kunti's* magnetic personality was of a discriminating intelligence. She distributed love and compassion freely. Her perceptive and distinguishing intellect made her famous. *Madri,* who was *Pandu's* devoted younger wife, was gifted with a pious mind. She was expanding towards a spiritual life.

Years later, *Bhishma* suggested that *Pandu* who had just returned from many years of battle, relax in the Royal Forests with his two wives. While there, *Kunti* gave birth to their three sons. *Yudhishthira,* the eldest of all the brothers was good-natured and upright. *Bheema* was able to control Energy in Nature. He had overpowering strength over breath control. *Arjuna* was pure of heart and mind and had the fire and energy to ensure all his efforts are inspired and perfected.

Madri gave birth to twins. *Nakula,* who had the power to meditate and adhere to stillness in his mind, was the older twin. The younger *Sahadev* had the capacity to resist all temptations of the flesh and remain aware of his devotion to his duty in life.

When *Pandu* and *Madri* died suddenly, the monks of a neighboring forest monastery groomed the children to perform *Pandu's* last rites. *Kunti* then returned to the palace with the five sons. After *Pandu's* death, the five *Pandava* princes were raised with their one hundred evil *Kaurava* cousins. *Duryodhana,* the eldest of the *Kaurava* sons, had enduring jealousy for the *Pandavas.* In time, the immoral *Duryodhana* succeeded in ostracizing the family of five brothers. In the long run this also proved fruitless.

When the five *Pandava* brothers connected with *Draupadi,* she adjusted five houses. She rejuvenated all their creative actions, and made them express their nobility through all types of ordinary and worldly actions.

Yudhishthira, the eldest of the family of siblings, was to be crowned King. *Duryodhana,* the eldest of the *Kauravas,* expressed displeasure. *Dhritarashtra* sent for the *Pandavas* and commanded them to move out of the palace. They spent many years in a newly built house at the edge of the forest, before *Yudhishthira* was crowned King.

The *Pandavas* left willingly with their mother *Kunti.* However, unknown to the *Pandavas,* their new home in the forest was made of wax. Uncle *Vidura,* who was always aware of what was going on in the palace, warned the *Pandavas* of the danger and directed them to build underground tunnels beneath the wax palace.

When the *Kauravas* scorched the forest house, the *Pandavas* escaped. Convinced that *Pandu's* family was destroyed, *Duryodhana* and his father *Dhritarashtra* rejoiced.

During their twelve years in the forest, the *Pandavas* spent their time in ascetic penance and embarked on spiritual journeys into themselves. The rest of the story is about a war between the *Kauravas* and the *Pandavas.*

3. Arjuna's Grief

Vyasa has documented in the *Mahabharata* that *Dhritarashtra, Pandu,* the *Kauravas* and the *Pandavas* or *Pandus* are all from the lineage of King *Santanu.* He had two wives, *Ganga* and *Satyavati.* Eight sons came ashore from first to last using *Ganga's* womb. *Ganga* smashed seven in the current of her own waters as soon as they were born. The eighth son *Devavrata* or *Bhishma* when he reached adolescence was left behind with the father. In these, his formative years, *Devrata* was ready to be a king. *Ganga* then disappeared.

Bhishma was powerful and mighty. When *Pandu*'s son *Yudhishtra* was too young to rule, it is *Bhishma's* daring that saved India repeatedly from marauders, He never wasted time in high living or benefiting from the kingdom. Sage *Parashar* fathered *Vyasa* with *Satyavati* long before she married King *Santanu.*

Immersed in a *mantric* invocation she petitioned with petals to become King *Santanu's* Queen. *Santanu* saw the lotus petals in the blue waters of the river. He followed the trail and came across *Satyavati.* Captivated by her beauty, he proposed marriage, but withdrew the offer. *Santanu* was challenged to remove *Devrata* from ruling the kingdom. When *Devrata* relinquished all his rights to the throne he pledged never to marry or have children of his own, *Devrata* was now rendered out of affirmative action, as *Bhisma.*

He brought *Satyavati* to the palace and joined *Santanu* and her in marriage. There was great rejoicing in the palace. Two sons were born to them. *Chitrangada* died in warfare. *Vichitravirya,* the younger son, married King *Kashi's* two daughters, *Ambika* and *Ambalika.* He died while delighting in his wives.

Later, *Vyasa* fathered *Pandu* and *Dhritarashtra.* Because *Ambika* avoided seeing *Vyasa,* she gave birth to a blind son *Dhritarashtra.* Because *Ambalika* was apathetic towards *Vyasa,* she gave birth to *Pandu,* who was born refined.

Pandu had two wives, *Kunti* and *Madri.* A curse of death condemned him to celibacy. Unable to sexually have children *Kunti* invoked children of heavenly beings by incantations of special mantras. While still unmarried and living in her imperial father's palace, she learned the technique from a visiting sage.

Unknown to anyone, she experimented tempting the Sun god *Surya,* and gave birth to a male child – *Karna.* He was born with a sun-emblem imprinted on his chest. With the help of her maid, she bundled the infant in a basket and set him afloat on the river. A childless couple employed at the palace fostered him as their own child.

Kunti revealed her secret to her husband. After consulting with the younger spouse and her husband *Kunti* invoked *Yama,* the lord of virtue, and gave birth to a righteous son, *Yudhishtra,* She then commissioned the mighty wind god *Vayu* and gave birth to the awesome resolute *Bheema.* Finally she called on the god of rain and heavens *Indra,* and a son with exceptional qualities *Arjuna* was born.

At the request of her husband, *Kunti* taught the mantra to *Madri.* She called on *Ashwini kumars* – the celestial twins, and gave birth to twin sons *Nakula* and *Sahadev.*

It was springtime. *Pandu* went for a stroll with *Madri.* Overwhelmed with love, *Pandu* embraced *Madri* and died instantly. Despondent, she desired and achieved *sati-hood. Kunti* revisited her husband's kingdom with *Pandu's* five children.

Except for *Kunti* and her late husband, no one at the palace knew of *Karna's* existence. The infant grew up to be a fearless soldier. Oblivious of his birth, mother and five siblings, *Karna* joined with the *Kauravas* when *Duryodhana,* the eldest of the one hundred brothers, befriended him. Together they tried ways to destroy the *Pandavas*. When the five brothers tried to get back their kingdom, despite help from their cousin *Krishna*, they were denied their constitutional rights and war was declared.

Karna learned archery and rules of armed conflict from *Arjuna's* teachers. He too became a powerful warrior. In a public show of strength, the *Pandavas* unintentionally snubbed *Karna*–calling him a common herd. In spitefulness, *Duryodhana* befriended *Karna* and crowned him king of *Anga*. Together they tricked the *Pandavas* and struggled to ruin them.

These victims of deception were forced to live in exile for thirteen years. To regain their kingdom the *Pandus* and *Krishna* repeatedly urged the *Kauravas* against war, but *Duryodhana*, the eldest son of the blind pedigree *Dhritarashtra* and *Gandhari*, would not accept any advice.

The blind king knew of the many grievances against his nephews, the *Pandavas*. He was also mindful of the relative strengths of the two armies. *Dhritarashtra* felt assured by the indisputable greater strength of his sons' army. Yet, the viciousness of crimes committed by his sons weighed heavily on *Dhritarashtra's* heart. He hesitated about the outcome of this war. He could not honestly expect fulfillment and civility from a dishonest confrontation. In battle, when virtuous actions connect with evil inclinations, outcome is defeat for immorality.

Vyasa gave *Sanjaya* the power to witness the events in far-off *Kurukshetra*, while seated at the *Hastinapur* palace, besides *Dhritarashtra*. Blind *Dhritarashtra* ordered *Sanjaya* to highlight the activities of the five *Pandus* on the battlefield of *Kurukshetra*. After surveying the battlefield, *Sanjaya* is in contemplative stillness.

Dhritarashtra asks, "O *Sanjaya*, assembled in stillness and silence on the battlefield, what are my sons doing? What are the two armies, those of *Pandavas* and the *Kauravas*, doing on the plains of *Kurukshetra*? How and where have they assembled to fight? Did you know, their teacher *Drona* is determined to do whatever it takes, to give the royal lineage to my son *Duryodhana,* even though the kingdom rightfully belongs to my nephew *Yudhishtra*?"

Sanjaya, who has divine insight of self-analysis and introspection, understands the source of the blind King's questions. He knows that although the king normally operates from his cowardly mind-sense, his indiscreet emotion and self-serving ego, is anxious and hesitant. This is what punctuates *Dhritarashtra's* skepticism.

Sanjaya replies, "The *Pandava* armies are in battle array". Still preoccupied with his self-indulgent needs, *Duryodhana* has approached his teacher and mentor, *Drona,* and says, "Oh teacher, look at this great army. These sons of *Pandu* are skillful with noble talents and innately uncorrupted aptitudes. The well-endowed *Dhrishtdyumna,* is the *Pandava* General. He has true understanding of warfare. He has gained this knowledge through personal tutoring by Inner Radiance. It guides his every action. Not enslaved by disrespect for anyone he is fixed in his inner serenity. He controls all unnecessary annoyance and applies himself along a clear path of action, both in war and peace"

Duryodhana's survival at war depends on armies who understand his deceptive tendencies and wicked practices. They recognize why he surrenders to his unpredictable educator *Drona,* who also tends towards depravity. The pupil empowers the teacher with his logic for earthly satisfaction and assets. *Duryodhana* however seeks reassurance that despite misgivings about matters that are underhanded and deceitful, he is not at all responsible. He therefore consults with *Drona,* knowing fully well the teacher also has a shielded inner drive for unrighteousness. *Duryodhana* privately recognizes that fear of a *Pandu* retaliation keeps his army with him.

Events surrounding *Dhrishtdyumna's* and his sister *Draupadi's* birth are well known. Unable to have children,

King *Drupad* kept counsel with monks and sages for a long time. He learned about righteous actions and meditation. Established in this practice, he subdued all mental restlessness and evil tendencies. With the grace of gurus, his wife gave birth to two children, who were granted with the power of discrimination. Early in their childhood, they learned that the world is an illusion and therefore kept to themselves. They detected facts about the all-pervading Universe inside themselves. Through reverence and self-absorption, they discovered deep-rooted innate knowledge. They discovered the Universal Being in the *kutastha,* between and above the eyebrows.

Their father King *Drupad* was once *Drona's* student also. Encouraged by his wife, *Drona* once visited the king for wealth and land. This he was denied, but it so insulted *Drona,* that he pledged revenge some day. His brother-in-law *Kripa* was the palace priest. He also swore vengeance sooner or later. Both later joined the *Kaurava* army against *Pandavas.*

Drishtdyumna and his sister were born as gifts of extreme spiritual ardor. *Drishtdyumna* received rare guidance from an awakened Inner Light, which prevented him from doing harm through ignorance. His capacity for attracting and leading honest armies made it easy to enlist them for constitutional rights sought by the five *Pandava* family.

Duryodhana recognizes *Drishtdyumna's* inclination for goodness and his skill in psychological combat. The blind king *Dhritarashtra* has now assessed *Dhrishtdyumna* is fit to lead the *Pandava* forces with discrimination. They will likely win the war.

Sanjaya reports that *Duryodhana* has concerns about the brave qualities in his opponents. He is heard enlisting examples of winning powers of such selfless qualities. *Drona* pays attention to his student. But he also knows *Kaurava* tendencies will deter *Duryodhana* from listening to his intuitive mind. Distracted by need for name, fame, possessions and indulgences, his pupil will remain deluded. *Duryodhana* says to *Drona,* "Look over there at the *Pandava* army – present there are mighty heroes of resourceful actions. Their intensive and thoughtful practices of combat make them extraordinary archers. They are equally skillful in conflict."

"Bheema, the second *Pandava* brother has the ability to silence any weakness or agitation, through perfect breath control. *Arjuna,* the third *Pandava* has spent a lifetime perfecting existence through self-control. He possesses expertise in fantastic weaponry. The veteran warrior *Yuyudha* has mastered faultless action, through devoted determination. The strong-minded *Virat* trusts the power of concentration and *Drupad* is skilled at selfless action – his ardor and composure make him an authority on spectacular weapons also," *Duryodhana* says.

Although wayward, *Duryodhana* is a gifted student himself. He is granted with divine insight and understands the powers of right conduct. In spite of everything the same mentors educated the *Pandava* and *Kaurava* cousins – in straightforward action.

Duryodhana then enlisted the superior qualities necessary for strength of character. He had in any case learned these techniques of living honorably in the world. *Drona* who taught them self-control and conquering restlessness had now himself become unreliable. The teacher who has lost respect, potency, recollection, is now obsessed despite his learning for virtuous action. "*Duryodhana's* loss of discrimination will cause harm to the dynasty," *Sanjaya* thought.

Duryodhana goes on to give *Drona* examples of why the *Pandu* soldiers are superior to those of his own army. "*Dhrishtaketu* is empowered by restraint alongside temptations and indulgences. His guide is the reliable reverberation and symphonic directives of Om. *Chekitana* experiences *Krishna's* brainpower, which reveals aims of selfless action. *Kashiraja* has perfect logic, which he nurtures through discrimination. He transacts only that which is righteous."

"Eminent among these men is *Purujit.* who succeeds

highly by injecting intuitive guidance in all actions. He undertakes engagement by integrative deliberation. *Kuntibhoj,* who remains still in *asana* for long periods despite physical discomfort, wins even in action if they are mighty and honest conflicts. Then there is *Shaibya* who adheres to all rules of self-control and right action. All of these soldiers of righteous living give the *Pandu* army greater integrity and sanctified potency."

Drona listens carefully. As mentor, he has taught both groups of siblings, now facing one another in battle, the supremacy of right action. He has private reasons for encouraging this unrighteous war. *Duryodhana* continues to prattle.

"Then there is *Yudhmanyu* who worships the Cosmic Mother's Energy. It is said She makes available her powers to all charioteers. She gives them competence, control and ability to galvanize their weapons. Through lifelong purity the heroic *Uttamaujas* has become an expert on safeguarding capabilities of his chariot. *Krishna's* sister *Subadhara* who delivered *Arjuna's* son *Abhimanyu,* has been tutored by his father and uncle. He mastered unique techniques to fight worldly combats including attractions for lust, food, possessions, and pride. His ability to invoke the staggering power of sense control is legendary. *Abhimanyu* is declared remarkable, as are the other sons of *Draupadi* and the *Pandavas.* Their aptitude for controlling senses, habits, desires, anger, greed, attachment, pride, jealousy, and ego make them noble and desirable combatants," *Duryodhana* tells *Drona.*

Sanjaya, granted with clairvoyance and clairaudience, declares to *Duryodhana's* father, "O King, by cataloguing these heroes, *Duryodhana* infers that although the *Pandava* forces are fewer, their effectiveness will be much greater than the larger and better-equipped army of the *Kauravas.*"

But the blind king *Dhritarashtra's* mind is preoccupied with aggression and ambition. Passion and hatred towards his brother *Pandu's* children and his attachment towards his own *Kaurava* siblings spell disaster for the dynasty.

During their thirteen-year exile in the forest, *Sahadev* and *Nakula* the fourth and fifth *Pandu* sons together practiced and cohered to moral *[yama]* and ethical restraints *[niyama]*. They were now competent foot soldiers against all temptations. *Arjuna* the third *Pandu* underwent strict bodily sacraments with intense devotion *[abhyas]* to overcome covetous demands of the body. *Bheema* gained complete control over his breath by perfecting *pranayama* until he gained complete detachment from name and fame. He withdrew from worldly contacts, at will in *pratyahara*. This capacity to adjust his being with determination came from life force or *prana*. *Yudhishtra*, the first *Pandu* brother and rightful heir to the throne, had grasped every capability on hand in his family but he remained inconspicuous in humility. This gave him the genius to combine the power of concentration, meditation and integration *[dharana, dhyana, and samadhi]* with Universal Intelligence, *Krishna*.

Duryodhana, the eldest of the one hundred *Kauravas*, knows that his spirit vouches for goodness, but his sense-motivated selfish appetite refuses its advice. *Duryodhana* chooses instead to ignore noble pressures. He turns instead to *Drona*, who already is a casualty of corrupt dispositions.

Because he is his preceptor, *Duryodhana* addresses *Drona* as a twice-born *Brahmin* – a term signifying the teacher has succeeded in quenching a spiritual thirst, through learning and working with the *Vedas*. *Duryodhana* needs assurance and justification for his actions.

"Know also, O best among the twice-born, the names of those who are more famous among ourselves. These are our own leaders in our army. These are their qualities. I name just a few," *Duryodhana* says to *Drona*.

"Yourself *Drona*, whose nature from past experiences and deprivations has convinced you to remain on the side of the *Kauravas*. You cannot afford *Pandava* inspired righteous and religious changes. Your present birth demands comforts. The brave *Bhishma,* who is grandsire to both the *Pandava-Kaurava* siblings, is attached to his personal sense of duty to the crown. His disposition is therefore, a good guide for us. *Karna* is unswerving in friendship. His innate worldliness and bonding tendencies, fortunately for us, are born of what and whom he likes *[raaga]*. Then there is *Kripa* who avails himself to others because he is so awkwardly impulsive – thankfully his warmth makes him unfit to detect right from wrong. All our leaders have been prosperous and have deserved life's materialistic needs. Then we have *Ashvathama,* the talented warrior, whose secret wish for materialistic dominance motivates all his actions. *Vikarna's* endurance and creative determination are born of his dislikes [*dvesha*]. Then there is *Somdat's* instability and *Jayadrath's* fear of death and discrepancies. They are both motivated to fight for our cause – even if it is for mercenary authority."

Duryodhana's individuality and self-complacency are striking in this bravado. He even claims that a vast array of heroes is ready to lay down their lives for his sake. He declares to *Drona,* "And many other heroes who combat with ingenious competence are strongly encouraged by their own selfish rules for worldly riches. They have agreed they will give up their lives if their wishes are strengthened with riches for them and their families. They are all outfitted with various weapons and missiles. Their skills will be sharpened at battle for they hope to win worldly happiness and comforts."

Sanjaya tells the blind king that his son, *Duryodhana,* intuitively knows that his soldiers are obligated to fight. They are motivated by ignorance, ego, passion, hatred, attachment, past tendencies, ambitions and wants. *Duryodhana* promises the soldiers many desires – motivated guarantees including protection from *Bhishma* who is the only general qualified to contend with the purity of the *Pandava* forces.

Duryodhana sees for himself the small *Pandava* force is not defeated by restlessness and doubt. They have learned the technique of performing and fighting in the world. The *Kauravas* might be more able to destroy the *Pandavas,* since they have with them the powerful *Bhishma* protecting them.

He therefore says, "*Bhishma* has the expertise to protect our forces – the larger *Kaurava* army. Even though my army is limitless in numbers, it may still be inadequately weak. The smaller *Pandava* army, led by *Drishtadyumna,* although small has an adequate amount of strength. They already seem ready to triumph even before the combat has begun." Therefore, *Duryodhana* cautions, "All of you, take position and remain stationed in your own places, in each division of the army. Shield *Bhishma* and safeguard him from attacks from the back."

Through distinction of real from the unreal, the *Pandavas* are familiar with viewing the world as an illusion. By remaining in soul awareness with each breath, they have learned to experience themselves in the all-pervading Universe, – Mother Nature on display.

Duryodhana recognizes he has a habit of expecting protection from the invincible, expedient and superior *Bhishma,* his grand sire. He must now rely on him again because of apprehension about consequences of this conflict. Unlike the *Pandavas* he must seek *Bhishma's* help by appealing to him with reverence, perseverance and persuasion to achieve and hammer out his own survival.

Duryodhana knows that because of his own obsession with self-gratification, his mentor will come to his defense. After all, *Drona's* inclinations correspond to his own secret desires. *Drona* can inspire everyone with new ruses for earthly survival. Besides, *Duryodhana* is sympathetic towards authority of companions who themselves are enslaved by predispositions – such as *Karna's* likes and *Vikarna's* dislikes or *raaga-dvesha.*

Although *Krishna* offered model companionship among all the cousins, he cautioned *Duryodhana* against a war that he foreordained *Kauravas* would lose. Even so *Duryodhana* calls on his armed forces to prepare for warfare. Since cooperation is the backbone of an army's success, *Duryodhana* the clever strategist coaches his various commanders to work out a single scheme for protecting *Bhishma.*

Sanjaya is describing these scenes of *Kurukshetra* to King *Dhritarashtra.* He notes there is shortage in *Drona's* usual confident responses. This on a battlefield triggers the freethinking *Bhishma* to send a promising message to prevent the self-possessed *Duryodhana* from becoming brokenhearted. *Bhishma* elatedly blows his conch, expressing his restlessness and dissatisfaction – this deafening battle cry interrupts *Duryodhana's* reflection. It stirs him to warn his army to fight and destroy all.

Aiming to cheer *Duryodhana,* the grandsire *Bhishma,* the oldest of the *Kauravas,* blows his conch shell again with a resounding roar of a lion. Suddenly, a great chorus of sounds comes from shells, kettledrums, cymbals, tabors and cowhorn-trumpets from the *Kaurava* side. This collective fanfare stimulates their mercenary needs and intensely energizes their senses to fight.

Duryodhana, unhappy with his own improper motives, is invoking flawlessness by conscripting all trustworthy forces, even if his own conduct is unrighteous. The painstaking *Bhishma* understands *Duryodhana's* obvious agitation. He tries to revive *Duryodhana's* victimized mind. *Duryodhana* suddenly suspends the stresses on his senses. He gives his mind an objective and an expectation of success at war. This immediately gives him ambition for achievement and satisfaction.

Sanjaya now turns his attention to the *Pandava* forces. He sees *Arjuna* normally of fervent resolve, suspending all demands made on him for action. *Sanjaya* witnesses *Arjuna's* charioteer *Krishna* speaking. He describes his own understanding as he follows *Arjuna's* mind-set, guided by his soul. While trying to free his mind from rambling thoughts, he sees *Arjuna's* heart pierced by the unbroken sound of the *Pranava.*

Krishna is directing *Arjuna's* chariot harnessed to ten white horses. *Arjuna* seems free of all physical hindrances, and seems mindful of the direction *Krishna* is taking on the battlefield of *Kurukshetra*. *Sanjaya* witnesses this marvel and elatedly reports to *Dhritarashtra*,

"*Krishna* and the son of *Pandu* – *Arjuna*, are seated in their magnificent chariot with white horses. *Krishna* first blows his divine sounding conch. From *Arjuna's* conch emerges a spellbinding sound of *Om*, which seems to emanate from its core. *Arjuna* witnesses and experiences an expansion into the *pranava* from the *Panchanjaya* – *Krishna's* conch. Having introduced *Arjuna's* mind to become aware of God's presence on the *Pandava* side of the battlefield, *Krishna* looks back at his friend."

Sanjaya, who is a reclusive ascetic himself, recognizes and experiences the symphonic vibrations of *Om* all around. Long practices at concentration and contemplation have spiritualised many of *Arjuna's* lower inert tendencies. Instead of rampant desire-motivated actions for materialism, cravings, lust, jealousy and conceit, *Arjuna* has almost successfully replaced them with self-control, adherence to restraint, constant practice in contemplation, and intuitive execution of all actions. *Sanjaya* reports to the blind king *Dhritarashtra*, "*Arjuna's* common past tendencies have been nearly substituted. The transformation is so marked that even the subtle spinal plexuses or *chakras* are vibrating with *Om* at different tones and in different frequencies."

Sanjaya continues, "*Krishna*, who is granted with limitless intelligence, is blowing the *Panchanjaya* again. Once upon a time, it supported the formation of five primitive elements of Creation."

"*Arjuna* now blows the *Devadatta*, his personal conch, which has always given him the power and joy to remain in Divinity. *Bheema* is blowing the *Vrikodara*, to give him power to perform superhuman deeds. He has the ability to disconnect his emotions, senses and organs of action through *pranayama* and *pratyahara* when dealing with unpleasant actions. He has now blown the conch *Paundra,* which gives him the power to destroy all states of desire, anger, greed, and attachment."

The blind king demands he hear the original vibrating sound of *Om. Sanjaya* says, "*Krishna's* conch *Panchanjaya* and those of the *Pandava* forces cannot be heard unless the spinal plexuses become genial to contemplative training."

Sanjaya continues, "King *Yudhishtra,* the son of *Kunti,* has blown the *Anatavijaya* which conquers anything in infinite space. *Nakula* and *Sahadev* have blown the *Sughosha* and the *Manipushpaka,* capable of protecting the pure ones."

Sanjaya now feels confident the *Pandava* family consists of trustworthy and honest leaders. He warns King *Dhritarashtra,* it is impossible to overthrow them, whose perfection is conserved through long years of exhaustive cooperation, dedication, self-control, patience and a deep reliance in a comrade and mentor like *Krishna.* He next speaks of integrity and strength of the best from *Hastinapur.*

"That determined King of *Kashi* is an exceptional archer. The faithful *Sikhandi* is a powerful commander of eleven thousand archers. The self-controlled *Dhrishtadyumna,* the clear-sighted *Virat* and the ever sincere *Satyaki* are unconquerable," *Sanjaya* reminds the blind king.

"Long years of sanctified performances have made *Arjuna* withdraw from all personal feelings for the results of his actions. He has learned to become accomplished in progressive stages. He acts only for a common and universal good. While in the company of *Draupadi,* he has documented right action by withdrawing life force. He witnesses all while in his own divine cave." *Sanjaya* persists.

Sanjaya continues to describe the superior abilities of the *Pandava* forces: "*Krishna* trained all of *Draupadi's* children in fairness, self-denial, contentment, austerity, and dedication to Truth. He also coached his nephew, the high-minded *Abhimanyu,* son of *Subhadra* and *Arjuna,* to remain free of cravings, miserliness, greed, pomposity, jealousy, and selfishness. Armed with complete submission to Truth – look, these mighty *Pandava* sons have also blown their conches."

Dhritarashtra understands *Sanjaya.* While developing with his two younger brothers, *Pandu* and *Vidura,* he also was educated in the art of victory over mercenary instincts. *Sanjaya* reminds *Dhritarashtra* that contemplation on Truth while seated stationary in any chosen posture or *asana* will reveal to him the right course of action. Such concentration or *dharana* will lead him to become skillful at dealing with the confusion about the conflict.

He was reminded that breath control or *pranayama* triumphs over all yearnings and restlessness. Sense withdrawal or *pratyahara* becomes unwaveringly effective. Concentration, meditation and assimilation *[dharana, dhyana and samadhi]* comes easily, *Sanjaya* promises *Dhritarashtra* Truth will guide him to revoke this ungodly war he has approved.

Dhritarashtra interrupts *Sanjaya,* "I understand such efforts dispel impurity of thought and action, and true knowledge is illuminated through the eight-limbed yoga. With establishment of discrimination the cause of all injury is crushed. Man then arrives at emancipation. But, my son must reign as king of *Hastinapur.* I am the eldest son of the dynasty and therefore *Duryodhana* deserves to be king, even though *Yudhishtra* is the oldest of all the princes."

Sanjaya had given the blind king a vivid description of the excellence of a collective *Pandava* force. Perhaps, he thought, the blind king can be convinced to stop the war. A long continued roar of bells and cymbals ravaged his heart. In response, the frightened king says, "That turbulent sound, which resonates throughout heaven and earth, pierces and intimidates the hearts of the *Dhritarashtra* clan."

Sanjaya's heart shudders with anticipation as he watches *Krishna* and *Arjuna* and declares, "*Arjuna,* the third son of *Pandu,* bearing the flag of *Hanuman* – the son of the Wind god, has taken up his bow and is now addressing *Krishna.*"

Sanjaya watches *Arjuna's* decency with close attention. The mind is clear and heart rooted in virtue. At the edge of the battlefield in *Kurukshetra Krishna* guides his chariot; *Arjuna* studies the scene before him. Then he says, "O *Krishna*, please take me between the two armies, so I may see those who stand in this battle formation. On the eve of this war, let me clearly understand with whom I must fight."

Sanjaya sees *Arjuna* ride amidst the two sides, seemingly obsessed with a goal for combat with the hostile army. He acknowledges the army that must be destroyed. He wonders who will he fight with first? *Arjuna* notes the *Kaurava* soldiers seem nervous and fearfully uncertain about why they are assembled in battle. He notes there – their bond towards their lineage, appetite for materialism, bitterness towards imagined wrongs, a decision to remain muddled, and obligation to constraints of *Maya*. All are cursed by Nature's power of deception.

Seeing his own people are engaged in war while deluded, *Arjuna* is astonished. *Sanjaya* watches *Arjuna* redeem his own center of morality. In this genteel state of mindfulness *Arjuna* looks around under *Krishna's* watchful eyes.

Sanjaya once more convinces the blind king that seeing as both armies are descendants of King *Bharata*, the common ancestor of both the *Kauravas* and the *Pandavas*, the impending battle be halted. *Sanjaya* fails again.

Krishna declares, "O noble *Arjuna*, you, the son of *Kunti* my aunt, are made with her chaste earth. I wish you to eyewitness the *Kurus [Kauravas* and *Pandavas]* gathered here."

With that, *Krishna* steers *Arjuna's* chariot into the middle of the battlefield of *Kurukshetra*. Here *Arjuna* becomes contemplative. He allows himself to identify with enigmatic conflicts entrenched in his person. *Arjuna's* bewilderment seems fixed in memories and fancies about lineage, alliances and property.

Arjuna speaks, "Let me pay attention to all these nobles who are ready for war. Let me see with whom I am engaging in confrontation. Let me see all who side with this battle. These brave ones who agree to fight, have assembled on this battlefield because of *Duryodhana's* greed and desires. Let me see and become aware how the evil-minded ego assisted by vanity compels this entirety to combat for control and ownership."

Arjuna admits he knows what he must do when confronted in combat for honor and dishonor, truth and untruth, right and wrong. However on the battlefield he sees instead the same instructors and ancestors who modeled his brothers and cousins. He recognises *Drona,* their shared mentor and his favorite but egotistical grandsire *Bhishma.* Despite his thirteen years in the forest for spiritual restoration, *Arjuna*'s opinions are overcast by old recollections of kindred kinship.

Sanjaya marvels that even an unblemished spiritual aspirant like *Arjuna,* who conquered sleep and sloth, can be found wavering. Instead of soldiers *Arjuna* sees, family and old companions. He does not see enemies or opponents with negative urges and delusions ready to fight him and his honest constitutional rights. Deluded by sects of close blood relations, *Arjuna* is ready for a truce.

Sanjaya reports an unexpected and abrupt change in the arrangement. "Overcome by compassion and empathy *Arjuna* examines both armies wanting war. Paralyzed with confusion and bewilderment, he sees fathers, grandfathers, teachers, maternal uncles, family, sons, grandsons and in-laws too. He does not see them as enemies!"

Arjuna appreciates the full import of sacrifices being made, while waging war against unrighteousness and immorality. *Arjuna* realizes the extent of damages the citizens of *Hastinapur* will be called upon to make. Instead of a much -needed transformation leading citizens towards freedom, equality, and truth – they will in its place avenge the wrongs of *Duryodhana's* cruelty.

Sanjaya assesses *Arjuna's* predicament. He knows from experience that very few virtuous applicants voice morality in earnest. What *Arjuna* considers true, is that one cannot be free of minor evils, especially if addicted to them. Although the role of sympathy and forgiveness are natural and inborn, *Sanjaya* knows they are not necessarily for ever and a day noble emotions. An impulsive tendency is a defect but is termed by some as benevolence. Knowing that forgiveness causes a mental splintering of intellectual equipoise, he watches *Arjuna* lose his detachment and objectivity.

Arjuna is intelligent enough to know the difference between right from wrong. He nevertheless says, "My relatives, O *Krishna,* are bedecked and enthusiastic to fight us. My control fails me. Suddenly my mouth is parched, my body shudders and my hair stands on end."

"The *Gandiva* bow, which is usually my scaffold of integrity, slides from my hand and my skin feels scorched all over. I am incapable of standing and my mind is spinning. I am unsteady and I believe this war is a mistake. This, what is happening is an armed conflict against kith and kin. That, to me seems contradictory."

In a few sentences, *Arjuna,* the candidate of veracity and virtue, sees his own character overruled by a selfish pretentiousness, intrinsic in *Bhishma.* Inbred inclinations of *Drona* and dissatisfactions in *Somadatta* are detected in *Arjuna.* Ambitions in *Duryodhana* and fancies entertained by *Ashvathama* are also identifiable in him. Narcissism seen in *Karna,* and abhorrence in-built in *Vikarna* also is detectable. *Sanjaya* sees all current inclinations towards dishonesty built into his own personality also.

Arjuna's breathing becomes erratic. His body cannot be still. He says. "I am seeing terrible omens, O *Krishna.* Why do I need a kingdom? What advantage is there in staying alive while I slay my kinfolk and friends? I neither want glory of victory nor the kingdom. What is the use of enjoying this kingdom or even life?"

Krishna knows *Arjuna* must center himself while in the battlefield. He must erase all subliminal memories of past immoral actions he is oblivious about. *Arjuna* feels an intense sense of disconnection. He is in a mental wasteland, created by abandonment of materialism.

He refuses to contest unrighteousness and declares,

"O *Krishna,* I do not see any good in killing my relatives who are present here. They seem ready to sacrifice life and wealth. All these noble relatives and friends, even if they wish to kill me, I have no wish to stop them."

Sanjaya was giving the blind king a true description of. the condition experienced by devout seekers like *Arjuna,* who have traveled some length on the frail trail of morality. The early soul contact is with eager happy beings basking in the flush of intellectual contacts. The initial change in personality revels in universal intelligence. *Sanjaya* knows that for *Arjuna* to make further progress in his fight against injustice, his dedicated wishes, sense cravings and reactionary inborn dispositions and tendencies need extermination.

Arjuna continues to justify his retreat from the post of duty and repeats what he said earlier in response to *Krishna's* pregnant silence. *Sanjaya* knows *Krishna's* silence is itself a criticism of *Arjuna's* disposition.

"These *Kauravas* – I do not wish to kill though they kill me. O *Krishna,* I will not kill even for the sake of dominion over the three worlds – how then can I kill them for a mere kingdom on earth?"

Feeling he had not stated his case strongly enough,

Arjuna declares in a spirit of mock renunciation, "Killing these sons of *Dhritarashtra,* what pleasure can be ours, O *Krishna*? Sin and misfortune alone will be our gain by killing these felons".

Despite all that *Arjuna* has said so far, *Krishna* remained silent. The wise *Sanjaya* understands that offence is a blunder committed by an indiscreet ego, against it's own eternal nature, the soul. *Arjuna's* seemingly learned disapproval originates from a dejected, impulsive, illogical understanding.

While addressing his friend *Krishna* who is gifted with higher intelligence, *Arjuna* imagines and rationalizes that it is wrong to destroy the guilty. *Arjuna's* objection to killing enemies is a gross misunderstanding of the sanctioned texts of enlightened cultures. *Krishna* understands his friend's fretful distraction has to be scattered.

He therefore allows *Arjuna* to continue talking.

"Therefore, we shall not kill the sons of *Dhritarashtra.* How can we be happy by killing our own people, O *Krishna*? Only sin will amass by eradicating their sanctuary. In what way will happiness be ours by hurting our relatives, *Krishna*?"

False reasoning and imagination has led *Arjuna* to wrong resolutions. His intelligence has lost its discriminative and perceptive powers. He has introduced fantasy, conceit, empathy, hostility, and flawed loyalty in his convictions. *Arjuna* declares, "Seeing through *Kaurava's* clouded intelligence, I see no evil in destroying families. They are a self-serving society, geared towards self-indulgence. Viewed from their perspective, I see no sin in their cruelty and treason towards friends."

Sanjaya watches *Arjuna's* mind accept ignorance. *Arjuna* sees finite as infinite, impure as pure, misery as happiness and no soul as soul. With his soul entrapped in worldly matters, the power of his opinion and the quality of his observations has abandoned the Inner Light. Dutiful work in worldly life could have given him sublime happiness, but enslaved to mundane existence, *Arjuna* is constrained by past habits and inclinations.

Arjuna gives himself two choices: intellectual complacency or pure passivity. He is so confused that he feels a number of arrangements can be made so that both virtue and unrighteousness can coexist. *Arjuna* has met many who believe obliteration of senses; mind and ego destroys an individual's ability to enjoy happiness. He therefore continues to address his own consciousness and declares, "O *Krishna* why should we who see evil in devastating friend and kin, learn to turn away from such sins, even if this war is against unrighteousness? They like us, are ready to kill, but can I not turn away from this sin?"

When lust, desire, anger, greed, possessiveness, and pride, eclipse the irrational mind, a mortal does not see decay of his own human personality. *Arjuna* rationalises that sense inclinations are indispensable to experience the world, as decreed and designed by the Creator himself. He sincerely presumes that sense-indulging dispositions can live side by side with good habits. Both tendencies make realm of living complete.

The *Pandavas* took over a decade to substitute bad habits for good tendencies. *Krishna* knows Man is plagued by soul-humiliating defeats at the hands of old habits, until *self*-consciousness becomes securely anchored in *Self*-consciousness. He therefore allows *Arjuna* to rant and rave.

Sanjaya knows there is an inaccurate belief among those who practice morality and spirituality that sense urges are reformed through internalizing and meditation. *Arjuna* may have learned to regulate external circumstances, but prevailing influences of individuality, past habits, opinions, and tendencies are not permanently erased.

Mortals like *Arjuna,* who lack a knowledge base to confront conflicts caused by desires, former habits, and submission to the powers of individuality, need intuitive guidance. *Krishna* knows *Arjuna* needs essential advice on how to control physical, emotional, psychological and intellectual urges. Once Man is armed with such behavior adjustments, there is conservation of psychic energy, and automatic dispassion for materialism.

Even contemplation does not help *Arjuna* arrive at a tranquil clear inner centre where he can get insight and knowledge of growth into soul-awareness. *Krishna* knows need for spirituality entails progressive transformation in every atom of the body, from the nails to the core of one's being. *Krishna* knows the whole clan of cravings needs destroying. These yearning senses and their progeny of inclinations need elimination.

Arjuna reasserts an oft-repeated fact that culture is a technique by which morality is upheld by a family and ultimately the community. If communal actions do not unfold into an orderly culture with righteous tradition, a nation's heritage stagnates into confusion and destruction.

Arjuna therefore declares, "Killing relatives creates destruction of enduring skilled traditions of a family. Codes and morals become redundant and overwhelm surviving families. When experiences are adulterated, delusions arise. Their mind is exposed to grave hazards when families lose everyone and everything that once kept them together and alive."

Arjuna stops to think before continuing with his tirade,

"Chaos in social standing escorts the slayer of the family to hell. When leaders of families fall, there is none to explain about rites and traditions. Forefathers and ancestors are dispossessed and ritual offerings of food and water stop. These evil deeds by the destroyer of families cause disruption in their own rank by dissolving their own old rites performed by the family."

Krishna listens while *Arjuna* continues to defend his resolve not to fight. "We have heard, O *Krishna* that it is fated for these families to become extinct when their religious rites and traditions are destroyed. When family virtues are destroyed, they linger in hell for a longtime. Therefore they spend their time in eternal suffering."

He therefore tells *Krishna,* "Alas! We are involved in a great sin. We prepare to kill our relatives, for the sake of greed and for enjoying a kingdom."

Sanjaya was watching *Arjuna's* shenanigans. As a beginner at seeking through self-unfoldment *Arjuna* needs self-realization all the way through searching within. His craving for soul culture at first forces him to be silent. He peers behind the veil of darkness and ignorance. The seeker in *Arjuna* wonders about the folly of renouncing tangible pleasures for a likely glimpse of the Spirit. When he inspects the infinite cosmic vision, between and behind his eyebrows, he becomes hesitant..

Arjuna knows that suppression of innate personality traits cannot be a permanent condition. He must challenge and transcend all obstacles unresponsive to self-unfoldment. He has two choices. First becoming knowledgeable through study of scriptures and second reflecting until his past character cancels itself in the experience of an intimate enlightenment of the sublime.

At this stage, the rational in *Arjuna* is dissatisfied, both with the lack of serious progress and the disconnection from routine sense habits. He even dares to express this inaccurate notion that training and adjustment of impulses might result in corrupt results. *Arjuna* cries in desperation, "*Krishna,* even if the armed sons of *Dhritarashtra* slay me in battle I will remain unresisting and unarmed. That would be better for me, because I will incur no sin."

Sanjaya continues watching this communication between *Krishna* and *Arjuna. Arjuna's* moving argument has taken the form of dejection, anguish, and grief. Overcome by a sense of futility in continuing the path of action and reflection, *Arjuna* slumps forward, willfully dropping the upright bow. He throws away his decision and resolution to fight immorality.

Sanjaya now speaks to *Dhritarashtra,* the blind king of the *Kuru* clan of *Kauravas* and *Pandavas.* "Having thus spoken amid the battlefield, *Arjuna* is sitting down. From near the seat of his chariot he has cast away bow and arrow towards his feet. His mind is unsettled and overcome by grief."

Sanjaya's intuitiveness makes certain judicious observations about *Arjuna's* thoughts, prejudices, sensitivities, tendencies, and involuntary inclinations for likes-and-dislikes.

A raging battle is happening inside *Arjuna* – between his society of outer environment and his inner growth for soul-consciousness. For growth to take place, *Arjuna* must blend understanding and inner satisfaction, to re-establish wholeness of body, mind and spirit.

Krishna ensures that *Arjuna's* old personality can be dared to transform. The armed conflict on the piains of *Kurukshetra* between virtue and unrighteousness is similar to the terrain that is *Arjuna's* body, mind and intellect. Both are perfect places for self-development. Through self-cultivation, *Arjuna* can become a successful go-between to change his faulty disposition, humor, impressions, past sense tendencies, and ambitions.

With the right information and continued self-discipline, *Krishna* knows, *Arjuna* will give up unfocused actions, false thinking, fantasy, and dissipation of dynamism. Mindful of correct knowledge, *Arjuna,* the spiritual seeker and practitioner of dedicated action, can transform his physical and psychological body through philosophical study and meditative exercises. He can be convinced to surrender to concentration Universal Intelligence and finally to Cosmic Consciousness.

Once *Arjuna* securely settles in the *Kutastha Chaitanya* or center of Universal Intelligence with each breath, he will no longer wish to share experiences in societal performances. Such misgivings, confusion, inactivity, falseness, and untold conflict can be transcended. Guru-instructed meditation will immerse him to arrive at the endless Universe of the Infinite.

Without help lifelong companions who have given *Arjuna* sensory pleasures will not be destroyed and abandoned. Worldly happiness will not be renounced. Control will be prescribed and restraint cherished.

4. Self-Knowledge and Equanimity

Sanjaya understand
everyday
life's
action
duty
knows
percep
rites a
superi
know
compe

As
recogn
highes
Krishn
four
and th
pass o
solace
army o
Life a
discrim
what is
pathetic

Sanjaya
Dhrita
of tear
Having

4. Self-Knowledge and Equanimity

Sanjaya understands *Arjuna* is spun-out on a moribund everyday flare-up. He was turning away from the stage of life's battle. He knows all about the principles of selfless action for a greater good. *Sanjaya* hopes this deviation from duty will fade away. This new bias will resolve. Everyone knows he is a distinguished symbol of aptitude and perception. *Arjuna* was trained in conventional protection rites and mercifully and overwhelmingly engulfed by superior prenatal tendencies. At this point he does not know he is already living a righteous state. He has the competence to repulse negative tendencies.

Arjuna is an approachable seeker of *Sankhya Yoga.* He recognizes the Knowledge of the Imperishable Self as the highest Yoga of Wisdom. The stirring conversation with *Krishna* will have to include the essence of the ponderous four *Vedas,* one hundred and eight important *Upanishads* and the six systems of *Hindu* philosophy. *Krishna* will have to pass on the universal message of Cosmic Wisdom, for *Arjuna's* solace and deliverance. He must identify with his duty to the army of humankind already assembled on the battlefield of Life and Existence at *Kurukshetra.*

"I cannot see, I feel powerless and my power of discrimination is lost. I take refuge in you *Krishna.* Teach me what is accountable and what is not," *Arjuna* suddenly wails pathetically.

Krishna responds to *Arjuna's* entreaty for leadership. *Sanjaya* reports all conversations to the blind king *Dhritarashtra,* "*Krishna* addresses *Arjuna,* whose eyes are full of tears, and is overcome with immoderation and opposition. Having gained contentment neither from the senses nor from reflection, *Arjuna* weeps, dispirited and yearning for a blameless and righteous but pious development."

Krishna, the obliterator of impetuousness, comes to the aid of the troubled conscript, *Arjuna,* who begs consideration. *Sanjaya* understands *Arjuna's* grief. It is the regret experienced by all freshly dedicated competitors of elusive secular action. *Arjuna* learned no real advantage from his early striving to gain from union *[yoga]* with duties to right action and to divinity. He failed to interpret that inner development comes from inflexible and balanced efforts at reflection, as anticipated by his faultless mentor, *Krishna.*

Although *Arjuna* at this moment feels his attempts to direct the mind are ineffective, he is confident if he persists at putting faith in his friend and teacher, he will find an answer to his problem. He wants time for calm deliberation and consideration. He knows the universal convention that the Spirit of integrity counsels all believers by assuming the form of a friend, a *guru* or saint. He is also familiar with the belief the Lord speaks in the course of the devotee's own intuitive analysis.

Krishna consequently expresses his disappointment. "In such a critical moment amid war, from where comes upon you, O *Arjuna,* this delusion of dejection? This behaviour is inappropriate coming from an *Aryan* soldier. It is damaging to the achievement of virtue. What is this delusion that brings so much disgrace, O son of *Kunti*?"

Feeling he is receiving a divine response, *Arjuna's* attentiveness soars to the *kutastha.* While centred here, in the middle of the spiritual eye, he senses proximity with the Spirit immanent in all creation and displaying in each being.

"Do not become weak, O son of *Kunti.* Even a trivial disadvantage of the mind does not suit you. Abandon this and get up and do battle," *Krishna* orders *Arjuna.*

Any determined seeker can sense the propelling Spirit but only an exceptional disciple like *Arjuna* can hear the intelligent voice of counsel. The Lord censures *Arjuna* for dejection.

"Great enemies of Man remain seemingly inoffensive within understanding, as friends, only to usurp Man's sacred and honourable competence. By lowering the bridge of compassion, over the moat that separates the wise-castled soul and the nearby senses, you are allowing psychic enemies to break through the ramparts of self-control. When challenged to make choices, intuition reveals the path of action. But our past tendencies allow individuality, to follow the path of unfortunate decisions," *Krishna* states.

"The universal command is to do no evil and to disallow depravity through others, whether through our own bidding or by tolerating corruption through silence. Cooperation with mischief through ambivalence is a conceited display of our own pretended virtue. A negative image originating from a flawed awareness of our spiritual self is expressing in you as fear of failure, and dread of what others might think of you, regardless of your actions. This is hampering your ability to exercise self-will and obstructs your capacity to act righteously," *Krishna* adds.

Sanjaya understands Man's life is a puzzle. He can be satisfied with godly satisfaction that he is a soul made in the image of the Spirit. Yet, the body that has incarnated through so many lives has learned only sensory preference. *Arjuna* needs discrimination to distinguish between, real soul and illusory pleasures of the senses.

Krishna knows that Man is steadfastly submissive to sense enjoyment of the body. He advises *Arjuna* to abandon apathy. He wants *Arjuna* to become convincing and productive, so he can experience the just satisfaction of courage.

"O *Arjuna,* agree not to such frailty! It does not suit you, who are always decisively critical of foes. Cast off this weakness of the heart." *Krishna* said firmly to his friend.

Without achievement by preference, *Arjuna* would surely succumb to cowardly neutrality. *Arjuna* is warned he could become individuality-centred, which could and would inflate his instinctive weakness. He must neither, warns *Krishna,* become impartial towards spirit nor must he increase his affinity to the senses.

Arjuna is not convinced. "O *Krishna,* you who are a slayer of foes, how can I in this war, direct my skills as an archer against *Bhishma* whose egoistic individuality I cherish and also against *Drona* who left me with gratifying memories of concrete worthy habits? Is it not more fitting they be worshipped? Individuality and self-esteem have been my companions for so many lives," *Arjuna* pleads.

Arjuna is overcome by his false self-belief but he still has the ability to intuitively turn towards his honourable and therefore true nature. He calls on *Krishna* the slayer of demons of Ignorance and Temptations. *Arjuna* is finding it difficult to veto his individuality and past inclinations. To justify his judgment he cites his past existences when he was parented by his egoistic grandfather *Bhishma* and taught by *Drona* who inculcated and reinforced in him, all past tendencies and habits. *Arjuna* admits it would be a frightful task to destroy even a deluded soul's identification and attachments.

Arjuna carefully rationalizes about these two foes, individuality and habits, both authoritative. Unable to transcend his own delusive criminality, he continues to rant and rave. He has so far not mastered the art of withdrawing from his familiar mental faculties, now breathing in his body.

"Even a life of extreme poverty would be better for me than an existence injured by slaying my most dignified educators. Even if I do wipe out these mentors, who are engrossed in wealth and possessions, then surely, here on earth all my own would-be satisfaction in tangible indulgence will be soiled appallingly with the blood of remorse," *Arjuna* continues.

Everyone is listening to *Arjuna's* conversation that in traditional mercenary and materialistic consciousness, ego and past habits guide Man's thoughts, feelings and desire goals. *Krishna* understands they are the preceptors of all human activities that are able to mould for old needs, new ambitions, and give continuity to Man's mundane individualised existence.

Arjuna lacks the wisdom and insight that misplaced compassion can turn away a dutiful mind from Consciousness revealing existence and experience. Understandably, he asks if destroying ego and habit-inclination will cause him regret.

Krishna knows that depravity exists, only in the misapplication of authority on the reserves of Nature. In all bad inclinations the freeing ego, makes an opinionated demand on the human character.

Disagreeable tendencies have eclipsed his intelligence and desensitised *Arjuna's* early resolution to fight the enemies when he says, "I can hardly decide which closure would be better - that we should defeat them or that they should conquer us. Disagreeing with us are *Dhritarashtra's* one hundred craving children. They perfected the art of indulgence, made materialistic gains through need, anger and greed, fought for jealousy, and displayed conceit and enviousness, among other inclinations. Their death would make my own life unattractive without the company of these well-known kindred members."

It is only when one sense-gratification after another fails the materialist that Man wonders if blessedness is ever possible through the senses. This thinking has a releasing effect. The mundane in *Arjuna* has the spunk to detach him from this distraction.

When the materialist finds satisfaction in the exercise of contemplation, he directly experiences in his own inner silence an incredible wisdom that he is in Him and He in him. United with the Whole, he is delighted to serve God with ease and self-control. Without effort, he abandons his old uneasy hunting grounds chasing after desires. His accomplishments now become an army for freedom, equality, and fairness, for the total universal family. Understanding involuntarily un-encumbers him from his old stubborn folly and sense servitude.

Normally, a worthy student like *Arjuna* judiciously follows the leadership of the spiritually intelligent. Wise preceptors such as *Krishna* do not impose their ideas or sentiments on the seeker. A genuine teacher leads the soul towards its own inherent bliss-producing qualities to unearth its own unfolding.

To release the mind from the outgoing senses through meditation is to automatically wipe out the bodily importance and inclination prejudices. *Krishna* would not stop *Arjuna* from his illogical reasoning or his hesitation.

Even though the senses in unison cry out "Please us, never mind the soul," *Arjuna* intuitively understands the senses are never satisfied with their ever-increasing wants since before birth. The sense demands troubled him even while penniless in the forest for twelve years. There, he practised monumental self-denial and fearless penance. *Arjuna* was a continuing spiritual practitioner, to whom sense pleasures are well known and soul happiness, extraordinarily uplifting. But amid the silent cry of the bliss-demanding soul, he experiences the familiar clamour of life energy flowing out through the senses, demanding to experiences that are pleasing to tamed feeling.

The teacher only asks Man to control the senses. A teacher like *Krishna* knows that a sense slave will eventually find himself a victim of disease, and thus will not be able to assign his broken body to soul-search. *Krishna* therefore allows *Arjuna* to drain himself in a futile mental uproar until he surrenders, because *Arjuna* cries, "My heart is overpowered by the taint of self-pity; my mind is perplexed about my duty. I beg you *Krishna* to advise me what the best path for me to follow is. I am your believer. Direct me, who has taken sanctuary in you."

Arjuna, after inviting the cause of the senses, is filled

with anguish and drained of energy to do any work, leave alone fight his enemies. He admits his inaptitude and surrenders to his inner Spirit - the *Guru*-preceptor. In the seat of meditation, the voice of Inner Silence lacks clarity; therefore, the advice from a *guru* is desirable. The devotee in *Arjuna* is willing to listen to the *guru* in *Krishna,* learning from him the deep truths of soul development. *Krishna,* however, would not teach unless asked.

Arjuna therefore declares, "I see nothing that will remove my private affliction that pounds at my senses. Nothing eases me. Not even my possessions of unrivalled and prosperous kingship help. My lordship over this perishable earth does not satisfy any of the sense deities in my earthy heaven."

Sanjaya follows and reports to the blind king, all of *Arjuna's* confusion. As long as one lives in the body, one must experience through the senses and enjoy the pleasures they give. It is natural therefore for *Arjuna* to ask why he needs to engage in battle with unrighteous materialism.

Sanjaya understands when *Arjuna* speaks of the earth; he is referring to Man's perishable body. Its prosperity is health, total well being, and happiness. This threefold wealth is unhealthy when the inner life force is misused to provide for indulgences. Physical, psychological and physiological illnesses leave bad *karmic* influences on the causal body, from past wrong actions and inclinations. Compelling sense preferences are revived as unfavourable habits in the next life, only to become impediments to spiritual practices, in the future. Even if a seeker wants to launch on a spiritual expedition, the physical body that has been mistreated would be unfit to follow and perform physical and contemplative activities.

Sanjaya, who through the *yoga* of meditation, has become seasoned with insight and is impermeable to physical ailments, is in permanent communication with *Om,* the origin of all life's abilities. Because he constantly experiences spiritual plenty on earth, he is able to talk to the blind king who practices loyalty to materialism and attachments.

Sanjaya discloses *Arjuna's* bizarre psychological state to the blind king. Although *Arjuna* resists entertaining righteous action, he is fully cultured to regard *Krishna* as the Lord of Insight. *Arjuna* is stilling the mind and silencing his senses, so he can understand and live, according to the teachings he has received all his life. *Sanjaya* says to *Dhritarashtra,* "Having told *Krishna* that he will not fight, *Arjuna* has now become silent."

Arjuna remains mentally stagnant, neither progressing nor withdrawing. *Sanjaya* apprised the blind king, that even though *Arjuna* is assailed by hesitation, he has surrendered unconditionally to *Krishna* in inner silence, and is able to distinguish the Light, across the firmament of his inner understanding. *Sanjaya* tells the blind king that *Arjuna* is an unblemished seeker who has led an uncontaminated spiritual life. He practiced correct eating habits, amended conduct, and deep meditation. He is therefore fortunate enough to witness the smile of the Spirit and to detect the voice of Wisdom in *Krishna.*

"O King *Dhritarashtra,* to *Arjuna* who was lamenting between the two armies, the Lord of the Wisdom *Krishna,* smiling, speaks these words."

Sanjaya then heard *Krishna* say, "*Arjuna,* you have grieved for those not worth mourning over. Yet you utter words of wisdom. The wise agonise neither for the living nor for the dead."

Krishna knows that *Arjuna* needs to reflect on the enigma. He must be convinced that his affinity to individuality, old habits and old friends are deceptive affections stemming from fickleness. *Arjuna* needs to know that life-and-death are ruled and measured in Time and Space. Therefore, *Arjuna's* reasons and conclusions are false. *Krishna* knows that he must awaken *Arjuna's* intelligence.

Krishna begins by reminding *Arjuna* they have both lived

and moved together as teacher and taught, through different platforms of reincarnation. With every reincarnation, their causal souls enticed a suitable physical-astral body covering, needed for their onward spiritual journey through space and time. *Krishṇa* therefore said, "It is not that we both and your royal sense relatives, have never existed before, and will not exist in the future. For that to happen is impossible. Neither is one ever born nor does one ever die. Because of this conflict in understanding there are an appearance and a disappearance only. It is absurd to lament over this."

With this statement, *Krishna* announces in clear terms, the embodied self is set on a great pilgrimage, in which it comes to identify itself with varied forms and temporarily gains a limited, but determined set of experiences through the senses. Man's quality of creativity or *rajoguna* is ever moving away from the stupor of inertia or *tamoguna* to achieve a still and tranquil state or *sattvaguna.*

Krishna continues, "Just as in this body, the self passes through childhood, youth and old age, so also does he pass into another body. The wise are not disturbed or grieved by it. By *guru*-instructed meditation Man has an innate creative ability to aspire and become a reflection of the divinity that he has forgotten that he is."

Krishna reminds *Arjuna* the contemplative prudent shift their responses away from errors of the intellect. Ignorance, which seats itself on inert torpor then, stops to exist. He must stop indulging himself by safeguarding the forces of unrighteousness. They are only impediments to his creative ideal for a moral and spiritual perfection.

He further enlightens *Arjuna* there is only one *prana,* the life force, *Om,* coursing through the Whole and the objective state of affairs he is surveying from his own mind, which is transient. *Arjuna* is encouraged to seek the subjective Oneness in the Whole view of many happenings. Once he has experienced this Oneness within himself in meditation, *Arjuna* will understand why he must fight his habits, tendencies, and his intense need to preserve his egoistic grandsire, *Bhishma.*

Krishna reminds him that he has already learned this knowledge, while banished in the forest, when he sought and experienced enlightenment through the scriptures.

"O son of *Kunti, Arjuna* the ideas of heat and cold, pain and pleasure are produced by the contact of senses with their objects. Such ideas have a beginning and an end; they are impermanent. Endure them with patience, O descendent of the *Bharata* race!"

Krishna explains the evanescent nature of temporarily unpleasant sensations and circumstances. Because physical sense organs and the emotional mind are reactively sensitive, their innate nature is to respond pleasurably or painfully to stimuli. Pre-programming triggers emotional and physical responses to strong likes and dislikes. However, if endured patiently until knowledge dawns on how to improve conditions, conflicts resolve and emotional and physical stability is restored.

Krishna tells *Arjuna* that feelings and thoughts are external to the soul and need a backed up evaluation. Sensations being transitory, fickle and evanescent, when threatened resolve themselves casually to fulfil mental evenness *[titiksha].*

"O chief among men *Arjuna,* he who is unperturbed by the pulls of the senses qualifies to embark on this journey. He is calm and even-minded during pain and pleasure. These do not bring him distress and he alone is equipped to follow the path of liberation to arrive at Immortality," *Krishna* says.

Krishna tells *Arjuna* that his calmness is not the result of disinterest. Once spiritually aware, *Arjuna* should know there is no eternity in fleeting things and the enduring everlasting Consciousness has no death. Aware of this undeniable fact the wise learn to endure. He too is expected to remain unruffled, irrespective of the outer conditions. This higher understanding will make him sensitive to inner evolution.

Once this understanding illumines the unenlightened *chitta* personality, *Arjuna*-like seekers will meet their own immortality passing through a view of circumstances.

Once enlightened his *chitta* or personality will never again surrender as a subservient response to circumstances of minor significance. *Krishna* tells *Arjuna* that his happiness lies in the constant state of unruffled peace during all experiences of earth's changeable creation. It is by meditation alone that Man can expand into omnipresence, and so *Krishna* continues, "The unreal has no existence. Of the Real there is no nonexistence. The truth about both these states is known by men of wisdom."

Only Consciousness exists. *Krishna* re-educates *Arjuna* when he asserts that expression arises from Infinity as the all-pervading life-force, *Om*, which is undying. These fleeting belongings and beings are creative statements of the imperishable permanent Awareness. The existence of them and the superficial adjustments happen because of its presence and in accordance with the Total desires of the Cosmic Whole.

Despite *Arjuna's* earlier scriptural training he identifies with mutation, and fails to acknowledge the substratum of perpetuity. Had *Arjuna* understood this, he would have perceived as real only the enduring substratum. He would have unravelled the mystery of the real from the unreal.

Through inward perception, *Arjuna* is being encouraged by *Krishna* to trace the cause of all activities in creation. Vision directed outward, he sees the waves; turned inwards, he sees the ocean. *Krishna* therefore states, "Know That to be permanent by which all this is pervaded. None can cause the devastation of That - the Imperishable."

Krishna stops to allow what he has said to sink into *Arjuna* and then continues, "They have an end, it is said, these bodies of embodied souls. The Self is Eternal, Indestructible, and Incomprehensible. Having known this wisdom, O descendent of *Bharata* - *Arjuna,* fight!"

Arjuna is still struggling with his beliefs and fancies about his own bodily attachments. Afraid to renounce his human emotions, he is like a bird of eternity sealed in a little cage, fearful of claiming his freedom, even though the enclosure is wide open.

Krishna recognizes unearthing the Spirit and intuitive wisdom is possible only through direct understanding in contemplation, and not through the rationality of intellectualism.

Arjuna is spurred to strive for spiritual growth. *Krishna* admits the state of affairs on the battlefield is potently forceful but he also recognizes *Arjuna's* hankering for righteous action. *Krishna* nonetheless suggests – better a death of virtue than an ordinary base death, on the comfortable bed of excessive self-indulgence.

"He who considers the Self to be the slayer and he who thinks He is slain, neither of these knows the Truth. He slays not, nor is he slain!" *Krishna* says.

Krishna reassures *Arjuna* that he dreams who thinks the Self soils its hands with birth, death, expression, non-manifestation, existence or nonexistence. The immortal Self remains untouched when its cosy cloak is destroyed, just as a man does not die when his house crumbles away. And *Krishna* continues, "This Self is neither born nor does He ever die. After coming into existence, He will not stop to be. He is birthless, eternal, changeless and old, and not killed when the body is killed."

After stressing the embodied soul in essence is reflecting the Spirit, and never undergoes the pangs of birth and death *Krishna* states it is the body which undergoes the six changes of impermanent Nature. They are birth, existence, development, change, decay and annihilation. Just as the rays of the sun are expressed but never created, so too, *Krishna* says, the eternal soul remaining in the perishable body expresses itself but forgets the imperishable source. Enmeshed in the body, mind and intellect, this self is only aware of these six matter conditions in Time and Space.

Arjuna is already taught to distinguish between the indwelling immortal soul and its perishable bodily encasement. During their twelve-year banishment in the forest, the *Pandavas,* who are students of *Vedic* texts, discovered the three bodily wrappings of the soul. It was important that *Arjuna* frees his awareness from his matter envelopment, before he can achieve final liberation.

Kunti, Arjuna's mother raised the five young *Pandu* children to believe the physical food sheath was born of the ever-witnessing *Shiva.* His energy, she said, gives form to five elements, five senses, five organs of action, the five life forces or *pranas,* the mind, intellect and the ego. *Kunti* spent a lifetime metamorphosing her children's innate wants or *vasanas,* and their past inclinations or *samskaras,* towards higher accomplishments. The result was a gradual character transformation, which did not readily enmesh her five sons in seductive indulgences, or prematurely speed bodily decay.

Arjuna also grew to grasp the creative mental-physiological astral body specified under *Brahma,* the Creator's control. *Kunti* taught the *Pandus* that creativity gives pure life or *prana* to the inert and perishable five senses, five organs of action, five subtle elements, the mind, intellect, ego and feeling *or chitta.* The inert physical bodily encasement now has a likeness of life.

Arjuna had also been introduced to his ideational causal body, entwined with wisdom and bliss of the ruling deity, *Vishnu. Arjuna* was taught that *Vishnu* allows the needed transformations of the astral and physical bodies. As the boys grew up together, *Kunti,* who is *Krishna's* paternal aunt, exposed all his cousins to this knowledge.

It was therefore natural for *Krishna* to say, "How can he who knows the Self to be imperishable, everlasting, permanent, birthless and changeless possibly think the Self can cause destructing another? O *Arjuna,* whom does it exterminate?"

Krishna urges *Arjuna* to lift himself to a higher plane of mindfulness and enter his own centre of awareness, where, he will see himself mirrored in his own immortality. Repeatedly *Arjuna* was gently censured that while he exists in his own individuality, a smoke screen of illusion clouds his awareness. Because of this perceptual error, *Arjuna* has become identified with his senses, his organs of action, his individuality, habits, desires, and thoughts.

Krishna cautions *Arjuna* the ascetic life in the forest and austerities of restraint, self-control, breath control, sense withdrawal and meditation overthrow sense pleasures only temporarily. Forces of outgoing senses are first made unresponsive with spiritual practices and then must be transcended. *Arjuna* is encouraged to continue and persist in his spiritual endeavours. Only on arriving at the Self, will he sense a higher state of bliss and happiness.

Krishna tells *Arjuna* that pleasurable experiences should be enjoyed, not destroyed. They can however be excelled and made loftier through contemplation from the plane of torment to God-attachment. *Krishna* is fully aware of *Arjuna's* aptitude as a student of meditation and his knowledge of the *Vedas* was reportedly extensive. Because *Arjuna* is distraught it was necessary to remind him of his scriptural scholarship.

Krishna therefore first refers to the doctrine of reincarnation. "Just as a man casts off his worn out clothes and puts on new ones, so also the embodied-self casts off its worn out bodies and enters others, which are new."

Krishna reminds *Arjuna* that he will repeatedly cast off his bodily costume for new ones until he awakens first into Awareness and eventually into Consciousness. When the individual self changes his fleshy physical bodily costume, it is not recognisable by those who were familiar with its identity in a previous life-role.

Krishna did not force this opinion on *Arjuna* who had already detected it intuitively for himself.

Arjuna is familiar with the Law of *Karma* or cause and effect that fixes the life span and durability of a physical body, in any one incarnation. *Krishna* therefore reminds *Arjuna* that from happiness we are born, for true happiness we live, and in happiness we melt at death. Death is an ecstasy, *Krishna* says, because it removes the load of the body and frees the self of all pain arising from body identification.

"No weapons can cut or pierce this soul. Fire cannot burn it. Water cannot dampen it and the wind cannot dry it," *Krishna* says.

Because the unseen is explained with the seen so the unknown can become defined, *Krishna* repeats himself and goes on to describe the Changeless with the mutable and ever-changing world, so familiar to *Arjuna*.

"This Self is impenetrable, not flammable, cannot be moistened, dried or eroded. It is always present and inextricably existing within everything in the world. It is eternal, all pervading, ever calm, immovable and eternally the same."

He waited for *Arjuna* to absorb the import of what he was saying and then continues, "The soul is unmanifest and therefore cannot be experienced by the senses of perception. The organs of action cannot corrupt it. It cannot be made aware through the mind and therefore is imponderable. It is known only when one becomes aware of Consciousness. Therefore there is nothing left for you to grieve over."

He reminds the learned *Arjuna* that the secret soul remains forever. It is never changing not even when the cosmos melts into Infinity. *Krishna* points out the subtle being remain as the substratum in every blade of grass, in every nook of creation, and even in the honeycomb of atoms.

Krishna smiles compassionately, when he said the Self loves to remain in grottoes of change, but is ever steadfast and immovable. It ecstatically dreams there only of Eternity. Only non-meditating individualists suffer incarnations of soul-oblivion, *Krishna* muttered, as if to himself. *Arjuna* understands that body-identification leads to individuality, and the self undergoes rebirth, with its attendant miseries.

Only through deeper and deeper meditation could *Arjuna's* embodied soul arrive at ecstatic communion with the Self, and thus forget the limitations of his body.

Arjuna was silent. Here in the middle of the clamour of *Kurukshetra's* battlefield, his mind became still and silent and he realized that during meditation he does not think. He only realizes. He grasps that he is formless, omnipresent, and omniscient, far above and beyond bodily changes. *Krishna* assures *Arjuna* that his meditative practice can be expanded into Cosmic Consciousness.

Arjuna already knew through self-study that before the self spews its thought waves, the soul can be made to rest in its own bosom as an inconceivable thought, undisturbed by change. When Spirit casts its dreams of the Universe, the soul, with or without its physical and astral covering, is still the same.

Arjuna therefore understands when *Krishna* describes the state of a deeply meditating *yogi* – who as soul intuition – delves deeper until all thoughts are dissolved and sees the unruffled reflection of his soul. Although *Arjuna* cannot yet see the image of his soul, he intuitively knows himself to be unchangeable, unmanifest, and ever calm like the Spirit.

At an important moment for decisive action to fight, *Arjuna* has already unexpectedly refused to contest his cousins, for half their combined kingdom, all which belonged to the *Pandu* princes any way. The *Pandu* family endured years of unjust tyranny and although *Arjuna's* faith agonized for integrity, his inherent tendencies have taken him to damaging circumstances. Overwhelmed by despondency, he has abandoned his potential to think or act decidedly.

The *Mahabharata* war has not yet started but was impending. In such strained moments of crisis, *Krishna* must rejuvenate *Arjuna* to fight this righteous war. He now argues his case with *Arjuna's* materialist standpoint. "But even if you imagine this soul to be born and dying with these faculties over and again and endlessly, then renouncing these faculties should not be a cause for grief, O mighty-armed *Arjuna.* For that which is born must die and that which is dead must be born again. Why then should you grieve over the unavoidable?"

Krishna argues that for both the atheist and the theist, elemental life is but a repetition of births, appearance for a little while, and deaths of subtle substances of Nature into which they merge back. While asking why grieve over the unavoidable *Krishna* says, "The beginnings of all creatures is veiled because it exists in the unmanifest form. Then the middle having become obvious will become unmanifest again. Therefore the end is again subtle. What then is there to grieve about *Arjuna,* O descendent of the *Bharata* dynasty?"

Krishna now deals with virtue, as seen by an enlightened atheist. Man wonders from what mysterious chamber came the original man, bird, beast, stone, flower, river, light, magnetism, electricity, worlds, stars and the universes. What happens to the population of the globe when in every century, it vanishes without a trace?

The atheist understands the stage of the earth is well supplied with food, air, water and fire. Man has heard there is a Director of this mysterious play of lives on the earth, hidden somewhere. *Krishna* knows humans like *Arjuna,* granted with a questioning intelligence, who ponder over the entire mystery. The atheist has inferred that if the world follows the law of cause, then the world must be the revealed effect of creation.

Krishna argues with *Arjuna* for the materialistic atheist. If creation is obvious just for a while, it will one day dissolve again into the unmanifest. Both the unmanifest origin and that, into which the display dissolves as the unmanifest is described, studied, heard about again and again. Still it is not understood and remains unknown. Recognising all this, why is it we do not know it, even when repeatedly explained?

"Some behold the soul in amazement. Others describe it as marvellous. Still others listen about the soul as wonderful.

And there are others who, even after hearing all about the soul, do not understand this at all. Then there are those who do not have the wish to know even after hearing about it!" *Krishna* says.

Arjuna was musing over his deep friendship with *Krishna*. He wondered if *Krishna* was a true teacher. *Arjuna* wondered if he would someday go beyond explanation to realisation and experience the Truth. *Arjuna* wondered if *Krishna* was his *guru*. *Krishna* picked *Arjuna's* thoughts.

Krishna tells *Arjuna* one needs a true Master, to see the vision of the soul, as a brilliant wonder. Materialists must be led to reach the shores of meditative ecstasy to hear the *Om or Amen or Amin* vibrating within them and echoing through the entire revealed universe. Only in a feat of wisdom, does the soul feel and experience the exquisite continuous joy of the soul.

Krishna explains to *Arjuna* there is only one-way of making out the soul: by developing the power of intuition, and by deeper and deeper meditation. By intuitively beholding the Light of Awareness, one can see the wonder through an inner vision and hear the symphonic *Om*, which makes known to the self, the wisdom and communion of soul-bliss. *Krishna* then went on to say, "O *Arjuna*, the one who remains in the bodies of all creatures, is the *Kutastha*, the brilliant Self. It stays as the witness of all creatures and is eternally indestructible. Grieve not, therefore, for any creature!"

Krishna reminds *Arjuna* that soon, soul triumphs over the self-serving egocentric nature. Although habituated to ego, senses, bad inclinations and cravings and usually hesitant to destroy these sociable enemies, who deceive Man's consciousness for a while, materialism can never demolish the soul. The embodied soul awaits a rallying call of a determined divine soldier seeking self-unfoldment and self-realization.

Krishna was carefully directing *Arjuna* towards the duty of a spiritual man who has worked at meditation and invoked the grace of the *kutastha.* When awareness finds out the grace of meditation, there is no other way for the embodied soul seeking liberation. By performing his duty, *Arjuna* can fight all fleeting pleasurable sense attachments.

"Even your own duty or *dharma* dictates that you should not inwardly waver. There is nothing more favourable for a fearless hero than righteous work and performing Consciousness revealing meditation," *Krishna* is heard saying to *Arjuna.*

Krishna warns against the tempting use of abstract principle of nonviolence as a ruse for allowing the slaughter of innocent people by conscienceless bandits.

"O *Arjuna,* fortunate indeed is the trained worker and soldier when called to fight a righteous conflict, which was not provoked, but becomes his lot. He finds in it opportunities of an open door to kingdom come. Having received secular or spiritual training and neglecting it can cause self-harm."

"Why is *Krishna* encouraging my nephew *Arjuna* to fight my children?" suddenly asked *Dhritarashtra.*

Sanjaya replied "*Krishna* is telling *Arjuna* the fighting back of evil by good, and not by evil is the ideal method of abolishing war. Armed conflict with aggression is wrong because it breeds more fighting. Warfare in self-defence is not wrong. But a greater feat is to defeat the conquerors with nonviolent resistance".

"*Arjuna* has now found himself on the scene of an inner psychological war. When individuality, sense inclinations and habits threaten inner peace and spiritual victory, this should be viewed as an opportunity to conquer them and to settle within the *kutastha,* the paradise of perfect happiness,' *Sanjaya* continues.

"But, if you decline to undertake this righteous combat, then, having abandoned your duty and fame, you shall incur sin,' *Krishna* is heard saying.

"Now *Krishna* is advising whether one enters a secular

or a spiritual path, Man must not become lazy, impractical or foolish about worldly affairs. It would be absurd not to honestly protect one's interests against dishonest rivals," *Sanjaya* recounts to the blind king.

Arjuna was welcome to practice unselfishness but *Krishna* is urging him not to neglect his duty to family commitments and to protect his mercenary interests. If he chooses to neglect his duty towards worldly promises, *Arjuna* would be inviting the sin of uncalled-for and unnecessary losses and failures. *Arjuna* is being told not to seek eminence by promoting double-dealing generosity and undeserved giving of plenty that has been earned dishonestly by others or by him. A wise professional makes for a competitive living.

"*Krishna* is advising *Arjuna* to balance his life with spiritual practices until his ego and self-consciousness transforms by contemplation into soul-consciousness," *Sanjaya* reports.

Arjuna knew his senses have no power of their own to invade his inner sanctum. Although he is still vulnerable *Arjuna* has been commanded to remain willing and vigilant in waging a righteous war against the restlessness of body consciousness. If he abandons his duty he would succumb to the awareness of the flesh and commit sin.

Arjuna is reminded that it is his duty to let his innate inclination of the soul to unfold as he engages in spiritual practices. To be skilfully effective and promote a rapid spiritual metamorphosis is to respond to *Krishna's* call in the affirmative. It is therefore *Arjuna's* duty as a warrior to uphold and defend the way of goodness.

"A warrior is presumed undedicated to his duty, if found to shrink from it. He would be overthrown by self-serving tendencies. *Arjuna* is stronger than the more influential, individuality-ridden habits, and sense tendencies. *Krishna* will only rejoice when the soul's unwillingness to centre itself on the side of virtue is exiled," *Sanjaya* said.

"Refusing both secular and nonsecular duties, you will

be assessed a failure. Man will forever speak of you with disrespect. This example of yours will suffer everlasting dishonour. To a man of repute, dishonour is worse than death!" *Krishna* said.

Krishna is gently calling *Arjuna* a coward for allowing sense enslavement to devastate his bodily kingdom. As a moral deserter, he warns his own conscience, as well as the hordes of 'holier-than-thou' materialistic people would constantly criticize *Arjuna.*

"The great battalion commanders will think that you have withdrawn from the battle through fear. And you will be looked down, by them who had thought so highly of you and your heroism in the past!" *Krishna* warns.

He goes on to explain that not only would the world denounce *Arjuna* and histories recount his infamy, but also it will deride him for his weakness. The commanders well known for their self-gratifying individuality like *Bhishma,* corruptly sinister *Drona,* bigoted *Karna* and *Vikarna,* and the covetous *Duryodhana* in the enemy lines, will brand him a coward.

Sanjaya recounts the strengths of *Arjuna's* own commanders. "Family members *Sahadev* and *Nakula* are both truthful and controlled in all their actions. *Bheema* is able to pace with perfect breath control, which gives him divine grace. That gift of intuitiveness *Yudhishthira* is so well known for will direct him to travel the high road to Truth and fairness. *Drishtdyumna's* self-control makes him an excellent commander in chief of the harmonized humanitarian *Pandava* army. *Drupad's* power of concentration and *Paundra's* courage make for a healthy combination. With that clear illumination of *Sikhandi's* intelligence, he will make the right decisions in combat. They have all always fought with *Arjuna* for virtue and rejoiced with him in his victories. If he refuses to fight, they would assume that *Arjuna* has deserted a righteous cause out of fear."

"Your enemies will speak contemptuously about your powers. What could be more painful than this?" *Krishna* asks.

It is natural that a retrogressing student of work and meditation is doubly criticized for both good and bad conduct. Blameless tendencies silently rebuke him when he becomes a casualty of a brazen invasion by his own past evil inclination. And *Krishna* warned, "If you should die while battling the enemies, you will gain heaven. If you are victorious, you will enjoy the earth. Therefore, O son of *Kunti – Arjuna,* stand up and put yourself boldly into the fray determined to fight."

"I object to this conversation between *Arjuna* and *Krishna,*" *Dhritarashtra* complains.

"Life is a battle – each man must struggle for his physical and psychological existence and is therefore subject to his or her own specific problems. Everyone who conscientiously fights these problems with objects, emotions and thoughts will either win or lose at the take on. *Krishna* as friend, confirms that those who die while engaged in a righteous battle to banish evil sleep on a soft bed of meritorious inner satisfaction. They are lifted to heaven," and thus *Sanjaya* justifies the conversation of the two cousins, on the battlefield of *Kurukshetra.*

"After becoming even-minded and not giving attention to pleasure and pain, gain and loss, victory and defeat, or happiness and unhappiness, it is fitting to engage in battle, knowing them to be the same. There is no sin in this action whether secular or spiritual," *Krishna* says.

The basic principle of *yoga* is that practicing mental equilibrium neutralizes the effects of delusion. Once suffused with inner calmness and even-mindedness, the seeker views life as a dream without emotional involvement. He does not become an automaton. *Krishna* assures *Arjuna* that he will remain in control of all contrary emotions, attachments, repulsion, longings and unwillingness. Even when seeking material fulfilment, *Arjuna* needs to keep his mind unruffled both during success and failure.

"The supreme wisdom of *Sankhya* philosophy of the soul I have already explained to you. If this does not take you to Consciousness, then listen and hear about the wisdom of the *Yoga* of *Karma* or Path of Action. Equipped with this, O *Arjuna,* you will destroy all cause-effect bonds and reach God," *Krishna* states.

Until now *Krishna's* advice to *Arjuna* is based on the soul-searching *Sankhyan* philosophy which through logic and reasoning allows him to judge the true nature of the Self while dedicated to sanctified action for the good of the Cosmic Whole. If a seeker understands this method of inquiry, it ends all sorrows and fear arising from expectation and attachment with the wanted action.

Sanjaya reports that *Krishna* is now explaining the Path of Meditation or *Yoga.* Training and determination on the path of yoga needs only a point of convergence and dedication. Seeking Self-knowledge without apprehension about the outcome and Self-realization through inner searching is attainable, *Krishna* is saying. When by yoga the ego is shackled to the soul, the seeker united to the Spirit and individuality loses its delusion.

Krishna is assuring *Arjuna* that by dissolving himself through meditation he is sure to merge his feelings of awareness or *chitta* into the original cosmic vibration of *Om* while revelling in his own consciousness. If he persists, *Krishna* promises he will unite with the Cosmic *Om.* When he reaches the Crowning Unity, the One from whom sprang the many, *Arjuna* will have arrived home.

In gradual steps, *Arjuna* was converting all awareness of the body into impressions of the Spirit. His powers of logic and imagination did not help him arrive at this opinion. It came as intuitive experience, which in turn seemed dependent on intense meditation, as taught by all great Masters of the world, *Sanjaya* tells the blind king *Dhritarashtra.* A seeker who knows the art of meditation or yoga cauterizes his past tendencies with the experience of bliss.

"Actions or *karma* are tied in with cravings and wants. In the Yoga Meditation there is only desire-free devotion and wisdom. Here there is no loss of effort, nor is there creation of contrary effects. Even a little of this real knowledge, protects Man from the great fear and suffering inherent in repeated cycles of birth and death,' *Krishna* says.

Krishna continues with his discussion on the *Sankhyan* philosophy. He tells *Arjuna* that yoga of meditation is the path of spiritual action and is the only way known in which an idea metamorphoses into an accomplishment. He is assured that for those who embrace the path of virtue, there is no loss of effort. When calculated, right spiritual enterprises produce remedial breakthroughs, in contrast to materialistic pursuits, which are, like trekking in blind alleys and shaping uncertain choices.

When this knowledge of the *Vedas* reveals itself in meditation, the soul removes itself from the mundane happenings of the body, mind, and intellect. A subtle transformation in the inner being happens. Distanced from actions, *Arjuna* can expect freedom from the Law of Cause Effect. Progress, *Krishna* says, is measured according to the peace-giving qualities meditation gives to *Arjuna*. And to preserve such peace within, despite the ever-changing circumstances of life, is being happier than a king.

Krishna discusses with *Arjuna*, the Path of Knowledge or *Gyana*, which lights the way for a seeker. Here, *Krishna* points out the difference between the meditating follower intent on searching and finding the Self and the restless person content with abstract instruction.

Krishna speaks of seekers who are content with descriptions of rituals or *karma-kanda* recounted in *Vedas* and described in flowery words. Because some cannot even think of the existence of higher works other than acquiring pleasure, they aim to fulfil all their wants and wish for heavenly enjoyments by performing these rituals.

Those who succumb to these wishes and imagine

reaching heaven through good actions during this lifetime, perform ritualistic action to gain pleasure and wealth. Addicted to enjoyment and wealth, such a man is sidetracked because the mind cannot remain determinedly absorbed in soul-search. They are reborn only because of their actions.

"O *Arjuna,* no single pointed resolution for Oneness in meditation is possible in those who cling to a need for flattery and debate about the words in the *Vedas.* Those who are full of such need, their discriminative intelligence is led astray by flowery dissertations of the spiritually ignorant. They promise new birth as the reward of their ritualistic actions and prescribe various specific actions for gaining power and a pleasurable heaven of the astral world."

Krishna now goes on to define the difference between the religious practices of the materialist and the meditative practices he was outlining to *Arjuna.* The materialist's spiritual activities are self-serving, ritualistic, and outward observations imposed by their chosen scriptures. Materialists, *Krishna* says, pray to a Higher Power for health, prosperity, name and fame.

In contrast, the meditating seeker first seeks self realization and then God realization. He holds the inner assurances that he will receive both grace and everything else he needs for his materialistic and spiritual fulfilment.

"For those who cling to pleasure and power, whose minds are drawn away from spiritual wisdom; these are neither decided nor are they fit for meditation and Unity," *Krishna* continues.

Arjuna is told he should avoid imprudent belief in the convincing words of the unwise. Advice for protecting his spiritual distinction can get stolen. The worldly promote the philosophy of various heavens, pointless discussions about scriptures, blind rules, discussions on abstract ideas, and sensory aggrandization.

Involvement in magical practices to control the

elements or to manipulate the lives of others is dangerous, *Krishna* advises *Arjuna.* To be seeing even while practicing meditative practices demands that there should be no wish for heaven after death, for he who yearns for other heavens, also is in delusion.

Arjuna cannot experience the soul-freeing results of meditation, which is contentment and peace, if his intellectual powers are clouded with want, conflict and restlessness. *Arjuna* is therefore asked to surrender to the practice of meditation until he experiences Oneness with the Source of Bliss.

Krishna next respectfully approves the *Vedic* Worship of Mother Nature or *Prakriti,* who reveals in all expression, as the quality or *guna* of Creativity. She, *Krishna* says, is either idle *[tamasic]* or creative *[rajasic]* and when decorative, toils towards equanimity *[sattva].* He advises *Arjuna* to transcend these qualities and concentrate on the Spirit or Self. He tells *Arjuna* to free himself from all emotional compulsions of Nature's dreams, wants and attachments. Instead, *Arjuna* is coached to fix himself firmly in the *Paravastha State* of God realisation through contemplation and meditation.

Krishna reminds *Arjuna* that external rites, no matter how harsh and faultless, are unable to deal with Man's need for liberation. Only inner catharsis through deep contemplation has the ability to unfetter Man from the characteristic compulsion or *gunas* of Nature.

"For those wanting their cravings fulfilled, the *Vedas* describe many kinds of rituals based on the quality or *guna* of their desires. O *Arjuna,* free yourself from Nature's compulsions and transcend Her triple qualities. Remain patient, and keep the mind free of wants. Harbour no thoughts of receiving and keeping. Become fixed in the Self," *Krishna* says.

Krishna tells *Arjuna* to learn how to detect the difference between the soul and the mind and its ramifications, and to identify the influence of the magnetic qualities of Nature on his body, mind, and intellect.

"To the knower of *Brahman* or God, all the rituals described in *Vedic* scriptures is like describing the usefulness of a little reservoir of water in a well. When there is a glut of water in the lake and everywhere in the ocean, why give importance to the well?" *Krishna* asks.

Sanjaya realises *Arjuna* needs to learn how to battle mental and physical passivity with right action. His dissatisfaction would have to be counterbalanced with dispassion and inner tranquillity. Reflection and self-illumination could promote superior ideals and mental equilibrium.

Sanjaya explains the relevance of *Krishna's* discussion to the blind king, *Dhritarashtra.* When enduring observation is arrived at, an *Arjuna*-like follower, who has combined his impressions with those of Cosmic Consciousness, experiences an abundance that transcends the theoretical world scriptures.

Fixed in Cosmic Consciousness, Nature's qualities, once obstructive, become appreciative of the seeker's spiritual practices. The contemplative pursuer goes into the depths of stillness and sees his embodied awareness withdraw from body-consciousness. He glides first into soul-awareness and finally into cosmic-consciousness. Enthroned in that palace of bliss, he never again yearns for the suffocating sense pleasures.

Having explained the Yoga of Meditation, *Krishna* takes *Arjuna* to the art of liberation from the cosmic forces of Nature and the establishment in Soul Awareness. *Krishna* now advises *Arjuna* on the Yogic Art of Right Action or *Karma Yoga* that leads a mortal to infinite wisdom. The actions of a seeker of the Divine are for the Infinite alone, and not to please humankind or to satisfy his own material wants. *Krishna* cautions *Arjuna* that he must not concentrate on expected rewards, but instead, perform right action for its own sake.

"Everyone only has the human right and authority to work. No one has the authority or control over the fruits of action. It is therefore unbecoming to be engaged in action wanting its fruit. Also one should not abandon action when noticing delay in coming about its fruit," *Krishna* states.

Krishna teaches *Arjuna* that to work towards emancipation is to delight the Divine. Man is on the right path when he concentrates on performing duties to please the Eternal. Knowing this, *Arjuna* is warned not to surrender to idleness, which is, in reality, the ego's escape for apathy. Nor should he perform action to fulfil his own egoistic wishes.

Krishna promises *Arjuna* that once he reaches the shores of deep meditation, he will experience the joy of an embodied-soul distanced from body-identifications. This feeling of satisfaction can make the seeker stagnant, with no further wish to progress. *Arjuna* is advised to burrow even deeper into meditation, to reach the seacoast of Cosmic Consciousness.

"O *Arjuna,* remain immersed in yoga and perform all actions. Abandoning all attachments to the fruit of action is being indifferent to both failure and success. This mental evenness and knowledge is termed yoga. The practice of Truth is lacking of motive. The wretched perform deeds for the fruits of action. Dedicate all, steady the mind and take refuge in the wisdom of sanctified action. Need for results is base," *Krishna* says.

Krishna has just reminded *Arjuna* that activities motivated by material wants are an inferior way to perform life's duties. They ambush the doer in an ever-tightening trap of increasing needs, which need to be worked out in future reincarnations.

Actions guided by the soul's inner intuitive discrimination and disciplined intelligence are for satisfying the Cosmic Plan, and thus leave no trace of the law of cause and effect. Since right action for necessary duty helps soul-qualities unfold, *Arjuna* must act without apprehension about the outcome and without claiming ownership.

"One who unites with cosmic wisdom goes beyond the effects of virtue and vice, even here in this life. Therefore, devote yourself to yoga. Yoga is the art of proper action. The mind is stilled by right action and suffering through hellish work gets destroyed. Freed from the fruits of action and self- satisfaction, Man becomes freed from the chain of life-and-death. He reaches the highest peace who performs the highest of all actions, in work and in meditation," *Krishna* states.

Krishna's advice to *Arjuna* that he must strive and contribute to the Cosmic Plan, is the right endeavour in life to contribute to the path of spiritual awakening. While constantly merged in divine union with Self, *Arjuna* is asked to remain observant of both actions and their results. By doing this, he will experience progressive degrees of unity, harmony, and Oneness with the Whole. He will become aware there are no real psychological compulsions of individuality, habits, or desires motivating his actions. While grounded by the self in the Self, he will become permanently centred within. This is the supreme art of proper action or *Karma Yoga.*

"When you transcend delusions of the mind and become engrossed in infinite wisdom, you will have no further interest in the fruits of action. When the intellect goes beyond such deception, you will transcend whatever you hear, whether good or bad. From this detachment you will free yourself from the cycle of rebirth. Therefore perform meditation, the highest of all actions," *Krishna* continues.

As soon as *Arjuna* understands the true aim of his existence, he takes the first step towards liberation. Human suffering because of interacting individuality with creativity in Nature is not part of Mother Nature's plan. The unhappy man is one who is out of touch with Reality and involves Man with Her creative compulsions and his own dictatorial authority of likes and dislikes or *raaga-dvesha.*

While in exile *Arjuna* discovered that deluded mortals are habitually compelled by their own individuality and sense identified minds. *Krishna* did not have to remind *Arjuna* the materialistic man grieves over the unaccomplished experiences of his past and is greedy for future possible satisfactions. Bound like a prisoner, life's experiences are ones of a dismal sense identification and indulgence.

Arjuna was already on the path of meditation. He had experienced soul contentment of a seeker as well as the restlessness of a worldly man. Now guided by a guru, *Arjuna* was gradually moving up higher into the realms of the Self.

Experiencing the staggering symphony of *Om* within himself, *Arjuna* was abandoning the conflict of the senses and body awareness. Serious reflection took him beyond the confines of his embodied soul. His intelligence outdid his fanciful delusions. Detached, he blended gradually with *Om.* His objective was to discover and probe the Light of Consciousness and become One with It.

Krishna knows that *Arjuna* is overloaded with information. To reassure him, *Krishna* says,

"When your mind and intellect are perplexed by the variety of truths being revealed, both secular and religious, then, detach yourself from it all. Become absorbed, secure, tranquil and anchored in the oneness of soul bliss. You will grasp the insight of such matters."

Arjuna granted with a refined learned intellect however is buffeted by many theological opinions. He is now penetrating the oneness through perfection. Entrenched in self-knowledge, *Arjuna*'s appeasement and indifference about the various learned explanations and assumptions suggests his deliberation is by one yet not spiritually attentive. *Arjuna* espoused his own self-knowledge and had become immovably set in the state of detecting Self-realization.

Arjuna had only just started to understand Oneness with the Whole and wanted *Krishna* to elaborate on how to recognize one fixed in *samadhi* or Oneness. He therefore addresses *Krishna.*

"O *Krishna,* whom shall I call steadfast in mind and settled in *Brahman* or God? What are the characteristics of a sage who controls an ever-calm wisdom and settled in superconsciousness? How does this man of steady wisdom speak, sit and how does he walk?"

Curiosity inflames *Arjuna.* While engrossed and in companionship with Reality, how should this sage think and speak to others? What would motivate his actions? How does he view himself with others? What is it to be a self-realized man of steady wisdom?

Krishna now describes one settled in wisdom or *sthitaprajna* and Self-realized. "O *Arjuna,* when a man is comfortable in the Self and is absorbed in the *kutastha* or the ever-witnessing Inner Self, there he experiences all he wants. He discards the mind and intellect. Fixed in Intelligence he is One with the *kutastha.* He is settled in wisdom."

Krishna's description of the inner and outer life of a Self-realized man of steady wisdom helped *Arjuna* understand for himself the right Master able to take students of meditation along the path of spirituality. He knew *Krishna* was for him his right guru. He had recognized *Krishna's* spiritualized ego, which was satisfied only by the joy, and rapture experienced by his disciple. Only a man of steady wisdom who has cast off all human cravings can protect and be protected by the Infinite.

Krishna continues to describe a true Master. "He experiences this realization through the *kutastha.* He whose mind is not shaken by suffering and who in prosperity does not hanker for pleasures is free from attachments, fear and anger. He is a *muni* or sage of steady discrimination. Knowing good and bad as colourless, he is everywhere without affinity, neither excited by facing good nor disturbed by evil. He neither rejoices nor hates but remains fixed in wisdom."

Arjuna realises that this Mastermind remains within the calm depths of his own Inner Being, beyond the reach of conflicting circumstances and emotions that might overthrow ordinary and mediocre beings. Afflictions of desire, anger, or fear do not distract him, nor do favourable circumstances rouse want and attachments in him for pleasure.

Because psychological unrest is absent, this Master senses neither impending misfortune nor feels any alarm. He recognises the nature of the soul to be different from the nature of the body and remains inwardly unruffled, watching and witnessing his breath from the ramparts of the *kutastha.* His meditative awareness is spontaneous and uninterrupted.

Desireless, content, wise, and of unruffled emotions, a Master is able to enjoy and is not blindly attached to anything. He does not react to good or bad, and to the pleasant or unpleasant. According to *Krishna* this man is insightful and understanding in all circumstances.

Arjuna realises that such a Master distinguishes, not through the excitable prism of Nature, but from the calm view of pure soul-wisdom. He ignores all opposites as afflictions that are not his. He therefore can control his body, mind, intellect and ego – the true agents of restlessness.

Arjuna wondered if a Master suppresses the natural urges of the materialist. *Krishna* explains the wise one does not suppress, he merely transcends urges.

"A yogi effortlessly withdraws his sense limbs like a tortoise. With removal from the senses of sight, sound, touch, taste, and smell, the objects of perception also leave when a man of wisdom retires in the *kutastha,*" Krishna said.

This, *Krishna* asserts is a state of soul contact through Interiorization. This is where real satisfaction is found. The yogi goes from the bodily coverings and into the cavern where the symphonic cosmic sound of *Om* resonates and eventually fuses into Cosmic Consciousness.

Arjuna wonders how a man of wisdom abolishes memories of past tastes, experiences and cravings and *Krishna* responds. "It is true that for the spiritually uninformed who is body conscious, the senses can be enfeebled through fasting. He discards demands of the senses. His mind blemished by memories of past indulgences returns to claims made by the senses. A man, who remains in the *kutastha* leaving behind all wants, finds the sense objects fall away automatically, leaving behind only a memory of past pleasures. But he who beholds and arrives at the bliss of the Supreme, destroys even these recollections and ambitions."

Arjuna recognises that renunciation of the world without practicing the yoga of meditation, which controls the life force to the senses and the mind, results in outward renunciation with the inward torment of sense temptations. He was on the battlefield of *Kurukshetra* and was already a victim of his past recollections, obsessions and singularity despite his twelve years of amends in banishment. *Krishna* recognizes the difficulties faced by a spiritual combatant with conflicting overtures when he says,

"O son of *Kunti* – *Arjuna,* the tumultuous senses do effectively seize the mind of even the wise one who has a high degree of discrimination and enlightenment and is striving for liberation. The senses cause him unhappiness also."

Krishna was cautioning all smug and self-satisfied seekers like *Sanjaya* and *Dhritarashtra* who might have arrived at some spiritual advancement and self-control. They may consider themselves immune to the lures of the senses. *Krishna* warns no one is safe from the senses, habits and individuality, not even a perfected being.

Even without seeming contact with sense objects, a seeker can still arouse the mind intrinsically, by feeding it with images from subconscious and unconscious memories. *Arjuna* knew he couldn't underestimate the formidable power of the subconscious mind, whose tentacles are more far-reaching than the conscious mind.

Krishna repeatedly reminds *Arjuna* that until illumination from the *kutastha* purifies the mind, he should not expect to be freed of wants, fantasies and hallucinations. These were to be resisted by *yama,* restrained through *niyama,* and substituted by disciplined energy and endless meditative exercises.

Krishna, the mortal reincarnation of Universal Intelligence, reveals himself to *Arjuna* when He says, "Having defeated all the senses, he who unites his spirit in me in the *kutastha,* in the centre of the Inner Being, remains immersed in me. My power steadies all the senses and the mind is stilled and under control. Those whose sensory and mental powers have succumbed to me, is called *sthitaprajna,* a pure man of wisdom."

Lack of understanding of the different states of consciousness, whether awake, dreaming or in deep sleep, the undulating emotion and an addicted mind, do not allow a yogi the necessary freedom from his obsessions and sense urges. Steady in contemplation of the Infinity, *Krishna* promises *Arjuna* steady Self-realisation whether working in the marketplace, in dreams, in sleep, or while in meditation.

Once Self-united, *Arjuna* can expect his senses to eventually abandon their revolt and follow their rightful sovereign. When not ready to abandon indulgences, *Krishna* warns that even a Master can become deluded by frustrations of real and imagined temptations:

"By brooding on sense objects, delusions and obsessions of attachment, to them they become obvious. Attachment kills memory as well as reason. When reason goes, all is lost. This then again breeds desire and cravings."

Sanjaya understands that *Krishna* is describing the fatal step-by-step descent of a potentially noble being, down the ladder of temptation into ruin. Brooding over sense pleasures, as is happening with the blind king *Dhritarashtra,* results in repression that clouds logic and awareness. Complex obsession is in the present the psychological spring source of want and the offspring of all its outcomes. *Duryodhana's* imagined righteous indignation has had the ability to inspire his father to extraordinary efforts to right a wrong self-serving anger. This anger has so blinded the *Kauravas* that they have become increasingly irrational while trying to fulfil unwarranted and blemished ideals.

Arjuna sees himself in *Krishna's* definition of a spiritual seeker gone astray. He therefore understands *Krishna's* next statement.

"Interruptions by obsessions for self-gratification fosters anger. Rage and disappointment breed mistakes. Error in judgment kills memory of the Self. Loss of power of recollection causes decadence of the cultivated intellect and reason."

From degeneration of discrimination, the power of perception is subdued, common sense is rejected and there is defeat of spiritual life. Enmeshed in anger a yogi can expect to lose his self-respect, as well as his health. *Krishna* reminds *Arjuna* that paroxysms of anger have physiological and psychological effects, which *Arjuna* is now already experiencing.

Physiologically, whole body systems metamorphose when the heart races. Inherent apprehension is felt as an excitement of the physique, nerves feel burdened and digestion is inhibited. Psychologically, hostility overwhelms the mind. Unsound motor pressures are apt to transcend all rational conduct noticed in normal placid states. Rashness shadows the mind and it now explores aimlessly. Man forgets how he should behave.

Krishna explains that in conditions of affliction and stresses, every unit of a society as a whole is subject to disreputable processes. If an individual like *Arjuna,* a constituent of community and society, refuses to fight unrighteousness, he should expect to devastate all these systems and tribes as well.

"Therefore free yourself from all likes and dislikes. Be free of obsession of the senses. Controlled by the power of the Inner Self, fixed in the *kutastha,* move among sense objects, empty of attraction and repulsion and gain unshakable inner calmness. Those who take part in objects of the senses in this manner reach a placid mind and intellect," *Krishna* says.

Man understands Life's Path courses through the territory of sensations and sense traps. It must be travelled to reach Reality. *Arjuna* is told a man of self-control wears the armour of wisdom and nonattachment. He performs his duties in the tricky sense world but while settled in the Self, this man of sense-control passes beyond. Freed of attractions of the world, he enjoys the bliss of the soul. His wavering reason becomes fixed on the soul, and he becomes rooted in unswerving discrimination. The light of soul-happiness finally dispels darkness from accretions of millions of reincarnations.

Krishna warns *Arjuna* that unsatisfied wants could be as dictatorial as the authoritarian influence of external objects, emotions and thoughts. Only useful needs, inspired by higher ideals for self-discovery, can prevent Man from alienating from the soul. This antagonism identified by displeasure, scattering of all sense and mind faculties causes untold strife.

Krishna reassures *Arjuna's* indecisive mind when he says, "When there is inner tranquillity from Soul-bliss, all afflictions and sorrows are destroyed. After that, wisdom stills the mind and discrimination dawns. To the nonmeditative, there can be no peace or tranquillity. To the not serene, how can there be happiness?"

Krishna reminds *Arjuna* that while in seclusion in the forest, he and the *Pandava* family were able to illuminate the intellect through learning. The gain was purely informative but distinctions are a product of intuition, earned only through soul-force, when there is union of the self with the Self.

Arjuna knows that discrimination ensures right judgment, under any circumstance, through the agency of intuition. Divine leadership, housed in consciousness as wisdom, is the cultivating faculty that path-finds itself to that intuitive Intelligence.

Sanjaya knew *Arjuna* has experienced harmony as a quality of his soul. He could not now be at peace unless he was in tune with the soul. The sadness *Arjuna* was experiencing had produced in him a mental apathy and he was in a pessimistic state of calm. *Arjuna* needs amity, the immune inner condition of his soul, to allow him feel real satisfaction born of ethical action. He would have to battle with unrighteousness to unfold within.

Krishna has already told *Arjuna* he will never feel content until he arrives at the state of uninterrupted accord. He must confront unrighteousness by active resistance, restraint, and disciplined endeavour. Only through repetitive experience of the Inner Self in the *kutastha,* can his soul gradually blossom into heavenly delight and infallible wisdom.

Krishna tells *Arjuna* that even a yogi who is rapidly nearing his goal might find himself among the storms of sense obsessions through blunders of past lives etched in the subconscious, or through the build-up of postnatal unfavourable inclinations. At such crossroads, *Krishna* advises *Arjuna* to invoke his will at the *kutastha* behind and between eyebrows. Here he can order the sensory tempest and wind to recede.

"Just as a boat on the waters gets carried off course by a gale, so also an individual's discrimination is driven away from the intended path when the mind succumbs to the wandering restive senses. Therefore, O Mighty-armed *Arjuna,* with every breath remain ever settled in the Self, and watch the senses become automatically restrained from the sense objects."

Sanjaya smiled when he hears *Krishna* address *Arjuna* as the scion of self-control. That too coming from the charioteer of the sense stallions of *Arjuna's* chariot; it voiced unspoken devotion for his friend and cousin, who was already well versed in the scriptures and worthy of *Krishna's* confidential direction.

Arjuna, the landlord of his own life's chariot was not asked to tie up his sense stallions and transfer them to inactivity. By training the steeds respectfully it allowed him to make all resolutions on their behalf.

Sanjaya understands that *Arjuna* needs to discipline the desires that escort Man's instruments of perception, action and the mind. Like a drunken sailor, the restless mind engages the intellect with the objects of the senses. There is erosion and impurity of action and because there is no stillness or tranquillity in awareness, there is no happiness. He is therefore repeatedly being told that his mind and intellect need freedom from sense bondage.

Sanjaya knows the way to soul contentment. To remain Self-aware when overwhelmed by materialistic duties in life, *Arjuna* needs to begin regulating his personal behaviour and decisively choosing encouraging relationships and circumstances. He needs to cultivate optimism, courage, and a will to live and excel in all that he does. He needs to develop the faculty of intentional positive thinking and expressing it verbally. He must also devise a balanced nutrition based feeding plan. It was essential his activity and rest periods are satisfactory. *Sanjaya* understands the commonest error Man makes is to have no awareness or conviction of a purpose to life. *Arjuna* is told that to be idle while pretending to be spiritual is a dangerous self-deceit.

Sanjaya also knows from experience that Man makes a common error on the spiritual path. He becomes complacent with his emotional conflicts and mental confusion. Such a seeker accepts his own shattered personality. He becomes engrossed in self-admiration and there is arrest in emotional growth. The seeker goes back into his childish objectives. Indulgences and sensual desires confuse him. Individuality-based self-centredness, rooted in illusions of complacency and independent existence, lead the seeker down the path of faulty beliefs and thoughts. Therefore, *Krishna* advises *Arjuna* to remain constantly aware of his divine roots during both worldly activity and intense inactivity in meditation.

Krishna now describes a man of wisdom who remains always in *paravastha* or the Supreme State. "It is night for objects when a *yogi* is immersed in meditation because they have been stifled in sleep. The soul however is awake and knowledgeable in its own Supreme State. When awake in physical affairs and involved with the sense world, it is night for a man of wisdom, for he sees nothing. The Knowledge of the soul has dissolved."

Krishna goes on to describe a *yogi* who is permanently fixed in Self-knowledge and is in the Supreme State. "Just as the sea that is already full of water remains calm regardless of the rivers and streams entering it, so too, those filled with the bliss of the Supreme State, can take part in the objects of the senses. Desireless and unperturbed, he behaves as if made by an unseen doer. This man of wisdom releases from materialistic enchainment. He is full of contentment who absorbs all wants within, just as the brimful ocean remains unchanged by waters entering it."

Arjuna has already understood *rajoguna,* the effective power of Mother Nature. Her qualities communicate as inertia, creativity and harmony in the organs of action. He also knows that Matter magnetically compels the senses and the organs of action to experience the five subtle elements - earth, water, fire, air and ether in Nature.

Arjuna has already understood that if Nature did not activate creativity, inertia and harmony, there would be no Creation. The atoms and sub-atoms would remain invisible. There would be no creation, preservation or destruction of planets and solar systems. The working quality of Nature in the Mind would not be able to reveal nor would the senses experience Man's satisfaction in Nature. A man of wisdom understands if he is born of Nature, is living in Her, he should be unaffected and unperturbed while remaining still and observant of Her Cosmic Play. His enlivening power of *prana* remains undisturbed and dormant. The soul or *jiva* understands he is an individualized part of the Cosmic Whole.

Krishna understands that *Arjuna* the soul must mature from just knowing his physical or food sheath. He barely understands and realizes the existence of energy sheath of matter in physiological, mental and intellectual sheaths. Living a life of a seeker lessens this flawed knowledge gradually. Once information becomes more entrenched in the intellectual sheath, *Arjuna* can fulfil the needs of his body and mind through meditation. Through the miraculous power of *yoga* he will one day experience the senses, the organs of action, the mind and intellect and his sense of individuality as part of the Cosmic Dream.

But *Arjuna* is like any modern householder who wants to perform worldly duties as well as find the Self. He can be taught to arrive at Wholeness but if he does not experience the silent Universe, *Krishna* knows that wishes for sense enjoyment will move *Arjuna's* mind away from its natural state of stillness. The power of creativity will once more magnetically attract him to substances his individuality craves to enjoy. Enlivening the active energy with *prana* will be invoked for sure!

Sanjaya knows the omniscient, omnipotent human Mind is so majestic that no power in the Universe can tolerate its unhappiness. The Universe waits eagerly to satisfy the Mind and quell its craving. Like a servant of the individual's willpower, the Universe fulfils all wishes to arrive at peace. What counsel will *Krishna* propose for him?

Sanjaya has himself experienced the smallness of a restive mind. One craving is followed immediately by another want, and then another. The individual mind remains endlessly disturbed and restless. The creative power of *rajas* scatters its operational force with many desires but is unable to apply its full power into anything in particular. What is viewable is a scattered, fragmented, conflicting thinking, but nothing is actually evident. The body stops functioning normally and death sheds his bodily sheath only to reappear in a new body, to fulfil amassed desires as unseen fate or *adrishta.*

Arjuna is in deep thought. He must learn to renounce *adrishta* by detaching from its roots of likes and dislikes or *raaga-dvesha.* He must learn to fulfil all the amassed desires without creating any new *adrishta.*

Krishna is following *Arjuna's* thoughts. He needs persuasion to perform action as willed by the Cosmic Whole. When the mind returns to its natural placid state, *Krishna* can expect the foundation of *Arjuna's* needs to end in self-fulfilment.

Krishna is heard saying, "O *Arjuna,* this is the way to established-in-*Brahman* [God] state. Anyone entering this state is never again deluded by the ego. His heart is empty of attachment. He fulfils his fated destiny and quenches himself in that Infinite State."

Sanjaya understands *Arjuna's* anxiety. He needs reassurance the gains he makes while on the path of spirituality are rooted in permanence. *Arjuna* wants to know what will happen to him if he falls halfway off the spiritual path. Does he lose the Knowledge of the scriptures he laboured so persistently at? Does he surrender the achievements of intensive years of atonement while in the forest for over twelve years? Does he preserve the developed achievements he shapes in this life? If he physically stops to exist while engaged in combat on the battlefield of *Kurukshetra,* will his next expression recollect the achievements of his present life? Is progress of Man towards super-consciousness universal? Even if he lapses once more into his sense identified physical state, will the incompletely smothered ego expand into the Self?

Arjuna's thinking encourages *Krishna.* He must tell *Arjuna* he might find himself successful even at the moment of death. "Listen about devotion to this Knowledge of God. Once it is grasped, the individual soul is never again captivated. Even at the moment of death, if this Knowledge reveals itself, the one who dies merges with and into the Infinite. The wise one who is fixed in the Self or the *sthitaprajna,* moves away from deluding death."

5. Yoga of Action

Krishna has already explained that no living
with body, mind and intellect should remain
Ending actions is a dedication to death. Th
must act.

Arjuna becomes naturally confused
discussions with *Krishna*. He wonders, if d
to Self is superior to work, why does *Krishna* e
such a dreadful undertaking? When an u
acts propelled by his or her wrong tendenci
for himself a new lease in the future, of a sor
He is told that while entertaining sensuous d
and earns inexhaustible mental impressions
invite new fields of existence in fresh fiel
through many reincarnations.

Arjuna understands Truth is a vibratin
the Spirit. As if in God's dream-creation
nijogana, innate in Nature or *Prakriti* b
and form of creatures big and small.

Arjuna also understands that althou
the discovery of the Self in the self through
this self-awakening is a daunting task. Ar
part of that creative vibratory activity and
the Cosmic Plan and God's dream. Fro
Cosmic Self. Man must shift back into th
To awaken into Realization, his activity m
with life's processes. Through action,
necessary adjustments. He should perfor
which is in harmony with the Cosmic Pl
in Nature.

Therefore *Arjuna* asks, "O *Krishna*,

5. Yoga of Action

Krishna has already explained that no living creature granted with body, mind and intellect should remain without action. Ending actions is a dedication to death. Therefore *Arjuna* must act.

Arjuna becomes naturally confused after his recent discussions with *Krishna*. He wonders, if devotion or *bhakti* to Self is superior to work, why does *Krishna* engage him in such a dreadful undertaking? When an uncultivated man acts propelled by his or her wrong tendencies, he is ordering for himself a new lease in the future, of a sorrowful existence. He is told that while entertaining sensuous desires, Man acts and earns inexhaustible mental impressions or *vasanas*. These invite new fields of existence in fresh fields of expression, through many reincarnations.

Arjuna understands Truth is a vibration-free region of the Spirit. As if in God's dream-creation the creativity or *rajoguna,* innate in Nature or *Prakriti* becomes the name and form of creatures big and small.

Arjuna also understands that although Man is allowed the discovery of the Self in the self through spiritual practices, this self-awakening is a daunting task. *Arjuna* knows Man is part of that creative vibratory activity and an integral part of the Cosmic Plan and God's dream. Projected out of the Cosmic Self, Man must shift back into this Universal Being. To awaken into liberation, his activity must be in harmony with life's processes. Through action, *Arjuna* must make necessary adjustments. He should perform prudent action, which is in harmony with the Cosmic Plan already intrinsic in Nature.

Therefore *Arjuna* asks, "O *Krishna,* I have understood

the logic of your previous discussion. After examining all the facts you have previously presented, a question arises in my mind. If you consider Wisdom about Nature's creativity to be superior to action, why then, *Krishna,* are you asking me to perform this distressing operation, fighting the *Kauravas*? Have they not harnessed creativity for self-gratification? One time you said Knowledge is superior. Then you say action is worthy of praise. Your conflicting statements are confusing my understanding. Therefore, tell me of a single path by which I can arrive at the Highest. Give me your opinion about what is best for me."

Sanjaya, while watching *Krishna* and *Arjuna,* understands *Arjuna's* confusion. In the early stages, while receiving knowledge and during meditative practices, it seems difficult to grasp the meaning of what is learned. *Sanjaya* recognizes through experience that *Arjuna* has partial knowledge of the scriptures but not necessarily an intimate understanding. *Arjuna* must act according to the dictates of his friend and teacher who has the wisdom of the *Vedas.* The crowning wisdom of action-in-inaction and inaction-in-action is possible only through intuitive contact with the Infinite Intelligence – the changeless, Free-of-all-vibration State.

Sanjaya reporting to the blind king *Dhritarashtra* had received similar training on spiritual practices and understood what *Krishna* was saying. To climb onto the Wheel-of-Action or *Karma Yoga, Arjuna* must involve both his bodily and mental characters through action or *karyam* in a spirit of devotion or *yagna.* Once meditation and knowledge remove bodily delusions, *Arjuna* will verify the wisdom of action.

Righteous action or *karyam* conquers sensual consciousness. By perfecting endeavors and following do's and don'ts or *yama-niyama* of morality, *Arjuna's* actions should become virtuous.

Although *Krishna's* counsel is wise and eloquent, it sounds contradictory. Having admitted bewilderment, the advice appears ambivalent; *Arjuna* wants *Krishna* to tell him exactly what to do next. *Sanjaya* sympathises. Spiritual advice appears paradoxical because mortals improvise their understanding of Awareness in Nature. To *Arjuna,* the Unmanifest Consciousness is invisible but he also rationally knows it as the source of Creation. Little wonder he is confused.

Krishna replies, "In the beginning during contemplation when awareness was completely focused in the *kutastha* above and between the eyebrows, a twofold path of salvation was given to the world. The wise ones, who are purified by Knowledge, arrived at liberation through the Path of Wisdom of *Sankhyan* philosophy. Those who had not yet been purified by this Knowledge, were engaged in performing the act of meditation or inaction, to receive this Science."

Arjuna is astonished! *Krishna* was around at the start of Creation? This is when Man was given two paths to retrace his steps back to the Self? If both paths have the ability to reveal the soul, the first through pure discrimination or *Gyana Yoga* and the second through practical activity or *Karma Yoga,* which should he, *Arjuna,* engage in?

Sanjaya knows the highest form of **knowledge** is wisdom or **Knowledge** gained through intellectual and intuitive examination and insight. Also the uppermost form of activity is engaging in the processes necessary to make this knowledge a personal experience in meditation. *Sanjaya* understands that most seekers do not embrace such distinctions. *Arjuna* must use scriptural knowledge to erase his psychological and physiological obstacles. Awareness cannot advance along the path within the divine cave when there are obstacles of wants, old habits and individuality hampering the progress.

Only transformative changes allow experiences of supreme knowledge as wisdom. *Sanjaya* understands meditation is the foundation of the house of wisdom. Yet, many aim for Knowledge without meditation, in the hope of securing such freedom. He knows gaining knowledge without the tempering effects of inner wisdom leads to conceit and mistaken beliefs. *Sanjaya* knows *Arjuna* is on the inner highway of Self-realization, which will someday end in the union of the soul with the Cosmic Self or Spirit. Therefore *Sanjaya* is not surprised with *Krishna's* answer to *Arjuna.*

"Without action, one cannot arrive at knowledge and without Knowledge one cannot reach liberation. One does not gain actionlessness, meaning awakening to freedom in deep meditation, just by avoiding action. Performance of action by renunciation also does not lead one to perfection."

"Projected out of Unmanifest Consciousness or *Purusha* is the Cosmic Plan of Creation of Nature or *Prakriti.* Integral to this Plan is the power of Her qualities or *gunas.* Through the harmonisation of Creativity or *rajoguna* and Perishability or *tamoguna* they allow the ascent of Man and of Creation into an Unmanifest or *sattvaguna* state. Endurance here leads to a Revealed state"

Sanjaya knows, while projecting the Unmanifest an intelligent vibrating life force supports the Universe. The Word – *Om,* knows of this. If one does not perform *guna*-dictated actions, Man falls into an abyss of Nature's stresses. Enslaved by Nature's tribulations man experiences fluctuations of affection-hatred, likes-and-dislikes, me-and-mine, and hot-and-cold. He becomes caught up, unaware of the motivation behind untested relationships.

Masters like *Krishna* understand the enigma. Established in the Self, they return to serve the world. They accommodate their thoughts and holy vibrations for the benefit of unenlightened beings. *Sanjaya* understands *Krishna's* admonition when he says to *Arjuna,* "No one can stay without acting even for a moment. Everyone is compelled to act helplessly. Urges are triggered by qualities or *gunas* innate in *Prakriti* or Nature."

Krishna had just defined work and action but each understands it differently. To *Sanjaya* work is physical action performed with a mental purpose by thinking, planning, deciding, or selecting. To *Dhritarashtra* action is useful for destructive adjustnents and imagined outcomes. To *Arjuna* action is adjusting awareness to restore self-knowledge.

But *Krishna* defined compelling action. The entire universe is created and controlled by exploits of three *gunas* or acts in response to traits inherent, constant, and silently influencing all of Nature. This is the way Divine Mother expresses Herself in Her magical expressions.

Krishna earlier referred to Nature's qualities that are innate in Her expressions of matter. As positive or uplifting creativity She is *rajas.* As negative or obstructive inertia or destruction She is *tamas.* When the negative and positive are neutral She displays harmony or *sattva.*

Arjuna reminds himself of the three *gunas* or qualities of Nature. They pressure the entire universe with guided dealings. They also rule the human body. *Arjuna* knows Man cannot stand still because he is compelled to act. This universal flux cannot avoid even a stationary man, not even in his seat of deep meditation.

Krishna adds, "There are those who want to flaunt they are meditating and want restriction from working hard. They subdue all organs of action and remain mute as well as insensate. They are ignorant because their minds are bound to past habits and sense objects. Without internal stillness there can never be inner silence. This hypocrite deludes himself."

To conquer enticement by the senses, *Arjuna* needs freedom from physical, social, mental, and spiritual problems. If this does not happen the seed of desire grows again into a huge tree, bearing fruits of misery with it. Repetition of corrupt acts produce an aiding device in thought and therefore breeds habits and instinctive inclinations. *Krishna* says bridling both thoughts and actions needs effort.

"Mind control wants Man first to renounce sense objects and then the organs of action. O *Arjuna,* you can do this by meditation and by execution of action. He who knows this and engages the organs of action, without attachment, succeeds on the path of action that unites man with Self," Krishna said.

Dhritarashtra objects and reminds *Sanjaya* that Man has worldly responsibilities. *Sanjaya* tells him that a man of worldly duties who keeps his senses under control, and whose work identifies with the Cosmic Worker of Nature or *Prakriti*, remains unattached to his own wishes and ambitions. Eventually, such right actions take him to the right goal – to Unmanifest Consciousness.

"Unattached to fruits of action, he meditates for enjoying supreme bliss while in his mortal coil,' *Sanjaya* tells the blind king.

Krishna echoes this truth when he says to *Arjuna*,

"Therefore perform your eternal duty and perform actions that are compulsory, because, it is better than inactivity. Even simple bodily maintenance is impossible without activity. Be ever engaged performing consciousness-revealing action of meditation."

Having heard that action is superior to idleness, *Arjuna* must at least do those essential duties bound by the laws of Nature. He must contribute to the total wellness and remain harmonious with life-processes. *Sanjaya* recognizes that unless *Arjuna's* actions are self-directed and positive, he must expect to become a victim of subconscious and unconscious influences of his environment and Nature's qualities. *Krishna* further states it is *Arjuna's* divine duty to transform inertia to creativity and creativity to harmony. Only soul-elevating cultural activities have the capacity to nurture intuitiveness and self-unfoldment.

Dhritarashtra remarks that *Krishna* divided action under two categories. Actions that support mundane needs but they leave a scar of cause and effect and dedicated religious endeavors meant for evolution, but leave no footprints. *Krishna* promotes devoted action. *Sanjaya* agrees with the blind king's assessment.

"Actions performed for disclosure of the Self is *yagna,* O son of *Kunti.* Performances for worldly wants cause Man to remain bound to repeated births and deaths. Therefore do action that is free of desire for enjoyment of its fruit. O *Arjuna,* act without attachment, in a spirit of *yagna,* offering actions of meditation as oblations."

Arjuna is bewildered. His mind is concentrated on worldly action. He again asks *Krishna,* "Which is superior – diligence in action or its abandonment?" He also questions why he must act if action breeds bondage. Why act at all?

Krishna explains, "Both abandonment and application of action lead to emancipation, but application is superior to abandonment." *Krishna* then argues, "Renunciation of fruits of action and act of meditation with devotion are one, although some may argue there is a difference between the two."

Krishna further asserts, "Renunciation without devotion to meditation makes it difficult to conquer the body and subdue the senses. Only by devotion, when you *Arjuna* identify yourself with all Her creatures, will you be freed of the fetters of performing actions. You will witness the senses engaged in objects of these senses. You will renounce attachments while engaged in action." *Arjuna* resolves that he not to be touched by the sin of self-serving action. He wishes to remain unaffected just as a lotus leaf in a pond is untouched by water.

Krishna clarifies that he as the eternal witness is neither the cause of *Arjuna's* capacity for action nor is he the link between action and the fruit-of-action. It is Nature and Her qualities or *gunas* that are engaging him in action. Some parts in the *Vedas* speak of ways to harness these three qualities for temporary sojourns in short-lived heavens. The ignorant delight in these rituals described in the scriptures because their minds are attached to worldly pleasures. For those whose minds are not connected to contemplation, enjoying this greatest object through performance of ritual, promise higher births as fruit-of-action. To them these acts are the only means to emancipation.

This science of ritual is shrouded in ignorance and creatures remain deluded. When this simple-mindedness is removed by knowledge-of-the-self through meditation, the Supreme Self is revealed. Thereafter a man-of-wisdom casts an equitable eye of modesty and acceptance on all, beings and creatures. His steady, unattached mind and intellect thinks about the Self and enjoys the imperishable happiness born of absorption with *Brahman* or God.

Krishna now describes Creation of Nature. He admits that She or *Prakriti* is His dream-creation. In the beginning, there was first a *yagna* of a fire ritual. From this Cosmic Fire of *Om,* came the Light of Intelligence. From It was created the Creative Consciousness, the Creator or *Brahma* as *Prajapati,* in whom lives the seed of His Cosmic dream. From that seed was brought forth all, beings and creatures, each with a soul made of universal intelligence.

Arjuna is lost and *Krishna* repeats by elaborating further, "In the beginning, *Prajapati* the Creator of *Praja* or human beings, created humanity. With this *Yagna* or act of sacrifice He said, 'By this you will multiply. This will be the milch cow *Kamadhuk,* as a source of fulfillment of all your just desires.'"

"How did that happen," *Dhritarashtra* asks *Sanjaya.*

"The Creator was commanded to multiply and to follow the wisdom-image of the seed embedded within *Prajapati.* This Intelligence would direct and fulfill all the wishes of those creatures wanting expression. The understanding would be like a milch-cow offering her milk of happiness to all desires whether materialistic, mental or spiritual," *Sanjaya* explains.

Krishna explains to *Arjuna* that these sacrificial actions escorted him towards total actions and reactions for achieving the highest good for Nature. Propitiated with rituals and sacrifices, the gods granted creatures with pleasures they wanted. But, he who enjoys without philanthropy is branded a bandit.

Dhritarashtra turned to *Sanjaya*. "If the Creator has given us plenty for wealth and enjoyment, where then have my sons and I gone wrong? How have we offended the laws of living?" *Dhritarashtra* asks.

"The good eat and enjoy remnants of sacrifice like thanksgiving before meals. They are freed of the sin of cheating," *Sanjaya* explains. "The unrighteous eat for their own sake and incur offense. This is because from food and action all creatures are created. This sacrifice is also the outcome of work."

The king's discussion with *Sanjaya* is interrupted.

Arjuna asks how rituals help in arriving at desires. *Arjuna* is reminded of his twelve years in the forest. "Your efforts at studying and learning the *Vedas* were a product of work. *Vedas* come from Him who suffers no decay. Therefore *Arjuna,* understand the Supreme Being installed in every act which is dedicated as a sacrifice or *yagna,*" *Krishna* states.

"Therefore, by elevating action to a *yagna,* the gods, celestials and the performer of the sacrifice are benefited. Like the falling rain, the gods bless you in return. They give you what you desire. To enjoy without offerings is like being a thief. To use what the cosmic agents have offered for personal sense enjoyment only, leads to self-destruction," *Krishna* says.

"Through practicing the inner fire rites of yoga meditation, *Arjuna* must attune himself to the heavenly agents that govern the worlds. Harmonizing with the exacting laws of Nature, these agents respond favorably to justified and dedicated demands and wants," *Sanjaya* tells the blind king. "*Arjuna's* concern as a mortal should be with work alone and not with the fruit of action. Results must not motivate him. He is at the same time cautioned not to reject work," *Sanjaya* continues.

Arjuna understands that effects of past actions govern life because these cosmic agents govern the universal laws of Nature. By remaining devoted to work in the face of both success and failure and attuning to Nature's laws raises man. It helps him avoid past evil *karma.* Misfortune cancels itself through closeness and alignment with *devas* or celestials.

Then *Krishna* repeats what has been said before, "What I have spoken of is also in the *Vedas.* The Knowledge comes from the infallible wisdom of the *Kutastha* behind and above the eyebrows. By meditation, this Supreme Being is experienced and arrived at."

The blind king becomes thoughtful when *Sanjaya* spoke, "When Man identifies himself with his individuality, he takes it for granted that he alone thinks, wills, feels, digests, and is responsible for keeping himself alive." *Sanjaya* continues, "He never admits that in his ordinary life, he is nothing but a puppet of past actions and of Nature, directed and controlled by intelligent celestial agents. Out of touch with universal harmonies, he lives as a lawless pirate, paying no homage to the countless forces that provide for him during his life span."

"Those who eat remnants of offerings in sacrifice or *yagna* are free of sins. But sinners are those who cook food only for themselves, for they feast on sin," *Krishna* states. "From food creatures are born. From rain food is got. From *yagna* of the fire sacrifice rain comes. Fire is born of *karma* or action. Know O *Arjuna* that this cause of action comes from *Brahma's* Creative Consciousness, which originates from the Imperishable Infinite Consciousness of *Brahman* or God. Therefore, this Creative Consciousness of *Brahma* is all pervasive and is inherently and inseparably present in every *yagna* or sacrifice, which is the essence of all constituents of creation."

The blind king seemed confused and *Sanjaya* came to his rescue, "In the Universe, creatures and beings exist within the field of Awareness of Nature. Individualistic circumstances and experiences are revealed in that field of Mindfulness.

We follow needs by the choices we make, and the harmony we create with the individualistic-Cosmic creation. The efficient forces of nature nourish us and we nurture them when our awareness is clear and our actions are in the service to the Universe," *Sanjaya* says.

Then, *Krishna* states, "O *Arjuna,* he, who lives in this world and does not go with the revolving wheel of action and reaction, lives unaware of the real purpose of life. Content in his individuality he remains sense-oriented. He experiences only sense indulgences. He lives in vain."

"What then is the purpose of life?" asks the blind king.

Sanjaya then describes to *Dhritarashtra* the purpose of existence. "In this great revolving wheel of Time and Action, Nature allows Man to experience all his wants. Descending from Unmanifest Cosmic Consciousness into Nature's compelling qualities, Man is expected to act and serve Nature, all the while re-ascending towards liberation," *Sanjaya* explains. "He, who does not heed the liberating yet disciplinarian laws of existence as a mortal, misses the sole point of earthly existence. He who instead identifies with increasing needs and sense indulgences remains rooted in the worldly soil of materialism."

Arjuna has many questions. "Is the Wheel-of-Action for all? Is it only for those with faith in Knowledge? Without Nature's Wisdom of renewal and creation, do the ignorant desire-driven meditate and perform necessary actions as an unpretentious duty? What must a yogi do when working for basic needs?"

And *Krishna* replies. "When a yogi has renounced cravings and has experienced soul-bliss, he is satisfied. His passion and pleasure is for the Self only. He has no need for worldly actions. He has nothing more to gain. The bliss of *Brahman* or God realization prevents any scattering of the mind. Action or *karma* has no rights over such a yogi whether holy or worldly. He is not compelled by the compulsions of Nature's qualities."

Arjuna knew this because he had sporadically thought of it. He had occasionally experienced Oneness with the Eternal Self. But had he grasped the goal of life? *Arjuna* had previously understood that he does not need to perform actions. He was of the opinion he is not bound to any *karmic* law if he is entrenched in *yogic* practices. He wondered would Creation nurture him? Or, must he engage in dutiful action for a positive outcome from Nature? Is this the righteous action that he must engage in?

Krishna responds. "Therefore, always perform your eternal duty as Man. Practice good materialistic actions or *karyam* as well as spiritual actions or *karman* without attachment to the results. By performing all essential actions as your duty without obsession for the results, Man arrives at liberation. The preferred purpose of action should be for a systematic outcome benefiting Nature or it ought to be to gain the eventual union with the Self."

As a prince and seeker of Knowledge and meditation, *Arjuna* wonders if he could perform materialistic actions, as well as spiritual acts. His contemporary, King *Janaka* who lived many centuries before, was distinguished because while performing his royal duties, he also remained fixed in the Self. *Janaka* performed actions for his own progressive evolution and set an example to society. His liberation became known as a product of noble actions and constant awareness of an interconnected society. Leaders of society were shown how to lead decent and orderly life-styles so life force can flow in harmony in the enlightened as well as the unenlightened

And *Krishna* interrupted *Arjuna's* thoughts. "Sage kings like *Janaka* gained perfection and liberation. He realised Oneness by action. He performed action for the salvation of his people and kingdom. You also should perform right actions for the purpose of guiding mortals accurately."

Arjuna had earlier expressed concern that *Pandava* offensive would manipulate families and relatives for generations to come, if he went to war against his relatives. *Krishna* reassures him that righteous actions not only transform the doer of the action, mentally and intellectually, but coalesces with the Collective consciousness of Nature:

"Whatever a great man does with his power of creativity or *rajoguna,* other men will copy. All your actions dedicated as *yagna,* whether in meditation or as dedicated work, will leave impressions of a righteous symbols. Your actions will set a standard for people of the world to follow."

Sanjaya decides to counsel the blind king. Perhaps he can be convinced to stop the war.

"In a similar way, the force of an individual mind interacts with the Universal Mind comprised of so many individual minds. Rather than becoming bound by your selfish actions for self-indulgence, you can become famous for selfless action. As a vulnerable human, the Laws of Nature will confine you to *Kaurava's* egotistical war. O king, perform your duties with an attitude of virtue," *Sanjaya* said.

"Look, even a man like *Krishna* has no compelling duty to perform in the three worlds. There is nothing that he needs to achieve or to amass. Yet he is unwaveringly present in fulfilling all accountable actions," *Sanjaya* tells the blind king.

The blind king asked *Sanjaya* to explain why *Krishna* lives among us. "Through Time in Creation, *Krishna* – like sages have arrived in different parts of earth to revive goodness. Even the vulgar and the unrighteous will do whatever a great man does. Ordinary men follow ideals set by great men. Every educated mortal must behave like the Spirit image that he is – calm and transcendent in spirit but simultaneously energetic in the body without entangling desires," *Sanjaya* explains.

"If the Creator does not engage in righteous action, men on all sides would follow his example and the worlds would perish," *Sanjaya* says. "*Arjuna* is being urged to serve his origin and establishment constantly. He is being counseled that in contrast to the ignorant that work having partiality, the wise must work without affinity. His determination should be to make men mindful of their duties. The wise should not cause distraction of understanding among the ignorant."

And then *Krishna* highlights the same goal.

"O *Arjuna,* if I stopped continual work, men would mimic my ways and my Path by example. If I did not perform actions, these universes would perish. I would be the cause of confusions in those born to do their rightful duties in life. I would therefore be the instrument of Man's ruination. O descendent of *Bharat,* just as the ignorant act because of attachment for reward, so the wise should act with dispassion and nonattachment, only to serve as guides for the welfare of the multitude." And *Krishna* adds, "O son of *Pandu,* under no circumstance should the wise disturb the understanding of an ignorant person who is attached to fruits of actions. Instead the illumined being, by conscientiously performing selfless activities, should inspire in the ignorant, a need for dutiful actions."

Dhritarashtra asks why the ignorant must not be disturbed.

Sanjaya repeats what *Krishna* explained earlier. "All works are compelled by the unique qualities of Nature in the actor. The deluded regards himself the actor. But he who recognizes the distinction of the self from the actor's qualities of Nature is not attached to the work he performs. He knows his senses and not the self are engaged with the objects of the senses. Those deluded by the qualities of Nature become attached to works done by Her creativity."

Krishna describes why a person of perfect Knowledge should not bewilder men of imperfect knowledge. "All action is universally brought about by the qualities or *gunas* of primitive Nature, *Prakriti.* Except for Harmony or *sattva-guna,* in meditation there is no other quality that takes Man to the distinction of Oneness with the Inner Self. After that, whatever action Man performs, the worldly senses and organs of action take their talents along the admirable examples of introspective actions. A man who is deluded by ego thinks, I am the doer. O Mighty-armed *Arjuna,* he who gains the Truth realises, that it is the senses, that are attached to sense objects, that keeps Man attached to actions and its fruits."

Therefore *Krishna* says, "A yogi of perfect wisdom should not bewilder the minds of men who have imperfect understanding. Deluded by features of primordial Nature, the ignorant must be allowed to perform activities caused by those qualities of creativity, dissolution and harmonization. Surrender all to me. Empty the ego and expectations, and with your attention concentrated on the soul, free from worry and anxiety, stay engaged in the battle of performances." *Krishna* further states, "Men, who with devotion, endlessly practice my teachings, without fault-finding, they too become free from all action and their reactions. But those who denounce my teachings and do not live according to it, they are deluded about true wisdom. They are empty of understanding. They are destined for a squandered existence,"

Krishna reminds *Arjuna* that even the wise act according to their own innate qualities and nature. *Arjuna* remains perplexed. What then is the purpose of fighting unrighteousness if all creatures and beings follow the dictates of their own nature?

Dhritarashtra began by justifying the need for the war. *Sanjaya* stopped him and said, "*Arjuna* is being told that those with faith in enlightened teachings of God find it easier to remain committed to righteous action, especially when it refers to the active spiritual practices of meditation. Many disbelievers refuse to transact thus because of their failure to understand the design of a human life."

After a quiet moment *Arjuna* states, "Even the wise man acts according to tendencies in his own nature. All living creatures go according to the predominance of their original Nature. How can a retreat from action help? Reactions to past actions are fixed and determined by individuality and past habits. They succumb to these tendencies because their likes-and-dislikes stand in the way of soul emancipation."

Krishna expects *Arjuna* to perform action with complete honesty and emotional maturity. *Krishna* further warns *Arjuna* that there is no one who has the ability to prevent the force of all the heaped wants awaiting fulfillment. Without their completion, the Total Mind cannot become peaceful until these are exhausted. The ignorant that enjoys fulfilling these wishes, hungers for more of the same or rejects those effects he does not enjoy. In this way, Man's individuality, his past habits, and Nature's qualities inherent in the senses and in the objects of enjoyment create more effects and Man remains enmeshed in repeated rebirths. But the wise one who agrees and fulfills his fated duties does not see himself as the doer of actions. He therefore works without creating new actions or reactions. *Arjuna* is advised to regulate his physical and mental impulses through restraint, adherence to restraints, and remaining still while in contemplation. Only through constant practice at remaining still and silent can a higher understanding of the purpose of life dawn on him. In this way, *Arjuna* can expect to reach the highest potential for excellence.

Krishna said, "Attachment and distaste by the senses for specific objects are ordained by Nature's compulsions. The deluded egotistical ignorant person thinks he is the doer of all work, which in reality is being done by quality-compelled senses. Such reasoning must not distress the wise. Otherwise there will be indifference for work by those lacking in knowledge. Beware of the influence of this duality. These two psychological qualities are one's opponents."

To transcend likes-and-dislikes, *Arjuna* is advised to stop considering them a problem but rather to become even more intent on awakening to the intuitive knowledge born of meditation. Remission of the pressure of Nature would then become involuntary.

Krishna tells *Arjuna* it is his duty to act under the Law of Creation, which has determined his nature and status in life, for the benefit of Common Good. *Krishna* considers dutiful action better than an action well performed. Death in carrying out one's own duty is preferable to adopting the duty of another:

"One's own duty or *svadharma,* though defective in merit, is superior to another's duty or *paradharma,* even if well performed. Better it is to die in *svadharma. Paradharma* is full of fear and danger."

Each person experiences bizarre predicaments. Even while undertaking virtuous actions, inducement oppresses Man, as if by compulsion. What then, must he do? *Arjuna* addresses *Krishna,* "O *Varshneya* of the *Vrishni* dynasty, Man is often forced into committing sin against his will, as if compelled by an unseen force. What is the cause of this?"

Krishna replies. "This reaction arises from an unsatisfied want which has left its footprints in the creative energy or *rajoguna,* as anger. Because the desire has remained unsatisfied, it remains in the memory. It displays as an enemy on the path of liberation."

Arjuna does not understand and asks for further explanation, "Born of the activating character of Nature or *rajoguna* it is desire and anger that is the impelling force. It is full of unappeasable cravings and a great depravity. Know this two-sided passion to be the foulest enemy of good designs and attempts at just endeavors, here on this earth. As fire is obscured by smoke, as a mirror by dust, as an embryo is enveloped by the amniotic membrane in the womb, so is wisdom veiled in worldly life by want and anger," *Krishna* explains.

Arjuna is told to do the best he can because it is the only way known to steadily grow in His grace. Copying another's future gives little if any contentment. The materialist endures existence until dead, but fears and distrusts life. *Arjuna* is told to live the needs of life with the understanding that, while constrained by Nature and Her qualities, he must live fearlessly, skillfully and successfully.

Krishna now defines ways to triumph over the two-sided sword of passion – desire and anger.

"O son of *Kunti* – *Arjuna,* this eternal enemy of even the sage is the unquenchable flame of want. Like fire it gives much sorrow and pain. This evil desire veils all rationalism in people. It is the eternal enemy of the wise because by this unquenchable need Knowledge and Wisdom are cloaked in the great heat of its fire. The senses, mind, and intellect are said to be the cause of all wants. Through these, desire deludes the embodied soul by eclipsing and covering Knowledge and Wisdom. Therefore, O best of the *Bharat* dynasty – *Arjuna,* first discipline the senses by meditation as taught by a teacher and the scriptures. In this manner destroy this unfortunate, insatiable and erring need."

Sanjaya understands that pure awareness in the meditating self is able to understand the compulsions of the senses and the mind as part of the Cosmic Person's Nature and qualities or *gunas.* In the depth of his soul, the seeker is able to intuitively find out and discriminate between goodness and unrighteousness. It can make out a clouded awareness when under the influence of passivity or *tamoguna.* He understands the workings of a well intentioned, energetic, purposeful seeker or *rajogun,* who becomes victim to conflicting and compelling wishes.

"The physical world-revealing senses are said to be superior to the physical body. The mind is superior to the sense faculties. Intellect is superior to the mind. But the soul is superior to intellect. Beyond the intellect is the ever witnessing intelligence, the Self," *Krishna* stresses.

Arjuna understands that for the individualistic ego, satisfaction of sense inclinations and emotional comforts decide and motivate behavior and give Man's life a direction. This intellectual determination has the ability to detect virtue from unrighteousness. The intellect therefore must be superior to both body and mind. It is the only instrument able to regulate the senses and the mind. It is the only way that soul can be calmed to make soul-liberating decisions to abandon obsessive compulsions and desire-motivated actions.

"O Mightily armed *Arjuna,* recognizing the Self to be superior to intellect, keep the mind disciplined by the intellect and mindful that it is want that is the enemy. Keep yourself separate from the senses, mind, intellect and ego and remain in the ever-witnessing Self or soul. Right at the beginning, destroy this harmful enemy – 'Want' that is so hard to capture."

Once meditative movements free the flow of life force from the mind, senses, and even the intellect, it retraces Nature's creative energy from the atoms to molecules, to cells, to tissues, and back into the spinal cord and brain. This physical transformation ensures there is also a progressive physiological, psychological, and intellectual transformation during meditative practices. Once this life-flow is unobstructed, awakening is progressive and uninterrupted. After that, whether meditating, sleeping, acting in the world, or playing, soul awareness is freed from the compulsions of Nature. Now *Arjuna* can begin to unfold.

6. Key to Karma Yoga

All new ideas, however logical and intelle
not readily agreeable to *Arjuna*. *Krishna* c
to perform necessary actions while reno
thereby. He gives a groundbreaking idea a
which is capable of being an explanatio
Science. *Krishna* has also given *Arjuna* a cosm
of all life's processes. By learning about the
of Nature on the senses and their chosen ob
and repulsion, and also on the mind, *Kr*
Arjuna is back on track.

Even after accepting that Life's purp
ultimate discovery of the Self's relationsh
Self, the deluded *Arjuna* still thinks that
is only for human happiness and fulfil
articulates that Man's persona is happin
anand. And discovery of this fact is possi
clarifications experienced during spiritual
is not the only purpose why Man lives in t

In his next discussion, *Krishna* makes
to fetch the Lord Himself. The Person
will talk to *Arjuna* in person. He promises
same old Truth and nothing new. He
many like him enter the grand archway to
of the Spirit, but none has ever seen or
about to witness *Krishna* for the first tim
his mortal garments. He puts on His divine
demonstrates He is the Supreme Self, th
of the Universe.

For that moment, *Sanjaya* sees, hear
the emotions of *Arjuna*. Here in themedit

6. Key to Karma Yoga

All new ideas, however logical and intellectual they be, are not readily agreeable to *Arjuna. Krishna* encourages *Arjuna* to perform necessary actions while renouncing the fruits thereby. He gives a groundbreaking idea about *Karma Yoga,* which is capable of being an explanation of the old *Vedic* Science. *Krishna* has also given *Arjuna* a cosmic understanding of all life's processes. By learning about the coercive qualities of Nature on the senses and their chosen objects of attraction and repulsion, and also on the mind, *Krishna* hopes that *Arjuna* is back on track.

Even after accepting that Life's purpose is to make an ultimate discovery of the Self's relationship with the Infinite Self, the deluded *Arjuna* still thinks that spiritual practice is only for human happiness and fulfillment. *Krishna* re-articulates that Man's persona is happiness itself or *sat-chit-anand.* A discovery of this fact is possible only through clarifications experienced during spiritual practices. But it is not the only purpose why Man lives in the Universe.

In his next discussion, *Krishna* makes an all-out effort to fetch the Lord Himself. The Person behind the *Vedas,* will talk to *Arjuna* in person. He promises it will be about the same old Truth and nothing new. He convinces him that many like him enter the grand archway to reach the Temple of the Spirit, but none has ever seen or heard what he is about to witness! *Krishna* for the first time divests himself of his mortal garments. He puts on His divine attire. He verbally demonstrates He is the Supreme Self, the Collective Lord of the Universe.

For that moment, *Sanjaya* sees, hears, smells, and feels the emotions of *Arjuna.* Here in the middle of the battlefield between the two armies he sees the kneeling *Arjuna* looking up at the glowing *Krishna.* The blind king intuitively knows the war has not as yet started. His person has deadly anchoring in want, rage, greed, possessiveness, jealousy, and pride. They are stronger than his sense of righteousness.

Sanjaya hears *Krishna* speak to the confused *Arjuna. Sanjaya* uses this conversation to once again convince the blind king to stop this unendorsed war.

Sanjaya knows that whenever a seeker like *Arjuna* questions the marvels of life and awakens spiritually, through His grace, the mystic faces a genuine *guru.* He or she is introduced to the art of divine union in meditation. *Krishna* speaks to *Arjuna* about the **Origin** of Conscious-awareness in humankind.

"I gave this imperishable and Eternal Knowledge to the Sun-god *Vivaswat.* He taught it to the Lord of Daylight, the first expression of Consciousness who is *Om.* Daylight taught it to the respectable *Manu,* the cosmic lawgiver of *manas* or the Cosmic Mind, who is also the progenitor of human beings. *Manu* taught it to the Cosmic Life Force, *Ikshvaku,* and this founder of the solar dynasty and lineage arrived at the perfection of *Om,* through meditation. He infused this Knowledge, which enlivens and governs all the creatures of Nature and then disappeared."

Arjuna is floored by this information but *Dhritarashtra* did not understand *Krishna's* statements. *Sanjaya* decides to explain the mysterious in scientific terms. "As you already know Sire, the Sun is a powerful electrical conductor which supports creation, nourishment and dissolution. This sun is seen at the *kutastha* behind and in between the eyebrows during meditation. The blue light surrounding it is the subtle energy embedded in creation, which emerges and dissolves, but remains hidden from the sense-inclined. The materialist sees this place as a dark and empty realm. It is the Sun who provides for all names and forms through the supremacy of *Om.* Mother Nature who is awarded with creativity preserves or dissolves Her displays as many conditions of existence. All this happens all the time in the Solar Universe or *brahmanda.* Here are found three states of existence, physical, subtle and causal, which present themselves as visible, partially visible and partly invisible planet. By meditation, these existences become increasingly visible because they are found within the miniature universe, in Man's body."

The blind king is overwhelmed by these facts. *Arjuna* is left wondering – "How old is *Krishna?*"

Meantime, *Krishna* explains the Knowledge of Consciousness inherent at every level of Nature's expression. Individual souls, who are units of the Cosmic Soul, are innately granted with this Knowledge of Consciousness, as well as of Nature's Awareness. But, Man is too preoccupied to heed this intuitive message.

About the Knowledge of Meditation, *Krishna* explains that he gave this imperishable method of devotion to *Vivaswat,* to *Manu,* and finally to *Ikshvaku.* Descending thus for generations, the sages were told the Knowledge. That is how it came into being. Because of a lapse of time, this science of devotion became lost to the world. *Krishna* reminds *Arjuna* that what he declares and describes this moment, is the same strategy of devotion, which to many today is a great enigma.

"Understanding this Yoga of Knowledge helps one to understand the Yoga of Actions. These enable a seeker to experience the Yoga of Meditation and also of Unification or *samadhi.* When an individualized soul unites with the Universal Soul, *Arjuna* you reclaim your birthright to the Yoga of Oneness with the Whole," *Krishna* said. "Handed down in this way in orderly and regular stages, royal sages acquainted with the sacrament and taught it to seekers. Through the door of the lunar channel, the mind is rid of its sense binding unhappiness. When the silent and still mind allows the filling of solar channels with knowledge, senses automatically renounce sense objects and become tranquil.

This knowledge makes him steadfast in meditation. But, O *Arjuna,* because of the long passage of time, this yoga has been lost to the worldly. Mother Earth craves for its rejuvenation."

"What does *Krishna* mean by what he just said to *Arjuna*?" asked *Dhritarashtra.*

"*Krishna* just made available the historical foundation and essence of yoga of meditation – the technique of uniting individualized Self and Cosmic Self in Consciousness," *Sanjaya* replied. The blind king nodded as if understanding.

"When knowledge is proved, all wants automatically disappear. When meditation, knowledge and renunciation are established, the mind moves into another location of inner peace. Now ceaseless Awareness reveals herself. The lunar family of *Ida,* the solar family of *Pingala* and the main spinal *Vrishni* family of *sushumna* meet at the Inner Universe in the *kutastha.* All bodily channels and nerves with outward projections of creativity recede into themselves in tranquility." *Sanjaya* continues to explain.

"When the causal body appears in the *kutastha* as the sun, Man knows he is always connected to Consciousness as *kutastha-chaitanya.* He knows his human body is created from Matter and exists as Energy and is enlivened by life force or *prana* that vibrates in a symphony of *Om.* He exists as *Manu.* He understands that *prana* enters and exits from the human body through the medullary or *ajna* center."

Dhritarashtra confirms what he understood and asks, "Although these links are forgotten, the memory is not. Because it continues to illustrate itself as different states in different depths of meditation?"

Sanjaya says, "The radiant Consciousness is seen in the spiritual eye as a five-star rays who *Krishna* identifies as *Vivaswat.* It vitalizes the *Manu* with Life and Energises both the gross and subtle bodies by coursing through the spiritual centers or *charkas.* These *rajarishis* vitalize using life force or *prana.* The soul's awareness is directed outwards towards attachments and desires. This happens because of a temporary loss of memory. He is the familiar individualistic self."

The blind king knew about this knowledge but his materialistic life style had left him disconnected from the truth.

Arjuna is a mature student of this Knowledge. He understands what *Krishna* is telling him, when he says, "I have this day told you about the same old yoga, because you are my supporter and my friend. The sacred mystery of yoga is that it is a creator of supreme benefit to humankind. This is a Supreme Secret which is self-revealing when a devotee is ready to understand it," *Krishna* says.

Krishna explains to *Arjuna* the meaning of different states of transformation, which eventually lead to the same ancient highway through which all followers must travel for final liberation. In the early stages, a seeker feels an awesome distance between himself and the Lord. But, as the disciple experiences consecutively higher states of ecstasy, barriers are broken. The devotee joyously recalls his long lost familiar state of oneness of the Self and the Cosmic Self.

He rejoices to hear the voice of Cosmic Consciousness in Nature. He is told of all the mysteries of the Universe. *Krishna* warns *Arjuna* that he needs to identify the different stages of awareness within himself. In time, he can expect to see his present state as a reflection of cosmic processes of stillness, satisfaction, enlightenment, renunciation and finally tranquillity.

Sanjaya decides to continue his discussion on delusion about the purpose of mortal existence. He still hopes to avoid the war. "Many souls experience a clouded awareness and while deluded forget the truth about themselves. They become increasingly identified with mind and matter. Yet, individuals have the ability to remove themselves from these external influences to promote a spiritual awakening through the practice of meditation," *Sanjaya* verbalises as if to himself.

"How is it that *Arjuna* has the intuitive capacity to see *Krishna* as a divine friend? Why do I only see *Krishna* as my nephew through the marriage of his aunt *Kunti* with my brother *Pandu*?" asks the blind king.

"This awakening occurs at different readings in the body. It happens in conjunction with the source in the soul. Here Knowledge, born of personal experience transforms all," replied *Sanjaya*. "Both teacher and taught are enlightened with such spontaneous unfoldment. *Arjuna* awaits this grace of soul liberation,"

Meanwhile, *Arjuna* is unable to conceptualize *Krishna's* assertion about the individualized self that came after Light or *Vivaswat*. Mind and senses come from *Manu* and life force or *prana* from *Ikshvaku*. He asks, "*Vivaswat* was born first, you say, and your birth occurred later? How then can I understand that you taught this Yoga in the beginning to the sun? Was this yoga not born in the beginning even before your birth?"

Like *Arjuna, Dhritarashtra* also seems confused. *Sanjaya* tries to explain the allegory. "In the *kutastha chaitanya* or the inner eye, the sun is experienced by the witnessing Consciousness in the silence and stillness within, while in meditation. Then only does the seeker see awareness and the sun united."

And *Krishna* answers also. "O *Arjuna,* many births we both have experienced together. I know about all of them, but you do not remember them *Parantapa,* O Scorcher of Foes. When your mind is concentrated in the *kutastha,* the *kutastha chaitanya* reveals itself many times. Because of a veil of ignorance, your soul has not experienced That. But when the veil of illusion or *maya* is conquered, all these will be revealed to you."

Sanjaya knew the questions and answers between *Krishna* and *Arjuna* were intuitional exchanges between wisdom and a knowledgeable seeker seeking perfection in action. In the experience of meditational oneness or *samadhi,* the seeker sees the Cosmic Light or *Krishna* and self or *Arjuna,* as having existed together through many incarnations. Though displaying to express in different ways, the Light never decreases within the confines of limited mind and matter. It regulates the cosmic processes of Matter and at the same time transcends them. On an individualistic level, the soul, identifies with mind and matter because of its false sense of ego and delusion. It becomes the individualistic self. In the process, memories are tucked away in the faraway recesses of the subconscious and the unconscious minds.

Krishna says he forever was and is the witnessing transcendent, revealing first Light and life in *Om* and the vibrating Energy in Matter.

It is He who grants intelligence and enlivens matter. He granted primordial Nature with qualities or *guna.* Nature displays as the individualized self. Veiled thus by the power of *maya* Her identity is Nature's compelling qualities. *Krishna* says, "Though I am free of birth and death and therefore unborn, and of changeless imperishable essence, yet, by becoming Lord of Creation, I remain in my own Cosmic Nature. As Nature or *prakriti,* I reveal myself in this world through a *maya*-caused body."

"Is *Krishna* asserting that He is both Matter and Spirit?" asked the blind king.

"Although the Cosmic Consciousness or *Krishna* is causeless and unborn, yet by entering Nature or *Prakriti,* He *Krishna* the witnessing *Purusha,* wears the cosmic apparel of a Self-created *Maya* or delusion, but is not affected by It," *Sanjaya* replied.

"But for what purpose does the Infinite get bound as Man?" Asked *Dhritarashtra.*

Krishna answers both *Arjuna* and the blind king at the same time.

"O *Arjuna,* because you who are a descendent of the famous and devout *Bharata* dynasty, let me tell you a secret. Whenever virtue or *dharma* declines and vice or *adharma* predominates, I take recourse of *Prakriti* or Matter and take birth - I reveal myself from me as an *avatar.* I appear in a visible form in every age to protect the pure and destroy those who think in directions other than that which is virtuous, to reestablish virtue."

Sanjaya understood *Krishna's* statements. *Krishna* witnesses the assembly of warriors on the battlefield of *Kurukshetra. Sanjaya* meanwhile, seeing through the eye of intuitiveness, knows there has been a rise of sacrilege and unrighteousness. *Krishna* has elected himself for guardianship of the virtuous and to destroy the evildoers so that sanctity might be reestablished. Human impersonations of Universal Intelligence have been born age after age.

Whenever human actors misappropriate their God-given sovereignty to create depravity and anguish for others, they create antagonism in His divine plan. Affiliate existences of humanity and their destinations are disrupted. At these times, the Cosmic Director of the Cosmic Plan appears on the platform in a human form to command them on the art of proper living.

And *Krishna* said, "He who knows that this visible world unloads from Infinite Consciousness, has experienced this in its true light. He or she knows about the truth of my orderly viewpoint. He understands because of my expressions and actions. He is not born again after death because he has experienced and realized me in meditation and in all actions. He therefore comes to Me, O *Arjuna.*"

"How does Man lose his way?" asked *Dhritarashtra.* "*Krishna* emphasises again that the Self settles into Matter through several orderly stages under the creative principles of Nature,"

Sanjaya replied. "Eventually the soul as causal body descends and becomes body-locked. This individualized self, when identified with his little bodily universe, becomes the mind, senses, organs of action and their worldly possessions. It is only by abandoning these wished for attachments, that

Man disentangles from conscious and subconscious cravings and enters a superconscious state. Here he realizes that he, the self, is a perfect image of the Cosmic Self. Once united with the Cosmic Self, the self is released from matter and becomes the realized soul."

"But how does this happen?" insisted the blind king. "By mindfulness and involving awareness in pure consciousness," *Sanjaya* replied. "Many souls who have remained engrossed in contemplation with the ever-witnessing Consciousness have surmounted all difficulties and awakened into the secret Knowledge. They have experienced tranquillity through spontaneous renunciation of all wants. They have realised liberation from all future expressions."

Krishna is then heard to speak to *Arjuna*. "The worldly are naturally dependent on sense orientation and do not cooperate with the path of knowledge that results in wisdom. Disengagement from such loyalties cause fear and anger. They therefore remain bound to them. Those who are fully absorbed and sheltered in me, and have been cleaned by enlightenment and austerity, these beings have reached my essential nature through meditation and have experienced their merging with Consciousness."

Sanjaya recognises that *Krishna* is an advanced yogi, who has succeeded in neutralising his personal emotions about the war of *Mahabharata*. In his intuitive mind, *Sanjaya* can see the dream pictures of life issuing from the Cosmic Beam radiating from *Krishna*. As soon as *Sanjaya* joins himself with *Krishna*, he loses his attachment to fear-and-anger-stimulating situations on the battlefield. Absorbed and secure in the presence of *Krishna*, he remains engrossed in the Infinite. He then suddenly heard *Krishna* speak to *Arjuna*.

"O *Arjuna*, in whatever way people approach me, in that measure I accept their reverence and devotion. I parade to reveal myself to them in the same dimension. It is my way that all men follow me in every manner of seeking, and from all sides. For Me, aim only for a Path to me, alone."

"Why does this nephew of mine expect me to worship *Krishna* as divine. In what manner does he become divine?" asked the blind king.

"The all-pervading witnessing Consciousness lives in every creature and being. Devotees worship the Cosmic Self variously and the Lord responds with grace, regardless of the outer rituals and practices. Rightly determined, souls awarded with devotion and knowledge adhere to their resolves to fight unrighteousness," *Sañjaya* replied. "Giving full attention to higher ideals, the meditating yogi opens himself to the grace of God who not only awakens him but also transforms all his soul impulses. Whatever he holds dear, the Self grants realisation according to the performance of the yogi."

Krishna understands that each person creates his own special screen of illusion for personal interpretation of Nature's qualities. A need by divergent intelligence has led to creating a medley of religions – all of which the Cosmic Being sanctions and sanctifies. *Krishna* states that all paths, theological, serviceful, discriminative, devotional or scientific, can in lesser or greater degrees give matching insights.

Krishna says, "They who wish success for satisfaction from their actions here on earth, adore the gods of their various ideals. Because satisfaction is quickly achieved from their actions, they move in pleasurable prosperity and arrive at the endless suffering intertwined with the senses and objects. It is want that breeds fear and anger, therefore to avoid this, remain in dedicated action to me or in meditation."

"Does that describe me and my sons?" asked the blind king. "The worldly materialist knows that fitting creative action will bring immediate success and fulfillment of personal wishes and endeavors. His thoughts and prayers propitiate the forces and reasons necessary to achieve his material goals," *Sanjaya* replied.

"But *Krishna* stated earlier that Man must erase his belief in limits, harness the creative mental forces and effectively focus actions to fulfill all wants. Learning to work skillfully to fulfill the aims of life, whether materialistic or for spiritual awakening needs a creative personality," the blind king pleaded.

"Materialistic interests and pursuits to satisfy individualistic needs may give man a quantitatively comfortable existence, but without any qualitative soul satisfaction. To fulfill his spiritual destiny, Man needs to withdraw from relationships with relatives and to expand his identification with the larger Universal Family of Nature," *Sanjaya* replied.

"The same creative skills used for materialistic gain must be harnessed to achieve a natural orderly style of expansive living," *Sanjaya* said. "O king, *Arjuna* is being asked to bring into play the creative skills of purpose, imagination, faith, expansion, and understanding that enable man to carry out activities to promote spiritual growth. *Krishna* expects *Arjuna* to live free of the compulsions of the qualities of Nature and in soul freedom, yet remain yoked with the Supreme Self."

To explain himself further *Krishna* gives details, "I have created four groupings of humankind. According to their past *karmas* they decide on their present life or *praarabdha*. Seeking different substances for wished happiness, I have distinguished Humankind according to their qualities or *gunas* and duties in life or *karma*. Though I am the designer of this division, yet, *Arjuna* know me as uninvolved in their actions-reactions. I am unperishable and beyond all change. I am continuous."

The blind king sat up to hear this discussion, but there was silence between *Krishna* and *Arjuna*. *Sanjaya* decided to voice the intuitive unspoken words between teacher and taught.

"Dominated by *sattva* or harmony and living constantly in awareness of Awareness are *Brahmins*. Those dominated by *sattva* mixed with creativity are of *sattva-rajoguna* predominance. They are classified as *Kshatriyas* who are constantly engaged in the battle for self-improvement. Those that are *tamasic-rajoguna* predominant concern themselves with the recruitment of bodily needs, study of scriptures and performance of rituals – these are *Vaishyas.* Then there are those who are devoted to the senses that are mainly *tamasic* or sluggish – they are called S*hudras.*"

"Humanity is divided according to their instinctive calling in life?" asks *Dhritarashtra.*

"Restated in another way, the Cosmic Creator's activities revealed as Cosmic Intelligence unfold as *brahmins.* Cosmic Energy reveals itself as the vigilant *kshatriya.* Cosmic life force fosters materialization of prosperity – these are *vaishya.* Cosmic Motion that displays the laboring are *shudra,*" *Sanjaya* explains.

"To reiterate, the four time-cycles or *yugas* of each creative cycle or *kalpa* are also under the influence of an Environment's qualities. They express characters of Nature but can be adjusted by *karmic* conditions of creatures or beings living in a particular *yuga,*" *Sanjaya* adds.

After *Sanjaya* describes compulsions of the Universe on a cosmic scale, *Krishna* is heard telling *Arjuna* about the Cycle of Creation and how it matches with many a person's wishes on a comprehensive level.

Sanjaya explains how awareness in dedicated activities undergoes oscillations from physical change to access into calming concentration. Here pressure becomes dormant. When Man sees the spirit shine, he becomes increasingly entrenched in soul-light and inner peace and the life force or *prana* attunes to stillness. He enters a desireless state of knowledge, renunciation, and tranquility. Man enters Oneness with the Whole. Many souls in a cycle or *yuga* are under the assertive influence of Nature's compelling qualities or *gunas.* During four Cycles of Creation or *yugas,* the *sattva* are enlightened, *rajas* are creative, *tamas* are dormant, and *causative-karmic* are clouded. Dominance of a particular tendency segregates and defines the cycle.

Krishna explains that when many souls experience clouding of awareness, the deluded forget their Truth. Their understanding is identified with the sense inclined mind and wonton materialism. When some individuals partially awaken to the Truth because of Nature's heavenly influences, there is a clearing of opinion as part of a natural external evolution over millions of years.

Sanjaya explains that some, like the *Pandavas,* withdraw from compulsive external influences of Nature and produce a speedy spiritual awakening. They seek a *guru* like *Krishna* to teach them techniques of glorified action metamorphosing their brain, the nerve plexuses or *chakras* in the spinal cord and the nerve tracts or *nadis.* Once these outgoing impulses are withdrawn within the brain and spinal cord, the path and the flow clears of all obstacles and limits. The current of Awareness is unencumbered and unprompted revelation of the Self happens.

Krishna explains that Man's activities exist as self-expressions of three *gunas* or qualities innate in Nature. *Sattva* is uplifting, *rajas* is activating, and *tamas* is degrading. These movements are molds from which all races are made. Humanity, however, displays a fusion of all types of *gunas,* thus accounting for the bewildering variety of creatures and humanity found in the world.

Krishna explains that motiveless impelling forces already inherent in Nature also influence Cosmic Actions. He goes on to tell *Arjuna,* "Actions do not touch me. I have no desire or longing for their fruit-of-actions. He, who identifies with me thus, is not impeded by my actions. Knowing my true nature, even men from ancient times desirous of emancipation, performed work but were free from the fetters of law of karma – of action-reaction."

Arjuna becomes reassured that his obsessive ideas, opinions and conduct while constantly fixed in the Cosmic

Self will not adversely affect his contemplative practices. He already knew that when he experiences Oneness with the Whole, he neither desires nor does he seek rewards for serving Mother Nature.

Arjuna is assured that once he permanently castes off *Maya,* the illusive power of God, veiling and projecting the Universe, he is sure to reach a personal realisation. He will intuitively know that the self is created in the same way as the Cosmic Self. In fact *Krishna* says, "Understanding this, wise men who have sought after salvation, since ancient times, have performed dutiful actions. Therefore, you too should act dutifully, discarding the ego and imprisonment by action, even as did the ancients in the antiquated old days."

Krishna tells *Arjuna* that just as the soul remains untouched by the traditional personality-activity it is born into, he is also unaffected by *Arjuna's* endeavours in spiritual practices. *Arjuna* gets forewarned to differentiate between Self-supporting actions and mundane-appetite instigated worthy conduct, which also have the power to cloud awareness.

He is deliberated to perform Self-inspired performances to triumph over his own spiritual destiny. He is cautioned that personal desires to be a servant humanitarian breeds fruit of that act.

"Does *Krishna* mean that I do not have the freedom to act the way I desire, even to benefit another?" asked the blind king.

"O king, *Krishna* is warning *Arjuna* that to do what one wants to do, does not constitute freedom. To do what one should do, especially when guided by the wisdom of a teacher, is what leads to complete emancipation," *Sanjaya* replies.

To emphasise these points, *Krishna* says to *Arjuna,* "Even the learned and wise are confused about what is action and what is inaction. Therefore I will explain what constitutes true action, so that knowing it you are freed of the evil of *samsara,* the action-reaction cycle that puts one on the wheel of birth and death. The true nature of karma or right action is difficult to know. Truly, to understand that fully one should remain absorbed in the *kutastha* in all activities. Here with a still mind, Man becomes aware of the distinction between dutiful and forbidden actions. One should also know the nature of inaction in meditation. The nature of the path of action is imponderable and incomprehensible"

Krishna explains that even sages become identified with the senses again when they disengage from their meditative state. They, like *Arjuna,* endure confusion as to what is right action. Only a saint who retains continuously That ecstatic state in the midst of action can perform Self-directed deeds that constitute right action. Conduct performed with an individualistic ego consciousness is and always will be wrong actions.

"Even mortals such as myself are therefore subject to temptations," the blind king said as if justifying his unrighteous actions.

"*Krishna* has asserted the difference between good and bad actions. They can be recognised only if the *yogi* keeps constant vigil during his wakeful state," *Sanjaya* censures. "*Krishna* has advised to vigilantly guard against sense indulgences, so that the reins are not unwittingly handed over to the ego. To an indifferent observer of the nature of action, this earth is full of discrepancies. The world's very existence seems, to him, to depend on relativity wherein interacting actions produce varying results."

"How then do I know if my deeds are righteous or not?" asked the blind king.

"*Krishna* says, an action performed out of good motive might be good. But the same action instigated by another motive could be evil. *Arjuna* is warned that Man's perspective is shortsighted, because he looks for immediate results. The same action through far-sighted wisdom may or may not produce a good result," *Sanjaya* said.

"*Krishna* therefore divides all human actions into three

categories: right or proper action; contrary or corrupt action; and inaction. Any deed that rouses soul consciousness and leads the doer's mind away from sense enslavement is proper action. Action harmful to the body, mind or intellect that causes one to indulge in the senses but gives him no satiety is contrary action. A *yogi* who endlessly enjoys the inner bliss of the Self, whether sitting still or actively busy, is inaction or non-binding action," *Sanjaya* said to the king.

As if continuing with the discussion, *Krishna* says, "He is a yogi – a wise one among men, who sees inaction in action and action in inaction. He controls devotion and performs pure action of contemplation without need for results and reaches the supreme goal of all true actions in tranquillity. He sees himself separate from his body and uninvolved in the work done by his senses. He who sees himself in this non-doing is satisfied in detachment. He is freed from the law of action-reaction."

Arjuna recognises that all human activities lead either outwardly to the sensory world or inwardly to soul consciousness. The worldly man harnesses all his activities towards increasing his physical, mental, domestic and social welfare. The *yogi* employs his time in meditation, introspection and service to Nature.

"I do not understand action-in-inaction and inaction-in-action," complains the blind king.

Sanjaya tells the blind king *Dhritarashtra* that when *Krishna* says, "Inaction in action" he is highlighting inner aloofness from outer bodily activities. By defining "action in inaction" *Krishna* is referring to an aloof *yogi,* acting for Nature and the Cosmic Being, inwardly disowning the fruits of his action. He does not renounce work because he is not afraid of dedicated action. But he surrenders karmic involvement as regards the fruit of action.

A yogi knows the true purpose of all human activity is to return to the Cosmic Being. He thus looks for *Krishna's* guiding hand in everything. *Krishna* is understood when he says, "The wise call that man a sage whose undertakings and efforts are all without desire of fruit and purposeful self-will. The fire-of-knowledge purifies his actions and there is wisdom arrived at through contemplation."

Krishna tells *Arjuna* that for the worldly man, his gods are ego and self-interest. He plans for success only for himself. The yogi plans his inspired activities to achieve the best results to accomplish His will, whatever that might be. The worldly man grieves when he does not reap the required results. The unsuccessful yogi keeps trying over and over again until he pleases the Cosmic Self. Nature ensures that all *yogis'* actions are cauterized in the flame of wisdom. As *Krishna* explains, "He resides in detachment who renounces and abandons all attachments to the fruits of action. He is content in the eternal bliss experienced in the *kutastha.* He does not take refuge in engaging his body and senses. He does not perform action while he is residing in detachment. He who is independent of worldly rewards, this wise one does not perform any binding actions even amid actions."

Krishna tells *Arjuna* that whatever deeds a *yogi* engages in are like impersonal 'carrying-out-orders' and not entangled in any personal karma. This yogi has joyfully reassigned his will to that of Divine Will. He, who without desire, with mind and senses under control, casting off all concerns, performs action only for preserving his own body, incurs no sin of cause-effect. He has renounced all sense possessions and is free from delusive human hopes and his heart and feelings are controlled by the soul."

When the Self in the *yogi* is in command, the body and mind work, but without the enslaving effects of actions. They are neutralised because of absence of the catalytic agent of delusion. The *yogi,* identified with Nature, has freed himself from categorizing with ego, body, mind, feeling, senses, habits and desires. *Krishna* emphasises, "That man of action is free from the law of karma if he is content with whatever befalls him. He rises above pairs of opposites and is poised above duality. He is without jealousy, envy or enmity, and is even-minded in success and failure. He is not shackled by action even though he works."

"This is an extremely difficult act to follow," the blind king said.

"Not true, O king," *Sanjaya* responds. "The yogi sees the Cosmic Being everywhere and becomes free of desires for the self. He has no will to gratify himself. *Krishna* explains that a yogi established in Him, is content to receive whatever comes naturally for fulfilling the needs of his body, mind and soul. He rises above dualities of good and bad. He has no awareness of me-and-mine. He entertains no adverse thoughts towards anyone. He is indifferent to worldly success-and failure and performs actions for and by the Deity within."

In fact, "All his actions-reactions perish who acts for the sake of service, who is free from attachments to fruits-of-action, whose mind is fixed in the *kutastha* with Knowledge and enveloped in wisdom. He acts for the sake of true sacrifice alone and is in a state of non-doing."

Krishna now describes the action of one who constantly lives in an awareness of the Cosmic Whole. When a yogic mind is free from attachments, it concentrates on Cosmic Wisdom. The yogi withdraws the life force and mind from the sensory-motor nerves as well as from the physiological life functions. He offers these into the fire of meditation or *yagna* and is heard to say, "*Brahma* the Creator is the urn with which this offering of butter is poured. *Brahma* is the oblation being offered. *Brahma* is the fire in which, by *Brahma* is poured the drink of butter. *Brahma* is the objective to which he proceeds by fixing his mind on *Brahma. Brahma* itself is the action. The fire and he who makes the sacrifice are manifestations of that Spirit. Absorbed in *Brahman* he sees *Brahman* in all activities. Truly, such a one goes back to Spirit alone."

Krishna says to *Arjuna* that since all manifestation is but a ritual of the one Cosmic Self, the soul/Self or *jiva* is no different from the Universal Soul. It is He who is the Giver, and the Receiver of all activities and rituals. He is the sacrifice and the offering. The yogi or Self who clearly understands this enters oneness with the Cosmic Self.

"What of those who honor family deities?" asked the blind king. "When specific sacrifices are offered in particular ceremonies for invocation of astral celestials or agencies in Nature, they invoke intermediaries that govern various utilities of the universe," *Sanjaya* replied.

Krishna tells *Arjuna,* "In truth, there are those yogis who sacrifice to gods. Others offer as sacrificial libation their senses, of which hearing is the first, into the fire of restraint."

Dhritarashtra does not understand what *Krishna* just told *Arjuna* and asks *Sanjaya* to explain the discussion. "Celibate monks are able to withdraw and control their senses through the act of *pratyahara.* These are unaffected by the lure of the sense-objects. Householders fulfill their life-duties by freeing themselves of likes-and-dislikes and performing actions without expectations. They worship the celestials first. Gradual evolution and progressive revelation of life force or *prana* in the mind awakens the intellect to realize the purpose why Man is born a human being,"

"After many births, Man fulfills his duties according to his karma or *prarabdha,* which determines his present life. He stops fluctuations in the mind, and seeks a guru who gives him sanctuary to perform action-in-inaction and inaction-in-action," *Sanjaya* concludes.

Arjuna knows *Ishvara* is the Lord of Creation who is a reflection of the witnessing Cosmic Self, governing the universe. *Ishvara* is the First Cause of *Light Energy* and then *Om,* the Life force or *prana,* permeates and enlivens all Matter. Cosmic Matter or *Virat* has embedded in it *Hiranyagarbha,* the effulgent and radiant cosmic golden egg with physical, astral and causal plans of all past Creative-and-Dissolution Cycles of Creation or all *yugas* of every *kalpa.*

Arjuna appreciates that on a microcosmic level, the equivalent of the witnessing ideational causal *Ishvara is*

Prajna. Of astral *Hiranyagarbha* it is *taijas* and of *physical Virat* is *Vishva*. These six *devas* are governed by a seventh heavenly being, *Maha-Prakriti* or Mother *Nature*. She is a reflection of Cosmic Consciousness as Awareness. Her ivory-like life-expression is a halo surrounding the blue energy field of matter-deities in the *kutastha-chaitanya*.

Krishna explains, "Knowing such knowledge becomes an agency to surrender to. Submitting individuality awakens self-knowledge for purposes of realisation. Those receptive to such core teachings need them for spiritual awakening. The vastness of this knowledge regulates and neutralises instinctive and conditioned tendencies of the egocentric individualist." *Arjuna* must renounce inclinations and habits that fetter him to worldly bondage. Once *Arjuna* reaches the shores of self-analysis, *Krishna* gives his word, he will salvage *Arjuna's* higher state of awareness.

Krishna explains, "Offering the senses in a fire ceremony is consecration. This symbolic fire is the deity. It is consummated by a worldly man, who seeks progress towards liberation through positive right actions." In many ways, he is saying, 'others offer objects of the senses. I am offering sound as my first oblation into the fire of sense-restraints.'"

"What sound is *Krishna* speaking of?" asks the blind king.

"The listening and offering the resonance of *Om* in contemplation, O king. To some this practice is better than coming up and gazing at the *kutastha*," replied *Sanjaya*.

The mechanical Man possesses sensory reflexes and he responds unthinkingly to sense objects and casts his energy into the fire of impulsive worldly efforts. An orderly Man sacrifices his energy in the fire of intelligent effort. He learns the self-discipline of concentration, meditation and oneness *[dharana, dhyana and samadhi]* and gains a proper perspective of discriminative knowledge experienced as an object of meditation. Senses do not rule him. Through interiorization, he dissolves his five senses, organs of action and objects of senses. If intense enough, he even cancels the work of breathing or *svasayama* and successfully eliminates the dissatisfaction of the senses and the body. In fact, given a choice, the intelligent being feels happy looking at the *kutastha* than offering oblations into a fire. He feels better still, while immersed in the ecstasy of meditation, where no outer world exists.

Krishna assures *Arjuna* that by deeper meditation, he gains inner self-control and succeeds in freeing his mind from his body and objects of his senses. He dissolves all opinions into one indivisible perception – the ecstasy of the Self. *Krishna* explains this state of rapture. "These followers of the Path of Knowledge after offering all the roles of the senses and breathing into the fire of devotion, remain steadfast in self-restraint, kindled by inner wisdom," *Krishna* says.

Arjuna realizes that his body and his substance are a dream. He discovers he is an eternal constituent of dreaming Consciousness. *Krishna* continues to list the various types of *yagnas* and devotees. "Some offer their wealth to help others as offering to the Cosmic Self. Some obey the dos and don'ts of self-discipline. Their *yagna* is their need for oneness with the Self".

"Other devotees offer wealth as oblation. Many perform penance of austerities and self-discipline. An added number prefer consecration by meditation, oblation through *Vedic* studies, appropriation of knowledge and wisdom, and yet others are ascetics of rigid vows," *Krishna* lists.

"Other devotees, offer as sacrifice *apana* or the downbeat *prana* and also the upbeat life-force, during *puraka* or inspiration. During *rechaka* or exhalation he offers *prana* into *apana*. In *kumbhaka* or retention and suspension of breath, the movements of *apana* and *prana* pause. Many perform this *yagna* as *kevali-pranayama* as an offering also," *Krishna* explains

"Then there are those who eat a little to weaken the senses. This also, I accept as sacrifice by another method.

The wisdom of such *yagnas* is meant to reach *Vishnu,* the god that permeates everything. Having completed such *yagnas,* they drink the immortal ambrosia and realize the Universal Person, of *Brahman.* There are therefore many types of *yagnas* and sacrifices described," *Krishna* says.

The blind king *Dhritarashtra* asks *Sanjaya,* to explain the practice of control and restraint of breath in *pranayama. Sanjaya* explains, "When a practitioner offers *prana,* into the *sushumna* as an offered oblation into *apana* at the bottom of the spine, movements of *prana* and *apana* neutralise spontaneously. This vitalises the physical, astral, and causal bodies with unmoving life force or *prana.* It redistributes itself from the brain and spinal cord through the spiritual centers *or chakras* and into nerve channels *or nadis.* The same now illumines Knowledge. When mind and *prana* are in repose, breathing and all bodily roles whether physical, physiological, psychological, mental, and intellectual become tranquil," *Sanjaya* says.

"How does one discover such heavenly tranquillity?" asks the blind king. "Loss of physical signs of visible activity decide the level of the seeker's consciousness and absorption," *Sanjaya* explains.

"Normally p*rana* enters the body through the medulla at the base of the brain, and after illumining the higher brain centers and the spinal plexuses it spreads into the body through regulated breathing," *Sanjaya* continues, "Inspiration is life and expiration is death. Delivering *prana* into the senses, organs of action and the mind are also the cause of both internal and external restlessness. Stilling *prana* and the mind through *kevali pranayama* described by *Krishna* therefore stifles uneasiness, reveals awareness, and illumines discrimination,"

The blind king confides in *Sanjaya* that he is unproductive with his efforts at meditation. *Sanjaya* explains that since the king is under emotional apprehension, physical uneasiness and mental agitation, ineffectual results from his spiritual practices are to be expected. In comparison, *Sanjaya* describes *Arjuna's* progressive physical mellowness and calmly regulated breathing, his emotional tranquillity, mental harmony, and undiminished mindfulness. Through determined concentration *Arjuna* penetrates superconsciousness. He unfolds into fuller states of Awareness and Consciousness.

The blind king asks *Sanjaya,* "Are there changes taking place in *Arjuna's* divine cave and in his body?"

Sanjaya explains again, "There are three *pranic* channels or *nadis* in the spinal pathway. The *Ida or* moon channel courses from the base of the spine through the left into the hypothalamus above the nostrils. This is a cool channel of parasympathetic nerves and is related to subjective emotional states and introspection. The right-sided *Pingala or* sun channel also arises from the base of the spine to end above the right nostril and into the hypothalamus. This sympathetic nerve channel also connects above the hypothalamus to the left-brain for intellectual and emotional input. Their connections to the creative right brain make these channels responsive to objective transformation through analytic introspection. The third channel, the *sushumna* courses through the center of the spinal cord. It takes with it the combined forces from the *Ida* and the *Pingala* to the center of awareness. It flows to the highest regions of the brain. When *prana* flows through the central channel, the flow in the moon and sun channels neutralises within the *sushumna.*"

Sanjaya tells the blind king, "Breathing ensures *pranic* flows in conduits, emotional and mental activities, and physiological works of the body – they are all interrelated. When *pranic* flows within channels are balanced and concentrated in the spinal passage, the physiological roles of the body are simplified. Breathing slows down, the heart beats at idling levels, passions are unruffled, and mental responses become purified and unclouded. On this crisp, transparent platform of concentration in the *kutastha,* self-satisfaction metamorphoses into soul awareness."

"How is this transformation experienced during meditation?" asks the blind king. *Sanjaya* reminds the blind king the *vajra nadi* is an astral channel of the *sushumna* with *rajo guna* and therefore has creative characteristics. When penetrated during meditation, expansion, contraction, light and sound are experienced. Within the *vajra* is the *chitra nadi,* also an astral channel with *sattva guna* or unanimity characteristics. When pierced during meditation, experiences of bright visions may become obvious. Deep within the *vajra* and the *chitra nadis* is the *brahmanadi* made of causal substance. When this is probed during meditation, astral sights are transcended, and causal discernment reveals insights and transcendental experiences."

Sanjaya suddenly realizes that *Krishna* is speaking with *Arjuna.*

"There are many ways to perform *yagnas* and many of these are described in the *Vedas.* Remember all *yagnas* perform action. Knowing the facts about action, and performing *yagnas* according to injunctions, the individualistic soul frees himself of worldly moorings," *Krishna* then says knowingly, "Even all those familiar with the sacrifice of *pranayama,* whose sins are consumed by the sacrifice of meditation, who eat meagerly the remnants of sacrifice, also win the house of *Brahma.* This happens because even faulty actions and their flaws become invalidated."

Having made adjustments to free of physical, mental, and intellectual difficulties, *Arjuna* is now free to enter the domains of superconscious meditation. He experiences a quickening of spiritual experience and soul unfoldment. *Krishna* confirms *Arjuna* enjoys the nectar of his sacrifice.

"Rather than shaping offerings in the fire sacrifice, O son of *Kunti,* it is better that you create a legacy of knowledge gained through the act of meditation. By realising knowledge there is dawn of wisdom. After that no further action is necessary because all deeds end in eternal wisdom," *Krishna* says.

"Therefore, O *Arjuna* go to the learned and wise ones and mindfully ask how you can be introduced to right action and become disciplined. Serve the sages who are already realised in the Self, as well as in God. Ask them questions about the soul and why it is bound to earthly moorings. Ask for a way out of this bondage. They will teach you the way to right action and about meditation," *Krishna* says.

Krishna adds that without inner adjustment, a seeker recognises himself only as the body, mind and intellect. When wisdom fixes itself through contemplation and meditation, Man is never again under the stupor of unawareness. He understands the nature of all things, creatures and beings in the Universe. The soul realises he is of the Cosmic Being. The self experiences himself as the Infinite Awareness and Consciousness. He therefore arrives at emancipation from constraints of Mother Nature and her compulsions.

"Knowing all this you will never again be deluded because you will see all as me," *Krishna* adds.

Sanjaya tells the blind king that *Arjuna* has experienced the tranquillity born of a hallowed past of righteous living and meditative sacrifice. Both know that *Arjuna's* performance of inner rites has given him an unpretentious spiritual reawakening. He has not yet reached the Self, but has learned that all actions of the body, mind and speech need offering in sacrificial *yagna* if he wishes emancipation with his new enthusiasm.

Krishna summarises what is needed to remove difficulties on the path of self-unfoldment. *Arjuna* understands that even the worst trespasser gets freed from the boundaries of worldly existence, through guru-instructed teachings on right action. *Arjuna* understands that through meditation comes knowledge and from this information comes wisdom. He must become a calm witness under all circumstances and not one driven by the qualities of Nature. *Arjuna* gets taught intense exercises of concentration to experience the Universe within himself. Such expected peacefulness can give him desirelessness. Like a burned seed, he will stop sprouting any new wants for himself. Action then bears no reactions. *Arjuna* should clear the path of personal feelings and opinions.

"O *Arjuna,* all sins are burned to ashes in the experience of this wisdom. Steadfast in this wisdom, with the passage of an interval, the witnessing soul gets automatically perfected. For purification, nothing is greater than this knowledge, arrived at through contemplation and meditation. The blessed reach perfection over time," *Krishna* said.

Sanjaya explains to the blind king that although *Arjuna* is a deep meditator, for aptitude, he must fulfill all preparatory exercises. Contemplative practices alone cannot be depended upon. He must learn and experience Spirit and Matter to promote soul unfoldment.

Krishna tells *Arjuna* he cannot reach any transcendence without experiencing this wisdom. "There is nothing more sacred than the purifying knowledge-revealing Consciousness already living in the body. The penance for knowledge is superior to all sacrifices and actions for the fruits of action, because O *Arjuna,* all action is understood to be for this knowledge. *Arjuna,* all action-reaction and the karmic effect is consumed in the fire of knowledge and wisdom," *Krishna* said.

Krishna explains that only seekers who are reverential and victorious over the senses realise this knowledge. Once this self-knowledge becomes settled, only then can he expect freedom from constraints of worldly existence, "One whose mind is single-pointed and triumphant over the senses, only such a one becomes a receptacle of such knowledge and wisdom." *Krishna* adds.

The blind king intuitively watches *Arjuna's* spiritual growth. *Krishna* is the blind king's nephew and wonders why he never recognised *Krishna* as an expression of the Spirit.

He voiced his anguish and *Krishna* spontaneously heard his pain.

Krishna decides to lay down the conditions and discipline of ethics followed by any apostle-master alliance. He tells *Arjuna* the Spirit in *Krishna* befriended him because he heard a plea for a discriminating teacher to escort him through spiritual unfoldment.

Krishna's, voice always guided *Arjuna* during spiritual journeys. He is sure every mortal, who attunes to the Self in self-surrender, with intelligent questioning and through service, can meet a spiritual master. This teacher is always able to activate astute rivulets of enlightenment.

"Destroy all doubts and by contemplation earn the power of certainty in the mind. Erase restlessness of the senses and control *pranic* abilities. Remain in the soul in contentment. Learn this knowledge by prostration, inquiry, and service to the teacher. Understand this well. By surrendering yourself to the guru, by questioning the guru about your own inner opinion, the sages who have realized truth make known that wisdom to you," *Krishna* advised.

Having learned the art of grasping true knowledge, *Krishna* tells *Arjuna* never to endure delusion again. "Only by atonement, guidance, and blessings of a teacher can this Knowledge become fruitful. You will see all souls within One Field of Awareness. This awareness takes you into the lap of Nature and Her Grace."

"Once you understand this knowledge and wisdom from a guru, O *Pandava,* you will never again fall into the trap of delusions and illusion. By that understanding you will see the endless creatures of the universe first in yourself and then in me the Cosmic Self. When a doubt appears, cut it with the sword of discrimination," *Krishna* said.

Sanjaya adds, "A true seeker who receives this cosmic wisdom from a cosmic teacher can never again be deceived by the qualities of Nature. The deception of otherness of *maya* is permanently understood. There is no separation of the one from the whole. The spiritual view of the enlightened teacher like *Krishna,* allows the devotee in *Arjuna* to see the entire cosmic dream within him."

"Although *Arjuna* is overcome by memories of past errors and serious misdeeds, *Krishna* explains that sins or errors committed in ignorance, distortion of reality, and illusion are redeemed by righteous actions that have the ability to transform and set you free. By gaining ecstatic wisdom, all the darkness of karmic slavery vanishes instantly, just as light banishes darkness."

Sanjaya continues to explain, "To emerge from this self-revealing knowledge is progressive. Blooming of the innermost essence needs removal of every veil of Nature that shrouds the Self. *Krishna* tells *Arjuna* that many recognise this fact, but continue to ignore or doubt such instructions. They are ignorant because they refuse the knowledge. Others, who lack devotion towards matters spiritual, including the need for a guru, never reach a life of sacrifice because doubters have unsettled ideas of soul value. These three reasons hamper their natural evolution here and thereafter. They suffer the effects of their actions, hardly aware of their ignorance."

7. Renunciation of Action

Despite the advances made by *Arjuna* he raises yet another problem about action. *Arjuna* is unable and cannot decide whether action has any place in the search for the Self. He therefore asks which of the two, prudence of renunciation-of-action while in seclusion or participation-in-action while serving in the world, is the nobler?

Sanjaya realizes from the question that *Krishna* has persuaded *Arjuna* accurately – he is interested in right action and *Arjuna* has salvaged some psychological equilibrium. *Arjuna* understands that action, intelligently followed, is the legitimate path for advancement and self-development.

For *Arjuna* self-development must metamorphose through three stages: desire-prompted action, desireless deeds, and action-free activities in meditation. Here, in action-less meditation, *Arjuna* has already transiently experienced the innate joy of the Self. Engaged in manoeuvres for divine union, *Arjuna* connects his soul in worship with the Cosmic Self, and has experienced the evanescent but imperishable rapture.

Arjuna was mentally becoming a renunciant, with a lessened appetite for the sensory world. With passions and mind better controlled he hopes to become Self-realized one day. He knows if he persisted on the path of spiritual unfoldment, he will become unencumbered from this world and the realm beyond, but he has to first clear his doubts.

Arjuna therefore asks, "O *Krishna,* when all that you have explained and described earlier is experienced in the *kutastha* between and behind the eyebrows, a question arises. You describe and applaud *sannyasa* of renunciation of social ties for the sake of meditation and at the same time you advise *karma yoga,* to perform action. I cannot understand what you are saying. I have recognized that all action must be equally ended. Yet I must perform action through meditation as my pressing duty to stop all swings in awareness. Convince me, which of the two, is the better path? Please tell me for certain."

Arjuna, like many seekers of Truth was not free from bewilderment. In the early stages of meditation, he was content with his new surroundings of inner perceptiveness. He even wondered if he should stop his daily activities and remain in secluded meditation. For now, does he serve the world or end meditation, in favour of seeking knowledge of the scriptures?

Krishna answered, "Listen carefully and attentively, *Arjuna.* For liberation, whether you renounce action or perform action, there is no conflict between the two. From the point of *sannyasa, karma* according to one's *svadharma* or inherent nature is of greater value, especially when devotion is directed towards desire-less action. For purifying awareness, action or *vikarma* when the mind and heart are in the action, is greater than knowledge or *gyana.* Remember without purifying mind's awareness in *sadhana,* there is no knowledge. When the mind fixes in the *kutastha* at the centre of Universal Consciousness, the experience cancels all types of actions. Both renunciation and performance of action find salvation and emancipation. But of the two, the *yoga* of selfless action is better than renunciation of action or *akarma.*"

The blind king is still confused. He wants *Sanjaya* to restate what has been said in simpler terms. "*Krishna* has clearly asserted that Man should practice *yoga* of meditation to realize his own Self's oneness with the Cosmic Self. At the same time, he must perform his worldly duties as a consecration before the altar of the Cosmic Worker of the Universe," *Sanjaya* explained.

"Having said that, *Krishna* also thinks that liberation is arrived at by understanding the scriptures. But *Krishna* understands that the average person does not have the time, the command of concentration, or the psychological and intellectual clarity to reach the shores of self-realization through the study of scriptures only. For most of us like *Arjuna,* the path of meditation is the most suitable route to follow," *Sanjaya* added.

Arjuna needs to adhere to what he intuitively knows must be done on his spiritual journey. He already knows his own personality and temperament. He has the power of concentration for meditation and an intellectual inquisitiveness for the study of Nature. *Krishna* allows *Arjuna* to make his own choice and said, "O mighty-armed *Arjuna,* the one who lives in peaceful nonattachment and whose awareness is beyond conflicts of wants and dislikes is on the way to emancipation. He performs actions only to preserve the normal bodily roles. He is a renunciate from all types of actions. Such an ascetic is easily released from the bonds of action."

Krishna's comment that salvation has a twofold foundation is clear. Man must renounce all mortal wants provoked by Nature's cosmic illusion of *maya.* At the same time Man must remain working, but in continual contact with the Cosmic Being. Therefore, the path of right action without wish for its fruit, plus meditation on the Cosmic Self, is superior to a life of meditation without outer activity. *Arjuna* is told that it is better to live in the world but not belong to the world.

A true renunciant, whatever his place or duty in life, is a Self-centred devotee. He experiences the world as a play of ideas in his own mind, made pleasurable or painful by the warring contrasts of the mortal attached to the body. *Arjuna* is told to maintain the body and serve it. But he needs to remain unperturbed in *titiksha* and to control his sense entanglements, always, even while engaged in action.

Krishna warns *Arjuna* that only the unenlightened see a difference in knowledge, meditation and action.

"Fools say the knowledge of *Sankhyan* meditation and *Karma Yoga* of action is different. While performing one or the other, they both lead to reaching liberation and tranquillity. Reactions of self-centred action corrupt the purity of awareness. By destroying the compulsions of worldly life, one becomes united with the path of a *yogi* who understands the knowledge of meditation. They therefore yield the same results. He alone sees who is settled in *Sankhya* and *Yoga* as one and the same."

Those who study scriptures intellectually, for knowledge alone, make distinctions between the paths of knowledge and action. A true *yogi* sees no division. *Krishna* assures *Arjuna* that he who follows one path receives the benefit of both paths. Traditionally, this is true if earning wisdom involves listening to the scripture as explained by a Self-realized master. Meditating on what the seeker reads and meditates on allows the seeker to become one with the knowledge and the Self. But without devotion to a true teacher and without his or her compassion, Man fails to reach his goals.

The compulsions of Nature's qualities make it difficult for the average person to become detached from worldly work and employment, relatives, and ingrained habits and tendencies. Mental analysis and intellectual reasoning are propelled by ingrained subconscious habits. Bodily demands are insistent and have a way of causing emotionally and intellectually confusing situations.

Krishna therefore insists that devotion to meditation and selfless action is the only way to emancipation, "Attempts to renounce action and sitting in meditation without first purifying mind's awareness only causes sorrow, O mighty armed *Arjuna*. Without devotion to action when a *yogi* surrenders to God, he cannot rise above the compulsions of worldly life. Spirit-uniting action of *yoga* meditation is difficult to achieve. By the practice of *yoga,* the *muni* or sage who keeps silence, whose mind is absorbed in *Brahman* quickly, reaches the Infinite Cosmic. He is engaged in devotion by action and has a pure soul. He has conquered his body and subdued his senses. He identifies himself with all creatures and is not fettered by the law of action and reaction, though he performs action."

Arjuna expects to awaken to spiritual knowledge and experience the Infinite Cosmic Self if he remains devoted and disciplined to the *yogic* practice of meditation. Once he transcends compulsions of Nature's *gunas* he should experience Cosmic Awareness. Intuitive understanding then allows *Arjuna* to see circumstances and family demands in the correct perspective.

Krishna reasserts that it is difficult to reach renunciation without contemplative activities. When a *yogi* has arrived at the Self-to-Cosmic Self-ecstatic State, the fire of wisdom after that purifies his descent into the body-mind-intellect and its activities. Satisfied with scant needs of the body, he reverentially performs all necessary duties or *vikarma,* without entanglements in *karmic* results because he sees all beings permeated with the same Self.

Having described a *yogi, Krishna* now tells *Arjuna,* "Those who become purified by meditation, who bring the bodily senses under complete control and live separately from them, realize that Awareness pervades the Universe as Consciousness or God. He realizes his awareness is the same Consciousness in himself. This man of devotion, who knows truth while united with the Spirit, automatically realizes, 'I do nothing' – whether he sees, hears, touches, smells, moves, sleeps and breathes. He speaks, rejects, holds, opens or closes his eyes – he realizes that it is the senses, activated by Nature that engages the objects of the senses. He therefore does not stop normal actions."

Dhritarashtra turned to *Sanjaya* and asked, "How can *Arjuna* come to terms with being a puppet of Nature's compulsions?"

"*Arjuna* is being grounded in the understanding that he was and is propelled by Nature. With that information,

Arjuna should be able to disassociate himself from his actions, feelings, thoughts, and his relationships with beings and creatures. *Arjuna* is being advised to arrive at right understanding. This would then enable him to remain alert for bodily activities. *Arjuna* must lessen his mental swings. He must transform his emotional and intellectual skills," *Sanjaya* explains. "Once *Arjuna* realizes that he, the individualistic self, is not the operator of himself, he will have a clear intellectual insight of sense control."

"What are the characteristics of a *yogi* with a transformed personality?" asked *Arjuna*.

Krishna now restates what he had previously said to *Arjuna* about a true *yogi's* changed personality. This is also a response to *Dhritarashtra's* implied query. "Just as a lotus remains unsullied by polluted water, he programs all action, for renunciation and surrender to Infinite *Brahman*. He remains untainted by the entanglements of actions of senses. Those who are devotees, cast off attachment, perform action and arrive at purity of the self, with the body and mind. Their understanding is that even the senses are free of want. They do their work as is befittingly suitable for them, never attached to any action."

Arjuna's mind was analyzing his different states of alertness. He realizes that while asleep, he is not involved in the group of five *pranic* physiological life force. He is intuitively aware that sense consciousness of the mind and the discriminative intellect are not conscious while he sleeps. His individuality, memories, habits, and tendencies had receded into his sub-consciousness where he dreams. These then were all absent in his deep-sleep. His feelings or *chitta* seemed suspended in the causal-state while in deep-sleep but are distinctly observable as Awareness of existence-knowledge-bliss when roused.

Arjuna detected a 'Doer' behind all his actions, whether acting, dreaming or sleeping. Through the transparency of his feelings or *chitta*, he achieved the insight that it is Awareness

–Om, that enlivens all his states and activities.

Krishna wanted *Arjuna* to grasp that his senses are divinely guided by the compulsions of Mother Nature's Awareness. Once he understands and experiences this fact, *Arjuna* would work to serve the Cosmic Being. Emancipated, *Arjuna* would labour among the senses floating like a lotus in the muddy sensory waters of *maya,* but unsoiled by the entanglements of *karma.*

Sanjaya turned to *Dhritarashtra* and said, "*Krishna* is explaining the sanctification of the self through worldly and meditative actions. He inculcates work requirements without fruits of it."

"It seems as if materialism and working for the self contradicts all rules of idealism and right action," protested the king.

As if he had heard *Dhritarashtra, Krishna* said, "He, who is controlled by way of devotion, performs *vikarma* or actions necessary for the body, has his mind immersed in contemplation of worship, has the right attitudes towards action. Renouncing the fruit of action, he reaches the highest tranquillity and his awareness is purified. He, who does not have devotion and is attached to the fruit of action, is fettered by action or *karma* even if performed from necessity. Through such attachment he remains in bondage."

Inspired by the idealism of right action and the experiences of self-discipline, *Krishna* expects *Arjuna* to act in the spirit of duty to the Cosmic Mother.

"Those who are successful at realizing they are disengaged from the senses and the organs of action are successful at renouncing their deeds. They live enthusiastically within the temple of nine gates [mouth, two openings each of eyes, nose and ears, and the two sets of excretory systems]. These self restrained embodied souls, who renounce all actions in their minds, remain free from anxiety within the house, neither acting nor causing anything to act. The Self is not the foundation for this talent for action by acting men, or for connecting action and its fruit. It is Nature that engages in action. Delusive Cosmic Nature of *Maya* with Her *guna* qualities is the originator of all such activities."

Krishna tells *Arjuna* that his meditative movements will allow him to see the Universal Self performing through him, other beings and creatures. He will also someday take pleasure in living His Cosmic Dream poised and fashioned by the Cosmic Creator, who is also bound by the imposing Laws of Nature. *Krishna* advises *Arjuna* he must mirror the dream the same as an artiste but without internal entanglement. Once he triumphs at becoming spectator of all bodily operations through these nine gates of the body, he will have lived an intrinsic guesstimate of all the sheaths and its expression, whether physical, physiological, psychological, mental, or intellectual.

Krishna is leading *Arjuna* to an intimate understanding of the Cosmic Doer. Mother Nature is the surrogate who completes all performances. She is also the Cosmic Delusion of *Maya* who allows Man to misappropriate the gift of free choice. The mortal hankering for sense satisfaction becomes enslaved by Nature's qualities or *gunas.* There is therefore neglect of the purpose of being born a human being.

Krishna then adds that neither He, nor Nature is responsible for the ignorance man suffers. All things whether mobile or stationary, follow their instrument of command and keep on getting assembled according to their own inherent qualifications. Yet Awareness-Consciousness permanently exists everywhere. The metamorphosis inherent in nature is also intrinsic in the body, mind and intellect and has power over souls. Man becomes deluded only to remain bound to worldly life or *samsara.*

"The Lord receives no one's sin, nor also their merit. By ignorance, this Knowledge is shrouded. It is because of this Cosmic Delusion of *Maya* in Nature, that creatures are deluded. But in whomever this ignorance about Nature has been destroyed by Knowledge of the Self, that Knowledge which is like the Sun, discloses the Supreme Being."

Krishna said about His and Her omnipresence, "He is ever as He should be. Nature is also as She should be, granted with qualities and Her compelling creativity. Mortals preoccupied with their own wishes are unaware of the causative compulsions of individuality, habits and personality inclinations. Fragmented, deluded, and confused they are shrouded by illusions and delusions and keep stumbling in the twilight mirage of *maya*".

Arjuna understood he can never move up towards spiritual growth while emotionally involved with conditionings of self-conscious attitudes. These restrict the soul. Only by rising above these tendencies and assuming the position of witness could he hope to witness *Krishna's* Cosmic Dream.

Krishna tells *Arjuna* his only hope to gain wisdom was to understand that, "Those whose mind is on Him, whose soul is He, who remains in Him, and who have Him for their goal, go never more to return, their sins all destroyed by Knowledge."

Krishna assures the *yogi* in *Arjuna* the soul is made of immutable Consciousness substance. Nature in the presence of Consciousness creates new types of created substances that are Aware. These display as many things, beings, and objects, all imbued with the three *gunas* or qualities - inert *tamas,* creative *rajas,* and amicable *sattva.*

Nature's Awareness is an expression of the ever-witnessing Consciousness. In order that a soul experiences the manifestation, it feels through the mind, senses and organs of action. Man invokes Nature for this get-together to happen. He wishes for more of the same delusion or he develops discrimination and frees himself from Cosmic Dream identification.

Past habits and tendencies force Man to pursue

momentary happiness entrenched with qualities of harmony, creativity and inertia. He now experiences the Cosmic Drama through his own Cosmic Light. He sees contrasting Shadows of delusory *maya* playing on a substratum of *Krishna's* Light.

Sanjaya speaks to the blind *Dhritarashtra,* "*Arjuna* needs to concentrate on the radiance and effulgence of the Cosmic Sun. In this absorption, he will experience the ecstasy every soul feels when it returns to its source – projecting and withdrawing into itself repeatedly through so many births. Such a one does not return to the dream stage again."

Krishna describes the transformation caused by such illumination; "Those who are wise cast an equal eye on a learned and humble Brahmin, on a cow, an elephant, and an outcaste. They know the four *Vedas* and understand the secret underlying all these things and beings. They experience themselves as the Self in the entire Universe and realize themselves as pervading all. These wise students with pure natures do not experience themselves as separate from the Self. They understand all these are only variants of Mother Nature."

"How is such a state achieved?" asks the blind king who was listening circumspectly.

"Individual souls gradually experience their Awareness as a reflection of Consciousness by guru-instructed meditation which has the quality of destroying non-awareness and ignorance. The self-revealing knowledge has the power to reveal the entire Cosmos," *Sanjaya* replied.

Krishna tried to make *Arjuna* realize that all seeming appearances are only comparable to each other. Besides, all states of being, whether conscious or waking, subconscious or dreaming, or unconscious in deep sleep are performances of the egotistical and therefore relevant in that context only. Only in pure super-conscious states of meditation will *Arjuna's* soul understand and recognize the Cosmic Life Substance underlying and pervading the Universe and its appearances.

"If Mother Nature's distortions do not crop up in a

mortal's mind and individualistic souls do not get contaminated by uniting with Her compulsions, these ones experience the Universe as unalloyed and equal. Here those minds rest on sameness. They have conquered birth and death. Since *Brahman* is faultless and equal-minded, therefore, they remain in *Brahman*. They are worthy and in the Cosmic Self, they are taintless. They are balanced in the Cosmic Self," *Krishna* says reassuringly.

Krishna reminds *Arjuna* that he need not wait for an unrehearsed revelation in meditation. He can unfold by intellectual discrimination and direct himself to gaze beyond things, beings and creatures. He should recognize and approve the existence of the common thread of Oneness coursing through the Many. By so doing, *Krishna* pledged *Arjuna* an inner calm of pervasive serenity. *Krishna* describes this consistent awareness as fixed firmly in the Immutable Infinite.

"He whose mind is steady and stilled, who is not deluded, who knows *Brahman* and who rests in *Brahman*, is neither jubilant on getting anything that is agreeable, nor does he grieve with an unpleasant experience that is disagreeable."

While *Arjuna* was on his spiritual path, he accepted duress as effects of his past actions. He faced good and bad happenings, as well as health and disease, in the same way. Although immersed in the wisdom of his ecstatic experiences, *Krishna* told *Arjuna* to watch all appearances with indifference, because, "He whose mind is not attached to external objects of senses, gains happiness which is in the Self. By concentrating his mind on the contemplation of *Brahman*, he enjoys a blessedness that is indestructible."

Krishna has just described to *Arjuna* the ecstasy experienced by a *yogi* who learns to control his feelings or *chitta* when he detaches from the external world. He focuses his attention and remains united with the Self-Cosmic-Self State. The bliss is that of the soul who knows he is free because of a self-perceived enlightenment of sovereignty from all his hindrances, whether physical, mental or intellectual.

Krishna gives *Arjuna* the rationalism of such bliss when he says, "O son of *Kunti, Arjuna* my dearest cousin, the corrupted delights born of contact of the senses with their objects are inventive of suffering. They are bondages with unhappiness. No seeing sage seeks happiness from them."

Krishna did not disagree with *Arjuna* enjoying a normal life. He needs to engage with other opinions but he is cautioned not to become inured by them or to their motives. He is warned to remain ever watchful against creating strong attachments to them. Vigilance against compulsions of matter is advised. Designing moderation in all indulgences should be based on knowing that transitory pleasures of the material world end in sorrow if fostered.

Arjuna is told to find never-ending satisfaction in meditation, for *Krishna* says, "He, who is wise O son of *Kunti,* never takes pleasure in these objects that have a beginning and an end. Even if Man has natural tendencies, know that they are also quality compulsions of *Maya.* The discriminating wise, this yogi refuses to be attracted by them and he is a happy man."

Sanjaya is listening to the advice given to *Arjuna. Dhritarashtra,* habituated to a life of indulgences, questions *Sanjaya* about the logic of *Krishna's* advice. The blind king is not convinced that even advanced yogis could be prone to impulses of lust and anger because of effects of *karmic* impulses in previous incarnations.

Sanjaya explains that a man on a spiritual journey must remain engrossed in the ecstasy of divine view. It is the godly secret of combating prompting of past harmful impulses buried in the subconscious mind. *Krishna* was heard telling *Arjuna* the secret of rightful living when one discovers success both in meditation and in worldly activities.

"One who is an unmoving body even before death and lives disconnected from his body, mind, intellect and senses, who is unruffled by lust and anger, pleasure and sorrow, he lives in the quarters of freedom. Such a man, who is able to withstand agitation and is fixed in contemplation, is contented – he owns the inner bliss. He reaches complete liberation in the union of Self-Cosmic-Self state even while living in flesh," *Krishna* states.

Krishna then goes on to describe the state of emancipation, "Those who see the soul within are contented and are careful to abdicate from all tangible riggings. They labour at becoming Truth only to reach Consciousness or *parabrahman.* He who finds happiness within himself, whose sins are destroyed, whose doubts are removed, his senses subdued, while contributing to the welfare of humanity, he gets absorption and liberation into *Brahman.*"

After that only *rishis,* who are released sages, may choose to be reborn by divine permission, to serve as ideal human beings to serve confused mortals. *Krishna* describes the future path of realized souls who wish to serve mortals or remain absorbed in *Brahman;* "Those who have arrived at the highest state of absorption understand the form of *Brahman* within. Having gained liberation, they abandon duality and remain engaged in actions that are good for all. These saintly people whose sins have been destroyed, whose doubts have been dispelled, who see the oneness of things, they are engaged in the righteousness for all creatures."

Krishna now describes the framework and method for discovering of soul peace. *Arjuna* already knows that he must withdraw his attention from the body, mind, and intellect. Regular practice would make him move from individuality-attentiveness to inner-contentment and to self-awareness. And *Krishna* adds as if to reinforce what he has already said, 'If these devotees are freed from the forces of want and anger they become disconnected from sorrow and pleasure. Their minds are under control because they have the knowledge of the Self. They arrive at liberation even while there is still life to live. Their absorption into *Brahman* frees them from action, both here and thereafter."

Krishna pauses to allow this to sink in and then gives *Arjuna* pointers in meditation. "Those seekers who have embarked on the path of liberation, who have abandoned all sensory indulgences should focus on the connecting points of the two eyebrows. They must equalize the up-going *prana* and the down-going *apana* within. The performance is targeted on emancipation. He is freed from want, fear and anger, and is liberated."

Sanjaya tells the blind king that a *yogi* such as *Arjuna* who is linked to the Cosmic Self can have only one goal, that of emancipation. *Arjuna* watches his own ego-identified soul undergo physical and mental misery because of ignorance of the Truth. Nonetheless, he is intent on freeing the soul from the clutches of his ego.

Krishna reinforces what *Sanjaya* has surmised and says what he has already said earlier, "When a seeker sees Infinite Consciousness as existing in everything he learns all actions and spiritual practices. He sees all in the cosmos as a Cosmic Experience of the Universe. This *Arjuna,* is what sages call liberation."

Krishna stresses that it is every man's destiny to realize this Truth. "Knowing Me to be the enjoyer of all sacrifices and ascetic austerities, the great Lord and friend of all creatures of all the worlds, go and earn tranquillity."

"There are many obstacles and riddles to performing actions," the blind king complained.

"Let me try again," Sanjaya replied.

"A *karma yogi* has climbed up a series of steps and has reached the top. He does not have to take another step nor does he have to lift his foot off the step. He cannot shake off the already performed action because it is second nature to his legs to move those limbs. He therefore continues to work to show to society the value of these extremities. The legs are performing action by their inherent nature or *svadharma.* The actor, meaning the legs, neither thinks they are doing anything exceptional, nor do they think the act is spiritual. The act is seen as a conduct and fragrance of the doer, their *svadharma,* in this case of the legs. By surrendering the need for fruit, the actor receives endless rewards of inward purity and a perfect life."

"What is the inner attitude of the true *karma yogi*?" asked the blind king

"The *karma yogi* does his work much better than others because to him his actions are a worship or *vikarma* and its payment is a reward noteworthy of the Self," replied *Sanjaya.* "The action is moist with love and dedication to God. He has surrendered to Him."

"But desireless action must track one's own *dharma* or *svadharma. Arjuna's* indigenous nature as a fearless hero is to fight *adharma* or incompatibility to virtue," *Sanjaya* continued.

"How then can action be made free of want?" The king asked.

"By nourishing one's own innate nature and performing action according the characteristics of one's inclination," *Sanjaya* said.

"Is then combating my sons in this war not *adharmic*?" asked the blind king.

"Let me talk of fury, then," *Sanjaya* said. "To a devotee of nonviolence, outrage is inconceivable. But disturbances can breed in the mind, as is the case with you, Sire. Drawing a sword proclaims an attitude of injury, but it is also not true that by dropping the sword a man becomes nonviolent. To be free of want, it is essential to keep clear of another's *dharma.*"

"Desirelessness is a quality of the mind and this understanding needs to be cleaned first," *Sanjaya* continued. "*Krishna* has used the term *svadharma* or inherent activity and *dharma* or action, interchangeably. He has also spoken of *vikarma* or actions purifying understanding and therefore the mind."

"Give me an example of *vikarma*," the blind king interjected.

"It is natural to perform one's *svadharma* when feeding the poor and destitute. The act is according to the principles of righteous action or *karma.* The disposition of action must be pure, as if attending to one's own family. When the mind and heart's action or *svadharma* is united with physical performance or *karma,* the deed is a *vikarma* purifying the heart. When in devotion, hands and a heart work together in dedication, there is no fruit of action – the transaction is *akarma,* or inaction in action."

The blind king seeks further clarification, "So you are saying that by carrying out *vikarma* or pure action into *karma* or activity, it becomes *akarma* or inaction?"

"When action or *karma* is combined with *vikarma,* then no matter what you exert at, the mind remains still and the performer feels no strain," *Sanjaya* replied.

"How does action become inaction?" The king asked again.

"My power of communication is exhausted. Sire, you have to go to the saints and sit at their feet. Though engaged in a thousand deeds, they do not allow a single wave to rise in the still reservoir of the mind. To understand this marvel, one needs to sit and experience this," *Sanjaya* replied, exhausted.

8. Controlling the Mind

"In front of me is a mountain of desires linked with anger," the blind king cried out in despair. "Far away on the high mountains, lives the Emperor of the Creation. Behind him are the inventories of Wisdom, which remain privileged information. Although surrounded by books and knowledge I remain without enlightenment of their legacy. I have had no time to interpret the written word or to reflect."

"Sire, you have been listening to me for far too long and your understanding is bewildered. Unless the mind is balanced, you will not understand the book of life. Only unspoken speech has the ability to clear doubts in the intellect. Go there, O king. See how serene this recollection can get, even when a battle rages outside," *Sanjaya* replied.

"But *samsara* and attachment to worldly life, enfolds me on all sides. No matter what I resolve, it pitches its canopy on all sides and monopolizes my mind," the blind king added in desperation. "Even while living within the bounds of *svadharma, samsara* never lets go. One can give up every distracting action, but Man remains filled with possessiveness," *Sanjaya* responded.

"How did I get into this mess? By *svadharma* alone one does not become unattached to *samsara.* How then does one achieve detachment?" the king asked. "Without the mind's help, Man cannot succeed. To give mind a shape, its cooperation is essential. For this growth, both performing dutiful external action or *svadharma,* and the inner attitude of the mind or *vikarma* are necessary. The mind must then be tested for its stillness," *Sanjaya* replied.

"How does one test stillness of the mind?" asked the king.

"Actions speak a language all their own. Spontaneous action is a mirror, which proclaims anger, selfishness, greed, and deceit, in fact, our true mind-form. Our actions therefore should be a progressive effort to purify the mind. When flaws come to light, frequent efforts must be made to wipe out these. To decontaminate minds perform *karma* or action with the help of chaste action or *vikarma*, according to one's *svadharma* or inherent duty in life," *Sanjaya* replied.

"Then what is the mental state of a *karma yogi* and that of a *sannyasi*?" the king asked. "Service to others or *karma yoga* is natural to a *gyani* or a man of knowledge, just like eating or drinking. The act in itself is inaction or *akarma*. While acting he does not think of it, so he is a *sannyasi*, or a renunciate. Even though acting, he does not act, being given to eternal goodness," *Sanjaya* replied.

"Your explanation is inadequate," the king complained.

"There are two ways to characterize *sannyasa*, O king. In one you can be doing nothing while toiling all-day, the other is accomplishing everything while not active even for a moment. The first one is like silence in speech and the other is communication through silence," *Sanjaya* replied. "This idea of renunciation or *sannyasa* is the highest point reached by Man's intellect and his power of thought. Beyond this point nobody's thought has ever extended. When it comes to speech and action, there is nothing nobler than doing everything by doing nothing and doing nothing by doing everything," *Sanjaya* adds and became silent as if in contemplation.

"The first is then *karma yoga* and the second is *sannyasa*?" asked the king.

"My examples are not perfect O King. Let us assume your understanding is," replied *Sanjaya*. "In their precise states, both are of equal worthiness, but the efficient value of *karma yoga* is higher. When Knowledge is added to each, their worth becomes equivalent and infinite. No matter what you add to Infinity, their appraisal estimate will always remain Infinite."

Meanwhile, *Krishna* was rationalising it must be difficult to understand action through inaction. *Arjuna* however had grasped inaction through action. In *Karma Yoga* it seemed *Arjuna* could find both the path and the goal. In *Sannyasa Yoga,* he discovered the goal but not the path. The goal *Arjuna* surmised is to achieve the perfect state of beatitude.

Dhritarashtra meantime has chosen to build a fence around him. Wallowing in worldliness, he keeps raising the height of these boundary walls and perseveres in degrading himself. *Sanjaya* has tried hard to push him forward with courage, imagination and his inherent power of growth.

Krishna persists and declares that true renunciation needs connecting with the whole. In yoga this is a function of meditation.

"While doing dutiful action and not paying heed to the fruits of action, a *sannyasi* or renunciate who understands the essence of it all, remains immersed in the *kutastha* having renounced all cravings. He is both a *sannyasi* or renunciate and a *karma yogi* also," *Krishna* said. "Regardless of the fruit of action, he performs dutiful actions, which should be carried out with a mind-set of an enthusiastic devotee. He is not one who rejects the sacrificial fire of spiritual actions nor does he abandon action or *karma.* Understand O *Arjuna* the best of the *Pandavas* that what is spoken of in the scriptures, as renunciation is devotion. It is the same as *yoga.* For, he who has not renounced selfish thoughts as a resolve or *sankalpa,* cannot become a *yogi.*"

Sanjaya hoped the blind king would take heed of this repetitious guidance. *Arjuna* was mentally surrendering his individuality and mentally practising only noble movements to promote a consolidated goodness. Dedicated to this resignation, *Arjuna* can expect to become loyal to the Cosmic Whole. A mind faithful to collective good abdicates its mutated self-conscious singularity to the adventures of an otherworldly state.

Krishna echoes *Sanjaya's* thoughts.

"To the sage rising towards devotion, action is the means. When he has risen to devotion, end of action is the means. Ascent is fulfilling *yoga.* Meditative action is the *karma* or act to perform for a divine union or *yoga.* When one is no longer attached to the objects of the senses, or to actions, and when one renounces all resolves of ego-instigated thought schemes, then this *tyagi* has risen in devotion. This man has arrived at a firm union of Soul with the Supreme Self through *yoga.*"

Arjuna understood terms such as *sannyasi, yogi* and *tyagi.* Unless Oneness is experienced, impediments must be removed through rejecting individuality, which is got by *tyaga,* or abandoning the merits of action.

Arjuna has a vision and he strives for it with admirable conviction. He must alter and adjust the approach. His actions and mental attitude must be constantly retailored as an instrument of self-effort or *sadhana.* He would have to ignite the fire of devotion, inquiry, analysis, character evolvement, meditation and discrimination. Only a *yogi* can experience an internal condition of view of the Self.

Sanjaya has already told the blind king of unrighteousness and indulgences. A true student of action and renunciation depends on the act of regulating the mind itself. To succeed in the *yoga* of meditation or *dhyana yoga,* he lays down the groundwork for intellectual improvement. This distinctively unique mind state is prefixed with boundaries to one's existence. To achieve this state, the understanding basks in pure calmness.

As usual, the blind king does not understand the steps of a spiritual life that needs augmenting with self-effort. He therefore asked *Sanjaya* to clarify this further.

"O King, one cannot expect to improve until the mind's deeds and misdeeds are controlled. Life's movements must be set within the boundaries of duties; in fact, every act should be vigilantly found out and carefully thought about. Lastly one should have the loftiness to think for the Cosmic Whole. To carry out all this, Man must exercise aloofness," *Sanjaya* said.

Krishna meanwhile coached *Arjuna*, "For ones who want to move up in *yoga*, desireless activity is the way. Performance of desireless action is the proper way to rise towards liberation. Remaining in the Self is the bridge to tranquillity. Seekers who wish to still rise and fall in the mind should perform guru-instructed meditation. To destroy all causes of changes, remain in the unknowable oneness and practice nonattachment again and again. This is the means to come to rest. It is the means to end all past *samaskaras* or reactions to past actions. Meditation will cancel past physical and human karma."

Sanjaya is hoping the blind king understands that he must lift himself by his own self, by the ego itself. He cannot afford to lower himself through self-degrading actions of unrighteousness. *Sanjaya* asks the blind king to employ his individualism to become his own friend just as he has used his self, the ego, to become an enemy of righteous actions.

Krishna goes on to confirm this advice *Sanjaya* gives to the blind king. Describing how Man achieves progressive states of oneness and experiences them, *Krishna* says, "One is one's own friend and benefactor and one is one's own enemy. Without effort by oneself one cannot do kindness or harm to anyone. Therefore to save yourself from endless suffering of a worldly life, you must make the effort yourself. One should not become dissatisfied in matters of Awareness and Consciousness. To him only one who has subdued his self – the ego, by himself is a friend. But to him who has not defeated his self, his self adversely behaves like an enemy."

After a pause, *Krishna* continues, "One who is able to silence himself through meditation, is his own friend. O son of *Pandu*, one who cannot triumph over himself is his own worst enemy. Man must end his own conquering by the mind, intellect and the senses. Once emancipated, he becomes firmly incorporated in Soul-Consciousness. He has been triumphant in assuming his undistorted identity. He knows the greatest patron of himself is himself, his true companion. Ones who break away and are controlled by tendencies and imprisoned by desire-filled endowments, are themselves their own supreme enemies."

"How does one succeed over worldly matters, never mind about spiritual matters?", asked the blind king *Dhritarashtra*, "Success is difficult without an extraordinary application of the mind, no matter how aged the body becomes, because the brain has both the vitality and the enthusiasm to soar to great heights." *Sanjaya* replied. "The body may get frail but the seed, the soul within gets stronger. Concentrating and fixing the mind in the Self prevents it from engaging in details of worldly life. But the mind cannot concentrate unless it is pure. To purify the mind, daily actions must have uncorrupted motives."

"How do I do that, *Sanjaya*?"

"By setting up order and discipline. By turning away from the destructive, and remembering to avoid excesses, is disciplined conduct. It is setting perimeters to one's life. A poised perspective is a helpful one that all creation is favorably placed. Behold this constantly also in the world within, O king,"

"These are difficult practices," complained the blind king.

"For *dhyana yoga,* the way to meditation, detachment from worldly affairs and constant practice or *abhyas* is essential. When one realizes that all sweetness in expression gain their courtesy from the Self, indifference fills the mind."

Krishna adds, What is Knowledge but a vision of permutations of the Self, realised at the *kutastha* between the eyebrows? Wisdom, which goes even further than

Knowledge, is achieved while remaining steadfast in the *kutastha,* while in meditation."

After a pause, "Only those who have been triumphant over the senses can remain padlocked in *Brahman.* Like one drunk, he now sees a lump of clay and gold to be the same. Then, these good-hearted well-wishing friends who are aloof from pleasure and sorrow, cold and heat, honor and dishonor, wish goodness for all and see all beings as the same. The placid sage victorious over the egoistic *chitta* or self is fully fixed in the Supreme Soul."

They all understood that a persevering *yogi* eventually succeeds in metamorphosing his egoistic self into a true soul, the *enlightened chitta.* In this pure Awareness already inherent in Nature, *Arjuna* can expect to realise and experience the omnipresent Spirit of Consciousness.

"What is the *chitta*?" asks the blind *Dhritarashtra.*

"*Chitta* is the combined human personality of mind, intellect and the ego. It is unenlightened until a true *guru* teaches Man the rules of *sadhana* and spiritual effort," replied *Sanjaya.*

Having gained this self-knowledge by an *enlightened chitta, Arjuna's* efforts are propelled by unwavering self-confidence, enthusiasm, self-discipline, and attentiveness to meditative practices. He awakens in Consciousness. Having experienced realms of superconsciousness, he reaches the shores where Awareness and Consciousness merge as Matter with Spirit.

Sanjaya now stops to listen to *Krishna's* advice about incremental movements in spiritual gains towards superconsciousness. The route from subjective *savikalpa samadhi* to non-subjective *nirvikalpa samadhi,* love and devotion are that inner melody. Once *Arjuna* touches the fringes of this oceanfront in meditation, there are no traces of mind, intellect, or ego in the *chitta* personality. Awareness then merges in the Wholeness of Oneness.

Krishna now gives some advice and describes the external lyrical masterpiece of a meditating devotee.

"Think always of the yearned-for Lord of the heart. Remain in a lonely place and keep your awareness and mind under the power of the Soul, the Self. Renounce all material wants and do not struggle for another's wealth. Remain in a meditative state unceasingly. The riddle of the Self will burst on you as Wisdom. Here there is no night or day. Remain here, emptied of expectations. Even while among everybody, do not go anywhere and look at nothing else."

The *yogi* in *Arjuna* would gladly remain absorbed in Truth and Self-realization – essentially merged with the Supreme Self. He would like to consider equally well-wishers, patrons, friends, enemies, and even strangers that are indifferent to him. He wants to take part with both army sides as a negotiator. Those who are objects of his distaste and those who are related to him need his consideration. Those who are good and virtuous and those who are wicked should be dealt with as distinguishable only by the virtue of his duty in life. The purity of his action should be judged as being above all these issues, among others.

Krishna interjects, "Take your person to a solitary place. In a clean place, spread out a seat or *asana* of the sacred *kusha* grass. Next, spread a skin and cover it with a clean soft cloth. Sit on this *asana.* Concentrate the mind and subdue the senses and remain sitting straight with your body, neck and head such that it does not move. Focus your sight at the root of the nose and do not look around in any other direction. Remain here in intense peace with your mind and awareness in Me. This technique and the method will stop changes caused by *Maya* or Mother Nature in the mind and body parts."

"I have not been able to grasp the bliss of the Soul despite many efforts," the blind king complained.

"When Man is mentally scattered, he adopts many tendencies, Sire. The physical experiences of an indulging

Man produce physical ailments and mental problems with inability to make out differences between good and bad. Such aloofness, lack of devotion, inactivity, and endless apprehension over happenings are imaginary deceptions. They lead to unbearable obstacles in the physical and subtle bodies. Lapses in discipline are associated with unfulfilled desire for the bliss of the soul," *Sanjaya* replied.

"How can this be overturned?" asked the blind king.

"By practicing *ekatva* or unity with Oneness," replied *Sanjaya* and then continued, "By its very nature, the mind cannot live in an environment of emptiness. It needs to hold on to something that gives it lasting happiness. If that does not happen, by its innate tendencies, the self goes on life's merry-go-round seeking worldly pleasures for happiness. To make happiness long lasting, *Krishna* has given us the techniques of breathing or *pranayama* and of contemplation/ meditation that purify tendencies and create long-term inner happiness."

"What is this inner experience of bliss?"

"Keeping the mind happy by these techniques, Man experiences the all pervading sound of Space. A touch of the *pranic* air within, the sight of an inexhaustible Light, the nectarous ambrosia flowing from the crest amid a divine scent, fills Man. The mind no longer runs after external joys. He remains steadily in That. Once revealed, Awareness surrenders to it and the mind becomes silent and still."

Sanjaya understands the advice given to *Arjuna.* Having realised his soul through meditation, the fully appeased *yogi* rests in the single beam of Light and follows all parallels as diversified vibrations of the one Light. Canceling all false sense of individuality while in existence as an enlightened soul or *chitta,* Man must solve the difficulty of the mind while on a spiritual journey. *Arjuna* needs to decontaminate his egocentric state by becoming more skilled with his Knowledge of the true soul. Cultivating optimism and contentment would strengthen his psychological health and transform both his physiological and physical health. Given a chance, the *chitta* can be expected to agree to positive metamorphosis. The subtle influence of a stilled mind and a content placid intellect can be expected to mature into a long-lasting inner bliss.

At this stage, the oneness experienced in the *yoga* of meditation is not permanent. *Arjuna* needs to become incorporated into the confines of pure Love for the sake of Love alone.

Therefore, *Krishna* advises *Arjuna,* "Always meditate in this way, you will effortlessly cross the ocean of worldliness or *samsara.* You will thus quench worldliness by immersing all names and forms into a visionary understanding. The mind will assert neither am I nor is anything mine. Intellectually you will succeed in stilling the mind, senses and the body. Later you will go beyond this intellect and into the lingering place of tranquillity."

Then he continues, "If you eat too much, there cannot be *yoga* or union. If you do not eat at all, there also cannot be *yoga.* Sleeping too much and inadequate sleep is unhealthy. There also there cannot be *yoga.* Remain absorbed in the bliss of yoga, eat and enjoy life and work. *Yoga* or union does not happen if this is not done in moderation."

Krishna is clear with his instructions. *Arjuna* must learn to center his concentration, calm the swings of thoughts in his mind and intellect, and awaken his self-consciousness to soul-consciousness.

As *Krishna* says, "The one whose awareness is stilled in the Self, he is called a *yogi.* He or she is empty of lust and want. Saints who are knowledgeable in *yoga* of meditation compare the awareness of such a seeker to a lamp, the flame that steadily burns unperturbed in a place empty of even a breeze. The union of his Awareness with Consciousness remains in motionless equipoise."

Krishna assures *Arjuna* that his prevailing composure should make him fearless. His perseverance in *brahmacharya* of self-control will discipline the mind to remain unperturbed and thought-free. Content with soul-awareness, *Arjuna* will rise into the realms of Awareness for a meeting with transcendental Consciousness.

Krishna therefore continues, "The place where *yogic* services are done, in that place where changes of the mind have ended, the mind transcends everything and the Self is seen. Having surrendered the wants of the senses, mind and intellect, the Self experiences the true eternal form of the soul. The one, who realizes the Soul's true form, does not heed hot or cold, or relationships with pleasure or pain. Know therefore that these are characteristics of a *yogi*. You will arrive at *yoga* or Oneness."

Krishna senses *Arjuna* wants reassurance. "Resolve to renounce and smother all lusts and control all roles of the senses and organs of action. Patiently remain steadfast of mind and end connections with worldly life, little by little. Settle the mind in soul-awareness. Casting off thought, remain in inner contentment."

Krishna continues, "Whenever the restive and unsettled mind wanders, bring it back. The mind wanders because of its inherent *rajoguna* or creativity and can become distracted. Exercise coaching and practice meditation and withdraw the mind until the Self controls it. By such a repetitious procedure of retraction of the senses, the mind becomes placid and its purity becomes a *sattvic* condition. It cancels both the creativity of *rajoguna* and laziness of *tamoguna,* in the mind stuff."

The self-governed *yogi,* whose mind is fully under control, engages his soul in endless meditative union with the Supreme Self and reaches the peace of being. This results in the final deliverance and total liberation in *nirvana.* Past habits and demands return to their causal origins to make their self-discovery in the cusp ego-consciousness. Here, they merge and are washed because of soul expression.

Krishna describes this type of devotion; "Man must live

in harmony with the rhythms of life and his interactions with Nature. Cultivation of physiological and psychological balance within the body-mind-intellect complex ensures that this is spontaneous and effortless."

"By becoming righteous, the mind is under control. By repeated practice of this restful poise, the mind is able to remain in soul consciousness. He experiences the created cosmos in its perfect infinity. In all the elements he sees the Self and the Self in the elements. The *yogi* witnesses them as the same. He is freed while alive and crosses over. Fixed thus, he experiences Infinite Consciousness in everything in the Universe. He experiences the subsisting of all things, creatures and beings in this immovable *Brahman* or Supreme Reality, infusing the world as the Self."

Sanjaya shudders. *Arjuna* realises *Krishna* is going to utter all in further revelations.

"Whoever sees Me in everything in this way, that all is Me and I is himself also, then he is in an awakened state and is never unconscious. He lives ever awake. Having followed his *guru's* instructions, he sees *Brahman* embodied in even the immovable elements as awareness. He sees it abiding in all of Creation. There is nothing around that is lacking of Awareness. Whoever sees Me in everything, making all One, grasps the tranquil state even while remaining among things. He lives in Me, *Arjuna*. And if he sees all in oneself, including pleasure and sorrow, he is indeed a supreme *yogi*."

And *Arjuna* decides to express his unspoken anguish, "In describing the yoga of meditation you spoke of an important instruction. I must make a firm resolution that I promote myself by my own endeavor. You have guaranteed me that I will rise and reach the galaxy above. You have also convinced me that I will not be unprotected in this body of mine. You tell me and I will then be able to advance towards God because I have made every effort needed to reach there. Although I have experienced momentary composure as an after-effect of equipoise, I do not see this as enduring."

"O *Krishna,* I cannot see inner strength coming out of my fidgety mind. How then do you expect me to transact *yoga*? This mind is the cause of want by the bodily senses. Who has the power to win over such a fractious and incorrigible mind? Just as a pot cannot hold a raging wind, the mind cannot be steadied while turbulent," *Arjuna* cried out in despair. "It is impossible to hush the mind for a stretched period of time, just as it is unworkable to stop inhalation and exhalation," and with that he sat down on the chariot seat.

"Arjuna, what you are saying is all true. The turbulent and uncontrollable mind is restless and has the power to compel it back. Wherever the mind goes practice repeatedly to bring it back until it becomes fixed in Me. By non-attachment, the mind eventually becomes disinterested and will remain in Me," *Krishna* replies.

The blind king intercedes with his own judgment, "My sympathies are with my nephew, *Arjuna.*" *Sanjaya* becomes thoughtful before responding.

"It seems necessary to explain what *Krishna* is saying, Sire. Constant practice or *abhyas* and nonattachment or *vairagya* are the two preparatory additions of *yogic* methods," *Sanjaya* replied.

"When enjoyment mingles with external matters like sound, touch, sight, smell and taste, there is transformation of the mind into an adulterated reprogrammed state. If awareness is able to refrain from obstacles to regain its own natural state, mind undergoes a gradual adjustment. It discovers itself vanishing periodically. Man becomes appreciative of the fact that the mind is living in a perverse state. The mind now makes an effort to secure its own genuine state and labours to remove the foundations of all mutilation. Early efforts are often ineffective because the mind is constrained by habits of previous tendencies or *samskaras.* The burning want for peace compels the mind to struggle until even these tendencies are removed. The mind through constant practice does in fact arrive at its natural non-wanting or *vairagya* state," *Sanjaya* reasons.

"Without the experience of Bliss-Consciousness, it is unworkable for the mind to persevere in this almost unattainable condition. What is of principal significance is to take sanctuary at the feet of a genuine mentor."

Krishna intervenes with a similar reassurance. "Even if the mind is brought to stillness momentarily by *yoga,* the restive matter-oriented mind will assume its former adulterated condition. To quell the mind, prove its stillness and experience omnipresence, even if difficult. It is attainable by a *guru's* grace and continuous practice. Controlling the mind without meditation is impossible. Only when controlled can the mind arrive at wisdom."

Sanjaya then tells the blind king, "The condition in which the mind is restrained by practice and preoccupation with meditation, is complete tranquillity. He sees the self by the self, and is content in his own self. Here he experiences the highest happiness. It is sense-transcendence characterised by immeasurable bliss, which is beyond the senses. When he awakens to that pure intuitive intelligence, which understanding can only clutch at inefficiently, he remains fixed in that Truth. Gaining this he regards no other procurement greater than that. He becomes anchored and remains unmoved and immune to the mightiest grief. This state conditions devotion to *yoga.* In this condition there is a severance from pain. Such devotion should be practiced with perseverance and with a non-grieving heart."

Arjuna has doubts. "My days are over, *Krishna.* In a short while I will be killed in the war. What is the use of all this spiritual practice? Bound to wants and enjoyment of their fulfillment, mortals like me take birth again and again."

Arjuna continues, "When bliss of the Self is experienced by guru-instructed meditation, mind is filled with thoughts of knowledge and bliss. It wants to abandon lust of worldly wants. They move about like fragments of clouds scattered in the blue sky. Thoughts do not continue in *Brahman*. They remain ignorant. What is their destiny?"

"Then there are many whose minds have already earned dispassion and have known Bliss-Consciousness but are interrupted repeatedly by death. What is their destiny? Do they not end with a corrupted mind? What happens to them?"

"Please resolve these concerns now and allow me to present other concerns later." After a short pause *Arjuna* adds, "Without you O *Krishna*, there is nobody who can dispel this conflict in me."

The blind king was looking for similar answers and *Sanjaya* replied while *Krishna* gave the impression of being absorbed in the armies assembled on both sides of their chariot.

"Death is only a long sleep, Sire," *Sanjaya* said. "Everyday after a hard day at work, we sleep eight hours without any fear. We worry only when unable to sleep. Like sleep, death too is necessary. Just as we wake up from sleep to resume our work where we left off, our former spiritual practice is available to us even after death."

Krishna responds. "O *Arjuna* trust your inner experiences which have amassed their own bounty. The divine expression, no matter how transitional, can never be destroyed. Just because one is unable to stay for long periods in the Bliss of Meditation or is not fully able to succeed in dispassion for worldly inclinations, such efforts are not wasted. Such seekers are born in homes of fully developed beings whose minds are chaste and are successfully living in circumstances that lack wants. Such types of births in the physical world are precious."

"Having taken birth in such types of homes, *yogic* habits of prior births from previous bodies once again soar towards the *yoga* of Awareness. Some without any effort go beyond *Vedic* rituals. Their inborn tendencies compel them to inquire about techniques of *yoga* and they become united with Eternal Knowledge. They rehearse meditation as was practiced in the previous body."

"The *yogi* who after many births exerting in self-discipline succeeds in erasing the impurities of the mind is not dislodged from continuity. Such *yogis* re-exist in dispassion and eventually arrive at the supreme path that leads to the Bliss of Knowledge and *Brahman.*"

Having said all this to reassure *Arjuna, Krishna* goes on to give him some advice and recommendation.

"Since *yogis* are superior to the austerity performing ascetics or the scriptural students who seek objective knowledge, my advice to you *Arjuna,* is that you be a *yogi.* Enduring in the stillness and silence of Bliss Awareness is better than just concentrating in the *kutastha* behind the two eyebrows."

"Remain in this Bliss. There the mind is always in *Brahman.* Here the *yogi* will know Me. Knowing Me as Bliss-Consciousness the mind, intellect and the senses are all restrained."

After a pause *Krishna* continues.

"Practices of the last birth are usually disfigured by hallucinating greediness or *moha.* They interfere with former spiritual practices or *sadhana.* Ones who tread the path of uprightness never come to such suffering. The effort in all previous lives is never wasted. Whatever was left incomplete yearns for success and becomes perfect. Accept what I have said *Arjuna* my friend."

The blind king found *Krishna's* promise of a continuous bliss perception, whether in meditation or while performing mundane activities in the world, difficult to accept. *Sanjaya* therefore reminds the blind king it is far superior to aspire for the pure and enduring soul-joy than for worldly transient pleasures. Both *Arjuna* and the king are warriors of life and living but *Arjuna* is being taught the art of liberation through conscious and disciplined deliberation. He is encouraged to make out the One Supreme Spirit everywhere and in everything.

"O king," *Sanjaya* said "*Krishna's* reply is a monument of inspiration to sincere yogis. No matter how many times the *yogi* falls, he is eventually rescued in this life or in the life beyond. The memory of *yoga* practice remains lodged in the subconsciously hidden memory of experiences that sprout forth in spiritual inclinations even in infancy."

"Advanced and righteous but still imperfect *yogis* are given a chance to experience happiness in the astral spheres of the divine and are allowed to incarnate under better conditions of existence. Progress in the awakening path of spirituality is the soul's inherent impulse to connect with the Whole."

9. Surrender

Arjuna faces an earnest difficulty. His mind is bewildered. His bafflement is about dutiful action or *svadharma*. Covetousness and miserliness or *moha* have created a smoke screen in his understanding. He is pursuing ways to retreat from his duty in life as a fearless hero and warrior prince.

Krishna succeeded in convincing *Arjuna* that illusion governs him, which is his own and singularly private delusion. He understands his physical sheath is transient but he is inherently indestructible. This hallucination therefore gives him no right to abdicate his duty in life. If and when his peers come across his cowardly actions, history would remember him as one who subverted his duty.

To confirm and support what *Krishna* has already said, *Arjuna* is encouraged to silence his mind in meditation so he is able to grasp the magnificence and creative compulsion of Mother Nature. Man instinctively rationalises there is Consciousness threading all things, creatures and beings in Nature.

The knowledge of the Self, seemingly so wonderful to *Arjuna* is expressed so clearly and simply by *Krishna* that even *Arjuna* of limited intellect, imagines the Infinite Self in all Its contradictory conditions.

Krishna explains that those who are girdled by constraints of Nature cannot identify with this Knowledge. Yet, it is possible to awaken to this Knowledge while in meditation and fully come to terms with Nature's *Maya* that veils Man's intuitiveness with Ignorance. *Arjuna* must cast off his sense of a twin personality, of 'Me' and of 'I'. By lifting himself to the real 'I' through meditation he will grasp the import of such Knowledge.

Arjuna recognises that a definite solution to all his human difficulties is to have a purposeful knowledge of himself as a spiritual being. He asks *Krishna* to list God's real personality as both Nature and Spirit. *Arjuna* concedes he is becoming increasingly competent at fixing his mind in Him through the power of concentration and deepening meditation, but he wishes to experience Him as Spirit.

And *Krishna* answers, "O *Arjuna,* listen how, without doubt you may befriend Me. Fix your mind on Me, practicing devotion to meditation, and take refuge in Me. By following the path of *yoga* – hear how you detect Me beyond all doubts. You will see Me fully with all My qualities and powers. If your awareness is immersed in the center of Universal Intelligence at the *kutastha* between the eyebrows, the pervading Consciousness with Its mighty miraculous powers will reveal Itself in complete clarity."

Krishna's assertion triggers a discussion between *Sanjaya* and the blind king. *Dhritarashtra* already recognises the path of meditation is only a means to reach the divine destination. He has a theoretical knowledge that a *yogi* must communicate with the Supreme Spirit, for the technique of *yoga* to fulfill its purpose. And *Sanjaya* says, "Just as a blossom precedes the fruit of divine realisation, so too, the fruit needs ripening through continued *yoga* practice to achieve complete union with the Supreme Self."

Dhritarashtra asks *Sanjaya,* "Everywhere I turn, I see both the ordinary physical and the abstract. I have seen this since my birth, then why is Man caught in Mother Nature's delusion? Why does Man see differences? An attractive Man is pleasant to look at and yet the sight of another fills one with disgust. Why is one attracted by one and repels another in abhorrence? Why do different people depict different emotions while looking at the same noteworthy scene? Why does remarkable music played by the same artist make one cry and another turn away in distaste? Why is the mind preoccupied with what is his and what is alien to him? Why indeed do such reflections arise in my mind? Why do responsible actions deflect from duty? What is the authority of this deception?"

"Only those who have surrendered to the Infinite Self will escape this play of *Maya* in Nature. You Sire, are experiencing it and so is your nephew *Arjuna.* For those who surrender to the Knowledge of the scriptures and follow the path of meditation, the waters of *maya* dry up while still living and breathing, here and now," *Sanjaya* replies.

Arjuna has his own doubts also. "What is this power of illusion, *Krishna,*" *Arjuna* asks.

Krishna replies, "I will tell you all without omission, both about theoretical knowledge and that which is experienced as wisdom. It is the highest knowledge written in the scriptures. Knowing this, there is nothing in this world left for you to know. If successful in experiencing this knowledge of Infinite Consciousness, then there is nothing left in the Cosmos for you to know or gain."

After a pause, *Krishna* continues, "A seeker must take refuge in Me. Among thousands of men, who strive for spiritual attainment, few among such blessed true seekers devotedly try reaching Me. Perhaps one of them has arrived at perfection? Rarely does one experience, make out and know Me at the *kutastha.*"

Dhritarashtra tells *Sanjaya,* "This priceless state of understanding seems difficult. I am a mediocre individual whose five sense perceptions are revolving towards my worldly needs. Even with free will I, like most, am habit-bound and identified with my mental and physical resources. My materialistic habits do not allow me to interpret the nature of my soul. I need practice in ever-increasing intensity to unfold. I wish for concentration and meditation, but do not have the will to act so. My Knowledge is inadequate. I feel more shielded with the self-knowledge of Me, my individuality. What is this deception that has bewildered me on the path of life?"

"You will yield to the divine pull. Your worldly conduct will be raised and exchanged for spiritual habits. You have to understand the power of God, His artistry, and the skill of His hand. Matter and Spirit is together Infinite *Brahman.* The power of Creation is *maya.* The skill of His artistry has allowed the Creator to use eight Matter materials to create things, creatures and beings and imbued them with Spirit. His artistry is what has you stupefied," *Sanjaya* replied.

"What are these eight matter items, *Sanjaya?*"

"*Krishna* is planning to speak of them to *Arjuna,* Sire – listen," *Sanjaya* said.

"Earth, water, fire, air, space, mind or *manas,* understanding or *buddhi* and ego or *ahamkar* – these are My eight-fold Nature or *prakriti,* threaded by my Indivisible Spirit. O Mighty-armed One – *Arjuna,* please understand this mystery. This Cosmos with its solar systems is created from two fundamental materials, Matter-substance of Awareness and Spirit-substance of Consciousness. The trinity of the Father, Son and the Holy Spirit are together the Eternal Substance before Creation, the *Purushottama.* He is God or *Brahman* – Cosmic or Infinite Consciousness."

"The three in the trinity are not different from each other, *Arjuna,* they are One. The Cause of Creation, Matter or *Prakriti* and Spirit or *Purusha* are also not separate from That Trinity. They are two *Prakriti* expressions. One is of power or *shakti* and the other of Awareness. Although Matter has Awareness, it is unable to work at Creation on its own. Spirit is attracted to Matter. It energizes and transforms Matter into the primary cause of creation, the *mahatattvas.* The two now become the great principle of Intellect or *Buddhi* of *Hiranyagarbha,* the golden egg that holds Knowledge of the Cosmos," *Krishna* continues.

"When Awareness of Material *Prakriti* is filled with Consciousness or *Purusha* it transforms into Intellect. *Mahatattva* whose inherent qualities are *gunas* – the principal of which is creativity or *rajoguna.*"

Arjuna is fascinated with what he is hearing and sits down on the chariot seat while *Krishna* continues to describe the descent of Man from God to mortal.

"Past inclinations and habits colour the *mahatattvas* and propel Mind to work contrary to duty or *dharma* and Intellect to work as self-centred logic. Awareness in *Prakriti's mahatattva* becomes self-conscious and decides it is 'separate' and the ego develops. The mind, intellect and ego together becomes a person's personality or *chitta.*"

"Is that how *Prakriti* as *chitta* gets polarized into *dharmic* and *adharmic* forms of the ego?" *Arjuna* asks.

"Let me clarify this further. Embodied *tamoguna* is inert earth, combined *tamas* and *rajas* become water, while *rajoguna* externalizes to become the fire energy. Creativity of *rajas* mixing with the harmony of *sattva* becomes air while *sattvaguna* embodies space. That is how the elements are formed, O *Arjuna,*" *Krishna* says.

"Therefore the Universe is built from permutations of all these quality or *guna*-components, the five elements, and the *chitta.* But this is only the characteristic of Matter. There is also another power. Consciousness or *purusha* or Lifeforce or *Om* is what makes the Cosmos living. Both are powers, of *purusha* and *prakriti,* and are the Power of Infinite Truth-Knowledge-Bliss Consciousness. It is from where the whole Universe emerges and dissolves in through the passage of ages."

"The lower form of My Nature is *apara prakriti.* Different from this there is a higher form of my Nature, which is breathing. This holds the Universe as *para prakriti* by *purusha.* Know that all creatures have these for their source. I am the source of evolution and the source of dissolution of the entire Universe. Understand that this dual Nature of Mine, the pure *purusha* and the impure *prakriti,* is the womb of all beings. I am the Creator *Brahma* and the Dissolver *Shiva* of the entire Cosmos," *Krishna* said.

Arjuna feels ensnared by worrying activities in the

Universe he lives in and says, "You have shown me your palace and the many inhabitants living there. How then do I know you personally? There are a cast of characters and the arena is nerve-racking because of intriguing tangles," *Arjuna* says.

"There is only one means to know Me, *Arjuna.* Through a purity of mind and with devotion to meditation," *Krishna* replies.

Dhritarashtra is now flustered. He needs *Sanjaya* to explain *Krishna's* statements.

"Just as shadows and lights together reveal the activities of actors on a stage through a single beam of light, so also, Cosmic Nature produces a dream picture of beings on a platform. Expressions of five elements, beings and creatures with mind, intellect and ego make up the eight forces of cosmic nature. They become animated on a bedrock of breath or life force," *Sanjaya* declares.

The blind king wants more details, and *Sanjaya* continues. "Matter, whether organic or inorganic, starts with the atom or *anu* from the realms of original Nature. It displays only after an inherent cosmic idea of causal electricity and magnetic essence arises as a sub-atomic energy or *param-anu.* This is the life force – *prana* that is able to employ intellectual and mental capacities for expression. It comes about and crystallises from thought consciousness or *chaitanya.*"

Pausing, *Sanjaya* realises the blind king is still intellectually sightless. So he continues, "*Yogis* assert that gross nature or *apara-prakriti* is a dream body of the Spirit. It has five elements, two perceptive processes of mind or *manas* and intellect or *buddhi,* and one feeling ego or *ahamkar* entity."

"Out of sight behind the *apara-prakriti* is the enlivened *para-prakriti* of pure Nature as Spirit. It is fabricated from the cosmic astral universe – a cosmic causal universe, which is intelligent. It is *Om,* the breathing Holy Spirit that supports both the *apara and para-prakriti* as an Eternal Witness – the intelligent Consciousness of Mother Nature."

Sanjaya finishes by highlighting more information on an interesting note. "The Spirit dreams Itself into the trinity: Father, who is beyond creation; *Kutastha* whose characteristic is Universal Intelligence is the Son – *Krishna* who reveals himself physically when needed; and Intelligent Cosmic Consciousness – the Holy Spirit who enlivens Nature. Using eight prospective agents, THAT creates, supports and dissolves three mansions of creation – causal, astral and physical."

Arjuna says, "Show me where it is You play a part in."

And *Krishna* continues, "O *Arjuna,* all these, internal and external, in the entire Cosmos as well as in its minutest form are existing because of *kutastha-chaitanya,* the Inner Self which is destitute of egoism. It is all-pervading, this self-revealing **Om,** that exists as breath of Life in all creatures."

"Know Me as the taste and liquidity of water, the radiance of the sun and moon, and the glowing essence of human beings. There is nothing that is higher than Me, or beyond Me. On Me are all these creatures and objects are strung, like a row of pearls on a string." He now gives an extensive portrayal of THAT which is all and everywhere.

"O Son of *Kunti – Arjuna,* I am the *pranava Om* in all the *Vedas,* the sound in space, and the strength in Man. I am the sweet fragrant scent in earth, the brilliance in fire, the life in all living creatures and the self-discipline in unyielding ascetics."

"Know Me to be the eternal seed of all beings and creatures, O *Arjuna.* I am the understanding of intelligence in all creatures and the glorious grandeur of all the magnificent things and beings."

"I am Eternal and without beginnings."

"Among the powerful, O Best of *Bharatas – Arjuna,* I am the strength that is beneficent and the ability that is free from longings and attachments and thirst. I am that lust where there is nothing depraved and desire that is consistent with duty in all creatures that obey *dharma* and goodness."

"And all existences which have the quality of goodness or *sattva,* I am That. Those that have the qualities of passion and creativity or *rajas,* and the quality of darkness and slowness or *tamas,* know that they emanate from Me. They are from Me, the Supreme Awareness. I am however not in them, but they are in Me."

"Why then is Your presence so illusive, *Krishna*?" asks *Arjuna.* "Because of the character of three qualities in Nature. Because of *gunas,* all this Knowledge has disappeared from Man's memory. They therefore do not know Me. But I am beyond the *gunas* of creativity as *rajas,* inertia when *tamasic* and in harmony but *sattvic, Arjuna.*"

Sanjaya is familiar with Nature's seductive power of *Maya.* He spent years working to experience Universal Intelligence for himself, without much success. The blind king needed further simplification and asks *Sanjaya* to justify what *Krishna* has just told *Arjuna.*

And *Sanjaya* says, "When a *yogi* banishes all thoughts and sensation, he finds in himself an intermingling of knower, knowing and known, as a single experience. It is then that a *yogi's* intuitive insight plainly experiences a swell of the cosmic sound, in view of an imposing radiance from omnipresent awareness. Being one with the Spirit, the *yogi* sees himself in the palpitation of Truth – Om. Man is then able to see himself in Cosmic Connection with the lifeblood of elements, in the genius and light of Creation, in the understanding of all creatures, and in the scent of all mental images emerging from That One fountainhead. He sees the fanciful appearances of good and evil in every screen of this grandiose delusion."

The blind king was reflecting over what *Sanjaya* had just said when they hear *Krishna* address the spiritual seeker in *Arjuna.*

"The uninformed who is stupefied by the *guna*-filled *Maya* is granted worldly existence and gains demoniac self-consciousness. In truth, this entire Universe becomes a vision of delusion because of these three properties. These three qualities are My own power of mirage, my *maya*. Although it is difficult to thwart the competence of *Maya,* those who take up the search for Consciousness are able to go across and beyond *Maya.*"

"Worldly beings are too deeply immersed in the drama-of-life to understand the propelling forces of Nature, the sole Doer. This Cosmic Self-deception, my *maya,* is my verdict. Its effect is like a hypnotic spell on all creatures, things, and beings. Fettered and driven they endure being packaged within the perimeter of sensory temptations, past habits, and their inclination causing all creatures to lose their peace."

Sanjaya reminds *Dhritarashtra* that it is irrational that Man, who is the reflection of God and is gifted with free choice, acts mechanically under the influence of these triple realms of *Maya*. Whether deliberate or unintentional there is an unethical act happening, which is in conflict with evolutionary teachings. They deny a need for higher Knowledge. They instead stake at deflecting the soul away from the Self.

Krishna reiterates the same truth to *Arjuna.*

"These basest of humans, these evil-doers are the lowest of ignorant men and perpetrators of wrong. These misguided fools who have been robbed of the knowledge by my illusion are wedded to the character of demons. Because they do not resort to Me, they wander about in the world."

In truth, Man seems like a joyless trekker who takes delight in false entertainment and inert gaiety. Is this true satisfaction, *Arjuna* wonders? Joys to the worldly man seem like violent contacts with sensory objects, whether they are intoxicating drink, tobacco, foodstuff, loud music, or intimate relations. Exhilaration with satisfaction cheats even the powerful with beguiling shadows. He expects to know the Universe with his five senses. Unless familiar with a known stimulation, senses decide to inflict oneself with distaste. Unless Man experiences the true joy of Nature's Reality, he cannot know how barren his autobiography has been. The best way to discover this joy is through worship, dedication and consecration or *bhakti*.

The journey is a lonely one. Contrary reflections prowl around and evaporate. The validated as well as the irrelevant Man seduces himself, evaluating all things that fill him with sweetness. The restlessness within keeps Man searching. Like moths confounded by the incandescent lamp, many perish in the feverish heat and joy of reaching the Light. Only a few lose their identity in the fire of harmony. But even with this consecration Man savours every frontier of joy. *Krishna* then goes on to describe those who are granted with the colour of devotion.

"The virtuous and the pure of character who reflect on Me are of four kinds. The desperate, the searching seeker, the materialist and the fortunate follower are the four classes of doers of good deeds who worship Me, O *Arjuna.* He that is distressed and afflicted with dissatisfaction, the one who has searched and possessed of systemized knowledge, and the one who seeks for power and wealth here and in the hereafter are the *artha-arthi.* These are preoccupations of the first three types of devotees. Only the wise follower who is constant has faith in Me. These are the four kinds of honest men who worship Me, whose virtue follows Me. Only one is superior to the rest because to the man of experienced Knowledge – the sage, I am dear to him above everything, and he is dear to Me."

Sanjaya knows that goodness demands a well-planned approach towards God based on an understanding of God and life. Most turn to Him when under personal pain or loss. Others wish materialism and worldly success. A few learn the Scriptural Knowledge to understand Nature. And an even smaller number awaken to the Knowledge through meditation and enlightenment. Every being and creature, *Krishna* explains, naturally changes towards its source. The key to spiritual fulfillment, he says, is steadfastness on the chosen path in life. Only devotion leads to Self-realization.

"Because they take up the path of self-awareness, all these types of devotees are meritorious. But among them, the one who has heeded the words of a mentor, thought about and deeply speculated on the Knowledge, he experiences the Unfathomable. He is on the path of Consciousness. He, the sage knows that Soul Awareness is the only essence worthy of his devotion. He offers all his friendship to Me. He takes sanctuary in My Self, and his mind co-mingles in Me. With his soul fixed in contemplation, he reaches his highest objective."

Krishna admits motives of men may vary, but all that seek to grow spiritually are in essence responding to their inner urges, to unfold according to their innate spiritual needs. An acclaimed devotee gives public services for name and fame. He does no harm and the need for recognition strengthens his belief he is doing no wrong. He finds joy in such identification and faith that he advances the Lord's work.

Pleading for the Lord is better than begging from the world. Many perform daily rites desirous of the Lord's grace. Some fast with petitions and others make contracts. It is in these situations that great souls like *Dhruva* have made notable beginnings. This also is a devotion of a wanting devotee and the Lord must authenticate his will. Whatever the justification, *Krishna* wants Man to enter the tabernacle of devotion.

Motive may be the first wish, but Man becomes generous when there is a disclosure in it of magnificence and strength. Even the most colorless of creatures, if he thinks and loves the Lord, earns homage from the Universe. His mental attitude is of a selfish wanting devotee. This first seeker who sees the world with the eyes of love alone is a *karma yogi.*

The restive devotee with a motive seeking compassion to fulfill life's purpose also acts in truth, sincerity, yearning and love. This impatient adherent who seeks wisdom has an uncontainable hunger for knowledge and an impatience to know the truth. He searches everywhere like a fish in water searching for water itself. He does not think to seek the Lord within and sees the world with the eyes of expectant unfolding.

The third devotee seeks meaning and purpose in all. This one applies money and all his faculties for the welfare of society. Such a one-would never act to harm. He sees the world with a view of happiness and welfare for the world. He sees the world through the eyes of knowledge.

All of them are desire-less and yet their approach to the Lord is not complete. The seer saint is a knowledgeable devotee. All that he sees is a form of God, whether in the ugly or in the beautiful. In his heart beat the waves of an endless ocean of bliss and happiness.

"How is this possible?" *Arjuna asks.*

"Because of the power of many lifetimes of spiritual effort, seekers understand worldly life. At the end of many incarnations, man possessed of Knowledge reaches Me as filling the Universe. He thinks and experiences that *Brahman* is all this - the Lord is all pervading. Such a high-soul, however is rare and hard to find."

"Though permissive and indiscriminate beings are most influenced by this cosmic delusion, even they can escape by separation and meditation."

All four types of seekers, *Krishna* stresses are traveling slowly or swiftly on the path of liberation.

Even those who are frenzied by want and blindly honor false gods like name, fame, power, success, materialism and idol-worship are loved because they perform above the supreme limits of their capacities. *Krishna* admits to this fact.

"Because these individuals are under the power of their

own *samskaras,* they are bound by these ordered and packaged inclinations. Their intellect is discouraged by their unfulfilled needs. They squander their lives trying to fulfill them for satisfaction. They who are robbed of Knowledge by cravings, their godheads, obey diverse codes and are self-possessed by their own structure."

"In whatever form an individual meditates on Me, wanting Me with reverence born of a steadfast mind, I am within all those gods and am the fruit of all. Whatever shape of godhead a worshipper needs to adore Me with constancy, I interpret his faith and stabilise it toward that form."

The blind king questions why *Krishna* is not more straightforward with his supporters. *Sanjaya* explains, "Led by their own preference, their excellence stolen by this or that craving, practicing this or that cultic demand, Man seeks lesser gods. But, *Krishna* does not reject them. Whether the expression is of a saint, or a deity or an incarnation, if a devotee strives faithfully to worship, *Krishna* considers him his dearest one because the motives of faith and devotion are firm and unflinching."

Krishna explains why. "Absorbed in faith and devotion, he who is intent on worshipping Me in that form, he gains temporary fruits from all that he wishes. I have ordained they reach heavenly homes suited for each according to his need for advancement and pleasure. Once these pleasures become disordered, the mortal re-attains the life of worldliness because the harvest of this person with little intelligence is insignificant and perishable. They that worship unending life and godheads go to the endless worldly life, while they that worship Me come to Me."

Krishna also recognises those who want interaction with past known souls or cosmic forces of the astral realms of heaven. They, in all sincerity, believe and presume these souls are enlightened. Unable to experience the ever-present essence of Infinite Consciousness in their own *kutastha,* they think I am concealed and unmanifest. These men of scant knowledge also worship lesser gods to receive finite results. The devotees of such deities go to them, the astral angels or *devas*.

Krishna calls his devotees who surrender their self to the Soul to come to the *Krishna*-center within, "I am in the devotee in a revealed form. In the presence of others, I am also openly there. I am without birth, decline or expansion. Caught in the power of *Maya,* they who have no insight to regard Me, who am unmanifest, to have become obvious. They do not know this supreme and cherished state of Mine."

Krishna knew that without wisdom those with incomplete knowledge consider His Unmanifest State as assuming some type of an expression. Although many are engaged in worldly and devout actions according to their inherent natures, because of inclinations and habits from past lives or this life, they devote their lives to worshipping money, fame and power. They deify the objects of their wants or adore lesser gods and forget to worship the God of gods.

Nonetheless, each seeker who expresses devotion through worship, *Krishna* stresses, will receive His grace too. Those worshipping astral deities hoping for fulfilling desires also have their wishes realised through them. He alone is the *Chintamani,* the jewel that grants all wants. But, *Krishna* says that seekers, who commune with the Supreme Spirit in this life, dissolve their rebirth-making *karma* in the fire of the highest ecstasy to reach His Eternal Abode.

Krishna repeatedly admits to *Arjuna* that many uninformed individuals have been seemingly eclipsed by His *Yoga-Maya,* because of a mirage born of triple qualities of Nature. Because He remains unnoticed by Man, the confused world knows not God as the Unborn and the Imperishable.

Sanjaya tells the blind king that *Krishna* is making no apologies but rather admits a Cosmic Dream of beings and creatures veils the Spirit's appearance. On the unseen screen of *Yoga-Maya,* soiled by the triple qualities, the mysterious dream pictures of Cosmic Nature become visible. The illumination remains cleverly hidden as an unseen Cosmic Breath.

Krishna in fact says, "Nobody knows me. Camouflaged by the subterfuge of My unimaginable power, I am not obvious or seen at all. This ignorant world does not know that I am unborn and undecaying. O *Arjuna,* I know all things and creatures that were in the past, and those who presently are, and all that are to be in the future. But there is nobody who knows Me, O descendent of the *Bharata* dynasty - *Arjuna.*"

"Having occupied a physical body because of affection for favorable matters and repulsion towards unfavorable matters, mortals remain enraptured by ordeals of cold and heat, pleasure and sorrow. This hallucination of pairs of opposites arising from want and distaste or *raaga- dvesha* is an affliction."

The blind king did not see the reason for these statements and suggested that *Krishna* had made many seemingly contradictory statements. *Sanjaya* therefore decides to describe the processes of descent from Whole to soul.

Sanjaya clarifies the pattern of Man's design. "As soon as a soul leaves the Whole, he develops a false sense of independence and individuality as the self. At first identified with mind and intellect, and later the body, the self becomes propelled by his likes-and-dislikes and is directed by the captivating influence of Nature's qualities. Identified with mind and matter, he undergoes a physical birth as he travels between first the astral and then the physical conveyances."

"When the unenlightened soul, who by now has forgotten his divine origin, presents himself as the partially enlightened *chitta* of a mind-intellect-ego complex, he undergoes a physical birth ensheathing the subtle and causal bodies," *Sanjaya* explains

"Some of these mortals change to a justifiably vindicated state. Once fully enlightened, they may reincarnate physically for the sole purpose of taking part in the evolutionary processes of souls who are struggling while on a spiritual journey. The Cosmic Teacher comes to such souls as materialisation of Masters on a foreordained mission," *Sanjaya* finishes.

Sanjaya explains to the blind king the fact that we are born in a physical body at all is evidence that Man is in soul-ignorance and has not realised his identity with the Formless Infinite Spirit. *Sanjaya* says, "To breathe at all is to inhale in *maya,* the cosmic delusion. God gives Man His illusion first and not Himself. This happens with an ambition of hauling Man through the drama of creation. Attachment to family, friends and objects is part of this great delusion."

As if reading *Sanjaya's* mind, *Krishna* tells *Arjuna* that seekers who live by their innate tendencies and in harmony with circumstances, who do not willfully make errors in thought and action, live blamelessly. Righteous in thought, behavior and action, they surrender the self at the feet of the soul. *Krishna* promises *Arjuna* such beings are worthy of grace.

"Among the righteous people are those who have been admitted into meditation. These people of virtuous deeds, whose sins have reached their end, are freed from illusions of pairs of opposites. They worship Me firm in their vow of that worship."

"Those who take refuge in Me, strive for release from birth, decay and death. They reflect on Me having become purified in the heart. They gradually know *Brahman,* the entire soul of the entire universe or *Adhyatma.* Effortlessly, they know all, having become self-realised."

Grace received from teacher and Nature leads Man to seek liberation from re-emergence. They awaken and transcend decay from old age and death by taking refuge in God. They realize that by clinging to Him, they will know *Brahman* as the Supreme Self or Spirit. They discover the all-inclusive *Adhyatma,* the soul as a repository of the Supreme Self or Spirit. They also become familiar with all secrets of action while serving Universal Nature.

Krishna continues, "In this way, they are able to experience Bliss-filled Knowledge of Infinite Consciousness. They know the lord of the physical as the *Adhibhuta,* and of the subtle bodies as *Adhidaiva.* They experience the Infinite leaving the body. They remain filled with Eternal Bliss having their minds fixed in meditation."

The blind king was perplexed. *Sanjaya* reiterates what seems observable. "Those who discover God in the *Adhibhuta* see Him as the motivating power of physical Nature. Those who see God in the *Adhidaiva* see Him as the astral life force animating matter. And, those who see God as *Adhiyagna,* know Him as the incomparable in all heavenly understandings."

Therefore, *Krishna* encourages *Arjuna* and *Sanjaya* encourages the blind king to perform actions dedicated to Mother Nature. Only moral actions have the power to allow Man to retract from trivial controlling reasons. *Krishna* promises that only a righteous one with his seat of passion affiliated to the spirit would be inclined to persevere to distinguish Him even at death.

Krishna assures *Arjuna* that a seeker who awakens in the Supreme Self realises that he has been dreaming under the influence of *maya.* The laws of *karma* or action-and-reaction governed his twofold experiences of life, the real and the unreal.

Sanjaya also promises this for the blind unrighteous king. He will get Knowledge over mis-understanding and insight into Truth. He will discover the presence of the soul in his own physical, astral and causal bodies. Even small efforts made by the self to learn to unite the soul with the Supreme Self, promises God's benevolence. Once the body, mind and soul are permeated with the Supreme Self, the seeker rises above all probation of human suffering, including death.

Sanjaya says, "The egoistic self enters a tug-of-war with death, as long as there is a wish for human existence. In such circumstances, the ego lodges itself determinedly in the brain, refusing to leave. By meditation, the soul even if partially enlightened, learns to detach itself from the individualistic self. With the power of will, and by engaging the life force, mind, and intellect, the soul unites with the Cosmic Soul."

10. Perseverance

Sanjaya realises that *Krishna* introduced new terms of reference for the soul. A man of wisdom or *gyani* who is intuitively distinguishes between the Higher or *purusha* and Lower Natures or *prakriti* of materialisation discovers his identity with the Infinite Consciousness – the *Purushotama.* He moves at will, supporting Lower Nature, but refuses to make inaccurate connection with his external world and therefore never invites affliction.

Sanjaya tells the blind king, "Agreeable with all circumstances of life, this man of wisdom understands that the highest and the lowest materialisation starts from an at atom of an inert stone. He understands they are all expressions of Awareness pointing on the compass towards Consciousness. That, O king is who you are."

Arjuna by now understands that human life is full of bad as well as good tendencies or *samskaras* developed by repeated actions throughout life. All leave links, impacts and built-up tendencies in the mind. Tendencies structure life from childhood to maturity. Then there is the compulsion of past births and rebirths, erased from memories of the present. Only outstanding events leave behind knowledge of a lifetime. The final release from worldly existence needs purifying and sublimating mind and intellect.

Krishna spoke of many things, which he declares firmly, must be experienced at the *kutastha,* between and behind the eyebrows, while settled in contemplation. *Arjuna's* mind has a flurry of questions. What is this *Brahman,* the *Purushottama* described as having the nature of Infinite Consciousness? If Created Universe is made up of higher and lower Nature, who are the gods of physical, astral and causal energies?

What categorisation of spiritual practices must a seeker perform to know these gods? Which of the two Natures grant Man with revelations? How and where do these gods live in a mortal's body? When the mind and intellect are immersed in meditation what is it that experiences the wisdom of *ananda* or bliss? *Arjuna* seeks answers and asks for clarification.

And *Arjuna* therefore dares to ask aloud, "O *Krishna,* please tell me, what is *Brahman*? What is *Adhyatmic Karma?* What do I need to know about *Adhibhuta,* and what is *Adhiyagna?*"

"O merciful one who is the slayer of the demon *Madhu.* Teach me about this and furnish me with your grace. What is *Adhiyagna* and in what manner is *adhiyagna* present in this body? And how does one remember God? How is He known at death, especially by those who have spent a life in control of oneself and away from whims of the individualistic self? Please tell me."

And *Krishna* replies, "I will tell you piecemeal, so you must listen carefully. *Brahman* is the preeminent and imperishable Reality, which is constant and without characteristics, but is intrinsic as the Supreme Substance. It cannot be substituted or demolished and nourishes the Universe. It is all pervading and self-revealing. All plants, creatures and beings are Its parts. Its passion, fire and combustion is the Spirit, the *Purusha* that presides in the different substance as a witness. Know that Its materialisation is of *adhibuta* or of original matter. The ruler of the solar systems is *adhidaiva* or heavenly gods. Actions or *karma* performed in these bodies are by a*dhyatma* or soul. The fruits of such actions by the Self, is *adhiyagna* or sacrificial achievement."

The blind king, who has lived an extroverted self-indulgent life, finds this discussion between *Krishna* and his brilliant nephew *Arjuna* confusing. So, he asks *Sanjaya* to clarify these statement made by *Krishna.*

And *Sanjaya* explained. "*Arjuna* has breathed, seen,

witnessed, experienced and heard the enlivening Cosmic Sound or *pranava* – Om while settled in the *kutastha*. He wants to know all about Om, Sire."

"But *Krishna's* answers are even more confusing," the blind king complains. "Perhaps I can try simplifying this discussion between them," *Sanjaya* replied.

"Om is **A, U, and M**, a union of three sounds – *A* is the hum of *Brahma* the Creator in the Trinity, *U* is the resonance of *Vishnu* the Sustainer and ***M*** is the symphony from *Shiva's* drum – he is the Dissolver in the Trinity. All are considered necessary for this Creation."

"I already knew that," the king interjected.

"Nature, that is Creation is known by eight names. They are *Vishva* and *Virat* or physical microcosm and macrocosm; *Hiranyagarbha* and *Prajna* or cosmic and microcosmic radiant awareness; *Ishvara* and *Chidabhas* or universal and individual reflection of Supreme Intelligence, and *kutastha-chaitanya* Individual Consciousness free of egotism. These are all states of the Energy of Awareness – the first six are the presiding gods of *karma* or action. The last two reveal creation."

"*Vishva* and *Virat* exist as *tamasic* or stationary energy of Awareness, which is constantly changing through destruction and transformation. Its god is *Shiva,*" *Sanjaya* patiently explains.

"*Taijas* and *Hiranyagarbha* exist in materialisation as *rajasic* or creative subtle energy. Its god is *Brahma* who is being adored as the *adhidaiva.*"

"*Prajna* and *Ishvara* exist in appeared creation as the causal seed of *sattvic* energy of harmony. Its god is *Vishnu* who holds and carries the universe and he is called *adhyatma* or soul."

"Why must I know these facts?" asked the king.

"When seekers such as *Arjuna* remain focused within the *kutastha* for prolonged periods of time, they gradually come to gradations of realisation. They feel their corporeal being connected to the *adhibhuta* or *Virat* as part of the Cosmic Being. Their subtle existence or *taijas* manifests as part of the *hiranyagarbha* as *adhidaiyva*. They experience their causal substance in the body of *ishvara* consciousness. When this happens, Man hears the *pranava,* Om. It is the experience of *ishvarpranidhan* or grace because of devotion for the Lord. It is this bond that connects Man to *Brahma, Vishnu* and *Shiva*. When dissolved in the Cosmic Sound, the subconscious is absorbed in the highest state beyond Creation."

"What you are saying then is that Creation is the amalgam of *adhibhuta, adhidaiva, adhyatma* by Om, the *pranava*?"

"The physical, psycho-physiological energy, and soul awareness cannot make themselves known by their own individual authorities. To self-reveal, Man needs concentrating at the *kutastha* for the grace of *Ishvara* where *chidabhas* reveals itself as Conscious Intelligence or *kutastha-chaitanya*. This is the *yagna* or *karma Krishna* is advising *Arjuna* to perform. He will experience all creation within himself," *Sanjaya* ended.

For his part, *Arjuna* has understood the propelling forces of Mother Nature and Her fields of activity. But he wants more information explaining how spiritual actions cause transformation in a seeker. He also wants to know more about the self-giving movements in Nature.

And *Krishna* says, "O supreme among the embodied beings *Arjuna,* the *Adhibhuta* or obvious form of Nature's elements exert influence of the *gunas* on physical existence. *Adhidaiva* the transforming energetic agent or *prana* is the foundation of astral existence. And I, the Self, within the body and the cosmos I am the *Adhyatma* – the Causal Origin, to whom all sacrifices, reach. All holy offerings as self-giving in *adhiyagna* are offerings to the indwelling true Self. The Infinite Consciousness is higher than all that I have spoken about. That remains as the Immutable Eternal *Brahman* or God without qualities."

"You have spoken about what happens while alive and in meditation. What happens at death, *Krishna*?" *Arjuna* asked.

"Because there is rise and fall in awareness at the time of its mortal death, the united feelings become empowered. A need for fulfillment for a particular condition directs Man's trajectory to death. He enters my Being who thinks only of Me at his passing, when the body is abandoned. Whatever uniqueness of relationship with Me occurs in the mind, at death that is what he gains and none other. This truth is beyond doubt."

In response to *Arjuna's* concerns, *Krishna* tutors him to reflect on this unceasingly, "Therefore, remain attentive to the *kutastha* and practice the religion of the Self and perform meditation as directed by your teacher. Surrender your doubting mind and intellect by remaining combined with and remembering Me always. Engage yourself in the battle of action. And surrender to Me your mind and your understanding. This is the only way to come to Me, without indecision. Thinking of the Supreme, with a mind not running to other objects, perform such practices uninterruptedly, O *Arjuna*."

Krishna reaffirms the need for experienced self-mastery in the seat of meditation. Once there, the single pointed mind allows itself to be progressively purified at the *kutastha,* behind and between the eyebrows. Once it has come to terms with the power of devotion, the energy in the wavering mind stills. This has the ability to silence the breath or *prana.* In the silence and stillness of the *kutastha,* both the energy and the life force are visible and experienced. The Omniscient Self arrives as the Universal Self-revealing as Infinite Consciousness, beyond the body, mind and intellect.

"Still the breath while in the *kutastha.* Practice with patience and in meditation. Listen to the cosmic sound. This is the Form of God. Concentrate on Me while venturing away from this physical bulk, and you will surely reach My house."

Krishna has already told *Arjuna* that He is the Energy of Awareness, which gives structure and permeates all veils of gross and subtle matter. This Energy merging with the enlivening Life Force or *prana* is Consciousness in meditation. It is here that transition from the physical body to the Omniscient happens. Destination is towards the Ancient *Purushottama* and Ruler of the whole world. By an act of will, the seeker merges with the One who is not only smaller than an atom, but is also the Supporter of all. Its Form is unthinkable. That which is beyond all delusions and obscurity, That shines like the Sun.

And *Krishna* adds, "Those who renounce all thoughts and remember Me constantly while united with me in meditation, they reach Me easily and joyously. Even at death, with an unshakable mind full of love and devotion and by the power of Yoga, he fully penetrates the *kutastha* between the eyebrows and he the Seeker, reaches the Supreme Resplendent Self, the *Purusha.*"

Sanjaya reminds the blind king there are three qualifying justifications by which a seeker advances from the physical body into the divine Spirit.

"Seekers ought to have always seen the *kutastha* during meditation. They are then able to merge with It at will. The *yogi* must be able to withdraw from circumstances, as well as from senses and mental processes. He should successfully retreat from objects, emotions, and thoughts. He must have the competence to will his life force or *prana* into the divine cave of the spinal cord and through the brain and into the seat of awareness in the *kutastha.* With commitment to the Spirit, competence over the science of meditation, and constancy of perfect control of the body-mind complex, the seeker's contemplation can then coalesce into Awareness."

Krishna next reveals some mysteries of existing in different degrees of spirituality, "I will tell you in brief about a recognisable locality in the divine cave. Description of this is written in the *Vedas.* Humankind is familiar with it. The scriptures declare it as indestructible. Ascetics who are unfettered by longings enter it. Such saints realise Consciousness and attain liberation. They do not have to take birth in worldly existence, which is the home of sorrow."

"Even after gaining the heavens in *Brahmaloka,* souls take rebirth to satisfy unfulfilled ambitions. But, after expanding into Consciousness they never return to worldly existence," *Krishna* adds.

Arjuna, Sanjaya and the blind king *Dhritarashtra* have all understood that ascetic lifestyle is one of voluntary simplicity. Even *Vedic* seers repeatedly declare there is no need for seekers to sequester themselves or become reclusive.

Seekers need a free choice to demand essentials from life. Yet undeniably it is through concerted inwardness and renunciation, of *brahmacharya,* that ascetics gain morally. Through declining empathy he covets little and leads a life of self-discipline. Once Man experiences rivulets of ecstasy welling up from the spring within, all other satisfaction becomes tasteless.

"Why then does Man feel dispossessed of plain blessedness? Is genuine satisfaction located in the outside world? Why does Man sacrifice himself in worldly pleasures?" *Dhritarashtra* asks.

Sanjaya replies, "Because Man does not know where his true joy lies. He is controlled by phantoms. He gains his satisfaction through the five senses. How can the complete significance of the universe be captured by five senses? And even among these five senses, Man uses just a few of them prudently. He gets wasted in those few connections which he likes or dislikes."

"What then is the solution?" asks the blind king. "The best way to detect real joy is through persevering dedication," *Sanjaya* replied.

Arjuna is lost in his thoughts. "As we march a suitable path we note the deftness of the Lord. On reaching the divine symbol, all other images evaporate. After that, enticements to further details dwindle. The entire world is filled with pure joy. Until the real is arrived at, Man keeps searching endlessly. Enraptured by the power of *Maya,* many lives are lived in ignorance for millions of years. Man keeps returning after so many stopovers in the galaxy of *Brahmaloka.* Why does transcendental meditation not lead Man beyond the grip of *Maya*?" asks *Arjuna.*

Krishna answers, "After Man journeys beyond *Maya,* he earnestly practices *pranayama* as previously taught. He revokes *chitta's* essence. One million earth years are revoked with each completed inhalation and breath control. Having reversed his *chitta* character, the reassembled entity becomes a worthy moral fibre of *Prakriti.* Over time and practice, the karmic debt vanishes into the extraordinary inconceivable linking body of the Infinite."

"Unseen, this happens again and again. This newest imprint of a laundered materialisation is never introverted. He knows how to cast off this body. He leaves by first closing all his sensory doors. He connects his concentration within his heart, and places his life-breath – *prana* between the eyebrows. He then rests there in a protracted meditation. He utters just this one symbol – Om – and while thinking of Me, he arrives at the highest aspiration." There is suddenly a pause of disbelief from *Sanjaya, Dhritarashtra* and *Arjuna.*

"Through fixing the soul in Om, the Word of *Brahman,* and remembering the Supreme Self, Man reaches the Supreme Goal? This final exit from the body is what you have just described?. But imprints of action stay forever? Why, *Krishna* are the laws of karma different for the meditating few?" *Arjuna* asks incredulously.

Krishna confirms this by repeating what he has said earlier, "He who continuously remembers Me with mind ever removed from all other objects, to that disciple, who is pledged to Me in meditation, I am O *Arjuna,* easily contacted. Only saintly people who have achieved the highest perfection, gaining Me, do not again contract rebirth in this transient house of sorrow."

Krishna's agreement is not only directed at *Arjuna* but also towards any *yogi* who is single-pointed, who relives Him daily, continually aware of nothing else but Divinity. Attainment of Self-realisation relies on determined and regular striving at meditation. Reliability harvests an ever-increasing deeper bliss. The beatitude achieved is the after-death state of supreme alliance with the transcendental Spirit.

Krishna then goes on to explain what he has already spoken about, "*Arjuna,* all the worlds emerging from the home of Infinite *Brahman* downwards, must go through a round of births. But those who know about the day and night of *Brahma,* each a thousand *yugas,* they know the Creator's regularity. They know ways to reverse effects of their karma."

The blind king is now thoroughly bewildered. He asked *Sanjaya* to explain the term *yuga* and how it relates to meditation and the spiritual practices already discussed.

Sanjaya explains, "Just as man lives a lifetime through days and nights, a period of one thousand cosmic cycles is *Brahma's* day and *Brahma's* night also spans through one thousand cosmic cycles. Universal processes occur in time-segments or *yugas.* For planet Earth and the solar system, their movement starts with and ends with every new cycle or *yuga.* All of Nature merges and emerges from an unmanifest field of original Nature. During a night of *Brahma,* Nature's qualities [*gunas*] are in equilibrium within primitive Nature. When an impulse disturbs this equilibrium, expression begins."

"*Yogis* as yet not freed from the world circulate back into the world, even from *Brahma's* galaxy, where the soul is in union with Self in *samadhi*. It is only on entering supreme Consciousness, that there is no rebirth. All worlds of *Brahma* – the Creator, are subject to the finite law of reappearance. But those seekers, who have merged into Supreme Consciousness while alive in the physical body, are freed from the cycles of Cosmic Creation. Even at this stage, *karmic* bonds, wants and attachments bind the *yogi* to the physical, astral and causal bodily encasements. The longer and deeper the meditations, the more the *karmic* bonds are destroyed for final emancipation," *Sanjaya* finishes.

The blind king is now able to follow the discussion. *Krishna* says to *Arjuna*, "On the coming of *Brahma's* day, everything that is obvious springs from the unmanifest. And when his night comes, into that replacement who is called unmanifest, all things disappear. That same assembly of creatures, springing forth again and again, dissolve on the coming of night and spring forth again, when day comes, but always constrained by the forces of action."

Sages know of the fields of Matter and Spirit. The soil of Awareness in Nature is as everlasting as that of Consciousness from which it emanates. Nature is not created nor is it destroyed. It is everlasting matter, emerging and then dissolving into it. Nature's *gunas* display as qualities of nature. When in disequilibrium, qualities manifest but return to an unmanifest state when *gunas* are in equilibrium. All of this exists in Consciousness.

Sanjaya tells the blind king *Dhritarashtra* that a seeker such as *Arjuna* must learn to experience the unthinking stillness. It is a condition of Awareness where one feels the enlightened subtle *chitta* or mind-intellect-ego personality. The practitioner must aim for an eventual self-revealing experience of Consciousness where soul-awareness is freed from a dormant *chitta* impression. Inwardly settled in enlightened understanding, the seeker goes into the estranged state away from Oneness.

Krishna describes the different levels of ecstasy, "There

is however another entity, unmanifest and eternal, which is beyond the unmanifest, which is not destroyed when all entities are destroyed. It is said to be unmanifest and indestructible. They also call it the highest goal, gaining which no one has ever come back. That is also my supreme focal point beyond the unmanifest. It is the field of Primordial Nature. That is a condition worthy of arriving at. He within whom are all things and beings, and by whom all this is permeated, is to be arrived at with reverence. I will now explain that timeless field of **Existence**."

"Inexpressible *Prakriti* exists as the material cause of creation. The mind and intellect, which is supreme in the cosmos, exists in *Prakriti*. Beyond all of these there is Eternity. Even when the total cosmos is wiped out, It is never destroyed. Eternity always exists as **Truth**."

"That inexpressible form is the Imperishable Essence beyond matter, mind and intellect. It is Infinite Consciousness. Individual Souls seek that **Knowledge**. Having gained It, this devotee does not have to experience worldly life again. *Arjuna,* therefore know this form also to be mine."

"The one who stays as the Omnipresent in this Creation starting with the atom in the elements to the final materialisation is also Infinite Consciousness. Know that to be also my form. It is experienced through devotion. There is no other way to grasp That also."

Krishna explains anyone who wills themselves away from the forces of Nature can choose their time of departure from the physical body. *Krishna* now continues to describe to such changed *yogis,* the paths of departure from the physical body.

"Dying while remembering Me is always consistent and uniform. There is a way *yogis* use, which releases them from worldly life. But then there is also another way by which they are repeatedly born for worldly experiences."

"One method is departing from the body during the bright light of day in summer, in the presence of the sun and its the fire. Auspicious is exiting the body during the moonlit fortnight – this is the best time but especially during the six months of the northern solstice. Such a departing person leaves knowing *Brahma.* He is fully awake who exits through this path and enters the galaxy of *Brahmaloka.*"

Krishna then goes on to describe a *yogi* who enters the realms of the lunar galaxy.

"If this *yogi* releases his life at nighttime when the dark fortnight is under the influence of lunar half of the month, especially if during the six months of the southern solstice, he enjoys the galaxy of *chandraloka.* This devotee wins the influence of the lunar light and returns into worldly existence."

The blind king is amazed to hear that *yogis* can plan their migration from the body during favorable halves of the month, year, and under favourable astrological conditions. The king is not aware that it is important for a *yogi* to have an understanding of affirmative and discriminating operations in life.

Sanjaya therefore tells the blind king about the meaningfulness of such subtle forces.

"The upper half of the human body is called 'north' while the lower half is labeled 'south'. An adulterated sheath earmarked as 'night' covers the soul when Man is slumbering. Fire and light are the vitality and luminosity of the awakened *yogi* in meditation that experiences day always. He has wiped out phenomena and has risen to experience Awareness."

"The bright half of the lunar month makes the *yogi's* awareness more perceptive of his bodily directions. His front is his eastern avenue for sense enjoyments. His spinal pathway is the western orbit of retirement in meditative practices. His lower body is the southern trajectory of decay and is the journey of indulgences. The northern passage of *udana* leads the *yogi* to the *kutastha* into awareness."

Sanjaya continues to explain what *Krishna* had been describing.

"*Yogis* who are still attached to cravings are unable to revoke worldly life and cannot experience this Awareness. They are shrouded in the darkness of illusions. Smoky views of knowledge are like the reflected lunar light of Consciousness. It becomes increasingly obscured if the uplifting experience of meditation is interrupted by intensified involvement with the descending southern forces of indulgences, illusions, and attachments. Leaving under such circumstances is unfortunate. He, who follows this path of *apana,* gets the astral and causal galaxies of expression. He then returns to earthly corporeal realms."

Then *Krishna* makes his position clearer still.

"For all manifestation to reach their final destination, there always existed two trails, the white or higher and black the lower. The bright and the dark, these two paths, are regarded as constructive and never-ending passages of the universe. By the one, he goes and never returns and by the other, he goes but comes back."

Arjuna recognises that he has just been shown the two trajectories for egression from the terrestrial sphere of materialism. The path of light would lead him to divine expression and release. The passage of darkness would escort him to protracted entanglement with the constraints of delusion and rebirth.

Krishna made cryptic and metaphorical references to the science of meditation. Competence in freeing the soul from its three encasements, physical, astral and causal, has to be earned by prior practice and perseverance in meditation.

Arjuna knew he had to persevere on the path of fire to reach *nirvana* or final liberation. He had spent a lifetime carrying out endless actions to achieve untold knowledge. His mind registered little of this knowledge after their productiveness ended. Those actions and knowledge that persevered have become part of his disposition as *samskaras.* These will leave with him at his physical passing.

He is not certain if these *vasanas* or habits will cause him confusion in his eagerness for liberation. *Krishna* has just told him the idea that is strongest at the moment of death commands his next beginning. The soul sketches its own journey ahead.

Remembering that death is the crowning glory of life, *Arjuna* is convinced that he should be constantly aiming for means by which the closing moments are sanctified, uncontaminated and faultless. He must rebuild the mind with nobler actions and tendencies. He must clean his personality of mind-intellect-ego or *chitta.* By scrupulously discovering errors, he must become answerable to them before obliviousness chisels them into his *chitta* disposition.

Filling the mind with noble reflections, performing *karma* as his inborn duty or *svadharma,* he must dedicate his mind in purity and devotion or *vikarma. Arjuna* must re-spin his life drop by drop, into an unbroken stream of divine reminiscence. With such constancy, he is sure to reach the ocean.

The first scientific step to be taken by *Arjuna* is to gain control of life by surrendering to the brilliant Inner Light of Discrimination. Only submission and perseverance reroute the natural flow of such energy away from materialism.

Krishna interrupts *Arjuna's* thoughts.

"Those who know about these two paths are never deluded. To arrive at liberation from the sufferings of worldly life or *samsara,* O *Arjuna,* always remain in Soul awareness. Whatever profit and satisfaction you earn by studying the *Vedas,* performing different *yagnas* and sacrifices, practicing austerities and penance and renunciations are prejudiced in comparison with the experience of Consciousness. Those who dedicate their lives and persevere at the realm of Consciousness go beyond *Prakriti.* They gain the highest liberation of *nirvana* in the realms of *Brahman.* Here the self effulgent Self-revealing Consciousness fully satisfies all wants and there is no need to come back. He remains in indestructible peace."

11. Dedication

Sanjaya had tried to convince the blind king that he can be released from worldly bondage or *samsara* by considering his profession or *svadharma*. It would then be an affirmation that he must act. If *karma* was performed as dutiful worship or *vikarma* to the Supreme Self, it would attain distinction. If this offering to Nature or *vikarma* was made with the right knowledge that It is Consciousness who is everywhere and in everything, yet remains distinct from it all, he would encounter Awareness through meditation.

Krishna, meantime, wants to summarize his discussion with *Arjuna.* He wants to explain and solve the mystery of simultaneous immanence and transcendence of the Spirit in Nature. Through meditation, the *yogi* in *Arjuna* can unite with the transcendental Spirit, beyond all expressions but he can also remain immanent and active in the Cosmic Dream of God.

And *Krishna* turned to *Arjuna* amid the cacophony and commotion of horses and the clamor of infantry members waiting in anticipation.

"What I am about to tell you next is not only the highest knowledge but it is the most pure. But it is a supreme secret. It has to be realized by oneself. This knowledge is beyond the power of words. It has been tested on the touchstone of direct experience."

Arjuna replies, "You have told me so much in the last few minutes, *Krishna.* You have mentioned different *yagnas* and *yogas* but you have also said these penances and practices need qualified doers. These rites are filled with subtle ideas. There is no real liberation except through the *Vedic* path, but even here you say, few have the fitness to study them.

What then happens to the rest of humanity, *Krishna*? What is the supreme essence of the *Vedas,* please tell me?"

"Because you do not dispute this teaching, I will now tell you *Arjuna,* that most mysterious knowledge as well as the experience, knowing which, you will be freed from effects of your past actions."

"When seekers are absorbed in the *kutastha* above and between the eyebrows, they become free of unfavorable inclinations of likes-and-dislikes, lust, anger, greed, possessiveness, pride, jealousy and individuality. The deeply embedded intuitive knowledge of Infinite Consciousness, about which has been written in the scriptures, becomes obvious. Knowing That, you can cross the impure world of worldly existence of *samsara,*" *Krishna* said.

Sanjaya senses that *Krishna* would speak about the rare power of the name of God. Personal opinions and experienced revelations reveal the secret knowledge of meditation. They need examination because of intuitive intelligence and support through knowledge of the scriptures. *Krishna* encourages honest questions but discourages the petty arguments that perpetuate ignorance.

Krishna admits that he has been revealing a higher knowledge, which may remain a riddle to those of minimum powers of understanding. But he also reassures all by stating, "This distinguished science of meditation is a majestic mystery, eminently cleansing, knowable, consistent with the sacred laws, easy to practice, and imperishable. The experience of Awareness is the greatest knowledge and grants the highest bliss. It is gained easily by **constant** practice. The information base of such activity is experienced directly and remains permanently engraved in the seeker. Know this to be the Knowledge of the Self. Of all the secrets this is the highest because it displays as wisdom."

When grasped, this intuitive knowledge purges the mind of mistaken beliefs and distortions. It has the capacity to advance evolution and to nurture inner growth and self-unfoldment. If this insight is used in the practical application of meditation, it becomes a permanent helper of spiritual growth."

Sanjaya assures the blind king that meditation is the king of sciences, in that it gives to the *yogi,* this royal secret. As a peerless purifier, it is the essence of *dharma* – Man's righteous duty to make efforts to shape a personal view of Truth.

Krishna encourages *Arjuna* to accept the revealed knowledge of the true nature of Awareness and Consciousness.

"O *Arjuna* my friend who forever has chastised foes, people who have no faith or reverence for this incomparable sacred doctrine which grants self-realization, do not reach Me. Empty of knowledge and the experience of My bliss, they remain enmeshed in the cravings of pleasure. Enslaved they return to the path of darkness of life-and-death again and again."

Sanjaya also encourages the blind king to have faith and not doubt what *Krishna* has said. Men lacking faith in this *dharma* cannot expect to understand or experience the metamorphosing influence on the self. Without devotion to the practices that grant realisation, they tread the worldly life or *samsara* in a deluded state.

Krishna backs the wisdom of Self-realization as the highest branch of all human knowledge. Because the Truth of Oneness can only be experienced intuitively, this conclusion is the essence or *dharma* of all religions and the core mystery of how the Self is both immanent and transcendent. *Krishna* echoes this Truth.

"From an Inexpressible Form I have created this whole expanse of worldly existence in an Expressible Form. All this Creation is in Me. I am not in them. I pervade the entire Universe in my unmanifest form. All entities are in Me but I do not remain in them. Nor yet are all entities in Me. See my divine power. The total cosmos exists because of

Infinite Consciousness. Supporting all entities and producing all entities, I do not stay in those created entities."

The blind king finds this assertion both paradoxical and disconcerting. *Sanjaya* is now forced to explain the Divine Mystery where all beings are seemingly not in Him nor does He linger in them. Yet He alone is their Creator and Preserver as well as their efficient cause.

Sanjaya says, "Even though all souls stay in His Consciousness, their physical, mental, and intellectual characteristics do not. They are effects of primordial Nature. Supported by Her delusory powers of *Maya,* She individualises them as the self, and keeps them within their wants, habits, and feeling of independent existence."

Krishna goes on to describe himself as transcending even original Nature who's Awareness sits in the cusp of His own Consciousness:

"The mystery of creation is such that even though Infinite Consciousness is the Self in all created things and It establishes them by holding and ruling over them, It is not bound to these plants, creatures, beings or things. It does not live in them. Soaked internally and even externally with Awareness and Consciousness, these beings travel worldly existence birth afterbirth. Just as the great and omnipresent infinity always occupies space, understand that all entities live in Me, in the same way."

Dhritarashtra is confused. "Just as air moves freely in infinite space and has its existence in space, yet air is different from space. So it is also for all creatures that have their being in God but are not omnipresent in Him," *Sanjaya* said. "Creation, although filled with God, yet it is not composed of Him, nor does it reveal His essence. He pervades it but does not live in it. His mysterious power is a vibration-less unmanifest cosmic consciousness, which underlies all of the obviously vibrating cosmic creation – a puzzle indeed."

Krishna tells *Arjuna* that this fact can be intellectually analysed and even understood but must be reflected upon until experienced in meditation. When knowledge and awareness agree, the inner experience matches the enlightenment. Then, *Krishna* says the unenlightened soul has no choice but to return to the field of Original Nature.

"Just as air within the sky can travel everywhere and is also powerful, it continues unmixed and separate from everything else. In the same way, this Cosmos, although staying in Consciousness, is bound by Unconsciousness and continues in that way. All entities O son of *Kunti* – *Arjuna* arrive at My nature at the close of a *kalpa* during every cycle of creation. Regulating my own independent nature, I create again. In this whole total of flexible entities, because of outcomes of actions, there is subordination to Nature."

"At the end of a cycle of creation or *kalpa,* when dissolution occurs after thousands of *yugas,* all things and beings return to the unmanifested state of Cosmic Nature as *Prakriti.* The three *gunas* become balanced and dissolve into Infinite Consciousness. Then, at the beginning of another cycle, the three *gunas* as matter-qualities are jolted and again spread forward into the next *kalpa,"* *Krishna* tells *Arjuna.*

"In this way all exist in the universe. Because they are bound by the power of previous habits or *samskaras,* they adopt the three *gunas* according to their particular conditions. They again come about in the form of created beings and things. This act, however, O *Arjuna,* does not fetter Me who sits as one unconcerned, being nonattached to these acts of creation."

The blind king is a deluded being of veiled understanding. *Sanjaya* had to explain the same facts, in a different way.

"Reanimating *Prakriti* or Nature, is His own emanation. Again and again He produces this host of creatures, all subject to the finite laws of Nature. At the end of a cycle, the Spirit awakens Nature and causes Her to resume her objective display, all the time supported and permeated by the vibrating enlivening Spirit – Om."

Krishna goes on to interpret the workings of Nature, "Because Consciousness is not attached to or within anything,

It remains in aloofness. Through Me the onlooker, the original nature produces the universe of movable and immovable. Even though they get dissolved and created over and again, they exist because of My nearness."

Krishna declares that He is divine and has taken on a human form. He knows he is not understood and is discounted by the ignorant that do not support that he is the Lord of All. This happens when Man lacks in devotion. This misunderstanding is never-ending in all religions and in all tribes.

"Benumbed by the enthusiasm of wants and because their temperaments permeate likes and dislikes, they become enthralled in pastimes that bring them transient worldly happiness. Made senseless by purposeless debates about the truth of scriptural knowledge, these unenlightened beings have not experienced the preeminence of soul awareness. Unconcerned they remain outside the knowledge of Consciousness while in a human body. Not knowing My supreme nature as the great lord of entities, ignorant people of vain hopes, futile acts, self-conceited knowledge, and confused minds become wedded to the delusive nature of *asura* and *rakshasa* or evildoers. They discount Me as having assumed a human body."

"How do mortals recognise divine beings then? Does He hide somewhere? If he is a gem among humankind, is he hidden somewhere? How does Man find him?" asks *Dhritarashtra.*

Sanjaya again explains *Krishna's* statements to the blind deluded king of extroverted interests, "Those pure ones who are *sattvic* saints are able to recognise a human expression of the Lord, Sire. Do not dishonor the person of the Lord who is obvious in the human form. It is the Lord that appears as all whether moving or unmoving. One does not need aids to see or find Him. Relate to the Lord in whatever is eaten, seen, felt, heard, or tasted. Relate to Him in every act, Sire."

Krishna explains the activities of the saintly, "Know that these *sattvic*or pure beings know that only Self-Consciousness is the indestructible eternal substance and cause of all that is created. Understanding that It is this sole filling presence that causes Mother Nature to give birth to the animate and the inanimate, they worship. Because of transcendent Consciousness, the Awareness immanent in *Prakriti* ensures the worlds revolve in alternating cycles of creation and dissolution. Saints take refuge only in the astral world of creation. They honor Nature as an *upasana* or worship while immersed and stable in the Self."

"How is worship or *upasana* performed, *Krishna*?" asks *Arjuna.*

"Worship of Infinite Consciousness has been written about in the *Vedas.* Different *upasanas* are prescribed for bringing the worshipper and God nearer together. Man seeks freedom from the sorrows of physical [*adhibhautic*], astral [*adhidaivic*] and causal [*adhyatmic*] sources. Therefore some worship Me by chanting and others perform many rites. Some endlessly prostrate to Me. Some believe he is separate from Me and others imagine Me in a Cosmic Form. Many worshipers use their senses to offer Me services. Only the wise know that sorrows born of lust and want cannot be permanently stifled by *upasana.* The partnership in worshipful want reignites suffering," *Krishna* replies.

"But *Krishna,* humankind who suffers these three types of sorrows want them ended. That is the most important objective of an individual self," *Arjuna* pleads.

Dhritarashtra echoes *Arjuna's* anguish.

Sanjaya comes to the rescue, "If one dies, he must be born again and if born, he must die also. Bound to worldly life, Man cannot reach *nirvana* or liberation. To arrive at liberation, Man needs to free himself from both life-and-death."

"Then what is the way, *Sanjaya*?"

"If the self cannot put up with the path of emancipation and its beatitude, he cannot meet Infinite Consciousness beyond Creation. To end suffering from physical, astral and causal sources, Man must worship measures that lead to Consciousness. By taking up the path of devotion and knowledge, Man is introduced to Soul Consciousness. Devotion imprisons and cancels mental and intellectual restlessness. Introversion leads to self-revealing *yogic* methods which lead him to experience Awareness first and Consciousness later, as a personal encounter," *Sanjaya* replied.

"Although the ignorant are oblivious to the immanent Nature of Awareness existing within omnipresent transcendental Consciousness, spiritual seekers must contact the creative force by devotion to **Om** as It expresses Itself in space and time," *Sanjaya* concluded.

Krishna again tells *Arjuna* that Consciousness is not the Maker of creatures – he is the origin.

"Knowledgeable saints, O *Arjuna,* who are possessed of a divine nature, and have minds directed to nothing else, worship Me, knowing Me to be the origin of all entities and as indestructible. Always glorifying Me, or striving with firm vows, or bowing down to Me, with reverence and ever devoted, they worship Me. Others again, performing the sacrifice of knowledge, worship Me, some as one, some as distinct, some as pervading the universe in many forms."

Sanjaya is asked to clarify *Krishna's* statements.

"Just as we can be aware of, yet indifferent to the contents of our field of awareness, so also Consciousness is the witness and neutral about the Universe."

The king looked at *Sanjaya* questioningly and *Sanjaya* continued, "Impelled by an impulse of need to express itself I Dream **Om** in Consciousness. **This Spirit** produces the field of original Nature. She displays the entire universe out of Itself. The impulse to reveal is the first Cause. All that happens are Effects of the original cause, the original impulse," *Sanjaya* says.

"Incarnated souls who are lacking in insight, who are unaware of the existence of the causative influences of Nature, can never accept the reality of Awareness in Consciousness. Their wishes and thoughts and actions are all in vain. They are self-serving because of egoism. They are empty of knowledge and remain tenaciously attached to self satisfying, ill-tempered, confused, and deluded states of awareness. Such men have the deluded nature of fiends or *rakshasa* and demons and *asuras,"*

Sanjaya continues, "While the ordinary person attaches great importance to the worldly spectacle, the *yogi* takes God's dream lightly. Spiritually awake, these souls intuitively know the origin of all souls and do not allow anything to distract their attention while concentrating on the science of meditation."

"These evolved *yogis* are ever absorbed in the awareness of Nature's divine qualities and offer their undeviating minds in homage to Consciousness, as the imperishable Source of all beings, through Nature," *Sanjaya* defines.

"Who are these *yogis?*" asked *Dhritarashtra.*

"Spiritually awake, these *yogis* are constantly absorbed in Consciousness. At the same time prostrating with adoration and serving Awareness in Nature, they remain fixed and determined in their high ambition, to transcend even the vibrating **Om** and into the self-revealing Light of Consciousness. They worship and praise in ever deepening meditation until they reach the vibration-less house of Consciousness."

Dhritarashtra was silent. To him it was inconceivable to transcend Om.

Krishna meanwhile continues to describe the offerings

and actions of the self-manifesting soul. The soul regards the Eternal Being as the all-pervading, all-knowing reality of all of nature. Therefore *Krishna* began by first explaining his immanence.

"Listen carefully to my words *Arjuna* and about the description that I am All. I am the *Vedic* sacrifice of the fire ritual. I am the sacrifice commanded in the *smritis* or codes of law. I am *swadha* or the offerings to the spirit. I am the cure faultlessness in herbs. I am the incantation as well as the sacrificial offering. I am the fire and my appearance is also of the sacrificial gift."

"I am the father of this universe, the mother, the creator and the grandsire. I am the entity to be known the means by which everything is unblocked by the syllable *Om.* I am the pure *pranava* Om spoken of in the *Rik,* the *Saman,* and the *Yajus Vedas*".

Arjuna's mind races to analyse the logic of *Krishna's* statements. Because God alone exists, He is in the performance all intentional actions. He is in acts of self-giving, in the herbs which nurture health, and in the truth-revealing scriptures. He is the scaffold in all-spiritual practices. He is in the transformative actions of astral enlivening energies of *prana,* and also in the self-erasing processes of the environment.

Arjuna reasons improved awareness about the presence of Consciousness forces seekers to perform inner rituals. In this higher state of awareness he naturally seeks knowledge and worships the Cosmic Body through selfless service. This *yogi* understands that he is immanent in the rite as *kratu.* He is immanent in the sacrifice, in the oblation of food offering to ancestors or *pitris* and recognises this immanence in offerings also. The giver, the offering and the receiver therefore must be one.

Vibration-less Consciousness dreams of creating vibrating Awareness, *Arjuna* thinks. God therefore can be realised by souls seeking liberation. He must first immerse in the enlivening Holy Spirit – the cosmic sound of Om, which supports all materialisation. After discovering the compelling influences of Nature by which all appearances exist, he must understand what motivates the self towards materialism. He must understand what it is that motivates a soul to turn for satisfaction and fulfillment in worldly pleasures. Yet, serving and nurturing Nature instead could also give this pleasure.

Krishna now clarifies his role as the supreme beginning of all happenings, the adjustment force in Nature, and the substructure of all exhibition and dissolution:

"In this world which is the fruit of *karma,* I am the governor. I see good and evil and keep order. In the place of enjoyment I am goodness. I create the world and again destroy it. I am the seed of all and the supporter of the Cosmos. There is nothing besides Me, *Arjuna.*"

"I am the heat of the sun and the rain in the clouds. I am the life in all, sometimes involved in creation and at another, in destruction. Everywhere I exist in physical and subtle forms."

"Although all that is perishable emerges from Me, that Beginningless Eternal Substance, I am still the goal, the supporter, the lord, the onlooker, the home, the refuge, and the friend. I am the source, the destruction, the support, the receptacle and the indestructible seed. I give heat and I produce and suspend rain. I am immortality and death. And I am existent and the nonexistent, O *Arjuna.*"

Sanjaya helps break the silence at the blind king's palace from where he is able to view *Arjuna* and *Krishna* in their chariot right in the centre of the battlefield between the two armies.

"The Supreme Self is the One repository where all dream-blueprints are stored at the end of a *kalpa* or cycle of creation. Here as the Imperishable Seed He urges Nature or *Prakriti* to return to Her kaleidoscopic form. He is the contradiction responsible for contrasts and opposites under the sway of *maya* – He creates *maya* hallucination. It is He who is the Cosmic Magician who dreams the Cosmic Dream."

"Who is to decide that *Krishna* is positively God? Should the world welcome him as worthy? Who indeed can make out the distinction between the blameless and the corrupt? Should humanity accept as factual only what they understand or is there anything more? Are we to presume that it is only the materialist worldly who understands what I want for my children?" asks the blind king.

"Sire, first why don't you accept there is nothing wrong with your ancestry and the governing reasons in which you were born? Creation of your family circumstance is only a reflection of your own mind. What you are and what you bring to the mirror is representing how you see the world. It is in the eyes of the beholder that decides what you covet from the form of this world. The sensitivity or *bhavana* you bring to the Lord's creation purify actions. This is what *Krishna* means. Whatever you do, whatever you eat, whatever rites or austerities you perform, whatever you give, do it as an offering to Me," *Sanjaya* replies.

"Why can I not do all this for me?" asks the blind king.

"Whatever actions you engage in whether good or bad, when giving to the Lord, a new dimension enters the action. The instance of surrender changes the act when it passes the formula of dedication. By the psyche injected into the deed, the significance of the act is burgeoned," *Sanjaya* replied.

"But there seems to be a classification of beginning exercises and awareness and of their appropriateness," complained the king.

"Once the sentiment of dedication to the Lord endures in the mind, you are granted an authorisation for emancipation. The reputation of the Lord has the competence of attenuating to cinders all deeds and moments of darkness. Offer the action and arrive at his grace revealing as Awareness," replied *Sanjaya.*

Krishna now explains the riddle of heavenly Awareness.

"The *Brahmin* who has studied the *Rik, Yajur* and *Sama Vedas* prays for Awareness. This *Veda*-ritualist takes up formally restorative rituals. After withdrawal from the body, he gains the paradise of his wants. According to his *karma,* he enjoys supernal ambition. He, who knows the three branches of knowledge, also drinks the *soma* juice – the nectar of life. His offenses are cleaned through sacrifice and he can seek admission into kingdom come. Having arrived at this sacred region of gods and having enjoyed divine pleasures of heavenly worlds, on depletion of his entitlement, he reenters the mortal world. It is thus that he who accepts the doctrines of the three *Vedas* and wishes for objects of wants, earns cycles of birth and death."

"Why does this *yogi* not arrive at *nirvana*?" asks the blind king.

"The delusions of those who aspire for liberation are not cleaned by Knowledge. They want to enter heaven and are promoted by influences of redemption through super-consciousness. They experience what they wish. There, in the sacred kingdom of the astral deities or *devas,* these devotees enjoy the subtle celestial pleasures. But after delighting in the glorious regions of heavens, these beings of flawed views, at expiring their good *karma,* return to earth. Thus supported by the scriptural rules, wishing the enjoyments of promised heavenly rewards, they travel the cyclic path between heaven and earth."

"Good dreams are still dreams of the astral spheres. A wise seeker seeks Oneness in vibration-less Consciousness as the supreme goal, beyond the spheres of Nature's vibrating Awareness," *Sanjaya* added.

Krishna describes the trajectory of a *karma yogi,* "Those people who thinking of Me without directing their minds to anything else, worship Me. Of those who are always devoted to Me, I make them gifts and preserve what they have. After enjoying huge amounts of heavenly pleasures, once the benefits of their good works are gone, they return to the realms of mortals. Bound to fruits of action, they forever come and go from worldly existence."

Krishna continues to describe a *yogi* who wishes Awareness. "Those who know there is nobody and nothing but Me to reflect on, I bring them closer and closer towards Awareness. I take care of their needs by reducing their sorrows more and more. Even these devotees who are infused with faith worship other godheads, even they, O son of *Kunti,* worship Me alone, though irregularly."

Next *Krishna* speaks of a *yogi* who worships other gods; "All seekers who preserve their awakened state by worshiping other gods are also united with the Spirit of Awareness. I am the enjoyer and the lord of all such sacrifices. They however, do not know Me. Therefore they fall off from heaven."

Krishna speaks in defense of those who choose to serve other aspects of God's expression. "Those who worship other gods, they worship only Awareness. All these reverential devotees do not seek liberation for Consciousness. Nonetheless I am indeed the only Enjoyer and Lord of all sacrifices. But they are worshippers of lesser gods who do not see Me in My true nature. Therefore, they also fall."

Krishna described self-controlled men who worship, ever united to Awareness through unbroken veneration. Nature supplies all their shortages and seekers make permanent gains in grace or *kshema.* Absorbed in Awareness they receive the attractiveness of physical regeneration, psychological and physiological transformation, and spiritual unfoldment. Life is wholesome and self-referring.

When the *yogi's* actions are in harmony with Nature's, he receives the grace to perform uplifting actions. Steadfast in the ambition to realise God, his awareness progresses through higher levels towards soul awakening. *Krishna* says even those devoted and faithful to other imagined gods worship Him alone, though not in the right way. "While foolish beings spend their valuable life seeking material wealth which must be abandoned at death, *yogis* use their efforts to find imperishable wisdom banked in endless time for future use. The strongest feeling at death decides their future address. Those who have communicated with the celestials, have nowhere else to go but only to come again."

Krishna next goes on to explain that Man who arrives at what he wishes.

"Those who devote to ancestral rituals arrive at their realm from where the elemental world of ancestors emerges. If attached to these gods of rituals, they win their heaven. But those who worshipfully meditate on the soul, they become filled with the Spirit and merge with Infinite Consciousness. They reach the house of God or *Brahman.*"

"Why *Krishna*?" asks *Arjuna.*

"They whose deeds are directed to the *pitris* arrive at *pitris* of the forefathers. Those who worship the domain of gods direct their homage to the minor spirits of matter. Worshippers of ghosts or *bhutas* win *bhutas.* They, who honor Me, will always reach Me, *Arjuna.*"

Arjuna understands that God clearly declares Himself through all that invoke Him with earnestness. Adherents who worship theories of God and the various forces of Nature discover their identity with them and meet them also. He knew of many friends who while dying wished to meet and communicate with these astral deities or *devas.* He was now being told, that too, was possible. Those who yearn to connect with family and ancestors or *pitris,* go to the manes in dependency. Those who worship elemental nature spirits or *bhutas* go seeking them.

Arjuna was unaffected. As a devotee of awareness he hoped he would gradually experience and awaken into God consciousness. Until awakened to Truth, his searching would continue to cling to beliefs partially revealed throughout his childhood. Still entangled with his mental daydreams, his illusory opinions were endless. Only souls devoted to knowledge and self-realisation could awaken into God-Consciousness.

"*Arjuna* I love the pure-hearted who reverentially offer Me their complete devotion. The one who offers me a gift of a leaf, a flower, a fruit, or water, if given with pure intent and a heart immersed in his soul, his reverential sacrifice fixes his with Me."

With that said, *Krishna* encourages Arjuna to come forward into His presence.

"Whatever you do *Arjuna,* whatever you eat, whatever you drink, whatever you give, whatever austerities you perform, manage it in such a way, O son of *Kunti,* that it may be an offering to Me. All those human endeavors with their good or bad *karmic* reactions should be performed with the intent of engaging Soul-Awareness. Thus you will be freed from the fetters of action and reaction having good and evil harvest. With self-endowed renunciation and devotion, you will be released and will come to Me."

Arjuna is deeply moved. He should dedicate all his actions as offerings to God. With the soul steadfastly anchored to the Infinite, every moment could be a harmonious renunciation and a relationship with the rhythms of life. He knew God is unprejudiced towards all beings because he is an identical breath of life expressing God's authenticity.

None is distasteful, and none is venerable to God. But, those who give God their deep attachment meet God in them and themselves in God. Even if a person does not agree with undivided dedication, as long as he exerts his best, he is on the right course of evolution. Therefore, *Arjuna* mentally offers all unjust incentives at God's feet and be helped to do virtuous actions. He knows if he uses this method of self-improvement, he can get delivered from the confines of indulgence and harvest of both blameless and corrupt actions. He craves to arrive at the Being of Consciousness.

Arjuna is convinced he can live up to his supreme potential even if he was a radical criminal.

Sanjaya notices that *Arjuna's* mind and heart have accepted the feeling that *Krishna* is his unswerving friend.

This friendship has ripened into a balanced affinity of assurance and loving esteem. *Krishna* will always be by *Arjuna's* side. He knows no anxiety because he has fathomed the Truth about achieving grace. It is not that *Arjuna* does not have the knowledge of devotion – he had not understood the instruction. He was taught not only to give of himself, but in what manner he was to offer himself at the feet of the Lord.

Krishna adds, "The Self lives equally in all. Whoever worships Me with devotion as Consciousness in all creatures, he lives in an awakened state. There is none hateful to me and none dear. They, who worship Me with reverence, are in Me and I also am in them. If even a person of wicked conduct worships Me, without worshipping anyone else, he should be regarded as admirable, for his efforts are well directed. Such a person soon becomes a virtuous soul and arrives at eternal tranquillity. Know O son of *Kunti,* that none devoted to Me is ever destroyed. For, O *Arjuna,* even they who may be of immoral birth and parenting, thorough charlatans, and those of disgraceful inclinations, even they, when they turn for help to Me arrive at the preeminent objective."

Sanjaya hopes the blind king can be stopped waging this unjust war against the *Pandavas.* Even one with a depraved personality can develop into a virtuous saint if mingled in Self-Consciousness. Intentional behaviour transformation might help remove unwelcome conduct and inclinations by cultivating contemplation and scrutiny of his selfishness. The intensity of his prejudiced instincts may be mild, moderate or severe – but they all have caused pain and suffering.

"O king, your actions need to be blessed by the Lord. The transaction will then pick up its own potency towards integrity and supremacy. With that competence, you will have abandoned not only your ambition for authority but also the outcomes of your misdeeds. Whether virtuous or not, you will have abandoned the circumstances of this immoral armed conflict. The act itself will fill you with delight and comfort," *Sanjaya* appealed.

Arjuna has rationalised that those who are unwavering to the practice of composure or *sattva* earn a determined steadfast mind. They are able to remain in the security of pledges made to their own Awareness.

Krishna augments *Arjuna's* convictions, "Take sanctuary in God and you will realise the Supreme Fulfillment. Even those who have been inbred in depraved surroundings, regardless of what or who they are can arrive at accomplishment. In your present condition, you have only been raised into the distinct culture of contemplation. Unlike fraternities and your elected constituents, the Eternal Self never cancels anyone because of birth, sex, racial or cultural governing reasons, or vocation."

Also, *Krishna* reminds *Arjuna* that his ancestors unceasingly defeated all practices of oppression and prejudice. They never feared to endure by the rules of Truth, "*Arjuna,* your lineage is both impressive and divine. Fundamental to your riches is the passage to ascension guiding you to self-unfoldment. Earnest resolutions to cast-off sense indulgences and needs leads you to effective existing and potent spiritual exercises. That is all that is needed. You will be discerning and be guided by your integrity to fight that what is unrighteous."

Krishna then goes on to describe his relationship with devotees who have or are awakening to Nature and Consciousness. *Krishna* compares *Arjuna,* his friend and devotee, to a pure mind. He advises *Arjuna* to come closer to him.

"Be assured that despite their tendencies they are all my beloved, *Arjuna;* the worldliness of *vaishyas,* the labouring and greed focused *sudras.* They are of gentle weaknesses who take shelter in Me, and will rise above worldly existence. What then shall I say of sanctified holy *brahmins* of pure minds and also of *kshatriya* warriors who fight righteousness for Me? Having come to this transient and strife-causing uneasy world, you be engaged in My worship. O *Arjuna,* fix your mind in Me. Be My disciple and My worshipper. Surrender to Me and thus make Me your sanctuary. Apply yourself to the preoccupation in meditation. You will come to Me."

Arjuna seeks further information, "*Krishna* you make this expedition an uncomplicated exercise. By consecrating all actions to the Lord, moment to moment, a pledge becomes shaped. You have assured me all self-dedicated routines will reach fulfillment. Such claims as You specify must be the result of endeavors of many births. The heart must have been previously drawn to and soon awakened into You through many lives?"

"Only inconsistent endeavours prevent self-unfoldment to result into soul-unfoldment. Therefore O mighty prince *Arjuna* of the *Kuru* race, fix your mind on virtue and through endless worship unite first with Nature's Awareness. Having served Her, transcend Nature and merge with Consciousness, the highest Goal," *Krishna* said.

"First learn to see God in the natural and the mighty. Having recognised Him in the Mighty, seek Him in even a grain of sand. This is the only way to resolve the mystery of immanence in Nature and transcendence in Spirit. In the *yoga* of meditation, the *yogi* is the real prince and king of peace. He rules and directs his kingdom of activity with a devoted mind and heart to Awareness, and by sacrificing his bodily actions at Mother Nature's feet as an oblation."

12. Contemplation

Having shown him the art of consecration for transfiguring his biography, *Arjuna* started to speculate if God positively exists. World doubts about violence, intimidation, hunger, homelessness, and poverty have discounted many fundamental principles of life and made devotion to the Lord problematic. What then is one to do? How can devotion become comfortable? *Arjuna* wants a condensed portrayal of how he can distinguish the eminence of the Supreme Self. *Arjuna* would have settled for an understandable portrait that could be grasped by any average intellect.

And *Krishna* expresses himself with persevering kindness, "Listen again, O mighty-armed *Arjuna,* and listen to my powerful words spoken from an aspiration for your good. I will tell you that with which you are contented."

Arjuna has not sufficiently been appeased with what was said previously, and *Krishna* now promises to reveal even more about the innermost self and the Cosmic Self.

"Even hosts of sages and gods who reflect regularly know not My beginning. Even the great *rishis* who are worshippers of *Brahman* do not experience Me. I am and have existed in every way before all these gods and great *rishis* or sages. He who understands Me as the Supreme Lord of the worlds, without birth and beginning, he the enlightened among mortals, is free from all sins. For your benefit *Arjuna,* I say you can meet Me at the *kutastha.*"

The blind king expressed his bafflement. He understood that what is existent in the simple must be present in the complex also. *Krishna* was describing the Divinity of Creation. It seemed like it is a sealed book, which is packaged in coverings of awe-inspiring statements. To the king, the form of the Lord has to be familiar. It must be an idealisation of caring and love. How else did *Krishna* expect humankind to worship the Lord? If the Lord cannot be seen or heard or understood where is He to be touched or found?

Krishna continues, "Those who worship, see, and understand Me, know that I have no birth and no beginning. I am the self-revealing Lord. Neither the multitude of angels or *devas* nor the great sages or *rishis* who have achieved temporary or permanent knowledge of God's Uncreated Nature, fathom the origin of their Source, because the Source is their derivation. But whoever realizes God to be Unborn and Beginning-less as well as the Sovereign Lord of Creation – that man has defeated the mirage and achieved the untainted state, even while wearing an impermanent physique. Enlightenment cannot be comprehensive unless the uninformed mask is erased through unwavering concentration."

"How is the veil of ignorance removed?" asked the king.

"By concentrated meditation when the breath stills, the Self realises he is above and beyond birth and death. The worldly plane of existence never again mesmerises him. His mind remains unscattered and rests in *Brahman.* This can only happen by withdrawing from physical distraction through breath control and lifting the life force to the royal seat of understanding. Here merging with the *pranava* is transcendental meditation," *Sanjaya* said.

"In this field of awareness, knowledge is experienced only through consummate contemplation. From this state of superconsciousness, the *yogi* can expect to experience even higher states of Awareness until he merges into the incomparable state of Consciousness," *Sanjaya* concludes.

Arjuna wants *Krishna* to describe the boundless beauty of this divine picture called *Brahman* or God. Meanwhile *Krishna* realises this portrait he is to describe must be of an expected and familiar form of God. "For you to recognise *Brahman,* you must still the mind. Self-revealing knowledge will become obvious, *Arjuna.* If your life is not deluded by worldly lusts, the forgiving intelligence will allow you to remain in the *kutastha.* Your intuitiveness will recognise that I am the intelligence in the intellect, the wisdom in knowledge, the absence of delusion, forgiveness, truth, self-restraint through control of the senses, and peace of mind with its resulting calm tranquillity. I am both joy and sorrow, birth and death, and fear and fearlessness."

"But I have been told this before, *Krishna.*"

"Remember O *Arjuna,* that one needs to be free of aggression and jealousy against the world. Until you are able to see all as being *Brahman,* do not expect to be at peace. A qualified teacher must admit you into the technique of meditating at the *kutastha.* Become armed with abstention from harm and noninjury, evenness of mind, contentment and serenity, reclusiveness with austerities and self-disciplines, open handedness with charity, and equipoise through fame and infamy. All these features will sway the worldly in you towards *Brahman.* You will recognise that all creatures arise from differences in My own Nature."

"*Krishna* I was once told that Creation is a Dream," *Arjuna* said.

"This drama and dream of Creation occurs in My Consciousness. It starts with the seven sages or *rishis* of Truth who represent the seven conditions of nature and the four *Manus* who govern and regulate all universal operations during the four quarters of a cycle of creation. They all begin with Me alone. They are the first ones born from My own seat of passion for insight. Nature's Awareness declares Herself agreeing with Her conditions at distinct levels of materialisation. Even these qualities of being arise from My Consciousness alone. *Arjuna,* nothing can exist independent of Me."

"What and how did they, the first beings appear?"asks *Arjuna.*

Krishna continued, "The seven great aspects of Nature are the five elements, the mind and the intellect. They are the ordinance and law of universal processes. The four emergences of a cycle of Creation are governed by the *Manus.* They were there before the seven *rishis.* They vibrated themselves with life force, cosmic matter, space, and time. The four *manus* are ancestors of the human race. They emanated from Me. From these progenitors came all living and immovable creatures and things. They are variations of My nature. Born from My mind thoughts, they are granted with My creative energy. All these in this world are my offspring."

"How do I realise this what you have just described *Krishna*?"

"By abiding with a stilled mind in the *kutastha,* O *Arjuna.* You will arrive here away from the elements and all My many expressions. You will behold here My essence, My unruffled state of Stillness. Having seen Me thus, expect to advance released of needs as well as doubt. Remain there in a protected state of being."

"The course of action you have spoken about is troublesome to carry through by a common mortal, such as myself. That kingdom you describe which is within is not that of the humanity I am familiar with. I see all Creation filled with objects of creation. I want all creation to communicate with me. Where is that heavenly vision I want to see?" *Arjuna* pleads.

"It is from Me that all that you see is revealed. That which appears to you exists in Me alone. He, who meditates as just described, witnesses this preeminence. My mystical power expresses and displays itself in the macrocosm and also in the microcosm. When the mind is in meditative equipoise, its personality remains united with that same state, far from worldly interactions. Possessed of unswerving devotion, you will see Me everywhere and in everything. Of this there is no doubt."

Sanjaya tells the blind king that although *yogis* are advised to spend time distinguishing knowledge of Nature and Spirit, they must also endeavor to become aware of their relationship with the Infinite. Restraint and adherence to the practice of restraint are the first steps. Concerted practice to energise the physical body, and transform the psychological and physiological body is the second step. Stilling the body in *asana* and withdrawing from the objects of the senses and mind through breath control is the third step. Lifting the enlivening life force up the spinal pathway is the fourth step. Having arrived at the *kutastha* in the spiritual eye behind and between the eyebrows, the *yogi* can expect to experience that which is Awareness. Here, the *yogi* hears the enlivening and vibrating **Om,** feels the life-giving breath, tastes the nectar of life, and witnesses the energy of Awareness. He merges with this Subject. He must now enter the territory and remain there preoccupied with Consciousness.

Arjuna is familiar with *ashtanga yoga.* He understands that *Krishna* was reviewing with him the technique of meditation, "By keeping your attention on the *kutastha* between the eyebrows, fix your breath in Me. Here you will realise your heart at Onement with *Brahman.* Having experienced Me you will know that it is about Me they speak of in all matters. Contented, you will experience My Bliss. I reiterate I am the fountainhead of all. From Me all possessions go. Thinking thus, the wise granted with My nature worship Me. Their hearts on Me, their lives devoted to Me, coaching one another, and glorifying Me they are ever contented and happy," adds *Krishna.*

Arjuna and *Sanjaya* realise that Man must be constantly united whether awake or while meditating, with the Lord of Creation. The gift of *buddhi yoga* is perfect stillness. The experience is *matchitta* or a feeling the sensory mind, intellect, and individuality are absorbed in an enlightening experience of intuitive knowledge. *Arjuna* now feels that perhaps he can now spend time proclaiming God always. Content and joyful under all circumstances, he could continue steadfast and confident that he will arrive at spiritual fulfillment.

Yet despite this knowledge, *Arjuna* protests that his individuality has a tendency for dragging his soul-awareness to self-awareness. *Arjuna* knows the ego cannot emancipate by itself and by his own mind. Although upright living and meditative habits help to replace some past physical and mental impropriety, inclinations towards extrovertedness are impediments. *Arjuna* wants the grace of both teacher and God.

Krishna does exactly that. "Always united with Me, those who meditate on Me with pure love, I grant them with Stillness. To them who are always devoted, and worshipping Me with commitment, I give them sanctification in the form of enlightenment by which they come to Me. Of them, for forgiveness sake, I destroy their corruption born of ignorance. By the brilliant lamp of knowledge they see Me lingering in their souls."

"In this way those who remain in the soul, without any wants and a stilled breath, I unite them with an awareness that is both extraordinary and wonderful. To those who continue to stay there in *Brahman,* they experience That Unknown Self who dissolves darkness. They remain in their subtle body with Knowledge and the self-revealing Light," *Krishna* said.

Arjuna had early on surrendered his soul and achieved preliminary insight about the immanence and transcendence of God. He was attentive and fired by a reinvigourated interest in Awareness in Nature and Consciousness of Spirit. *Arjuna* now asks a few more questions.

"Have you not said that you are the Supreme *Brahman* Consciousness who is experienced by connecting with *prana?* You have also voiced that you are the Supreme Home and Shelter, the Holiest of the Holy, the Eternal Divine Purifier, the God of all gods, Unborn, and Omnipresent. You have also uttered that the mind and intellect is made holy by this contact with You who is eternal and space-like. You say You are the final home and reality, beyond which there is no house. Is this reality beyond birth? You declare it is like a Great Void."

"You have also told me that all the sages or *rishis* proclaim You thus as expression beyond Space. The celestial *Rishi Narada* also repeats the same as You do. Other celestials like *Asita, Devala,* and *Vyasa* agree. All this You have also told me, O *Krishna.* Do You declare these statements are realised while meditating at the *kutastha*?"

"All that You recounted to me, I regard it to be as true, O Holy One. Neither the gods nor the unenlightened souls or *Danavas* are able to speak with You and therefore do not understand Your expressions. You alone know Yourself by you."

"Have You said that by working at meditation, the Supreme Person shows within oneself and can be known automatically? You say You are the essence in the state of deep meditation, and yet You are the Creator of all. If You are the Lord of all beings, O God of gods, and Lord and ruler of the Universe, none can know what You have said. O Infinite One before expressions, You are the Divine Cosmic Soul, the *Purushottama.* Please describe how You permeate the worlds and also stay in them. It seems only You Yourself know Yourself by Yourself."

"You should tell me clearly and without any reservations, that You are the one whose divine perfection stays in everything, as well as supports these worlds. Tell or show me that it is the Omnipresent You that upholds Your Space-like Form. Explain how You can be this wonderful active materialisation and at the same time be Your Tranquil Form."

"O Great Yogi of mystic powers *Krishna,* how do *yogis* get to know You and continually reflect on You? How should I be meditating? In what particular aspect and form, O Blessed Lord, are You to be imagined by me?"

"*Krishna,* tell me again and at great length, about Your mystical *yogic* powers and about Your perfection. I am never content with just hearing Your nectar-like words. Speak about that tranquil stillness while in the ecstasy of Oneness."

The blind king *Dhritarashtra* turns to *Sanjaya,* "The truth of the matter is that God is present in all forms of his dream creation. *Krishna* persuades *Arjuna* that he must direct his eyes to see within and without to receive Him. He also says he should be accepted in both the corrupt as well as in the virtuous."

"Yes Sire - the characteristics and behaviour of the disciple decides the assessment value of a devotee of God. There is no place where God is not. In every atom it is He alone who is present. The Lord who cares equally for all His creation is all compassion, competence and wisdom. His sanctity embraces and penetrates all," *Sanjaya* replied.

Krishna now describes a step-by-step portrayal of God. *Arjuna* is being given a revelation of an image, which he can treasure in his own heart. He will then realise how to pragmatically see Him within himself, as well as in that Being that pervades all in Creation.

"Very well, O best of the *Kuru* princes *Arjuna,* I will indeed tell you of My expressions and perfection. You will know Me because you are to Me one of the principal ones who is outstanding. There is no end to My variety. My wonderful revelations about the Self can be experienced through the *kutastha* only."

"O, beloved *Arjuna* with those delightful wavy hair, you conquered sleep to meditate on Me. Look, I am the soul seated in the heart of all creatures. I am the beginning before their origin, the middle in their existence and the end of all of happening events in their terminality. I am the Breath itself. It is in this that all appearances become quiet. This Breath is there within the boundaries of the duration of life. It is there again at rebirth."

Sanjaya understands *Krishna's* advice on keeping an eye

on the breath always, to stop straying of the mind. A speechless mind alone can reach the shores of inner tranquillity. The blind king meantime clues into the discussion. *Krishna* is describing himself as the image within.

"Among all the lights that exist, I am the placid Light seen at the end of meditation - that particle of sun is *Brahman* and the breath is a particle of my energy in the wind. Among the twelve effulgent planetary gods who are the supreme *adityas,* I am the preserver *Vishnu.* Among the self-shining luminaries, I am the radiant Sun. Among the forty-nine gods that control wind, water and earth or *maruts,* I am *marichi.* Among heavenly bodies visible in the sky my form is of the Moon."

Arjuna intuitively makes out the microcosmic presence of the self-revealing effulgence he has experienced at the *kutastha.* He will have to recognise Him in the macrocosmic person. *Krishna* goes on to describe *Brahman* as the Cosmic Being.

"Among the *Vedas,* I am the *Sama Veda* advising seekers to concentrate on the divine cave of the spine. Among the yearning gods within, I am the lord of the senses or *Vasava or Indra.* Among the senses, I am their swiftness expressing through the mind or *manas.* Of the living beings and creatures, I am the intellect. The resonance of **Om** that can be heard especially from the posterior or west side of the body, is my Form. It can be invoked from all the spaces and skies even without praying. Those are all My Forms."

"Of the eleven radiant beings or *rudras* I am their leader *Shankara* the well-wisher. Of the *yakshas* and *rakshasas* or astral demigods, I am *Kubera* the lord of riches. Of the eight vitalising beings or *vasus,* I am *Pavaka* the god of fire, with the purifying power. Of the mountain peaks I am *Meru.* In that stillness of breath, the crowned being in the *kutastha,* astride the triangular peak of mount Meru, are all my Forms, *Arjuna.*"

"Know me, O *Arjuna,* to be *Brihaspati,* the chief of

household priest or *Brahman*. Of the six spinal cord centers or *chakras,* I am *Skanda* and also commanders of forces. I am the Ocean among the rivers and all bodies of water."

The blind king continues to grasp the likeness between the microcosmic and macrocosmic person. *Krishna* meanwhile also persists in browsing through *Arjuna's* personal experiences. *Krishna's* description of the Cosmic Person can only be fathomed through inner apprehension in the dominion of Awareness.

Sanjaya sees a change in the blind king. He is still hoping that war can be averted if the blind king is made to understand there is nothing Man needs. Want for the sake of lust, greed, anger, possessiveness, pride or jealousy is unnecessary. Perhaps if he understands the eldest nephew ought to rightfully rule the kingdom. The spirit of virtue is always for a Common Good. The populace can then lead a life of harmony.

Sanjaya said, "The Spirit of God is the essence in every soul. It is also the all-pervading Consciousness in which all souls endure. In Space and Time the Spirit of Consciousness dreamed this created Universe on a substratum of the vibrating Om."

"As awakening in Awareness expands, the mind and intellect exert their influence on inner opinions. He develops ideas of the natural in Nature. Through insight he realises that all emanations in Nature are expressions of the First Expression."

"The *yogi* listens to the primordial Om, looks at the Cosmic Vision unfold all Her revelations, Her compulsions, and Her qualities. The *yogi* watches Awareness in the cusp of Consciousness and realises there is nothing worth owning. The Cosmic Person is only worth serving with devotion."

The blind king listens carefully but questions why *Sanjaya* has once again opened this controversy.

"The *yogi* knows the derivation of all understanding in

ancestry. He understands virtuous environments. His achievements in all engagements are exerted within omniscient and omnipresent awareness. O king, serve the Cosmic Being and abandon greed."

The blind king intuitively knows what he must do but needs the courage of his convictions.

Krishna describes the power of intuition, which self reveals its character within the field of Awareness. When displaying as the creativity of manifestation, It expresses itself as the immortal tree of life. *Arjuna* understands processes of cosmic expression as well as its return to unmanifest wholeness at the source itself.

"Of the mighty sages or *maharishis,* I am *Bhrigu* the beholder of *pranayama* at the *kutastha.* Among words, I am the one indestructible syllable **Om.** Among sacrifices and *yagnas* for holy ceremonies, I am *japa-yagna* – the silent, superconscious chanting. Among stationary objects, I am the mighty Himalayas."

"Among all trees, I am the holy fig tree or *ashvatha* seen reversed at the *kutastha.* Among the celestial sages or *devarishis,* I am *Narada* who also can be seen here. Among the demigods or *Gandharvas* who may appear as many visions, I am *Chitraratha.* Among the ascetics crowned with yoga-success or *munis* and are successfully freed beings, I am *Kapila.* All these are Forms of *Purushottama* Itself."

"Among the stallions, know Me to be *Uchchaishravas,* brought forth by the churning for nectar and thought of as revealed Fire. I am *Airavata* among the princely elephants. I am *Indra's* white elephant seen as a Vast Light. And I am indeed, King among men."

"Among weapons, I am the thunderbolt. The play of its lightning can also be seen. Of the cows, I am *Kamadhuk* the desireless heavenly cow that fulfills all wants. I am *Kamadarpa* the personified deity of ambition and commitment in patterned awareness. I am the foundation of reproduction.

I am king *Vasuki* among serpents who also may be seen here at the *kutastha.*"

"Is *Krishna* characterising himself as the abstract prototype of all things, creatures and beings?" asked the blind king.

"*Arjuna* is being educated about the characteristic expressions of Awareness, Sire," answered *Sanjaya.*

"But *Prakriti's* Awareness cannot display without the light of Consciousness, is that not so?"

Sanjaya started a discussion on She who is Awareness.

"She is enthroned in the cusp of Consciousness and sprouts back and forth into Its Source. *Vedas* elaborate on all divine displays of Awareness. When insight shows as *sattva* or serenity, She is able to direct and govern all wavering in sense apprehensions that are prominent in the mind and intellect of all souls."

"Here does She reveal a balanced state of Her compulsions, a state necessary for contemplation?" asks the blind king.

"When Awareness expresses as enlivening *prana,* She has the ability to purify all energies vitalising all Her patterned expressions in the gross and subtle bodies of all souls. Knowing such knowledge about Awareness allows humanity to accept Mother Nature's total nurturing influence on beings engaged in virtuous activity. Success in all undertakings then occurs in the omnipresence of Consciousness," *Sanjaya* stated.

"When Awareness reveals Herself to all souls as intuition, Mother Nature allows all souls to hear the vibrating resourceful force of **Om** in their field of awareness in meditation. Nature allows the *yogi* to see expressions of the immortal tree of life in the universe, which returns to its source in Consciousness. The *yogi* realises the image of this microcosm in his own spiritual eye is a replica of the macrocosm. It is where all manifestation and de-manifestation reveals Itself. It becomes a personal knowledge of Awareness and Consciousness. The *yogi* identifies the enlivening life force energising through the spinal pathway and animating all the spiritual centers and nerves from the divine cave. He accepts all levels of awareness until Awareness reveals the wisdom in gained and experienced knowledge," he added.

"In the fire of the field of wisdom, the *yogi* reaches the field of Light and Sound of **Om** expressing as the thunderbolt fabricating primordial Nature. Here the *yogi* realises he is the centre seeking and redeeming the self from attractions and propulsions of wants, habits and individuality. Dormant in the spiritually asleep, the *yogi* has the ability to awaken the creative life force of *Vasuki.*"

The blind king was deep in thought when he heard *Krishna* address *Arjuna* again. *Krishna* was sketching the illusions experienced by Nature-enmeshed souls. The blind king understood that although the compulsions of Nature are short-lived while the soul remains in the mirage of make-believe immortality, the self awaits the grace of self-mastery and soul awakening. He found it interesting to hear *Krishna* describe the illusions of mortality while already basking in immortality.

And *Krishna* continued, "I am *Ananta,* the causal being among the eternal *Nagas* or serpents. Among aquatic beings whose tranquil breath courses between the throat and the *kutastha* at the eyebrows I am *Varuna,* the god of the ocean. I am *Aryama* the ancestral parent among *Pitris.* I am *samyama* or Oneness that unites breathing, contemplation, meditation and absorption. Among all controllers that judge and punish I am *Yama* the god of death."

"Among the demonic *Daityas* I am *Prahalada* and Time among things that count. Among the beasts, I am the king of beasts - the lion. And among the winged creatures, I am the eagle *Garuda* who is the lord of the skies and the vehicle of *Vishnu. Arjuna,* please be assured there is true Bliss for those who can silence the breath into the *kutastha.*"

"Of the purifiers, I am the wind. Among wielders of weapons, I am *Rama.* Among aquatic fish-like creatures, I am *Makara,* the vehicle of god of the ocean. Among rivers, I am *Jahnavi,* the mighty *Ganges.*"

Sanjaya understood deluding mortality. The blind king was interested in immortality but, like many spiritual seekers, did not have the courage to embark on the spiritual path. *Sanjaya* encouraged the blind king and told him the famous story of *Prahalada.*

"All individualistic hopes for the highest goal must undergo the trials, agitations and obstacles attached to a path to soul-knowledge. Although of an individualistic demoniac birth, *Prahalada* analysed and used even the worst occasions wisely. Over time he learned to perform dutiful actions, as son of a deluded father of two differently motivated wives – one self-serving and the other soul serving. *Prahalada* understood, realised and experienced that omnipotence of Consciousness is supreme whenever extraordinary powers of Nature were used to destroy him. Only an awakening into such awareness had the power to dissolve all his delusions and illusions about both Awareness of Mother Nature and Consciousness of Spirit."

"The distinctly demoniac prince, *Prahalada* used his life force as a purifying device. It not only enlivened his breath, but it endured enough to revive him through the many attempts on his life with wind, fire, and other elemental forces. Despite confusion in his understanding about the Real, the mere intimacy and contact with *pranic* Om eliminated impediments in his domain of awareness. His self revealed itself in soul awareness as a spontaneous unfoldment."

Krishna interrupted *Sanjaya's* discussion with the blind king by describing His immanence in Time, Space, and activities in Creation.

"Of materialisation of assembled things O *Arjuna,* I am the beginning, the middle and the end of their serene state, all existing within Space. Among all branches of knowledge, I am the enlightenment of the Supreme Spirit. As Self I am the answer in all logical inquiry and controversies."

"Among the alphabets, I am the letter **A.** Of all totals, I am called *dvandva,* the connective of endless Time. I am the Ordained *Brahman* with face turned towards every side as the Omnipresent Creator. About happiness of worldly life, I am the all pervading Dispenser of every Destiny."

"I am the all-dissolving Death that seizes all and is also the Source of all. I am Birth, the origin of all that will be. Among females, I am of the quality of *Prakriti.* I am Fame, Fortune, Speech, Memory, Intelligence, Constancy, and Forgiveness. These are my Forms of gentle acts, beauty, and speech. I am the clarifying intuition and the steadfastness of divine tolerance."

"Among *Sama* hymns I am the stillness in exhalation, that *Vrihat-saman.* Among poetic meters, I am *Gayatri.* Of months, I am *Margasirsha* – that special month of winter. Among seasons, I am that which is productive of flowers like *Kusumkar,* the flower of spring. My enormous resonance is that of **Om** which resonates throughout the spinal cord like a feeling of springtime."

"I am the cunning in the game of dice that cheats. I am the radiance and splendour of those that are magnificent and filled with fiery energy. I am Victory and I am Effort and Industry. I am the *sattvic* goodness and truth of all that is good."

"Of the *Vrishni* lineage I am *Vasudeva.* Among the *Pandavas,* of the sons of *Pandu* I am *Dhananjaya* – O *Arjuna.* I am even *Vyasa* among the ascetic sages. I am the student *Usanas,* among seers and poets."

"I am the justice and discipline in rulings of morality. I am the Policy of those who seek victory. I am Silence among secrets. I am the Wisdom of Awareness in those that are possessed of Knowledge."

"That which is the Seed of all, I am that O *Arjuna.* There is nothing, moving or motionless, which can exist without Me."

There is utter stillness between the two cousins – *Arjuna*

and *Krishna. Arjuna* is processing what he has just been told and *Krishna* busied himself viewing both sides of the assembled armies. *Sanjaya* continues to speak to the blind king about the Lord's Immanence and His Transcendence.

"How does Time and Space happen while awake but dissolves with unconsciousness?" asks the blind king.

Krishna's description of the Lord's image was authoritative. Interestingly, the effects of this control were comprehensive and elegantly specific and precise. The central point of *Sanjaya's* discussion, he thought should be on Man's awareness of Nature.

"Time exists in Consciousness and is understood only when Self-knowledge dawns and reveals itself to those who wish to know. It is Consciousness, which is the *first* as the vibration-less source from which all vibrations emanate. Although Nature displays Herself in phenomenon, Awareness unifies all in Time and Space. It is Awareness that adjusts and governs the influential qualities of Her Nature," *Sanjaya* stated.

"It is in Consciousness that Universes expand forward and also dissolve. Parts and compositions of Awareness are made possible by Her intrinsic skills as creativity or *rajas,* idleness or *tamas* and harmonious purity or *sattva.* Upheld by Her vibrating sound frequencies, the influence of Om is felt in all valid knowledge, and mundane happenings."

"Unleashing influences of Nature express as *sattva* when prayers and rituals inherently embedded in Man disclose the self-illuminating capacities of wisdom. It is accessible in meditation. But, most deluded souls experience the awareness they are already entrenched in."

"Of the varied aspects of Awareness, Consciousness is its Source. The *yogi* expresses such awareness through self-control and ambition for the highest goal in meditation. He knows he must meet himself in a hidden mysterious place within his own divine altar where his knowledge is allowed to unfold. In that silence, the restlessness of past births is stilled and the mind's waves cease to exist. Here in the heat and seat of meditation, the *yogi* realises that no expression is possible without the seed. He understands the cause of the Cosmic Dream emanates from the field of Consciousness," *Sanjaya* concluded.

Sanjaya had just listed all the superlatives of expression. The blind king was mulling over the discussion when *Krishna* was heard telling *Arjuna* there was more to be said but the details were unending and the processes continuous. *Krishna* explained he had only allowed *Arjuna* to peep into the Cosmic Drama.

In conclusion *Krishna* said. "There is no end to My limitless and divine perfection *Arjuna,* O Scorcher of Foes. This recital of the extent of those perfections have been uttered by Me only as a concise declaration – it is a mere intimation of My expanding glorious powers."

"Whatever of exalted there is or glorious, or strong, understand that everything is born of a portion of My energy - know all such to be displayed sparks of My radiance witnessed at the *kutastha,* My third eye."

"But what need have you, O *Arjuna,* for the many details of this wisdom? Understand this simply. I, the Unchanging and Everlasting, comfort and permeate the entire cosmos with but one fragment of My Being. An atom of dust enters an atom of water. Water enters fire. Fire enters air and air enters space. Space enters *Brahman.* Know therefore the world is one fragment of the Particle of *Brahman.* How much more can I say?"

13. Cosmic Being

It is the strength of *Arjuna's* faith that allows him the right to receive disclosures made by *Krishna.* Having been educated to identify the Cosmic Form within the *kutastha,* he penetrates the incalculable marvel of this Universe. As long as he can remember, he has always coveted to make this boundless event his own insight. How could that be made possible? Can anyone see God?

Arjuna has diligently practiced the spiritual exercises of meditation all his life. He understands the reality of the Absolute without name or form. Now his essence wishes for a direct experience of the *Vishwarupa* – the Cosmic Being. He aspires to behold the numerous appearances of this Absolute, about whom *Krishna* has referred to repeatedly. He was told that in Many Universes as well as in the tiniest atoms, creatures and majestic animals, good and evil – are engaged in a special appropriate place in this Cosmic Form. *Arjuna* has understood that this earth is only a small part of creation, which to him is difficult to understand. This Infinite Universe that spreads below, above and on all sides, how huge is it? About beginning-less Time, what do we know about it before now, and the present? If Creation exists within a stretch of Time and Space, where is the Source and where is this Infinity seen in the beyond?

Arjuna therefore politely poses his questions in a logical sequence. His grasp of the Supreme Soul, the *Adhyatma,* has been developing. And he has achieved a realization of that, which before, he had only understood intellectually. He now wants a direct experience of the *Adhyatma* the Self.

"This conversation about the supreme mystery, called *Adhyatma,* which you have articulated for my benefit, has dispelled my delusion, *Krishna*. You have given me the secret spiritual science. I have experienced what You have spoken about. I sense this within the life and energy of the *kutastha*."

"*Krishna,* you whose eyes are like the lotus petal in the *kutastha,* I have heard from you about creation and dissolution of beings. You described also the greatness of Matter elements that are indestructible and know no decay. You also say you are immortal, unchangeable and divine."

"With what you have said about Yourself, you have truly acknowledged the Science about Yourself. Yet, O Cosmic Self who is *Purushottama,* I want to see You in your sovereign Embodied Form as *Ishwararupa.*"

"O Master, who is Lord of *Yogis,* if You think me deserving and capable of seeing that Form, then, O Lord of mystic powers, please show me Your Imperishable Eternal Form at the *kutastha.*"

Sanjaya realised that *Krishna* has taught *Arjuna* everything about himself with discerning kindness. *Krishna* has also disclosed the secret wisdom of the true Self and removed *Arjuna's* delusion. He comprehensively taught about Nature or *Prakriti,* about beginnings and ends of all creatures, and about the eternal majestic sovereignty of Consciousness over all. Having previously shown compassion, *Sanjaya* fully expected *Krishna* to allow *Arjuna* the spectacle of the Cosmic Being, the *Ishwararupa.* After all, *Arjuna* wished to experience this allness of *Brahman* as *Purushottama* – God.

Krishna replied, "Behold and experience Me at the *kutastha,* O *Arjuna.* Look at My Forms by the hundreds and thousands. I am in the atoms of various and many types of things and in diverse hues and shapes."

"Watch Me in the *Adityas* who are the twelve Sun deities and the eight *Vasus* who are the beneficient gods – the grizzly stars. Look at Me in the eleven *Rudras* who are the lamps of heaven and in the twin *Ashwins* who are the heavenly doctors of dawn and dusk. Also gaze at Me in the many guardian spirits – the *Maruts* who help creatures and beings. See all these astonishing wonderful Forms of mine. You have not previously seen these many marvels. O descendent of the *Bharata* dynasty – *Arjuna.* Look if you think you can!"

"Watch cautiously, O curly haired *Arjuna.* The entire universe of Creations both moving and immovable, are also my expressions. They are all together within this My body of *Brahman.* View That which you have wished to see."

"You are however not competent to look at Me with these your mortal eyes. Here, let me gift you with cosmic sight at right here in the *kutastha.* Recognise Me here where you have previously seen me as the Cosmic Eye, in meditation. Now see My sovereign mysterious nature."

Arjuna was invited to see the various displays of His Awareness in the one Cosmic Body, in which all the Universes exist. *Krishna* had to give *Arjuna* intuitive divine vision. *Vyasa* had given *Sanjaya* the same gift to allow them both, discovery of the magnificent authority and supremacy of such a *yogic* revelation.

Sanjaya described to *Dhritarashtra* the transformation of *Krishna* into the Cosmic Being or *Ishwararupa.* It was happening right there within their mind's eye, above and between the two eyebrows in the *kutastha.*

Having said this, *Krishna* the mighty Lord of mystic *yogic* power, exposed to *Arjuna* a fearful but an ultimately guiding and principal form. This Lord of Universes or *Ishwara* had many mouths and eyes with many wonderful expressions of beings within the cosmically displayed Form.

Sanjaya gasped at the awe-inspiring sight and said, "Many who are seated and reflecting at the *kutastha* are like *Arjuna* able to see, as I now see for myself. This is a spectacular emergence of the manifested Cosmic Deity. He is adorned with many saintly residents who are covered in celestial ornaments. Many have with them heavenly weapons lifted by so many hands. Their eyes and mouths are everywhere."

"Within the Cosmic Person are many who adorned with

outstanding garlands and robes made of Substance only known to space. The unguents are heavenly fragrances. They are of astonishing scent. Everyone, even those attached to worldliness and those who are perfected mortals are in the body of the Cosmic Being. They also are full of wonder. They too are gazing at their own *kutastha.* Right within the body of this Being, they are all viewing the resplendent Infinite. On all sides, all eyes and faces are turned towards the Cosmic Expression within their inner Self."

"The Spirit of the *kutastha* is like the splendour of a thousand suns bursting forth all at once in the sky. Without doubt, That is definitely the majesty and brilliance of that Mighty One."

Although the blind king could not see, *Dhritarashtra's* inner awareness was intuitively understanding and realising the Omnipotent, Infinite and all pervading vision of the Cosmic Person. His Grace could be imagined glowing in all directions of space, while wearing celestial robes and garlands. They were all in Him but He is not in them, the blind king reasoned.

Dhritarashtra's understanding confirmed the Cosmic Person fulfills only righteous activities that are in conformity with consecrated Laws and authority inherent in Nature. From every level of His expression, the Cosmic Person distributes the enlivening *pranic* life force. It vibrates throughout the Cosmic Man's Being. Like a scaffold holding all and everything together, it permeates matter to energise it layer after layer, in every creature, thing, and being. Although physically blind, *Dhritarashtra* can intuitively detect the corporeal body of Mother Nature. Her fragrance leaves him delightfully light-headed when earth, fire, and water are mixed in space. He is able to sense the feel of the soft wind and the whole void filled with the *pranava* – Om.

Souls of *Arjuna* and *Sanjaya* marvel at the display of Nature in Consciousness. They witnessed and experienced That about which they had only intellectually understood and meditatively realised. They testified and recognised the entire universe as an uninterrupted display of Awareness coalescing into Consciousness. From a vibration-less field, and conserved by the throbbing Om, Mother Nature"s splendour extends out of Infinity and spreads through and beyond her display. If a thousand suns glowed simultaneously in the sky, their light would only dimly resemble the splendour of the Mighty Cosmic Being, who is both Man and Woman.

Sanjaya now goes on to describe the experience *Krishna* has ordained himself and *Arjuna* to see, "This son of *Pandu, Arjuna* detects there in the body of that God of gods, the entire universe divided and subdivided into many parts. Each part is visible in the many different *kutasthas.* But also all together! This One body contains all of the five *Pandava* family."

"*Dhananjaya* – our *Arjuna,* who is a champion of true wealth, is awestruck and filled with wonder and amazement. His hair stands on end. He bows his head and begins to speak with joined hands. He is now addressing the revealed Cosmic Form. *Arjuna* is nervous. At first he describes the Cosmic Deity that he is experiencing with his God-ordained grace for an intuitive vision".

Arjuna and *Sanjaya* were both *yogis* born of spiritual endeavours and not surprisingly *Sanjaya* can hear *Arjuna* cry out in astonishment.

"I am experiencing You with the enlivened energy within the space of my *kutastha.* I see in there all the gods in Your body. All the varied hosts of creatures are therein. I see *Brahma* the Creator seated on his lotus seat, and all the *rishis* and sages also. The celestial snakes of *Shiva* and *Vishnu.* I see also. You are composed of many arms, stomachs, mouths, and eyes. On every side, I see Your marvel. Your Infinite Form is awesome and frightening."

"Neither end nor middle, nor also beginning of You, do I see, O Lord of the Universe. O You of Omnipresent Form, You are everywhere in this infinity. There is no end here. As far as I can see there is no conclusion to my seeing. I cannot see the beginning either of this Lord or of all the worlds in the Cosmos."

Sanjaya then tells the blind king that *Arjuna* continues to describe what he is seeing in his own *Kutastha.* "This day, I see Your Form with a gilded crown of stars on your head. You are wielding a mace in one hand and whirling Your discus of evolutionary Time in another hand. There is a mass of Infinite Light glowing powerfully everywhere. Its brilliance makes it difficult for me to look at You. All around there is a blazing burning fire of the Sun. It is all Incomprehensible."

"It is You who is the Eternal *Kutastha* that is worthy of knowing. You are the Imperishable One – the Supreme Cosmic Shelter, who is even beyond the Universal Form of the Cosmos. You are the *Vishwarupa,* the worthiest of Wisdom's Themes. It is here that is the home of Tranquillity where all starts and ends. You are truly the great treasure house of this Universe. You are the Imperishable Guardian of the Eternal Secret *Dharma* and virtue. I reason, You are definitely the Ancient Being that has uncovered Yourself within me."

"As previously noted, I see You without a beginning who is also without a middle and is therefore without an end. Therefore we are both Deathless. I see Your infinite authority, and endlessly working arms. Having the sun and the moon for Your eyes, and the blazing fire for Your mouth, I see this entire universe and worldly life aflame in Fire which appears unquenchable."

"The space between heaven and earth and also within my heart is pervaded by Your enduring and enlivening Light alone. This Existence of all Lights is revolving from and into all directions and at all points in horizons of all the three worlds. And from Your mouth I see You spewing flames. You utter the energising Om That is Your Own Cosmic Word. Your Self-born existence and energy shields and warms all creation from harm. This space between earth and the heavens and all the quarters is filled with You alone. Having seen this,

Your wonderful as well as Your terrifying Form, even the three worlds are awestruck by fear. O great Being of Cosmic-Soul I experience You as the Cosmic Eye in the *kutastha,* while in meditation, but only after rendering myself oblivious of my own being! But then You have allowed me to see this powerful Form of Yours inside whom are the three worlds. From Your feet to the navel is occupied by the underworld. Above this and up to the throat resides the mortal realm. Above Your throat lies the heavenly world."

"These hosts of gods are witnessing and entering You. Their eyes are still. Some who are afraid are praying with joined hands. Some who are perfected beings are saying 'Hail to thee'. These hosts of great *rishis and siddhas* are praising You with many hymns of praise."

"I see all the gods in Your body and the hosts of various classes of beings. *Brahma,* the Lord of Creation, is securely seated on a lotus and all the *rishis* are lingering in caves. The heavenly serpents inherent in Nature's creative life and energy are tame and dreamy as You support all. You who are of Infinite Cosmic Form and extending in every direction, with many arms, trunks, mouths and eyes, I cannot picture Your birth, Your reign or Your end. O Lord of the Universe, O Revealed Cosmic Form, in truth, into You alone enter these hosts of *devas.* All are awestruck. How strangely incredible, but all are at Peace."

Both *Arjuna's* and *Sanjaya's* souls continue gazing at this sight with awe. They understand, realise, and experience that their ego has no place in this present expression. Rather they seem propelled and compelled by Nature's qualities. They realize they are mere instruments of the Cosmic Deity's Total Will. They both experience firsthand the empowering influences that regulate all cosmic forces compelling each being and creature to become an agent of action. All activities in the displayed universe, they realise, are for a Collective good.

The two enlightened beings hear the creative Om

permeating and supporting the entire displayed universe. They, *Arjuna* and *Sanjaya* merge their awareness with Nature's Awareness and feel the need to serve Her, Mother Nature. Yet they remain incapable of seeing the entire view of Nature's expression and are unable to experience the endless processes of Consciousness that support Nature's Awareness.

Arjuna and *Sanjaya* experience the witnessing vibrationless Light of Consciousness as an all-pervading radiance permanently supporting Nature's entire vibrating exhibition. There are guiding principles and inherent orders governing the life-giving Awareness of Nature. Time and Space does not affect the laws inherent in Nature. The ever present, ever seeing Sun and planets helpfully watch over Nature's Laws.

Again they see the processes of physical, astral, and causal realms in the Macrocosmic Being and also in the microcosm. They are connected and pervaded by Awareness and supported by a witnessing Consciousness. They witness at every level enlightened beings existing within the displayed body of the Cosmic Being. *Arjuna* and *Sanjaya* see those who have understood the mystery and accept God with reverential gestures. At that time they see those who have realised the mystery, and are seers and sages who recognise God with rejoicing. And, finally there are others who have personally experienced the great mystery and know that what they see is a Dream of God. These are ordained gurus and teachers who have chosen to guide the deluded back onto the spiritual path.

Sanjaya tells the blind king that in the very beginning, even before the presentation of the Cosmic Being there was always God or *Purushotama* who by His mere presence gave every organisation vested powers to authorise specific activity. These agents remain in the Causal Universe as electricity, magnetism, energy, and light, all within this infinite space and backed by Om. In keeping with the Laws of Nature, they direct these processes within astral and physical Nature.

Arjuna and *Sanjaya* intuitively witnessed and experienced these intelligent impulses directing every aspect of every exploit in every part of Nature's expression.

Both *Sanjaya* and *Arjuna* are in awe. For his part, *Arjuna* lacks both courage and tranquillity to absorb what he sees in front of him. He once more exclaims what he has already stated before, "In front of this large form within the *Kutastha* I see the eleven lamps of *Rudra* in heaven. I also see twelve bright Suns – the *Adityas,* and the eight grizzly stars – the *Vasus.* The *Siddhas* who are aspiring hermits and the *Vishva devas* who are patron gods of the elements and the two *Ashwins* who serve You as twin heavenly physicians of dawn and dusk, I behold them all. I see the *Maruts* who serve creatures and beings as their guardian spirits and the *Ushmapas.* They are demigoblins of Manes. Hosts of faultless *Gandharvas* have arrived as demigods. I also see angels as *yaksha* and the *asuras* as demons. There in You are hosts of *Siddhas* who are perfected ones and at different levels on their spiritual pathway. They are all gazing at You, in astonishment."

"I now also see within that *kutastha* a Colossal Armed One. I see within this Infinite and Immeasurable Form, many eyes and countless cheeks. Their limitless hands and legs are adorned with lotuses, which are at Your feet also. Their mouths are like chasms with teeth suggestive of the primal doomsday. These yawns swallow swooning worlds below and above. This spectacle leaves me awestruck at its ferociousness and its grandeur. My own world and I are bewildered and distressed to see this sight."

"Many kinds of lights are appearing and pervading all space but are also radiating from all around the *kutastha,* that huge Eye which is in the middle of a dark oculus. I see in the bowels, a deep void filled with You. Your Cosmic Form touches the sky. Diverse colours of fiery hues emanate from Your lustrous body. I see Your gaping mouth, O *Vishnu* of fiery sight. You have overwhelmed me – I have lost both my courage and peace. My inner soul trembles with hurt. I can no longer command bravery nor peace of mind."

"Whoever sees You in this Universal Form, for whatever purpose, he sees You within his own *kutastha.* I see in Your mouth that which looks terrible because of those ferocious teeth that are like swords. I see the Form of Death at the end of Time. I see the all-destroying deadly fires of *Pralaya* at the end of a *Yuga* in cycles of Creation. I hear howls coming from Your mouth. It scowls at me. In all four directions everything is ablaze and my alertness is lost. My heart is in turmoil. Be compassionate, O Cosmic Guardian, Lord of gods. I feel alone and feel no peace within. Compose Yourself O *Kutastha* – accept my humble pleas. Be gracious O God of gods. O You who are refuge of the world's existence, spare me."

Arjuna has come to the realisation that every aspect and action of the Cosmic Deity is interconnected. He treasures the disclosure as awesome. He is inwardly disturbed with regret that his ego has guided his life. The extremist in him made all life's decisions. He acted so despite an intuitive knowledge of his known frailties and impending mortal extinction. He could not face himself.

He once more recognises the need for transformative spiritual exercises. He secretly decides to sincerely practice the eightfold agenda required for spiritual travels. Through restraint or *yama,* adherence to restraint or *niyama,* constant practice of self-withdrawal or *abhyas,* and stilling the physical body in *asana* he would learn to still his physical body. By concentration or *dharana* and regulating the breath *or pranayama* he would learn to tame the mind and energies of the subtle body. Withdrawing into the divine cave through *pratyahara* would help him concentrate and remain in *dhyana,* within the *kutastha above* and between the two eyebrows. With *Krishna's* grace he hopes his awareness could be merged with consciousness in *samadhi.* Despite his twelve years of penance in the forest, *Arjuna* knows he has more to do. He realises that he could not have gotten this far without the goodwill of his *guru.* He understands he must harness the cosmic forces that influence competence in soul-unfoldment.

Arjuna, like many *yogis* on the spiritual path, has had to substitute individualism for soul-unfoldment. He needs to trade-off his soul-destructive extrovert tendencies. *Arjuna's* blind mind is under the influence of past tendencies, *karmic* habits, and materialistic attractions. Propelled by sense tendencies and a delusion of egoistic selfhood, he has resisted soul unfoldment. His childhood and training was centred on fashioning an effective and prosperous being. It had to be familiar with worldly pleasures. He became a wealthy and distinguished individual. The impelling forces motivating him were for 'me and mine'. He has deliberately shaped his world for his own satisfaction by rigging the competence of Nature. His mentors have taught him only earthly subsistence.

Arjuna then sees an apparition of the battle-to-come. It begins with teachers who endured through materialism, "I see my one hundred naive cousins – sons of a mentally blind king *Dhritarashtra.* Led by the eldest lustful *Duryodhana* they enter Your mouth. Hosts of earthly kings also enter You. Look, I see *Bhishma* who nurtured my Ego and encouraged my individuality, also being swallowed. *Drona* my guru who explained to me my duty to Habits, is also in Your mouth. The charioteer *Karna* who illustrated the benefits of worldly attractions is also in there. I see being swallowed many warriors from both sides. They are hastily entering Your gaping mouth made fiercer by your teeth. The forces of unrighteousness wait to leap on our warrior chieftains – the *Pandava* discriminative forces."

"They are all riding towards a race to death – they hide but fall into Your devouring mouth, which is adorned with terrible crushing teeth. It is all too fearful to behold. Some are caught between Your teeth and others have shattered skulls."

"Your love will claim, the victor and the conquered. All are Your children of righteous and of the ungodly. Just as many torrential rivers flow through different channels and roll rapidly towards the ocean – so these heroes of men enter your mouth with flames all around. They must all someday sleep on a common floor."

"Like moths lost in beauty's game, swiftly and thoughtlessly they rush into the blazing flame to self-destruction. Passion fires pretend to glow like Your heavenly lights and draw mortals to attend to the trumpet call of their own death and destruction."

"Swallowing all these men from every side, I see Your mouths ablaze, Your leaping tongues lick the angry blood of both the weak and strong. You eat with infinite hunger, devouring all worlds on all Your sides. O *Vishnu,* You fill the whole universe with Your energy and Your fierce grandeur. You are ablaze with the all-pervasive torch, and are scorching the worlds."

"Greetings to You, O God of gods. Pray tell me, who are You and why You are in such a fierce form? You appear as the Cosmic Fiery One, yet I know you personally as benign and good. I want to know You, as the Ancient Original Being. What happened from what? I have not been able to understand this properly. I was seeing the *Kutastha.* What is this that happened? Tell me about Your Will, because I still do not know or understand your action."

Arjuna realises that all tendencies resisting soul-unfoldment are dissolved within this display of the Cosmic Being. Some are consumed more voraciously than others. Whether righteous or unrighteous, Nature absorbs both Her inert *tamasic* and creative *rajasic* qualities into Her own Being. Like fast moving currents, both enter Nature's vast display as if seeking *sattva* in harmony. She dissolves all Nature's qualities, habits, tendencies, and the self in Her Ocean of Awareness.

And *Krishna* replies *Arjuna* and *Sanjaya* together, "You are experiencing Me through the *kutastha,* O *Arjuna.* I now represent Time, which is engaged in destroying. Breathing is regulated at distinct multiples per day and night. *Yogis,* who learn to still the breath while in *samadhi,* still Time in the cosmic Oneness or *samadhi.* When Stillness has been reached in *Brahman,* Time is parked at Death. All warriors who are engaged in this war will not be there after the operation. Intent on evolution, every thing, creature, and being – all enter the fire, only to perish."

Arjuna is lost for words. *Sanjaya* concludes, "Nature makes no targeted preferences. She dissolves all Her beings into Her fiery transformative all-inclusive influence. Her resolve is to return all to Consciousness. *Prakriti's* Awareness dances Her ballet to make possible *Purusha's* Cosmic Dream. Nature dances first away from Her beloved's Consciousness. While weaving a dream, *Prakriti* remains aware of His immanence – Om. She dances on That platform and manifests a Dream Creation. At the end of a creative cycle or *yuga,* Mother Nature folds back into His transcendence," *Sanjaya* exclaimed.

The Cosmic Deity *Krishna* now wished *Arjuna* and *Sanjaya* to see the Cosmic Dance of Creation on a substratum of Om flowing out of God's mouth. First the platform filled with Time and Space with cycles of exhibition and dissolution. Once realised and experienced, *Krishna* hoped *Arjuna's* soul would perform all actions as a service to Nature. *Krishna* informs *Arjuna* that he has functioned and executed as an agent of his wishes. Now, after understanding the truth, all his actions must be for a Collective Good. He must unfold his own soul qualities through God's grace. Right action will allow him to overcome all obstacles on his spiritual journey.

To reassure both *Sanjaya* and *Arjuna, Krishna* says, "In the guise of the Endless Doom, I come as the acquisitive Time who engages in slaying the race of men and to destroy the worlds. Even if you refuse to fight the wicked foes, still, none of the hostile warriors displayed shall live. Therefore, keep performing your actions, including meditation. You are only an incidental justification for engaging in war. Even before the start of battle, they have already died."

"Therefore, stand up and triumph a victorious fame. Conquer the enemies and enjoy the wealth of a mortal's heaven and become the King of Peace. I know all the happenings of this mysterious future. I slew your foes and warriors a longtime ago. You be only My instrument - remember O *Arjuna* you cannot draw the bow with the hand you have, unless I will it."

"I work my Plans for the Universe through diverse paraphernalia. You become my emissary. I am neither causing you fear, nor excessive daring. I am encouraging you to hear what I now speak. I wish you to act for Me. I have already slain *Drona, Bhishma, Jayadratha, Karna* and all other brave warriors who are sense-attached to mortal existence. Through you, as in the past and in the future – transact for Me and I will carry out the extermination. Be not distressed with fear. I am only waiting for you to deliberate and serve Mother Nature – just fight unrighteousness. You must slay your enemies in battle."

Sanjaya understood the *Pandavas* will win the war of the righteous against the unrighteous. The blind king's resistance to counseling was a product of *samskaras* and inherent mental conditionings. All and every advice is blocked by the king's habits, deluded sense of individuality, attachments, and brittleness. *Pandavas* are already predicted victorious if challenged to war by the *Kauravas,* the sensuous sons of the blind king. Thus *Sanjaya* makes another attempt to describe what he has just witnessed. *Kauravas* are intended for death unless the blind king is convinced to stop the fight.

Sanjaya said to *Dhritarashtra,* "I can see both *Krishna* and *Arjuna* through my subtle vision. After hearing *Krishna's* words the predetermined victorious *Arjuna,* is trembling awestruck. This warrior who has transcended Nature's illusive *Maya* now joins his hands in worshipful prayer. In humble homage he once more addresses *Krishna* with a voice choked and overwhelmed with fear."

In a trembling voice *Arjuna* says, "My inner being is in fear and ablaze with Fire all around me. I see You as the

Kutastha of the Cosmic Being. O *Krishna,* rightly the worlds are delighted and rejoice in praising Your glory. The *rakshas* are demons who are terrified and are fleeing in all directions seeking safety. They are distancing themselves from You. And the hosts of *siddhas* and other perfected beings are bowing to worship You."

After a pause, he says, "And why should they not pay You homage, O Great Soul? It is You who are beyond Truth and Untruth. You are the home of world's Existence. It is You who are the indestructible *Kutastha.* You are greater than *Brahma* – the Creator who issued from You. O Infinite One, O God of gods, O Shelter of the Universe, You are the Imperishable One. You are both the Manifest and the Unmanifest. Also, You are that Crowning Mystery beyond both."

"You are the first Ancient God, that Primordial Womb of that excellent Primeval Man. Whether I call You *Purusha* or Spirit You are the Final Refuge of all the worlds. You are the Knower and the subject to be Known, the Supreme Fulfillment. You are where the Cosmos and Earthly world ends. You are indeed the Substance worth knowing. Your shining Omnipresence pervades the Universe. O Being of Inexhaustible Forms, it is from You that All is endlessly appearing."

"You are *Vayu* the wind and *Yama* the Lord of Death. As *Agni,* You are Lord of fire and as *Varuna,* the Sovereign of Sea and Sky. As Moon You are the Lord of the Night. O *Prajapati,* Father of countless offspring O Ancestor of All, prostrations to You again and again, a thousandfold."

Arjuna continues with his fear instigated tirade, "Greetings to You of Infinite Might, O Invincible One who is Omniscient and Omnipresent. O All in all, who is of infinite power of the Seed of Creation, I bow to You in front and behind. I bow to you on the left and the right. I bow to You above and below, and I bow to You enclosing me everywhere. There is no end to what I see. Your Form as the *Kutastha* has no boundaries. You are everywhere and gradually expanding into a point that has no end."

He now pleads with his friend, "Being unaware of Your Cosmic Glory, and thinking of You as a common comrade, I have often fearlessly called You my 'friend' or addressed you as '*Krishna*' and '*Yadav*'. I said what I felt in love for You. For all such rash carelessness and informality of endearment, I seek your pardon."

His next move is to ask for forgiveness, "In whatever way I might have insulted You in fun, while at play, while walking, sitting, resting or at meals, I seek Your pardon. When alone with You or while in the company of others, O *Krishna*–for all such unintentional slights, O Immeasurable One, I beg forgiveness. In my estimate this discovery of Your Seed *Kutastha* never terminated my earliest friendship."

"You are the Father of both animate and inanimate alike. None but You are worthy of worship, O Greatest Guru. You bring the Cosmos and the world from darkness into Light. I witnessed that life-giving Light and the Energy of *Prakriti*. I worshiped you in the *Kutastha* as both *prana* and *shakti*. How can there exist any power to surpass You? In the three worlds – physical, subtle and causal, there is nothing to match the image that I make out in my *kutastha*. There is nothing at all that can be like you."

After self-analysis of the third eye, he reasons, "Therefore, O Adorable One, I cast myself down at Your feet and beg Your pardon. As a father to his son, as a comrade of a close friend, as a lover of his beloved – you forgive me, O Lord. I will still my body, silence my mind to become calm and happy. With a stilled calm breath and remaining at the *kutastha*, I will await your grace."

Arjuna prefers the mortal *Krishna* and admits his uncomfortable state of mind, "I am overwhelmed that I have gazed on Your Cosmic Vision, never seen before. Because I have never seen this before, my mind is not free from terror. Be merciful to me, O Lord of gods, O Shelter of the Worlds. Show me your previous form as the benign *Vishnu.*"

"You were at first the four-armed Universal Form of *Vishnu.* Earlier I wanted to see you crowned and holding mace and discus. But now, please reappear in that mortal form, O Lord of a thousand arms who is presently the Person of the Universe."

It is proper that all beings thank and rejoice in the Lord's presence in even mundane affairs of things, creatures or beings. Oppositions resolve or are banished and goodness prevails. It is therefore natural for beings such as *Arjuna* to have constant devotion for their selected god.

Arjuna knows that all righteous actions have a transforming influence on a person. It begins with every atom, molecule, and tissue including physiological and mental bodily systems. In time the transfiguring reorganisation activated by spiritual practices is forever more etched into the causal being of the individual. These distinctively powerful forces cause Nature to grant the same in Her causal body also. Such microcosmic changes have the power to metamorphose macrocosmic records within Mother Nature's own Causal Seed.

Connected, empowered, and transformed the relationship between the meditative Man and Nature gradually involves trudging towards Oneness in Awareness.

This Knowledge of *Prakriti* and the march of Knowing but witnessed silently by the Knower – *Purusha* become One because of changes in the seeker. The intuitive interaction between these three forces allows *Arjuna* to see both the immanence and the transcendence of Truth as one experience.

Both *Sanjaya* and *Arjuna* have come to understand, realise, and experience the Great Mystery. Yet both have a great deal to achieve something ahead of them. Their meditative practices have become more intense. The Cosmic Vision has served its purpose and *Krishna* must now return to his human form. *Arjuna* has regrets but seeks forgiveness. He has surrendered his self-consciousness at the feet of empowered Awareness-Consciousness of *Prakriti-Purusha* when Matter and Spirit display togetherness. The Cosmic Deity as *Kutastha* must return to His familiar distinctiveness and comfort *Arjuna's* mind.

And *Krishna* said, "You experienced this manifestation through your *kutastha.* By performing the yoga of the soul, you were able to see this Form. My real Structure is greater than all that I have displayed. I revealed myself to you because I was pleased with the improvement you made in your spiritual practices. You saw My Light – it is my Life-giving Image, which creates both the Cosmos and Earth with My Energy. I have affirmatively exercised my own Yogic Powers to show myself to you and none other, O *Arjuna.* This Supreme Primeval Form of Mine is the Radiant and Infinite Cosmos which nobody has previously seen."

"No mortal other than yourself *Arjuna,* has seen this Universal Cosmic Form of Mine. This Form is not seen by sacrifice, charity, or good works or by rigorous austerities and the study of the *Vedas.* For normal mortals this Vision is unattainable."

"Your heart should not be fearing this Form. Do not be afraid, or bewildered at seeing My Terrible aspect! Dispel your fears and with a rejoicing heart, listen once more my familiar humming – my all pervading Form."

Sanjaya recognised the Cosmic Deity that displayed and revealed Himself to the receptive soul in *Arjuna* and in himself. Each experienced a soul-unfoldment conditioned by the purity of the mind, the degree of withdrawal from the compulsions of Nature, and the clarity of His own awareness. All external gestures of worship and adoration played no part in this revealing experience.

The blind king had heard *Sanjaya* when describing the Cosmic Deity but *Dhritarashtra's* view of the Image was substituted by his inherent overindulgent conditions. The blind king was not without fear or apprehension for his own one hundred children. By now he has realised that his children and friends will lose this impending battle. *Dhritarashtra* could not face *Krishna* as the Cosmic Man. He wanted word the Cosmic Deity had changed himself into his familiar nephew. He did not fear the familiar form of *Krishna*.

Sanjaya said to *Dhritarashtra,* "Having spoken to *Arjuna* thus, I notice *Vasudeva* the Lord of the Worlds, resume his own shape as *Krishna*. He, the Great-Souled One, appears to *Arjuna* in His gracious gentle Form, and consoles His fear-stricken disciple, *Arjuna.*"

And *Arjuna* says, "O *Janardana* – Grantor of All Desires – my dear *Krishna,* having seen you restored in your original human form, I feel composed in my mind and restored to my natural self. My heart has calmed down and my inner being has awakened to an enduring awareness of you, in all my activities."

Krishna replies, "This form of mine, which you have just seen, is difficult to behold. You have visualised the Universal Cosmic Vision of the Lord through your *kutastha*. Even the gods aspire to experience it. Witnessing this Form comes after many struggles. Neither by *Vedas,* nor by austerities, nor by gifts, nor by sacrifice can I be understood in this Cosmic Form. Only by undivided devotion and persistent thoughts on this One Divine View – a devotee is allowed to see what you have just examined, my Cosmic Form. Even sincere sages wish for this reality by which they can enter my embrace in Oneness."

"Whoever offers his contemplation while enduring in the *kutastha* and chanting Om, he works for Me alone. He makes me his goal. He lovingly surrenders himself to me, who am unattached to my delusive cosmic-dream worlds. He bears ill will towards none, which beholds me in all. He alone enters my being, O *Arjuna.*"

Although the blind king could not face the realisation

that *Krishna* was the Cosmic Deity, he wanted to understand what *Krishna* had just said.

Sanjaya therefore explains, "The Cosmic Deity is soul-revealed to one who in meditation has already practiced all the eight steps counted as necessary in spiritual practices. Studying the scriptures as you, O King *Dhritarashtra,* have done when tutored, only gave you their intellectual understanding. Charitable giving and ceremonial practices were for your personal psychological transformation. Only meditative spiritual practices lead to realising the Truth written in the scriptures. It is only with intuitive realisation that *yogis* such as *Arjuna* withdraw from their physical, psychological-physiological, and intellectual sheaths. They enter their causal sheath as an unenlightened feeling – *chitta.* There, by the grace of God and Nature, one may see the Cosmic Deity and experience the Mystery of God's immanence and transcendence."

Krishna adds, "Do my actions which have been taught to you by your guru. Remain in the *kutastha* with faith. Having seen this Form, all your wants will vanish. You will then be able to live in *Brahman* where you see all in All. You will then not battle wrong feelings because you will have reached me where the Self remains in the Self."

14. Devotion

Arjuna has displayed mental instability. Fearing the Cosmic Vision, he asks *Krishna* to return to his original form. He has seen the Cosmic Deity and wonders if it was easier to be on the path of spirituality through devotion to *Krishna.*

Sanjaya recognizes that devotion for a disciple is a means of corroborating his identity with the Lord of his heart. To speculate on devotion to the Unmanifest Formless God through *nirguna bhakti* can be forbidding, even though it is the Superior Path. But those *yogis,* who worship devotedly the obvious image of God through *saguna bhakti,* do so with intense love and are also able to dedicate all to Him. They are also one with Him, embraced in His bosom of transcendental bliss.

If one worships the formless unmanifest Spirit and another worships Him immanent in the revealed Cosmic Deity of Nature, which devotee is better at uniting soul with Spirit? All disciples of God are alike and their claims are equal. The names of the Image of God are different, but the substance is the same. *Arjuna* is in a crisis.

Arjuna therefore asks, "My inner being has a question, *Krishna.* There are those disciples who steadfastly worship you, and constantly remain in you in meditation as taught by a guru. Then there are those who meditate on you as the Indestructible Unmanifest *Kutastha* – who among these is better versed in devotion? Who is the better yogi?"

Krishna answers, "Your experience is a helpful communication at your *kutastha.* Here the remembrance is captivated after the act of meditation. Fine-tuning your mind on me, he who steadfastly cherishes me, while sheltered in serenity and is awarded with the highest faith, He is judged by me to be the most devoted."

Sanjaya knows it was possible to realize God through devotion alone. *Dhritarashtra,* the blind king, saw *Krishna* as his nephew, an imperfect mortal. In contrast *Dhritarashtra's* wife *Gandhari,* the mother of their one hundred *Kauravas,* discriminates and rationalizes that *Krishna* is the inherent undistorted Self, animating all beings. She roused the resident *Krishna* within herself by fixing her mind on Him. She adored Him constantly, affiliated with Him in unblemished devotion. *Dhritarashtra* accepted that *Gandhari's* dedication to *Krishna* was well placed and creditable. The best Master of Yoga penetratingly had trained her with unhindered blind devotion to God with a Form, be he *Shiva* or *Krishna.* So she too asked her own unseeing rational, what then of those who worship a formless God?

Krishna replied not only *Arjuna* but also to the unspoken inquiry posed by the blind king's wife. "Those who stay in the *kutastha* always, see Cosmic Person in the Form of the Universal *Kutastha.* They see this person in everyplace, in all matters, and worship Him as the Unmanifest, the All-pervading, the Inconceivable, the Indifferent, the Immutable and the Eternal Being. By restraining the entire group of senses they are equal-minded. Stilled inside, they are certain that all around them are worthy of His worship. They are pledged for the good of all creatures. They gain me. They who rejoice always in the welfare of all beings – they surely come to Me."

Sanjaya knows that devotion is a matter of psychological temperament, an expression of emotions connected to a mental-intellectual capacity to understand the All-powerful inherence in a God with features and form. While sympathetic towards scriptural Knowledge, if a seeker surrenders in devotion, he penetrates the essence of his own image while in contemplation. Such a disciple, who lives an effective righteous life while following strict spiritual practices, also transcends individualistic self-awareness. He too reaches the ocean of soul-awareness.

But then there are those who approach Knowledge of the scriptures without devotion. *Sanjaya* is convinced that *Dhritarashtra,* the blind king was one of them. He neither has the initiative nor the necessary resolve to continue his efforts at spiritual practices. His biography was injured by a powerlessness to achieve a grasp of his own life's adventures. He has never accepted that his physical blindness made him unsuitable to exercise authority over a Nation. Now his spiritual blindness has ambushed the Knowledge he was cultivated into. He feels self-righteous and injured. He cannot be persuaded to act rightly despite advice and counseling.

Those who worship the Imperishable, the Indefinable, the Unmanifest, the Omnipresent, the Immovable and the Ever-Constant and whose goal is the Unmanifest Being can augment mental misinterpretation. Their path to the Unmanifest Absolute is burdensome, especially for beings that are identified with the senses and their compelling demands.

Sanjaya saw God as innate Awareness and realised Knowledge of the scriptures as the substratum on which his reflections unfold into a soul-realization. To unfold into soul-awareness, Knowledge would have to be experienced as a personal Oneness of Awareness with Consciousness. The experience is with God without qualities. But as *Krishna* admits, this is a difficult journey for many, "Those who quench the senses and keep everything in equilibrium, have a seeing intellect that is stilled. They not only gain me but they teach others the benefits of meditation. Their minds are taught to remain in the *kutastha.* Difficulties of achievement can be greater for those whose minds are fixed in the Formless. The path to the Unmanifest is difficult to find by those who are in human form."

Krishna next spoke of those who dedicate all their actions at the feet of Nature. "Those who are unable to remain in the *kutastha* to see the Formless Deity, should dedicate all actions or *karma,* their wishes, and their fruits To Me. They who repose all actions into Me and regard Me as their highest subject of attainment, they worship Me. They, who constantly watch the breath, meaning perform controlled *pranayama* while meditating on me with devotion, worship me alone. When these minds are thus fixed on Me, I become their translocator from the ocean of worldly existence."

The unawakened individualized self occupies the field of Nature, propelled and driven to act for 'me and mine'. He dies and reincarnates in unending cycles. But those who worship Awareness immanent in Nature and Consciousness transcending Nature intuitively know the structure of the subtle realms. While constantly aspiring for higher knowledge and practicing understanding over the self, they renounce all actions and think of the Cosmic Deity as the Sole Doer. About the Supreme Self as the Goal, they meditate on the exquisite Soul with single-minded devotion and absorption.

For those whose minds are set on the most excellent Soul, He gives grace and becomes their redeemer rescuing them from the sea of recurrent mortal existence or *samsara.* Therefore *Krishna* said to *Arjuna,* "Fix your heart on me alone and place your understanding in me. I will take you from worldly existence and into tranquillity. After that you will stay in Me at the *kutastha* where I am permanently lodged. There you shall live in me. There is no doubt in this."

Sanjaya and *Arjuna* understand that feelings of tranquillity are born of spiritual practices. It is the early benefit of immersing the mind into understanding God alone. Concentrating the intellect in God merely takes the devotee in *Arjuna* to the doors of realization. Arjuna remembers that learning to reflect on God with qualities took place gradually. Eventually, in the presence of Awareness, *Arjuna* is being promised the experience of Consciousness without qualities. Once he has transcended Awareness to enter the characteristic superconscious state, *Arjuna* should experience Oneness.

His commitment to the *guru* given spiritual trail should take *Arjuna* to the final habitation.

Krishna therefore said:

"You should deposit your mind in Me, *Arjuna*. The stilled intellect in contemplation then penetrates the dominion of silence. If, however, you are still unable to fix your heart steadily on me, then, O *Arjuna*, strive to get me by devotion arising from uninterrupted operations. If you are unable to even do this continuous application, then let actions performed for me be your highest aim. Even by performing all your acts for my sake, you will reach perfection."

As a man of action, *Arjuna* might not have had the amenity of steadfastly practicing *abhyas yoga*. But, when *Krishna* asks *Arjuna* to perform actions for Nature's sake only and on *Krishna's* behalf, *Arjuna* could not refuse. But, if there happened to be periods when that was not possible, then *Arjuna* was told to stay devoted to *Krishna*. Remaining sheltered in this love while relinquishing the fruits of all actions would enable him to continue striving for self-mastery.

"If even this you are unable to do then, by resorting to devotion in Me and by overpowering your individuality and abandoning the fruit of all actions, wish to practice increasing meditation," *Krishna* voiced emphatically.

Sanjaya knew how difficult it is to become independent in life and productive in all actions. Living a worldly life and aspiring to do one's duty to family, friends and society involves a balancing act. Cultivating devotion and control of life for spiritual practices should be started early in childhood. Progressive spiritual evolution then becomes natural because a proper environment for learning has been set early on, even if the Knowledge is so far incomplete. *Arjuna* was an example of such a being and his experience was specifically addressed in *Krishna's* next statement:

"If you do not have the strength or the time to practice meditation, then perform actions for me. As one continues to perform acts of contemplation, desires for all things and for fruits of action quench themselves. That is how one arrives at *siddhis* or perfection in psychic powers. This Knowledge is superior to the practice of devotion. Meditation is better than Knowledge. Renouncing the fruit of action is better than meditation and the tranquillity that results instantaneously from such abandonment.

Dhritarashtra shakes his head. He admits he is confused with *Krishna's* advice. *Sanjaya* justifies this declaration to the blind king who has failed to grasp *Krishna's* logic. "Wisdom born of study of the scriptures can be applied during contemplation in meditative practices for soul-unfoldment. Therefore, it is superior to standardized yoga practice. Would you agree, sire?"

"Yes," answered the king.

"Then to unfold from understanding to achievement in meditation is more desirable than owning theoretical knowledge?" *Sanjaya* continues.

"Yes."

"When realization unfolds into the experience of inner peace and tranquillity, relinquishing fruits of action is preferable in the early stages of meditation?"

"Therefore, renunciation of fruits of action is followed immediately by peace and spontaneous soul-unfoldment and negation of the self?" asks the blind king.

"Once the tranquil soul is settled in his intuitive understanding, it gives complete attention to nurturing correct values through right living and sincere spiritual practices. It makes out the immanence of God in everything like a thread through a string of pearls. It also sees the transcendence of God while cooperating with God's dream. And, it is free from attachment and egoism about me and mine," *Sanjaya* ends.

Krishna continues to describe such a person of devotion, "If you still cannot do this what I have just described, then continue performing actions of spiritual practices, without hankering for their fruits. While settled in the Soul, perform contemplation or *dharana,* meditation or *dhyana* and assimilation in oneness or *samadhi.* He who has no hatred for any creature, who is also friendly and compassionate, is best suited for such actions. He, who is free from egotism, who has no vanity, attachment, and who is alike in pleasures and pain can meditate. He, who is forgiving, contented, always devoted, of subdued soul, and firm of purpose is devoted to Me. He, whose heart and understanding is fixed on me, he is dear to me."

"Besides learning symbols of worship or *mudras* and performing *pranayama* or restraining breath as taught by the guru, perform meditation without expectations. Remain ever content while steady in reflection, self-controlled, and hold firm conviction that *yoga* is the path of uniting soul with Spirit. With mind and intellect surrendered to me, remember neither is anything mine nor am I anything. He who remains devoted to meditation is ever dear to me."

The blind king heard both *Krishna* and *Sanjaya* but his understanding was clouded by his attachments to his kingship, the power he had over his subjects, his kingdom, his family, and especially his devotion to his desire-driven and sense-attached children. He repeatedly cast aside his wife *Gandhari's* guidance. *Dhritarashtra* depended solely on the guidance of his own individuality. His soul had already grasped and fathomed his righteous nephews, the sons of his skilled brother *Pandu.* He knew they would win the war of *Mahabharata* on the battlefields of *Kurukshetra.* But, he settled on trusting his own selfish ideals.

Sanjaya continued to revitalize *Dhritarashtra* to perform legitimate actions so he might have a heightened awareness of God. He hoped the blind king would experience peace inside, able to trigger qualifying reasons, even if transient, of purity and integrity. If this was understood, the blind king could be encouraged not to distort his worldly kingdom with more of his own fundamental character derangement.

Then both heard *Krishna* speak to *Arjuna* about the necessary mannerism of such a changing person.

"Do not hate anyone, *Arjuna.* See everyone as yourself within the Form of the *Kutastha* when absorbed in meditation. Keep rehearsing I am in oblivion and nothing is mine. By enduring in the *kutastha,* the ego is dissolved. He, through whom the world is not troubled, and who is not tormented by the world, who is free from joy, wrath, fear and anxiety, he is dear to Me. This devotee of mine who is indifferent, pure, diligent, and separated from worldly objects, free from afflictions of the mind, and who abandons all action for fruit, he is dear to Me."

Sanjaya wanted to reinforce *Krishna's* statements.

He therefore told the blind king, "Become a believer of *Krishna,* O king. Through devotion for *Krishna's* ideal you will be directed to use your life for valuable purposes. Ever ready to work for *Krishna,* you will become disinterested with and unruffled by the existing environment. Abandoning all self-initiated activities, there is bound to be calmness between your tormented person and the Infinite who *Krishna* represents. Have faith in *Krishna,* O king. Only trust and dedication have the ability to lift you from your troubled convictions."

And *Krishna* adds, "Such a person is content because my disciple endures in meditation. He has stilled his mind and surrendered his intellect to Me and does not waste his time on materialistic things. This happens spontaneously because the disciple has faith in the teachings of his teacher. He knows nothing else except me. His person feels no joys or distaste, he neither grieves nor wants, and renounces both good and evil. He has full faith in me and he is dear to me."

Sanjaya continued to speak to the blind king. He explained the benefits of one whose individuality is entrusted to *Krishna*. "The self changes in a gradual soul-unfoldment, O king. You will be able to renounce all kindred connections and in its relief will remain easily contented. Unattached to relations your tormented mind will transcend towards a calmer personality. Devotion to *Krishna* will allow you to live under the principles of righteous living and in perfect harmony with God's will."

The king is not sure he needs to change. He already knows that no Man has reached purity with the mind alone. His own personality would need to grow in strength through discipline and restraint. If he can do this for a character such as *Krishna,* his devotion would display as fidelity for the principle that *Krishna* stands for. The problem *Dhritarashtra* has is that he feels no attachment or loyalty for *Krishna's* standard of conduct. He neither loves him as an image of god, nor does he have the mental inclination to worship him. *Arjuna* however, was not only a friend but treated his cousin as an expression of a divine teacher. He performed his actions as dutiful deeds as deliberated by *Krishna.*

Krishna knows that an apostle must have the character of a devotee who can worship the wisdom of a *guru.* He therefore continues to speak with *Arjuna* and describes the personality of a loyal, devoted and worshipful person.

"The disciple who like a drunk person works on his own initiative without hurting anyone, is alike to friend and foe. In honor and dishonor he behaves alike in cold and heat, and pleasure and pain. He is free from attachment. To him censure and praise are equal. He is taciturn and is content with anything that comes to him while enduring homelessness or not. He is of steady mind and full of faith. This man is dear to Me, O *Arjuna.* They who resort to goodness go to immortality. It has been already declared, such devotees who are full of faith regard me as the highest. They know this subject and that this gaining of this Knowledge is dear to me."

"A disciple who remains in meditation experiences in everyone, the *kutastha*. By enduring in *Brahman,* he has discarded all personal wishes and lust for enjoyment. He works for the Universal Self. He is free of opinions on matters of the senses, which he finds the same. He refuses to condemn or praise because such matters arising from them are trivial and do not deserve any comment. He naturally becomes still and silent. He who automatically enters such tranquillity is dear to ME O *Arjuna.*"

Sanjaya is careful that *Krishna's* remarks are not lost on the blind king.

"It is not enough only to live life positively. One must understand both Nature and Spirit. Right action is lived by following with adoration the immortal *dharma* of the law of life," *Sanjaya* said. "Noble living is taught in childhood by righteous parents. Failing this, your life should be drenched with devotion for Lord with Form or for the Formless Lord. Become engrossed with the soul's impulses to serve the larger family of Nature, sire. You will then be instinctively led towards the right course of action. O King, this is the path of right action, if you wish to cure your anguish."

In conclusion, *Krishna* adds, "Practicing meditation without wants ensures that you receive and realize this Immortal Substance, God. O *Arjuna,* learn devotion and loyalty to the practice of meditation and the rules of living. Have faith in your teacher and you will spontaneously come to know about the Soul. You need to have the Knowledge of *Brahman* so He reveals himself and you can experience Him."

15. Matter and Spirit

Sanjaya and *Arjuna* both understand the overall theme of *Krishna's* discussion. From his perspective the blind king realises that *Krishna* used many terms to point out the two expressions of God – His transcendence and His immanence. He recognises the bodily physique of *Prakriti* and the identity of the soul as *Purush.* These, they understood are the two appearances of *Paramatma* or *Ishwara* – God.

Krishna makes many statements about life and living but he did not detail embellishments nor did he make lengthy and tiring speeches. The blind king understands that Knowledge of these three, *Prakriti, Purusha* and *Paramatma* and their interrelationship is the highest of all scholarships. Like *Arjuna,* the blind king wants his skills of Knowing *Nature* compensated with more hands-on information. He thinks he already has a thorough Knowledge about Nature. He now wishes to experience the witnessing Knower realised as knowing of Known Nature – that vibrating Om, that penetrates all.

Everything *Krishna* has stated so far can be put into action by testing life itself. The practice needs a necessary conduct of living. Emphasis on dutiful action as suits the personality and profession can be tested and verified by responsible actions. They are to be performed in a spirit of devotion for the Cosmic Being. Without an underpinning of a sound foundation this science is impossible to champion. *Krishna's* advice would be wasted. They have been told about and seen the macrocosmic Cosmic Person, the *Kutastha.* *Arjuna* naturally wanted to discover the location where the knower, the knowledge, and the field of knowing can be experienced within his microcosmic world.

Arjuna therefore asks, "O *Krishna,* I want to know more about *Prakriti* – the world of Matter and *Purusha* – the domain of the Spirit. What are these fields? I want to know about these regions meaning, *Kshetra* – the outer physical field of the individualistic self. Who is the knower of this field? I also want to know about the inner field, which you call *Kshetrajna.* I want facts about the body-mind-intellect assembly. Where do I find this Knowledge of Awareness and about the Knower of transcendent Consciousness? I was previously told about this wisdom, which I ought to know. But because I have not fully understood it, I wish a reassertion about all these matters. Tell me all this again. I will listen."

Krishna seemed lost in his thoughts. There was momentary silence, which seemed to last forever. *Sanjaya* already realises that in Nature, action flourishes everywhere in a very definite direction. It is opposite to what Man wants. He wishes fruits of action, which he must abandon. This is not only difficult to put into practice but near impossible to do. Man's actions flow opposite to the generosity of Nature. *Krishna* has highlighted that Man must perform action as a duty to Nature.

The blind king turns to *Sanjaya* and asks about the Self and the non-Self, "What is real and what is it that is unreal?"

Sanjaya is about to rephrase what he had rehearsed and understood as a student himself. He is asked to distinguish the inside from outside of both Man and Cosmic Being.

Krishna instead makes the right response; "Whatever you wish to know is experienced through the *kutastha* during meditation. *Kshetra* philosophically describes the holy physical bodily field. The individual soul, who knows this bodily field as the *kshetra,* is the knower or *kshetrajna* of the field, which he uses for spiritual growth and unfoldment. Therefore this body, O *Arjuna,* is the *kshetra,* the field where good and evil *karma* get sown and reaped in Matter. He who knows it, the learned calls him *kshetrajna,* the knower of Knowledge. Those who know both, matter and soul or *kshetra* and *kshetrajna,* are sages."

Krishna began by analysing matter and spirit.

"The bodily field or *sharira* includes three bodies with five sheaths. He the *kutastha* is the breath who knows all these fields. The physical body or *sthulasharira* is of the five elements. The astral body or *sukshma sharira* is physiologically enlivened by *prana*. Psychological or *manasic* and intellectual or *gyanic* sheaths are also energized with revitalising life force. The causal body *or karanic sharira* is of the *essence* of both the gross and astral bodies. Knowing about these bodily fields is Knowledge. O descendent of the *Bharata* dynasty – *Arjuna*, get to know that microcosmic atom of *Brahman* within the *Kutastha*. It is He who is knower of Matter the *kshetra* or *prakriti* and of Spirit the *kshetrajna* of Knowledge, the *purusha*. Understanding of *kshetra* and *kshetrajna*, I regard to be true learning. True wisdom comes from becoming the Knower of the dominion of Consciousness sustaining the Known jurisdiction of Awareness.

"*Kshetra* includes all expressions and includes the causal, astral and physical bodies. Whatever form Man or creature takes in this world, hidden within is the soul. Because of worldly attachments, mind and intellect mutate with consequential effects. This combined body is where Man experiences himself as the self – *kshetrajna*. *Arjuna* let me tell you first about what the external *kshetra* is like, where it comes from. Let me also tell you what changes it undergoes through spiritual efforts. Let me also clarify who the inherent *kshetrajna* is and what its powers are. Hear about this from me in brief. *Rishis* have described and discussed the rationality and imprints of *Brahman*. These are all described as creditable expressions in various scriptural verses. All such communications are mentioned and written about. Through the ages, many sages have repeated them at different times and in many writings. Without exception they re-affirm the same experiences.

"Here, through study Man collects knowledge of Nature's Awareness and Her compelling qualities or *gunas*.

Spiritual transformation takes place through meditation. The three bodies start metamorphosing. The physical scene invigorates through spiritualised energisation. Continued efforts eventually permeate the astral and causal bodies also. Through spiritual instruction and meditative training, sages who meditate at the *kutastha* are able to teach the different paths of contemplation and reflection.

"Through skillful endurance the teacher shows them the Presiding Deity in the *kutastha.* The student is taught to see the *kshetrajna* who is the Cause of this body, the *kshetra.* From this site in the *kutastha,* the student who becomes sage, experiences 'I am That Brahman'. It is through That that all is revealed. The still and silent Consciousness knows itself as the ever-witnessing, transcendental *Sat-Chit-Anand.* This experience of Existence-Knowledge-Bliss is of the immanent *Purusha.* He *is* indistinguishable from Awareness – Om, It is the enlivening Om that permeates and courses through the quality awarded Nature of *prakriti.* It enlivens and energises the Manifest Universe with the effulgence of life force or *prana.*"

Arjuna and the blind king listen to *Krishna's* long discourse patiently.

Dhritarashtra interrupts the talk, "Why do I need all this information?" asks the blind king and *Sanjaya* replies with, "So that Man achieves the inclination of looking at the essence of all things, creatures and beings, Sire,"

Sanjaya continues, "Man must unlearn his conviction that he is the body without a Spirit. He worships the physique and in this idol worship ignores the essence of the soul, who he really is. Man fears the death of this body and pampers it with concern and devotion. Man should be working in dedication for the Essence of mortal existence."

Society expects Man to examine himself and remove all visible blemishes. He must make the distinction between soul and body. Unless there are such queries, he cannot fathom the body as a tool for self-improvement. Separated from senses, Man becomes more skilled at removing his own flaws. His inner attitude of devotion triggers nobler performances. He detects both merits and defects in his actions but remains aloof.

Arjuna and the king modeled themselves for cherishing the body. Man's chief concern in life is the body aging and decaying. He wants it preserved and kept alive at all cost. Until death arrives at his doorsteps, he collects and uses every trick to delay death, knowing full well nobody ever succeeds. "Honouring the body as a temple and an instrument of service is a better way of living," *Sanjaya* mutters to himself. "Human birth is then worthy of existence. Man would then understand the purpose of human existence, which is so difficult to arrive at." *Sanjaya* asks, "What is the cause of this tyrannical and mysterious misunderstanding?"

Sanjaya, an enlightened soul, understands and realises these experiences are various expressions and exhibitions of *Nature. Arjuna* was taught all of this but still remains baffled about self and soul. He too needs repeated explanations and therefore *Krishna* must answer.

Krishna now reveals the mystery of Nature's field. It must be explained that *prakriti* is the physical source of all materialisation, including Man. Details about what, where, why and how Man reveals himself is necessary. *Krishna* therefore discusses the mysterious intertwined subject of Knower, Knowledge and Knowing. He must point out the science of self-discovery to enable soul-discovery. All this was described many times before by sages who explained their own spiritual journeys. The transformations they experienced support such methods of personal Knowing, *Krishna* affirms.

Krishna explains the reason for worldly materialisationof a pure soul who is experienced as the Self in the *kutastha. Arjuna* and *Sanjaya* were both granted with a self-illuminating Light for this understanding. It was here that the subtlest atom-like essence was experienced as an indivisible core of a whole. This essence carried the gist of all the senses and organs of action. Unmanifest and indistinct, worldly events were experienced within a Cosmic Whole of Knower-Knowledge-Knowing. The witness, the knowledge and the experience united in meditation.

The blind king invited clarification and *Sanjaya* said, "Although *kshetra* or field of nature has qualities it exists as melodious invisible essence before flaunting the *gunas.* It is the cause-effect of actions that have adjusting influences. Effects are responsible for changes in the soul's causal core. The *kutastha* witnesses oscillations on this emerging field. Knowers of this Knowledge speak these truths about both *kshetra and kshetrajna.* These facts are stated in various chants in different *Vedas.* Sages have reasoned and analysed these facts in aphorisms about God's dream world."

Krishna speaks about these matters,

"Briefly, the *kshetra* is poised and unruffled Unmanifest Nature defined as undifferentiated *mula-prakriti.* She assembles within her womb essences five cosmic elements, five *pranic* life forces, five senses and five organs of action. Included within are mind, intellect, ego, and the *chitta* personality. *Arjuna* let me tell you about the origin of *kshetra.* I will also speak about mental characteristics of soul-identified and self-identified humankind.

"The five great elements, egoism, intellect, the ten senses, one mind, five objects of senses, want, distaste, body consciousness, courage – all these are pledged to the *kshetra as* changed structure. They are permutations of Matter-field of *kshetra.* Want, hatred, pleasure, pain, diverse bodily forces, awareness, intellect and fortitude also are the *kshetra."*

"How does this happen, *Krishna*?"

"When Man attaches attention on what he wishes, he is either fulfilled with pleasure or becomes malicious with displeasure. He either loves or hates the thing he covets but may feel happy or sorrowful with it. Death associates with grief and therefore there must be a rebirth and a living once more. All these are transmutations of the body, *Arjuna.*"

"Can all this not be avoided, *Krishna*?"

"It can be prevented by enduring in contemplation in the *kutastha.* Those who practice absence of vanity and avoid injury, uphold uprightness and devotion towards guru and trainer, avoid such grief. The genuine and persevering that show self-restraint and are drawn to worshipping their counsellor are also able to avoid such problems of living. They are made tranquil through the exercises of soul-search."

"But there must be more to keeping oneself in the search and experience of the Self?" *Arjuna* asked.

"Yes there is. There has to be indifference to objects of senses, absence of egoism, an understanding of misery and evils of birth, death, decrepitude and disease. These give Man the ability to reflect on the enigma of suffering and conflicts. Absence of want allows Man to seek out and decipher ego, birth, death, old age, disease, and dishonesty, *Arjuna.*"

"Where does a seeker find ego most conspicuous, *Krishna*?"

"It appears as attachments, excessive fondness and possessiveness for wife, son, home and the rest. Man must live in steady consistency in the presence of good and evil. This allows him to sort out undesirables from desirables."

"How does one do that?"

"By enduring in meditation, it all happens spontaneously, *Arjuna.* The attitude should be of unswerving devotion to the *Kutastha* when in meditation. Watch the breath while sequestered – that also helps. Spontaneous distaste for gatherings and unnecessary chatter leads this person to oneself. Faith in the *guru's* words makes it all possible. Remember putting affection elsewhere besides the soul, leads the mind to rogues and wrongdoing. Avoiding attachments keeps the mind focused on the Self and seeking Self-Knowledge.

"When truthful to the science of self and the Supreme, his intellect understands the structure of Knowledge of

Truth. This science is earned from an astute and wise *guru.* Such knowing and seeing happens through grace of the Self-revealing Knowledge at the *kutastha.* Looking elsewhere for other forms of knowledge happens with attachment. It is unconscious knowledge which is ignorant of the Truth."

Sanjaya turns to the blind king, "O king, observe *Arjuna's* humility and unpretentiousness. He wishes no injury and seeks forgiveness. That despite what your unrighteous sons have done to the *Pandus* over the years. His undertaking to friends and *guru* stem from a faultlessness of mind and body born of self-control. His wisdom, despite this frustrating state of affairs, seeks both self-knowledge of *kshetra* and soul-knowledge of *kshetrajna. Arjuna* has unswerving devotion to *yoga* and perseverance to know and understand the self and soul and all the opposite qualities that make up ignorance."

The blind king's thoughts had strayed and then he voiced his concerns, "O *Sanjaya,* what does *Krishna* mean by the misfortunes of birth and death, old age and disease, and attachment to family?"

Sanjaya answered, "Be mindful of misfortunes that belong to birth and decay. The exhaustion that escorts old age takes the form of inconvenience, discomfort and pain. *Krishna* is warning *Arjuna* to remove these circumstances through self-control and energisation of the physical and astral bodies.

"Right understanding promotes self-understanding and settles in soul-awareness. Interaction with family and friends should neither be disadvantaged nor calculating. *Krishna* is encouraging *Arjuna* to live in harmony with all and allow others the freedom to change and deliberate at their own pace.

"Your sons have prejudiced your unrestrained behaviour, O king. You have nurtured their egoistic wishes and addictive needs for self-gratification. Hear now O king, about the Cosmic Being – *Purusha,* the Creator *Brahma.* Every self can experience the soul. Awareness experiences that

Consciousness. It is the core of Man's essence. Therefore, O king, aim for That and do not revitalise anarchy for the sake of personal rewards."

Sanjaya knows, so long as the thought of the Self does not arise in the body, Man is absorbed in mundane activities. He is immersed in activities of the body. The soul remains a a helpless witnessing faculty until he wakes up. Out of the blue, he realises he has lived animal-like for the body. With this comes the power of discrimination and analysis. A starting point for ethics is drawn up and discipline replaces unthinking indulgences.

The Self now assumes the role of the eternal witness who has the power to reproach, approve and even reflect on Man's actions. Self-approval gives him inner joy and Man is firmly on the path of right action.

Dutiful actions clean both mind and heart. Man stagnates when self-improvement is slow. He begs for assistance that comes readily when the yearning heart cries out in prayer. The Self ensures that Man is firmly planted on a platform of ethics in all his actions. The mind is cleaned of all impurities and when Man stumbles, he is helped in a flood of grace. All this comes spontaneously as education of Truth.

"What then of education at institutes of learning which allow Man to work professionally and earn for the lives of his loved ones?" asks *Arjuna.*

"The highest education is that of the Self, *Arjuna.* Man must undergo utilitarian learning because he must fulfill his four duties in life: *Dharma, artha, kama,* and *moksha* for righteous living. Wealth helps satisfy needs for livelihood and eventual liberation. *Krishna* says and then continues, "But there is a higher learning for *moksha.*"

Krishna now feels it is time to describe the Self to *Arjuna,* "What I speak of now are of matters that should be known. Knowing it Man imbibes immortal nectar. All other information besides the knowledge of *Brahman* is neither truth nor untruth. All, which is dissimilar to soul-knowledge, is Ignorance. I will now give further details about that which, when known, gives immortality. It is about the Supreme *Brahman* who has no beginning and is neither existent nor nonexistent. I reiterate He is known only in the *kutastha.* By knowing its Substance, Man forgets his individuality. He experiences Eternal Certainty who is beyond truth and untruth because both the seer and seen are there."

Arjuna wonders "What is the temperament of this Man who realises this Certainty?" asks *Arjuna.*

"In this state Man is able to go anywhere he wishes and like one drunk, his subtle being sees *Brahman* always, whenever he wishes, both within himself and outside. He sees His hands and feet are everywhere, and His eyes, heads and faces are on all sides. He knows He can hear all that is said because He is in every place."

Krishna continues, "The qualities of all the senses are duties and roles of His Form. He therefore experiences them all. *Yogis* and *gurus* know Him in the *gunas* enjoying through the sense organs and detaching from them. All elements and their qualities are Immortal and in Him. He detaches from the *gunas* as well as enjoys them, *Arjuna.* He remains and pervades everything in the world. He is not controlled by senses, though empty of senses. He is without attachment yet suffers all. Although without qualities He enjoys their characteristics outside and inside all creatures, especially when Man is in contemplation and the breath is stilled."

The blind king again asks *Sanjaya* to clarify *Krishna's* ambiguous words, "O King, I will tell you about the science of Awareness which should be known because it grants immortality. Heed also about the beginning-less Consciousness – *Brahman* who is being spoken of. That is neither existence *or sat* nor nonexistent or *asat.* He is unattached to creation, yet is the Supporter of all three worlds – physical, subtle and causal. It is free of qualities of Nature, yet experiences them all as the eternal witness."

"All you must do O king, is to transact virtuous actions to erase the facade of deception that nurtures your individualistic self. Meditation lifts these soul-restricting veils. A clear view of Awareness allows perfect realisation and experience of the Truth."

"Who will remove the veil of deception and how?" asks the blind king.

"The Self is nearer than we think, sire. He is the one who makes perfect what is so far incomplete on this spiritual journey," *Sanjaya* reassured. "Offer all the flaws, doubts about the Self in complete dedication, even the fruits of that, and receive the grace of the Self."

"Who is this Self?" asks the blind king.

Arjuna in the meantime is asking the same question. "*Krishna,* describe to me the Form of *Brahman,*" *Arjuna* petitions.

Krishna's answer describes *Brahman.* "In all possessions and in all there is but one Substance, *Brahman,* existing at once and at the same time. Both inside and outside and in all of Creation, *Brahman* is within and existing separately in His skillful form. Because of this He is not knowledgeable. He is both near and far also. He creates, supports and dissolves everything whether stationary or mobile, and is not knowable because of His subtlety. He is remote yet near, and is undistributed in all beings, yet remains as if stretched.

"So He is subtle and immanent in everything and yet in transcendence also?" asks *Arjuna.*

"He is in separate and in different forms. He is the sustainer of all beings and the absorber and creator of all. He is beyond the darkness of utilitarian knowledge, the object of knowledge and the direction of knowledge. He is at the Source within the *kutastha.*"

"What is His Form in the *kutastha*?"

"He is the Light of all shining bodies, and is beyond darkness of the planets. There is no other light like Him when He reveals in the *kutastha*. It is He who is the thing to know. Know Him, who lives in all hearts as Tranquillity, *Arjuna*."

"How do I recognize Him in this bodily field you describe as *kshetra*?"

"He is the field of Knowledge, the subject of Knowledge, the end of Knowledge and is the wisdom that must be known. He sits as the Essence in the hearts of all. He is gained by Man who has faith in the teachings of the *guru*. Knowing this, the devotee remains within the sanctuary of the *kutastha*."

And then *Krishna* continues, "You see *Arjuna*, these discussions about the knowledge of the bodily field of *kshetra*, by the *kshetrajna* or seeking soul, have been previously described by me many times, succinctly. The knower or *kshetrajna* of the bodily field of *kshetra* is the *kutastha*. The extrovert Man looks outwards by employing and engaging the cranial and spinal nerve channels. My devotee knowing all this switches his attention inside and uses the *ida, pingala* and the *sushumna*. He fully develops in spirit with me."

Once Man gains information of the Self and the Non-self, he resolves to get better enlightenment with the Knowledge of the Self. He acts according to ethics of lasting enlightenment. Man experiences grace when such acts are dedicated to the Self. It flows endlessly towards the seeker. Man dedicates even his agitations at the feet of the Self.

The blind king is still flustered and confesses simple-mindedness. *Sanjaya* reattempts to explain this mysterious science of God, "The qualities of Nature do not have a separate awareness or existence. When in harmony, there is no manipulative pressure or energy. The enlivening **Om** permeates all matter and emerges as a vibrating current from the still and silent field of Consciousness. Awareness merges with the field of Om. Energy inherent in Matter and the enlivening *prana* – Om, are together the understated Indivisible One, Yet *Purushottama or Brahman* appears as if divided into countless beings."

"*Brahman* the Supreme Spirit is the witnessing Light

Energy of all lights, beyond all darkness. It is reached by Knowledge itself, which should be demystified. That is also the Subject of Knowledge and the goal of all knowing the Knower. He sits in the hearts of all as the Light of enlightenment," *Sanjaya* explains.

As *Krishna* spoke to *Arjuna, Sanjaya* not only heard but also witnessed the conversation, He felt privileged he could learn from and communicate the discussions taking place on the battlefield of *Kurukshetra.*

"How does *prakriti* become the doer of all action, *Krishna*? Why does Man experience joy and sorrow even with dutiful actions?" *Arjuna* asked.

Krishna replies, "Elements, mind, intellect and ego are the material cause of all action. When action is triggered by a cause, the doer identifies with the material cause and becomes attached to results of the act. It is sad Man does not know *kutastha* is un-involved. While self merges with joy and sorrow, Tranquillity which is the substance of the *kutastha.* Is as if non-existent." *Krishna* shakes his head in disapproval and says,

"There in the *kutastha* is where the doer as contemplator experiences all. Therefore the cause of experiencing pleasure and sorrow is in the 'self'."

"How does the Self as *purusha* become contaminated by the qualities of *prakriti*?" *Arjuna* asks.

"Know that Nature or *prakriti* and Spirit or *purusha* are both without beginning or end. Variations and qualities spring from disturbing harmony [*sattva*]in Nature. Therefore although She is the material cause, activity and doer-ship emerge from Nature. It happens when harmony is disturbed towards commotion [*rajas*] or indolence [*tamas*]. Because Nature is the source of such potentials the doer enjoys pleasure and pain. *Purusha* is a witnessing partner in this delight and sorrow."

"I am not sure I understand what you have just said, *Krishna.*"

"*Purusha* is coloured by tints and shades of *prakriti. Purusha* shares in the experience of sorrow and enjoyment as a witness. He is after all tinged in the colour of *prakriti*. The supreme *purusha* in this body is the surveyor, approver, supporter, enjoyer, the mighty lord, and the Soul. Depending on their attachment to different *gunas,* rebirth of Man takes place in good or evil wombs."

And *Dhritarashtra* asks, "As I understand it, *Purusha* or Cosmic Self is the Macrocosmic Universal Being and *Prakriti* is the material cause that is Mother Nature. *Purusha* is involved in Man's sorrow and enjoyment as a witness. Both are without beginning and infinite. I also understand that it is qualities or *gunas* of Nature that force all action-impelled changes. You have enlightened me that *gunas* are inherent in nature. Changes directed by *gunas* are natural but the law of cause-and-effect relates to those who embellish themselves with agency."

Dhritarashtra then continues, "About cause and effect, the 'self' experiences nature's qualities because it identifies with addictive attachments to *gunas.* How can I reverse my actions while impelled and compelled by *gunas* to create new effects? I wish to free myself from soul-bondage and reincarnation?"

"You tell me the Supreme Soul is the *Purusha,* who is immanent and transcendent in all. He is the enlivening life principle in energy of Matter. Then who is the Supreme Spirit? Is He, the detached witness, the approbatory sustainer, the enjoyer, the great Lord who supports both *Prakriti and Purusha*?"

Sanjaya answered, "O King, you speak of stages of spiritual progression from growth and understanding, to realisation and experience. Most self-conscious individuals have no awareness of spiritual matters. They pray to a chosen deity and act by their body's inclinations, memories, past habits, and earned life-style. Wrong self-identification allows them to think and feel they are limited. *Tamasic* and self-righteous, they work from the base spiritual centre. Driven by lust within their astral-causal *muladhara chakra* Man is compelled towards materialism engineered at the physical coccygeal plexus."

"Then there are spiritual seekers who while on the spiritual path are of agitated and spiteful disposition. These are constrained by addictions, dependency, and unpredictable emotional outbursts. Because of self-defeating behaviours, they blame others for their failures. Prominent *tamasic* and mild *rajasic* forces make them extroverts. These self-conscious beings are driven by subconscious wants, habits and memories lodged within the second astral-causal *svadhisthana* or sacral plexus along the spinal pathway," *Sanjaya* declared carefully.

"A practicing spiritual seeker, who develops an intense habit of study and meditation, is self-conscious and has transformed his physical, psychological, and physiological body. He becomes addicted and attached to intermittent states of calmness. His rational and skillful actions are intellectually motivated for pleasures. He directs himself towards nurturing relationships. Such a being is propelled by the creativity of *rajas* and works from the intellectual centre of astral-causal *Manipur,* located in the lumbar plexus of the spinal pathway. If Man refuses to nurture restraint, he reveals a selfish and grasping personality instead.

"When this changing *rajasic* individual reaches a degree of awareness, he is duty-bound to find a teacher. The type of *guru* who appears is captivated by the seeker's spiritual awakening whose individuality is destroyed to the degree he understands and realises the Knowledge. He gradually masters actions and nurtures activities and relationships thrust more by *rajas* than *tamas,* but aiming for a harmony in *sattva.* Activities are centred in the fourth astral-causal *anahata chakra* in the chest. Whenever Man refuses restraints and self-control he displays confusing emotions of unquenchable cravings, exasperation, miserliness and possessiveness," *Sanjaya* continues.

"The genuinely committed spiritual seeker, who gains partial attentiveness about the Knowledge and is a Knower of some wisdom, realises that the Cosmic Dream of God is sustained on a scaffolding of vibrating Om where Matter displays both enlivening *prana* and energy. He gains elation from his inner understanding which is intuitive. Propelled by *sattva,* this person experiences inner perceptiveness and realisation emitted from the fifth astral-causal *vishuddha chakra* in the cervical plexus. He hears Om, feels *prana,* sees the cosmic vision in the *kutastha* and watches the different levels of consciousness. The materialistic Man who has never practiced this science reveals only arrogance with pride from this centre."

"When the seeker reaches the medullary *ajnaa centre* of Awareness, selfhood changes gradually towards soul-unfoldment. The unenlightened *chitta* personality reveals itself as feelings. He is freed from many illusions and delusions and the seeker comes face-to-face with pure awareness. A soul-unfoldment from this centre now awaits the grace of a *guru* for complete realisation. *Kshetra* and *kshetrajna* fuse in the *Kutastha* with the enlivening *Om.* The seeker experiences God with a soul-Soul Form in *savikalpa samadhi,*" *Sanjaya* explains.

"In the final stages of meditation, the enlightening *chitta* personality transcends into pure vibrationless Consciousness - *chit,* the Formless God experienced as *Sat-Chit-Anand* in *nirvikalpa samadhi.* O King I have tried to explain the different terminology used by *Krishna* by following the spiritual progression of an aroused spiritual seeker. The path and its pre-eminence depends on his eagerness and dedication to connect with God's immanence in expressions and in His transcendence beyond exhibition," *Sanjaya* concludes.

Arjuna knows about stages of development in a meditating seeker. He has other issues to speak about, "You have spoken about three entities, *Krishna.* There are Matter and Spirit who are intertwined in immanence and then there is the transcendental *Brahman*. What is the use of this journey after understanding the Knowledge?" *Arjuna* asks.

Krishna first explains the advantages of spiritual endeavours: "The *Kutastha* is the *guru* of all humanity, *Arjuna*. Whatever you are searching in spiritual growth is found through the teachings of this *guru*. He leads you to the *kutastha* and in its stillness and silence, you see the microcosmic particle of *Brahman*. This Person is witness, patron, lord and enjoyer. He is *Paramatma* – the Supreme Self who is also called the *Kutastha*. Even after meeting Him, the foolish keep searching for Him in all places. They rummage around Him but do not seek Him within, even while looking right at Him." *Krishna* then says as if in exasperation.

"In the body of the *kutastha* are both *purusha* and *prakriti*, tied together by the Father Spirit. All this endures in all hearts. That is *Brahman* – the highest *purusha* or *Purushottama*. He is the best of the *purushas*. He, who thus seeks and knows the witnessing Cosmic Self, the enlivening Spirit and the energy infused Nature with qualities, in whatever state he may be, he is never born again. Some by meditation behold the self in the Self by the Self.

"Others find this by devotion – this is already stated in writings. According to the *Sankhyan* system Man experiences the Self through dedication. Others gain the Self by fidelity through enthusiastically performed works for the Cosmic Mother. Others, who do not know this, worship That about whom they have heard from others. Even these, devoted to what is heard, cross over death.

"If the seeker stays in Him, he becomes He, *Arjuna*. Even though He is brought into being in meditation in the *kutastha*, he must be ready to watch the breath constantly in *pranayama*. He is now on a path to secure the meeting place where he will meet with the Supreme Person."

Sanjaya once more must explain what *Krishna* has just said. *Sanjaya* must simplify some of what has been spoken,

"To behold the self in the Self as the purified ego, by the Self in the illumined mind, some people follow the path of contemplation. Some follow the path of *Gyana Yoga* or Knowledge, and some follow the path of selfless action in *Karma Yoga.* Some men, ignorant of the three main paths, heed the instructions of the *guru.* Following the path of worship in *Bhakti Yoga,* and depending on the old teachings as the highest refuge, these men also can gain immortality, Sire. Once established in awareness of God and an understanding of the self-propelling manipulation of life by compulsions of Nature, all seekers like *Arjuna* reach life's goal of God realisation."

Krishna now adds, "O *Arjuna,* the pride of the *Bharata* race, know that whatever entity immobile or mobile comes into existence, comes from the alliance of *kshetra* and *kshetrajna* or matter and spirit. He knows this *purusha* is the incorporated witness of the *gunas* innate in *prakriti.* He sees the Supreme Lord remaining identical in all beings, as the Imperishable in the perishable. By seeing the Lord lingering alike everywhere, he sees all actions performed only by Nature. He now stays amid everything knowing Matter has no death and he is therefore without fear. He has found the unspeakable that cannot be defined. He sees Him in the *kutastha* while searching for the Self. He knows the search should be in this physical body and this seeking will allow him to see the Supreme Person. He understands he must learn meditation from a qualified teacher to find Him."

"Is this the only way to meet the Supreme Person, *Krishna*?"

"A seeker searching for the Supreme Person by *pranayama* and *dhyana* is able to witness *Brahman* in every atom of the five elements, mind, intellect and ego, no matter how superior, inferior or average the quality of Man. And even if the seeker does not stay in the *kutastha* always, such a seeker becomes that *Brahman* Being and freed of rebirth."

"How can a seeker continuously arrive at the Supreme Person?" *Arjuna* asks.

"After watching the breath at one sitting for a longtime, a seeker is able to see the pure Self. Some persevere unceasingly on uninterrupted *pranayama.* They behold spontaneously and without a doubt, the Self, every time. Such people remain unattached from everything else by not allowing the mind to connect to anything else. By remaining steadfast in the *kutastha* in whatever they do, they see the Self automatically. Such people are consolidating the breath or *pranayama* with complete sense retraction or *pratyahara,* while in constant contemplation or *dharana,* and in meditation or *dhyana* while, aiming for Oneness in *samadhi."*

"How do such seekers steady their minds, *Krishna*?"

"Having heard all that is to be known, they steady the mind by concentrating on a specific object." *Krishna* answers.

"What do you mean exactly?" *Arjuna* asks.

"They sit in a quiet place and listen to the cosmic hum of Om while breathing and in the pauses also. They navigate into the tranquil stillness and silence of contemplation and meditation."

"What happens to these seekers and what is it that they see?"

"They see all what you see, both mobile and stationary, happening within the Supreme Person. He realises that He is the revealed Form of all, in the outward appearance of *prakriti."*

Krishna continues after a pause, "He is also the Knower of the field who is both the soul and the Cosmic Soul. On seeing the Cosmic Person, the *Purusha,* he realizes that a soul is only a microcosmic *purusha.* He knows the soul is not the doer. This seeker remains in meditation practicing *pranayama.* He sees the Self through the processes of Knowing. He who knows this Knowledge has reached the highest goal. He has understood the knowledge through *gyana yoga* and through *mudras* taught by a teacher."

"What then of the movements of event in Nature?"

"By seeing all in this way, he sees all marvels becoming one and the same. He understands there is Stillness within the heart of all happenings right here in the *kutastha*. He sees the stillness at the end of extinction of all destructible matter. He witnesses that *Brahman* has no obliteration. He realises that he is seeing that who is the one seeing. After that, he works for the Cosmic Being without any cravings for results. In meditation he sees who sees all actions as propelled by Nature alone in every way and recognises the self everywhere to be the doer. He realises *Brahman* exists equally in all. That which is destructible is being destroyed. Whoever sees this is the seer," *Krishna* replies.

"What then is this seeker's attitude towards worldly living?" asks *Arjuna*.

"In this way, the one who sees *Brahman* found in everything and everywhere is with the Self by the Self. Whoever sees the Self present equally in all, he sees the soul by the Self. When one sees the diversity of entities in one, and the issue of everything from that One, then is one said to have reached the stillness of *Brahman*."

Arjuna interjects, "*Krishna,* my understanding reels. What are you saying? Does this mean that all action originates from matter as well as spirit?

Krishna replies, "Everyone is acting because of *prakriti*. Whatever exists, whether animate or inanimate, is born from the union of *Kshetra* also defined as the field or Nature, and *purusha* the *Kshetrajna* who is the knower Spirit of Knowledge. He sees who makes out the Supreme Lord present equally in all creatures – this is the Imperishable in the perishing.

Whoever sees the soul in everything becomes his own lord. He becomes a non-doer while remaining in the Self. Through this Knowledge such a sage combines *Brahman* with circumstances to become One. Then even worldly existence or *samsara* becomes nothing other than *Brahman.*"

'Then in this One is All and All is in One?" asks *Arjuna.*

"There is nothing other than *Brahman, Arjuna.* If in this One is all, then where can there be a beginning? For that matter where are these *gunas* also? Because *gunas* have merged in *Brahman* while in the stillness of meditation, there is no destruction of them. He, who has experienced this Knowledge, while living in this mortal body of his, what he does and does not do, is also *Brahman.* He is not enmeshed in anything. He sees all actions as performed in their entirety by *Prakriti* alone and not by the action-less witnessing Self. Indeed he sees the truth because he beholds all separate beings as existent within the One *Brahman* or God. When viewing everything as same within the Knowledge of *Brahman* as the encompassing, he has grasped *Brahman.*"

"*Brahman* encompasses both Stillness and Movement, *Krishna*?"

Krishna adds to his earlier interpretation and says to *Arjuna,* "Just as space moves subtly through the entire cosmos in stillness, it moves nonetheless. Within the path of subtle Stillness is the path of physical Movement. In the same way, the microcosm, which exists in all bodies in its soul form, is pervading in Stillness. Even here, movement occurs, but in Stillness. But subtlety works as if not enmeshed. This Stillness of meditation is to be grasped by seekers. If this is not aspired for, Man only gains Movement. But remember O son of *Kunti,* this inexhaustible Self, being without beginning and without qualities, does not act when stationed as the *purusha* in the body. He is not commanded by anything."

And *Krishna* adds, "Just as space, which is widespread and everywhere, never suffers effect of contamination because of its subtlety, so too the Self as soul, stationed in everybody is never tainted."

"From the time of birth onwards, Man lives in movement. The way to stop the movement of the universe is through meditation, which a *guru* teaches. Man only has to remain in this region and the current of action pulls the seeker in the needed direction."

"How then does the searching seeker witness the Spirit of Consciousness?" *Arjuna* asks.

"O scion of the *Bharata* dynasty, just as the single Sun lights up the entire world, so too the Spirit lights up the entire matter of a mortal's body. The dweller of the field the *kshetrajna* reveals the *kshetra* or field. As long as there is darkness because attention is filled with wants and attachments, the sun-like illumination from the *kutastha* is not and cannot be revealed."

"One can know the field or *kshetra* and its knower or *kshetrajna,* through the instrument of insight, the Eye-of-Knowledge in the *kutastha.* They that by the eye of knowledge know the distinction between matter and spirit and the path of redemption from all elemental entities, get the Supreme. The eye of knowledge reveals itself by performing the *yoni mudra.* While enduring in there, the mind and intellect remains fixed in the Divine Sight in perfect Stillness. Intelligence or *parabuddhi,* which is combined *purusha* and *prakriti* sees itself as **'*I-Brahman*'**," *Krishna* explains.

"Here *purusha* takes *prakriti* into His own Form and with that He absorbs Her *maya* into Himself. This is what a seeker experiences in liberation, or *moksha.* The self sees the Self and merges with the Self," *Krishna* says and turns around to view the army on both sides of their chariot.

Krishna was busy assessing the assembly of armies. *Sanjaya* was lost in thoughts. A great deal had been said right there in the middle of Life's Battle. *Dhritarashtra* remained unconvinced. *Arjuna* was impressed. They were all told the same message. To experience the Self, they have been advised to recognise they all have a physical expression. They must learn how to manipulate this display. That is Man's duty, which if performed as directed by a *guru,* would leave them with no sense of separation from the Self. They must learn to do the Lord's work. Reliance on the Lord to guide and to learn how to recognise Self by the self, is Man's duty in life.

Man's life must be ethical and moral so actions performed are noble deeds to clean the subtle impurities of the mind. When the cleaning efforts are stubborn, asking for help allows the Self to rush to his aid. After that all actions become an offering of love at the feet of the Self. Resolves to surrender all actions fills Man's existence, which is the final goal of life.

Therefore they make the distinction with their eye-of-wisdom and discriminate constantly. They know the difference between the field of Non-Self *or Kshetra* and the knower-of the field of Self *or Kshetrajna.* He secures liberation through devotion from the compulsions of *Prakriti,* and goes to the supreme home of the vibration-less Consciousness, the *Purushottama* or *Brahman.*

16. Nature's Qualities

It dawned on the blind king that entire humanity is classified into three types. Based upon dominating qualities of *sattva, rajas* and *tamas,* behavioural tendencies influence Man's character and personality.

Sanjaya in the meantime is in a contemplative mood. A great deal has happened in the middle of a battlefield where two parties prepare to start the war. He experienced insightful revelations during *Arjuna-Krishna* discussions. However, he is distressed. How does he convince visionless king to avoid this catastrophe?

How does he influence *Dhritarashtra*? Can he be taught to detect souls who have unfettered themselves from Cosmic Forces in Matter?

Dhritarashtra is also in deep thought. How do mortals fiddle with such compelling influences during their unrelenting but worldly survival? He understands the Self need not do anything. The self completes itself into the Self as an innate movement of soul dominance. It is the weight and freight of the body, which drags the soul towards descent. If there is a way to shatter the shackles of *gunas,* he can free himself of the powers exercised over him. The monarch believes all he needs doing is to psychologically discard dominant influence of matter over his soul.

The king reasons there is no authenticated connection between matter and spirit. The unsighted king realises that he must discover the art of forsaking the three-*guna* qualities and become *gunateeta,* beyond *gunas.* The monarch surmises that although *Sanjaya* identified discrimination and self-control as the way, he disagrees.

Sanjaya knows the only way the blind sovereign might realise his blemished action is if he can be convinced, he acts the dictates of his individualistic self. A need to become an enlightened soul through contemplation should show him a way to transcend qualities and compulsions of Matter. The stance of an ever-witnessing agent must be encouraged. The royal personage might still be convinced to stop this war of unrighteousness.

Sanjaya is a perfected yogi. He understands the worlds are swirling with dances of shadows and lights. Expressions of three *gunas,* animate all energy in matter with enlivening Om. Nature seems as if made up of three strands of qualities: creativity of *rajas,* inertia of *tamas* and harmony of *sattva.* This truth enables the *yogi* in *Sanjaya* to detach himself and dwell in the omnipresent Light of the Self, away from the *gunas.* He knows they can be transcended. Their influence stands apart from the Self. He wants the blind king to experience the same. He must make every attempt to persuade him to ascend this committed pathway.

Meanwhile, *Krishna* tells *Arjuna* how *tamas* displays as slothfulness, disregard and too much slumber. It destroys harmony and contentment in society because of its humiliating compulsions. With *tamas,* humanity becomes idle in body and in mind. They lose bodily deservedness for peaceful rests. Recall and attentiveness die away. Imperfect attention and inattention allow the body to desecrate the spirit of Man. He becomes ineffective and diseased.

Krishna also discusses the powerful foe, *rajas,* when entangled with *tamas.* Together they ruin humankind. When *rajas* empowers Man with boundless aspirations for utilisation, self-indulgence takes over. Both instincts and passions are activated until the body is exhausted. He loses attentiveness, self-confidence and dependability. Indulgence makes him tremulous and agitated in body and mind. His wholesomeness is blemished. To avoid death from absent-mindedness and carelessness, *Krishna* advises Man to channel creativity or *rajas*. Performance should be towards normal activities. Service in action is of benefit. Such links dictate one's inherently natural duty in life. It allows Man to conserve his energy, strength and power for self-growth and development.

Arjuna hears about *sattva* also. *Krishna* says it displays as ego and pride when devoted acts are performed with desires for fruit of action. Unless this connection with action is discarded, *sattva* cannot and does not express in the harmony of kindness and thoughtfulness. *Krishna* warns that all three compulsions are powerful. Guarding oneself against them is advised. Grace of the Lord and *guru* helps.

Sanjaya, Arjuna and *Dhritarashtra* have all understood that *Prakriti* is intelligent. Matter unquestionably devises the destiny of Man as either the self or the Self. Both the visionless king and *Arjuna* have a blurred idea of what is said about the compulsions of matter qualities as *gunas. Krishna* must now explain how the inherent qualities in Nature direct *pranic* life force on the energy in matter. Manipulation of the self or *aham* is sketched by *gunas*. Personal behaviours are etched by compelling circumstances, as is the case with the blind monarch.

Arjuna is pensive in his chariot. *Krishna* looks at both sides of the assembled armies. *Arjuna* suddenly asks, "Who is it who works with and understands this supreme knowledge about Matter and Spirit? What does this study hope to achieve? Where and to whom is this especially addressed? That which is taught and about which you speak, is it truly the crowning truth? When and how does the Knowledge eventually disclose itself?"

And *Krishna* replies, "This Knowledge is experienced through the *kutastha*. I will once again declare to you that this is a supernal discipline. This is not a branch of knowledge. It is the most outstanding of all known and unknown disciplines, knowing which even sages have reached their highest perfection. They are unchained from the shackles on this body. Those who opt for this system of knowledge reach the destination of His Personality. They are not reborn even when a new creation starts. They remain undisturbed in universal dissolution. This body of information consummates all the way through to the *kutastha.* Many confirm this fact repeatedly. They expand into this Knowledge spontaneously, without even wishing for it. The sages remain silenced. This encounter confirms there is nothing outside this Knowledge."

Both *Arjuna* and *Sanjaya* previously heard all this. The visionless king has also heard the same discussion. By embarking on a spiritual trail through the study of Knowledge of the Scriptures is only an act of awakening. The journey is from self-awareness to soul-consciousness. Following one's *dharma* is a vocation. Prosperity once achieved makes unrestricted effort for liberation possible. Every ambition is included in the cosmic model, as a seed in creation. Once this seed consummates with Knowledge, Man seeks his own emancipation. *Arjuna* wants to know how the Lord of the Universe advises Man to do just that.

"What exactly is this cosmic plan, *Krishna*?" asks *Arjuna.*

Krishna pauses before speaking. He must explain how the seed of origin is fertilised in the causal womb of matter, "The powerful *Brahman* is like a mighty womb. In it are placed the living germs of every creature. When some are armed with this incomparable Knowledge, such people come unhampered and committed to their *dharma, artha, kama and mokshaa.* There is no destruction for them. O scion of the *Bharata* dynasty *Arjuna,* the birth of all beings takes place from this womb alone. Some of these sages have already achieved silence and stillness of meditation, which is so necessary for attainment of this Knowledge."

"Is everything and everyone in the womb?"

"This womb is the Supreme *Brahman* who put into it everything that is still to become. Whether in the atom or in the Universe, all this *Brahman* pervades and permeates. When Man reaches there in meditation, even if asked, he says nothing. He is silenced by the inexpressible."

"Then how does one know about such substantiality?"

"O son of *Kunti,* all is born in wombs. Those that are extraordinary are also *Brahman.* Of all the shelters, the mightiest incubator *Brahman,* is the unified womb and also the seed-imparting Sire. Therefore, He is the ancestor of the seed in *Brahman-Yoni.* He is the Self in the Self, granted with the power or *shakti.* It is the Form of the *kutastha.* From the *Kutastha, kutastha* is born. The Father is born as Son and Son is born as the Father. Father and Son are One"

"Who then passes on this knowledge of the Self to mortals such as me?"

"The reincarnating sages, the Sons of God return through the ages, era after era, to enlighten humankind who have strayed," *Krishna* replies.

"Please speak to me of Matter, Spirit and God, *Krishna.*"

"O *Arjuna,* there are three qualities of *prakriti – tamas, rajas,* and *sattva.* These are indestructible in the flesh made of elements, mind, intellect and the ego. Darkness, passion and goodness – they are qualities born of Nature. They imprison the embodied soul when linked to attachments. Unless attentive towards the *kutastha,* he cannot expect liberation from the bondage of Nature's qualities."

Having explained that all causal seeds germinate in the original womb of Mother Nature *prakriti, Arjuna* understands that the enlivening life force or *prana* comes from the Creator *Purusha who* is the Father. *Krishna* defines further, "Because of tendencies of elements, mind, intellect and ego, there is adulteration in personality. Their cloudy expression deflects light off the *kutastha*"

"*Sattva* although established in purity, illumines, but it binds the Indestructible to earthly happiness but does not bind him to real Knowledge. Because it is untarnished by nature's creativity, it is more enlightened and free from misery, but *sattva* still binds the soul. O sinless one, unless there is an attainment of happiness through Knowledge, even pure Light does not clean the mirror of the *kutastha*. When the self sees the Self by Oneself and the Oneself becomes *Brahman*, then All is *Brahman*. When all has become One, then there is neither mutation nor destruction."

"What of the skilful power of creativity?"

"*Rajas* or goodness is born of desire and a thirst for fruits of action. Know that passion, having craving for its essence, is born of yearning and attachment. That, O son of *Kunti* – *Arjuna*, binds the embodied soul by attachment to effort. Man wishes with great expectations, desperate with a thirst that awaits fulfillment in front of the *kutastha*. He does not see the Light there."

"If compensation by creativity can defile Man, what then of inactivity?"

"*Tamas* originates from unconscious ignorance originating from the parasympathetic *ida nadi*. Mesmerised by attachment, the embodied is bound to expectations. Like an inebriated fool, such a Man chases misrepresentations in the many forms of imprudence. Exhausted in energy and time, he loses all opportunities of doing worthy actions. Like one bonded to enslavement, life runs away, squandered. Know O *Arjuna* of the *Bharata* dynasty, that obscurity when born of stupidity, bewilders all such embodied souls and binds them by misunderstanding, habitual idleness and slumber."

"It seems all of Nature's qualities or *gunas* cause Man's struggles of life and living. Why is that so, *Krishna*?"

Krishna must now explain the effects of these motivating intrinsic worth in Nature. Personalities are assembled as you would expect, enlivened by inherent insufficiencies that announce themselves through borrowed omnipresence. Mindful of the laws of cause-effect and of likes-and-dislikes embedded within the reminiscence of the individualistic causal being, the Cosmic Causal Being responds to the demands of the germ itself.

The serious observer in *Arjuna* understands that every matter quality, whether *sattva, rajas* or *tamas,* they all imprison him in the perishable body of the Imperishable Dweller. Of the three *gunas,* it is only the the stainless goodness of *sattva* that motivates him to seek enlightenment. He is still bound to attachments for worldly happiness and learning. The quality of *rajas* has granted him with refinement and enthusiasm for winning and creating mundane opulence. They have determinedly anchored his embodied soul to exploit Nature's bounty. *Tamas* has coloured his life with all that is shallow in him. It has succeeded in deluding him. *Arjuna* understands *tamas* to be the basis of his own tendency to idleness and slumber. Although bewildered, he cannot find the underlying cause or cure for himself.

"If Man is coloured by the tint of his cardinal quality, how do they behave and what is the cure?" *Arjuna* asks.

Krishna describes these personalities.

"From *sattva* comes worldly happiness and from *rajas* comes craving for fruits of action. Keeping one away from wisdom causes *tamas* through careless intoxication with addictive substances, the worst of which is liquor. When Man remains in the Self in *sattva,* happiness displays all around him, automatically and naturally. Such bliss is known by oneself and is therefore left unspoken."

"When Man wants and gains the temporary fruits of *rajas,* there is no knowing who will enjoy it next. Most of humanity is caught in this a trap. Filled with these attachments, such a worldly person wastes life that is full of attachments and useless discussions. Whatever life is left is lost in the obscurity of sleep where there is no Light. Even though this Knowledge is known and heard about, such a one lives in the pleasure-seeking obscurity of falsehood and darkness until death grabs him."

"But what of the benevolence of *sattva*?"

"Goodness or *sattva* unites the soul with worldly pleasure. O *Arjuna,* although passion or *rajas* unites one with work, darkness that veils learning, unites Man with the errors of *tamas.* When passion and darkness are restrained, goodness remains and Man experiences this through the *sushumna.* When passion and goodness are restricted, darkness remains and empowers Man through the *ida.* When darkness and goodness are confined, passion remains and empowers Man through the *pingala.* This cycle is never-ending, *Arjuna* until death overtakes Man who has denied himself of true Knowledge."

Arjuna, Sanjaya and the blind king were many times tutored about the spinal pathways that enliven with five types of energy or *prana* for energising and revitalising the physical body through energy channels or *nadis.* A descending *apana* life flow of *tamas* sanctions decay and disease. The creative or *rajasic* expanding and positive flow or *udana* offers generosity and development. When *sattva* is strongest, both *rajas* and *tamas* become neutralised. Contemplative practices reverse the flow of energies of want and decay. Neutralising first happens at the lumbar plexus. *Pranayama* or self-control of breath lifts *prana* to the medullary plexus until the whole spinal canal is magnetised with *sattvic* awareness.

Sattva illumines the *unenlightened chitta* who is the individualistic self. The *mind* makes truthful emotional choices and wishes. The *intellect* makes choices of healthy lifestyles and companions, habits and likes-dislikes, friends and reading material. The physical *body* is re-energised with life force and the body transfigures into radiance and health. Every sensory opening, meaning the eyes, nose, ears, mouth, skin and two excretory orifices, are healthy and glowing. Metamorphosis of the physical, astral and causal bodies happens. The life force flow is upright. The *self* understands and realises he is the becoming the enlightening *chitta* – the soul.

Krishna confirms this philosophy when he speaks to *Arjuna,* "If Man's attention is at the *kutastha,* then Light dawns here and in all the sense openings. When a *guru's* ability to illumine Knowledge allows removal of ignorance, the radiance emerges through all nine doors. *Sattva* predominates and settles itself. When at all these gates in the body, this knowledge is actualised, then one should know that goodness has been perfected there."

"Knowing all this, what is it that deflects a knowledgeable mortal from his premeditated spiritual path, *Krishna*?"

"When parsimoniousness empowers activity, there is infatuation with performance of works. Even an inherent need for *sattva* or tranquillity is born of need, – O *Arjuna*. Anything born of wants sanctions passion. Therefore, *rajas* matures from want and craving for its fruit. Expansion of such is through successive reconstruction of ways to look into such motives, even if *sattvic* in nature."

"But Man constantly seeks tranquillity and happiness, does he not?"

"A need for tranquillity may be triggered by *tamas*. Unless attention is transfixed at the soul, ignorance, gloom, inactivity, and errors of carelessness and delusion sketch Man's actions. O *Arjuna*, great scion of the *Kuru* race, enraptured by them, blemishes become deep-seated when darkness is perfected."

"Whatever happens to those who have lost their way?' asks the blind king.

Sanjaya who had been listening to *Krishna's* conversation with *Arjuna*, turned to answer the sightless monarch, "The strongest qualities of an individual decide in what state and where the disembodied being goes to. Soul liberation from the clutches of Matter involves transcending even *sattva*. However, when a man with *sattvic* capacities dies, he rises to untainted regions in which live those who are mindful of the Highest. When a passionate *rajasic* one dies, he is reborn among those attached to domination and action. He who dies permeated with *tamas* enters the wombs and family environments of the deluded with life-suppressing existences."

"Am I right when I say there is no escape from the compulsions of Nature?" asks *Arjuna.*

Krishna explains in more detail, methods of severance, from such compulsions and demands made by Nature, "Intensification of true *sattva* is only possible when Man continues meditating in the *kutastha* and merges there with the Self. There he sees the Cosmic Being and is freed of all impurities. When the proprietor of this body goes to such achievement with perfected *sattvic* essence, he reaches a faultless mind and pure heart qualified to know the Supreme."

"What happens to Man unable to transcend the forces of *rajas*?"

"When Man merges with *rajas,* he performs actions with cravings for fruits. When Man goes to his leave-taking from the physical with a predominance of such passions, he is born among those that are loyal to achievements."

"What then of one bound to *tamas*?"

"When he merges with *tamas,* he arrives at ignorance and pretends he knows everything but knows purposelessness. When Man perishes in ignorance, he is born in wombs that beget the unenlightened."

Dhritarashtra is fully aware that sages repeatedly assert that fruit of actions performed while embodied decide the environment for future existences. *Sattvic* action breeds harmony and purity of wisdom. *Rajasic* action breeds pain from greed. And *tamasic* action breeds ignorance, neglect of duties and delusion

Krishna is mentally reviewing what he will say next, when *Arjuna* says, "And please speak of different *karmas* when influenced by the compulsions of Nature."

"If they perform action seeking tranquillity but without need for fruit, they resonate as taught by a *guru.* This work is *sattvic karma* of a quality seeking the Truth. If Man performs blameless actions, the fruit is virtuous and untainted.

Remember *Arjuna,* the fruit of passion or *rajas* is sorrow and misery and the fruit of darkness or *tamas* is ignorance."

"What of one who is dedicated to *sattva*? Also what of ones who have sanctified their actions?"

"Having remained in *sattva* for a long time and after a stage in meditation, Man reaches stillness within the *kutastha.* When the Knowledge of *Brahman* becomes clear, Man enters the *rajasic* path of creativity in the *pingala* and performs actions for attaining *yoga* or oneness. Unconsciousness of *tamas* in the *ida* is then removed. Therefore from righteousness or *sattva* is produced knowledge. From excitement of *rajas* comes greed; and from gloom or *tamas* are born error, delusion and ignorance."

"Man is changing constantly. Is this automatic and spontaneous?" asks the sightless king.

"The self is perpetually planning towards soul-awareness, Sire. True *sattva* experiences progressive emotional and intellectual growth, *rajas* experiences persistent involvement with activity and circumstances which are dedicated and *tamas* experiences fewer soul-restricting environments and circumstances. When a seer sees in creation no intermediary except the three *gunas* whether in ascendancy or in descent, he recognises only That which is higher than the *gunas,* and he enters Consciousness," *Sanjaya* replied.

"Where do those co-dependents with their over-powering *gunas* go to?" *Arjuna* asks.

Krishna replies, "They that live in goodness go on high into the domains of knowledge and wisdom. They that are addicted to passion remain in the middle, in the domains of greed, and are both combative and pretentious. They that are of darkness, being obsessed with the lowest quality, go down towards negligence and delusional ignorance of the underworld."

"How are they recognized?"

"A knowledgeable observer recognises the *sattvic* has

moved up like ether towards the head. He sees the *rajasic* equipped for battle for the sake of possessiveness with an airy dynamism originating from the heart region. The *tamasic* descends towards the lower regions of lust and greed."

"What of those who have adjusted their lives towards consummated *dharma, artha, kama* and are seeking *moksha*?"

"When the *ida, pingala* and *sushumna* have their attention fixed at the *kutastha,* Man transcends the power of Matter's compulsions. Sages, who are able to make out the predominance of such qualities and know what is beyond Nature's qualities, arrive at the essence of the Cosmic Being in the *kutastha.* When one transcends the three *gunas,* Man spontaneously goes beyond the intellect and grasps the Supreme Universal Intelligence."

"Having gone beyond these three *gunas* of Matter which bind the embodied soul, Man is able to live for long periods of meditation in the *kutastha.* By transcending these three qualities inherent within the three *nadis,* they disempower all human birth, death, decrepitude, and misery. Man enjoys immortality and is free from rebirth. He has grasped the Tranquil Substance and enjoys the nectar of immortality."

Arjuna was curious about the one who transcends the compulsions of Matter and asks, "What are the footprints, *Krishna,* of one who has risen above these three qualities? What is his conduct after he arrives at such a feat? What then happens to these three qualities still existing in such a changed being? Where the Self exists so prominently, how does the Self act and experience?"

And *Krishna* replied, "All experiences are made capable through the *kutastha.* Here a revelatory Light presides where there is neither night nor day. His heart remains immersed in this Light like one drunk. This Substance enraptures his whole attention. His entire fields of want merge in a wish to remain there where that Essence lives, mounted at the top of the head, well above where the *ida, pingala and sushumna* meet below the pituitary gland. Here, when reluctance, activity and delusion present themselves, he neither hates nor wants for them. He does not mourn over the absence of light, O son of *Pandu*. Seated as one unconcerned, he is unshaken by those qualities. Rather he sits and does not move, knowing by experience that it is the qualities and not he that are engaged in their respective works."

"He sees the *gunas* or qualities of Matter, just there. Everything is still and to him pain and pleasure are alike," he says. "He is self-contained in Oneself. He now views a sod of earth, a stone, and gold as alike. Those who are agreeable and the disagreeable are identical to him. He has insight and is silent because he witnesses from the parapets of Universal Intelligence where Matter and Spirit have become One."

"Censure and praise, honour and dishonour are the same to him. He regards friend and foe alike. By renouncing all want motivated effort, he is said to have transcended all qualities - he is a *gunateeta.*"

The blind king interjected at this point with a question. "This sage who has transcended the compulsions of matter, does he live in a transcendental state of Oneness. Is this the state when vibrating Awareness and vibration-less Consciousness merge?"

"When Awareness and Consciousness merge, it is a merging of Matter and Spirit. When *prakriti* and *purusha* merge, the experience is that of *Brahman* or *Purushottama,* Sire," answered *Sanjaya.*

Krishna had earlier described *Brahman* as both with features as immanent and without features as transcendental. *Krishna* also spoke about the home of Infinite *Brahman* where the vibration-less Spirit exists. From here emanates the Immortal *purusha* permeating as the Indestructible vibrating enlivening Om. Through every atom of Infinite Nature of *prakriti,* Om energises all with compulsive qualities of *gunas.* For *Arjuna's* sake, *Krishna* again describes the different types of devotees who worship the Cosmic Deity and those apostles who worship the Formless Infinite.

"Such a one who performs meditation as taught by a *guru,* who is focused and enduring in the *kutastha,* who has no attachments for worldly needs is able to stabilize himself in equipoise. Such a one whose conduct is proper and lawful, who worships the Lord with exclusive devotion, is able to transcend these qualities. His faith in the *guru* makes him fit for access into the nature of *Brahman.*"

"How does a devotee of the Infinite *Purushottama* or *Brahman* know he is in the presence of the Formless Being?"

"When there is true Stillness in *Brahman* found in the *Kutastha,* Man reaches immortality. He is able to imbibe the nectar that falls to one who has practiced his duty as Man. Being fixed in *Brahman* as a source of immortality, indestructibility, and eternal piety for Real Knowledge, he knows he is in the presence of the Formless Infinite. Because of unbroken aptness for *Dharma,* he becomes *Brahman* by such single pointed devotion. Such happiness has no end and should be the aspiration of all people who desire True Happiness." *Krishna* said.

17. Completeness

Krishna had just reasserted that the world is perishable and the mortal is a mixture of Matter and Spirit. The three qualities of matter manipulate the elements from these materials in space. Their refinement in association, exchange, and conversion into mortals contribute and share responsibility for entrapment in the cycle of birth and death.

If a mortal's lifestyle is to remain balanced, the physical, mental and intellectual sheaths supported by the *gunas,* must be in good physical shape for compliant daily living and spiritual growth. Dreaming inner growth and mechanical spiritual routines of prayer and meditation are not enough to carry Man to Higher Realms. Balanced lifestyles through adherence to restraint, constant practice, correct Knowledge and steady contemplation, alone take Man to the Universal Being, the *Kutastha.*

Arjuna understands most of what *Krishna* is saying. *Sanjaya* has also awakened into his inner reality within the core of his being. After separating the Self from the body, he realizes that although self-control frees one from *rajas and tamas,* he must develop *sattva* while overcoming connection with it. To achieve real success, he must learn to renounce the fruit of dedicated action.

Sanjaya wishes to achieve such success. *Arjuna* meanwhile feels he needs awakening to the *Vedas* that are expressions of *Brahman.* Realizing the Self by the self seems essential. Without devotion, such a feat seems impossible. Such effort needs Man's personality, which has been nourished birth after birth by the compulsions, freed from want. Taking cue from *Krishna's* recent discussions, the best means to control creativity and sloth is to develop *sattva* in an unattached state of wholesomeness.

Arjuna liked the idea of bringing together His omnipresence in every thing, creature, and being. Although *Arjuna* understood and accepts the Truth about Matter and Spirit, he needs literal information on the nature, power and role of the Cosmic Deity, the *Purushotama*. He wants to know where he can detect Him expressing Himself in and around and through every expression of life. *Arjuna* needs his intellectual ability to see beyond the seeming superficiality of self-consciousness and the ever-changing appearances of life and living.

Arjuna wants to awaken to this Knowledge through insight and personal experience of this Changeless Reality. He feels such an awakening could come if he gave the *Vedas* a Form of the Lord. He would then treat this Form as the source of Knowledge for which he already has the greatest of devotion. He thinks he could work for this Form in devotion. Armed with the three requirements – Knowledge, Devotion, and Dedicated Action, *[gyana, bhakti,* and *karma], Arjuna* hopes to distinguish this elusive *Purushotama.*

Sanjaya meanwhile also realises that without love and devotion there are great hurdles to overcome especially while dealing with the compulsions of Matter at the same time. Armed with Self-knowledge, *sattva* would emerge in its purity without the blemish of the ego. The Vision of the Self would ensure spiritual progress.

It dawned on both *Arjuna* and *Sanjaya* they require a Lord with a Form whom they would worship all the way through with love, service and knowledge. This would then take them to the Image within, of the Universal Being. Perhaps there is hope of meeting with the Cosmic Being also.

Krishna understood them and said, "As I have said many times before, the *Purusha-Prakriti* or *Purushottama* is experienced through the *kutastha*. This One *Brahman* of the Cosmos envisages as the *ashwatha* or a peepal tree. It has roots above and branches with leaves below. This eternal tree is indestructible. Its leaves are the *chants* and intonations of groups that one time lived in the underbrush of the *kutastha*. He, who recognises this science of permanence, knows the *Vedas.* Downwards and upwards are stretched its branches which like arms and legs of the human body are augmented by *gunas* and virtues. Its sprouting leaves seek objects of the senses. Downwards from roots and branches they are escorted by action into the world of men."

Arjuna realises that his dear friend is making it easier for him to perform consecrated service to the Supreme Person within, which is imperishable, unchanging and immortal. If he could show a method to steady attitude towards the Self while embodied inside this ever-changing layered sheaths, spiritual efforts can be easier. Acts would become worship he would not tire of performing.

Sanjaya also realises it is perishable sheaths that serve the imperishable soul. All creation is His glorious dream and Nature continuously dances to recreate this admirable panorama. Although Mother Nature is perishable, She is forever newly innovative and self-creating. No wonder She is worthy of Man's devotion and service. *Krishna* explains how She fashions Herself in the body of Man.

"All the pathways are *nadis* that run the length of the branches. They travel up to the top from the bottom of the trunk. They climb towards the head. *Gunas* journey with the *ida, pingala* and the *sushumna* to wholly expand into the *kutastha.* The branches support and contract with imperceptible *gunas.* When cut with the hard axe of indifference, this *ashwatha* tree with roots firmly fixed within the cranium should be sought after. After seeking and finding that place, no sage returns. But those who think they seek refuge from the ancient mystic, they travel the worldly life which binds them to action."

The blind king is pleased with *Krishna's* description of procedural technicalities of the human body, which resembles the banyan tree.

Krishna continues to describe the form of both the macrocosmic and microcosmic structure of the Nature. "This eternal *Ashvatha* tree, with its roots above and branches below, its leaves are like *Vedic* hymns and have no Form. No knowledge arrives by the side of it because all creation fills it. It is relentlessly moving. Nobody has therefore ever seen it. The certainty of its expression remains unstated. It is neither felt by the senses, nor is it easily understood what causes it to put on a show, as it does. Its beginning, end and middle or its entirety, is not found by any ordinary seeker. Only he who has removed himself from Matter's compulsions and their influence understands this tree-of-life. The one who has becomes the *ashvatha* tree by enduring in the *kutastha,* is as if mounted on its roots. He then stays in the head within the *kutastha* without any wants," *Krishna* says.

Arjuna is deep in thought. So, the branches that spread underneath and away from home are nurtured by the *gunas.* Its buds are the sense objects. Downwards, hooked on worldliness, expands the ancestral tree that forces Man into action. Emanating from the vibration-less transcendent field of Consciousness, regulating cosmic forces become immanent in the body manifesting as the extraordinary creative force of Om.

Krishna continues, "The wise, having destroyed the firmly rooted *ashwatha* tree with the powerful axe of nonattachment, realise that physical expression of Man and the spinal pathway is like the upturned cosmic tree of life. The brain-roots are embedded in Consciousness in the seventh spiritual centre in the *sahasrahara;* and Awareness is embedded in the sixth medullary or *ajnaa* centre which energises and enlivens the embodied. It is necessary to travel this road. Having traveled this path, Man never comes back for he has gained *Purushottama.*"

The descending sinuous brilliance of Om comes as the life force or *prana* to flow through the physical-astral-causal spinal shaft. It energises spinal cord, nerve plexuses and matching astral-causal spiritual centers *[vishuddha, anahaata, manipura, svadhisthana, muladhara]. Prana* moves out through nerve branches or *nadis* to senses and organs of action. Constrained by past habits, likes-and-dislikes, the self decides the life style it chooses."

"Does taking protection from the Cosmic Person persuade Man differently?" asks *Arjuna.*

"Merely wishing I take refuge in the Primeval Cosmic Deity is not enough. Man must seek internalisation, by withdrawal of senses into the mind, and keeping the intellect in the Self. Uphold disinterest in pain and pleasure, likes-and-dislikes, remain free of want, anger, greed, pride, possessiveness and jealousy, to reach the deathless essence in the *kutastha.* Having arrived at this Indestructible Eternal Substance, Man lives in Stillness always," *Krishna* answers.

Krishna tells *Arjuna* that with such a view of bliss where the energy and *Om* merge with the cosmic vision, it describes the Supreme Goal, from where none returns. Thereafter there is a spontaneous transformation in such a *yogi.*

Arjuna therefore asks for a portrayal of such a *yogi* and *Krishna* explains, "He is free of pride and delusion and has restrained the malevolence of attachments. He is steady in contemplation of Reality of the Supreme. From him want is absent, and he is free from pairs of opposites – of pleasure and pain and the like. He makes up for his delusions in the seat of contemplation. There, where the sun lights not the seat, nor the moon, nor fire, is where this *yogi* remains. Having gone there, none returns because that is the supreme position."

"Describe to me this most excellent space where such a *yogi* stays, *Krishna,*" *Arjuna* said.

"That is an unimaginable, awe-inspiring place about which many sages have testified and spoken about in the course of unambiguous direction. The *yogi* who remains ever settled in the *kutastha* experiences the Cosmic Deity, the *Purushotama.* When others hear of it, they disrespectfully express amusement because they have never seen it for themselves. Illumined by Consciousness, the sage does not need any outer source of light or understanding because he has seen it. Established in his own enlightenment, the *yogi* rubbishes all criticisms, illusions, and delusions that veil his relationship with his core foundation. He knows His supreme enduring position and does not want to return."

When giving a portrait of the Cosmic Deity, *Krishna* illustrated to *Arjuna* how he from Cosmic Soul became the individualised soul. He explained that even the Father begets the Son when he displays for a Collective Good. The motive of expression in every individualized self is desire. The self descends in stages to pick up instruments for its fulfillment.

Krishna adds, "All souls are eternal portions of the Cosmic Being, the *Purushottama*. By becoming an individual soul he draws to himself the five senses with mind as the sixth sense. They all depend on Nature. When the ruler of this bodily frame assumes a form or quits a body, he leaves taking all these away with him. He leaves like an airstream taking away perfumes from their seats."

"Remember *Arjuna, jivas* or individual souls are only fragments of that which is eternally present. After edifying, if Man refuses to seek *moksha* or liberation, he is bound by qualities or *gunas* of Matter because of attachments to sense matters. The mind is pulled by wants and induces a new birth in other suitable wombs."

"What attracts a particular soul to a specific womb?"asks *Arjuna*.

"By the supremacy of magnetism, like scent, *prakriti* presides and lives in the ear, the eye, the organs of touch, taste and smell, and over the mind to enjoy all objects of senses. When the body no more wanted, while focusing into the core of attachments, wants direct the self towards sense matters, as if attracted by a fragrance. Unaware, the self drags itself towards circumstances of unsettled mind, instead of the Self. The soul is trapped into an entanglement of worldly existence. He is reborn in wombs flailing between *tamas* and *rajas* and enveloped by the law of *karma*. Death succeeds and grabs him away from liberation."

"What causes Man to become enmeshed in worldliness?"

"The ruler of the senses is the mind who thinks the senses are important. People find entertainment in hearing, seeing, smelling, touching with an already stilled mind. The mind and intellect then reasons they have reached earthly blessedness. They crave for more of the same. Influenced by deception, Man begins to live like a naive child, looking for more of the same."

"What binds Man to his actions, *Krishna*?" asks *Arjuna*.

"Since birth, such a one has performed action for its fruit. He steadfastly remains there reaping according to his strongest *guna*. What he reaps is either pain or pleasure, hot or cold, or what he likes or dislikes. Only insight leads Man to a true teacher or *guru* who introduces him the science of liberation through knowledge and contemplation. Remember *Arjuna*, they who are deluded and do not at first see Him – of Spirit in Matter, go to intrinsic worth and are reborn. They, who see are controlled by the eye of knowledge."

The blind king wanted *Sanjaya* to elaborate and he said,

"The Supreme Self when revealing as individualised self personality earns a body, mind, senses and organs of action. The deluded does not notice the soul staying, parting, or experiencing qualities, incarnation after incarnation. They display in physical, astral, and causal realms with memories of opinions and experiences well embedded, as they journey through time and space."

"O king, righteous living weakens such nature propelled conditionings. Personal circumstances revaluated bring wellness in physical and astral conditions. Life-enhancing qualities allow embarking on righteous living, discriminative actions and using power of will to nurture qualities of goodness."

"Those whose eye of wisdom is open, see the Supreme Self. *Yogis* like *Arjuna* who are striving for liberation see Him existing right within themselves, as the Supreme Self in the core of the soul. Those who are undisciplined cannot see Him even when they struggle to do so. O King, follow the path of virtue. It is the only way you will understand what *Krishna* is saying," *Sanjaya* continues.

"Until committed to spiritual growth, self-awareness cannot unfold into soul-consciousness. Intellectual curiosity alone cannot reveal that Matter emerges from Consciousness. This has to be experienced in meditation," *Sanjaya* explains.

"Tell me about a yogi's experiences when he reaches for the *kutastha.*"

Krishna then described the experience of a *yogi* fixed on the spiritual path of meditation, "Whoever stays in the Self in Stillness brings the mind into him. If he is not still, he cannot see the truth because the heart is not still. A devotee exerting towards that end beholds Him remaining in himself. He, however, who is senseless and whose mind is not restrained, beholds Him not, even while exerting himself."

"But, if he is sheltered by concentration and contemplation, meditation and merges in oneness *[dharana, dhyana, samadhi]*, such a *yogi* lives in his own heart. His inner vision sees the self in the Self as instructed by a *guru*. Having discovered Stillness in the *kutastha,* he remains in there. Therefore, his early efforts are at bringing the mind and intellect into the Self. Only after he has lived here for a long-time does Man's self see the Self by the Self."

"When this *yogi* has reached the *kutastha,* what does he experience, *Krishna*?" asked *Arjuna.*

"Just as the power of the sun illumines all by its mere presence, so also the power of the *kutastha* reveals itself in the body, *Arjuna.* That authority has the Form of air in space.

It has the form of understated heavens displaying in so many atoms of *Brahman*. It is energy, which can be seen only when Knowledge speaks by itself as an experience and an understanding while remaining constant in the *kutastha*."

"I have not understood what you have just spoken, *Krishna*"

"The splendour residual in the sun, which illumines the vast universe, that which is in the moon, and that which is in the fire, know that magnificence to be that of *Brahman*, the *Purushottama*," *Krishna* explains.

Arjuna wonders to himself. If the proud display of the moon can become one with the sun, his only hope is to surrender to the Lord. It would not cause any suffering to the cradle of humanity if he did that.

"Where do I find this *Purushottama* in Creation and in myself?" asked *Arjuna*.

"By entering the earth; Lord *Purushottama* upholds all creatures by His enforcement. By becoming the moon, He nurtures all herbs with the elixir of medications. To find the Infinite, *yogis* with will and strength still their own breath and enter the *guna* pathways of their substance. By staying in this state, infinity reaches Infinity, meaning the self reaches the Self and becomes the Self."

"How does the Self show in individual bodies and how are they connected to Mother Nature?"

"By becoming the warmth as *Vaishvanara* He remains in all bodies of creatures that breathe. By uniting and equalizing life-breath, that is, upward going *prana* and downward going *apana* He digests the four kinds of food. When *apana* and *prana* are equalised in the body, assimilation is possible after chewing, sucking, licking and digesting. As long as there is fire of enlivening *prana* in the body of creatures, assimilation keeps it alive. When the energising fire begins leaving the form, life first leaves everything except the *kutastha*. This self sees and meets in contemplation of the Self. Careless ones allow this flame to burn up everything in its way, even after lighting the fire with *prana* at birth."

The blind king asks, "Who is *Vaishvanara*?"

And *Sanjaya* answered, "He is the enlivening awareness that nourishes the Supreme Self with *pranic* energy, light, magnetism, and the cycles and tides of all cosmic forces. As *prana* He exists in the body of all-living creatures. Acting through *prana* and *apana,* he digests all the foods that are eaten in four ways – by mastication, swallowing, sucking and licking. He transforms food into the atoms and molecules adapted for bodily consumption," *Sanjaya* said.

"Sire, concentrate the mind on the brain and spinal cord. The best place to concentrate is where the blind-mind remains in the upper zone of the brain. There, listen to the angelic sounds emanating from the seven spiritual centers within the altar of God."

Arjuna had spent a lifetime refining his intellectual skills for soul-unfoldment and is ready for the next discussion. He always wanted to know where the Lord had hidden Himself. Upon asking, *Krishna* replied, "He is seated in the hearts of all beings. From Him are born memory and knowledge and the loss of both. He is the subject of Knowledge known by the support of the *Vedas.* He is the author of the *Vedantas,* and He alone is the Knower of the *Vedas.*"

"Can one see Him in the flesh?" asks *Arjuna.*

"That which remains fixed in the Silence of all hearts can be shown by doing the *yoni mudra.* Many however prefer to wear amulets around the neck hoping they have Him near. He is in the Stillness of all hearts. He is recognised by experiencing Divine Knowledge. By enduring in that stillness, all objects of senses disappear. Nothing remains except the self, which grows to be the Self. That is all that is worthy of knowing and if Man stays in the *kutastha,* he is able to discern. He understands that both the perishable and the imperishable are One and not many. This state is attainable by looking at the *kutastha,* feeling the *prana,* and listening to the cosmic sound of *Om*-all at the same time in contemplation. The attainment is spontaneous and automatic. Those who reach there never turn away from the Supreme Substance."

"What do you see in the *kutastha* by doing the *yoni mudra*? What is taught about this by a *guru*?" asked *Arjuna.*

"There are these two entities in the world – the changeable and the unchangeable. The perishable are changeable, everlasting energy of creatures embroiled in worldly events or *samsara.* The unchangeable *kutastha* is both Immutable and Imperishable. The reflection of these is the *kutastha.* Although Man understands these two beings, the destructible and the indestructible, he lives with his attention glued to attachments. This is destroyable but the others who remain in the *kutastha* are without fear of destruction. He settles in the teachings of his *guru.*"

"Is That the Self, the individual soul? What of the Cosmic Soul?"

"There exists another, the Supreme Being, called *Paramatma,* who is the Eternal Lord, that is not only pervading the three worlds, but upholds and carries the Immutable and the Mutable. This *Purushottama* is *Paramatma* who transcends the *prakriti,* and the *purusha.*"

"How does one see Him?" *Arjuna* asks.

"With continued gazing into the *kutastha* Man sees the *Paramatma* who is *Purushottama* of all the three worlds in this body, as well as, of the body of the universe. The worldly puts on a dress of skin and takes his mind to all that he wishes to consume through the senses. The one, who knows he is the all-pervading indestructible subtle being, knows he is a soul. He knows *Jagadishwara,* the Cosmic Lord is everywhere and acting through the physical form."

"Is He the Lord of all humankind that Man adores? And who are you?"

"For reasons already explained, He is distinguished in the world among men and in the *Veda* as *Purushottama* –

the Highest or Supreme Being who is beyond destruction. I am the reincarnated Universal Being. By knowing all this, O *Arjuna* of the *Bharata* dynasty, they worship Me the *purusha,* every time. That Indestructible Being is seen through the *kutastha.* The *Vedas* describe him as the subject *Om.* By knowing the subject of *Purushottama* through the teachings of a qualified teacher, He can be reached in meditation."

The blind king has no confidence that he is in God and God is in him. *Krishna* showed *Arjuna* the way through the bodily kingdom in search of the Reality behind his delusional mortality. *Arjuna* knows how to transform his every cell into enlivened and rejuvenated energy. He can reduce the remoteness between God and him. *Sanjaya* repeatedly tries to convince the unrighteous visionless king to embark on meditative efforts to gain understanding and experience the wisdom of the *Vedas.* He is shown and identified the *pranic* life force in all aspects of his subtle body and the spinal pathway.

Nevertheless, he still asks, "O *Sanjaya,* why does the Cosmic Being reveal outwards as well as dematerialise inwards? What is the essence of the body, mind, and intellect? In the macrocosm, He is the *Vaishvanara* as well as *Purushottama.* But, how do I recognise Him in myself?"

Sanjaya replied, "Just as the Earth moves around the Sun, and the centrifugal balances the centripetal forces for expression to exist, the opposing forces of polarity are balanced in harmony also for the sake of pure love. Consciousness dreams the Cosmic Deity on the screen of *Om.* She, the Cosmic Mother Nature, vibrates and manifests Her creative energy as the *gunas.* He enlivens Her with *prana* and rejuvenates her created exhibition."

The blind king asks again. "Give me illustrations and uses of this essence."

And *Sanjaya* replies, "In spiritual exercises, the essence of the physical body becomes conserved through restraint and adherence to restraints, until the body is stilled in meditative postures. All this becomes known through the study of scriptures."

In the meantime, *Arjuna* asks, "Does Knowledge unfold all knowledge?"

And *Krishna* said, "O sinless one, experience this Knowledge for yourself. It contains all the great mysteries. I have already admitted them to you, O *Arjuna.* Knowing this, you can become talented with an enduring knowing of all things. Meditate on this and you will have done all that needs to be done as Man. Whoever meditates at the *kutastha* after ingress never forgets what he experiences. If he remains in there, he eventually sees the *Purushottama,* the Universal Being of *Brahman.*"

"After perceiving the Knowledge with your intellect, Man can become a sage when the secret science is understood by your intelligence. I have already explained all this to you. The one who has successfully fulfilled all his duties as a mortal and yet continues to perform them, reaches liberation."

18. Conflicts

Krishna continues to discuss intelligent survival as a way of achieving life's purpose. He has effectively detached the Self from the worldly body by explaining functions of the *gunas*. By recognising such qualities in behaviours of humanity, he has advised *Arjuna* to see God everywhere in Creation. By authenticating a technique to overcome the three-*guna* qualities, *Arjuna* learns about the science of life. Both *Sanjaya* and *Arjuna* discover the mystery of reaching perfection. They will see *Brahman*, the *Purushottama* or God without Form.

He offers them exact portrayals of the three types of deeds – *karma, gyana* and *bhakti*, each a meritorious method of attaining virtuous living. *Krishna* does not separate these as dissimilar but wants the energy of action pervaded by the essence of true knowledge. Man then serves the Cosmic Mother in a spirit of devotion with love.

To deliver flawless service, Man's exploits need motivation from a confident belief that this knowledge or *gyana* and devotion or *bhakti* animates *karma* in action. This must be so even in his seat of enthusiasm. *Krishna* wishes that *Arjuna* see the brightness of perfect life as well as darkness that Man battles against.

Arjuna wants to know how one recognises that Man's duty is awarded with the colour of love, devotion and knowledge of Truth? Having exerted on earth with a material body, how does Man estimate the worth of life's yield? How does Man know he experienced from and matured in his spiritual efforts?

Krishna identifies the three great vices of humankind – *kama* or yearning for anything which triggers *krodha* and resentment, or *lobha* manifesting as insatiability. He tells *Arjuna* that they all need subduing. Following set of laws laid down in the scriptures is necessary.

Krishna was inspecting the battlefield of *Kurukshetra* when *Arjuna* remarked; "This combat zone is both out there as well as within us, is it not? The conflict that is raging inside me has assumed a shape and a form out there on the theatre of war. My enemy is metamorphosing into every shape nearby. In me it is the shape of passion and anger."

Krishna responds, "Both battalions are accurately grouped as they should be. Some soldiers have blameless intrinsic worth and others are shady characters. Both need authority to steer them. Armed forces need navigators who are courageous."

"How does one recognise such an able and fearless commander?"

"A valiant leader stands alert and watches from the front but modesty guards him from the rear. No matter how great his eminence, if he is full of conceit and egotism he is worthless." "What then makes a leader fearless and humble, *Krishna*?"

Krishna replies, "As said before, all extraordinary contacts with courage, truth, humility and immortality take place in the *kutastha*. Armed with fearlessness and purity of *sattva,* and a heart filled with perseverance whilst continuing Knowledge and *yoga* of meditation, Man sees the Cosmic Being. *Karma* of action is typified by generosity towards the needy while he remains fortified with self-restraint, sacrifice, study of the *Vedas,* ascetic penances and uprightness."

"But there are conflicts about what is reverential. In the minds of the wise as well as in the deluded, there is disagreement, is it not?"

"*Arjuna* if there is no covetousness and belligerence in Man, there is nothing to prompt want in him. For this reason he remains in the *kutastha.* This does not mean his cravings are destroyed but he sees for himself the treachery of want. While within the *kutastha,* he is not overcome by feelings, 'I alone have a right to exist'. Then how can there be anger and against whom? If such a one has no desires to own sense objects, where does he harvest the fruits of action? If he has no opinions about himself and realises that fruits of action are not his, against whom can he express hostility? If he is immersed in love for Mother Nature and the Spirit in Creation, his commitment will drench all in merciful abandon. If all, including himself is *Brahman,* what other needs to be gained in covetousness?"

"My life obviously is founded on vanity and ignorance. How does one compensate against such crimes, *Krishna?*" *Arjuna* asks.

"The power of the mind by which all is seen and done grants mercy. Forgive the sins of others *Arjuna* but it is a sin to justify lack of knowledge in oneself. To arrive at serenity, practice nonviolence, truthfulness, freedom from anger, renunciation, and tranquillity. There must be freedom from condemnation and humiliation of other's faults. Practice compassion for all creatures. There must be no covetousness and lack of compassion. Absence of restiveness is another of the many characteristics of one who remains in the *kutastha* where there is no dissatisfaction. These are divine qualities. They are achieved by self-control and equipoise."

"What exactly do you mean by equipoise from restlessness of the mind?"

"When the mind interacts with others, he wilfully decides he will do no harm to others and will not seek to be honoured. He does this with vigour, forgiveness, firmness and potency in himself. He observes purity and is clear of combativeness and hatred. He has complete control over self-importance. Know these are all righteous qualities. O *Arjuna* who is the pride of *Bharata* dynasty, you are born with many assets that are god-like."

Having described the glow of a spiritually inclined

person, *Krishna* describes *tamasic* and *rajasic* individuals. *Krishna* saw arrayed in front of him two armies. The one with godly qualities was in front of the demonic.

Sanjaya saw the same spectacle, but he experienced Truth aspiring for nonviolence on one side and an army of Craving wishing for acquisitiveness even if through brutality, on the opposite side. He has made some progress with the visionless *Dhritarashtra* but there is room for more improvement. *Krishna's* discussion with *Arjuna* has given *Sanjaya* endless opportunity to develop an idea of non-violence and truth in the blind king. He knows if he succeeds on an individual level, the people of the kingdom will also grow. The society and the nation would benefit.

Krishna has already warned that many lives will be lost in the aggression. *Tamasic* tendencies born of ignorance avoid and justify faults that inbred in some. Nonviolence is useless if it cannot sway vindictiveness and flaws. The conduct of Man must be truthful and free of secret messages born of a demoniac nature."

"How does Man oppose unrighteousness? What are the blemishes in an ignorant person who is of *rajasic-tamasic* nature, *Krishna*?"

"Man and society should oppose violence but progress is impossible when there are defects in that decision. First, there must be correct knowledge of high merit, second there must be devotion for Truth and third the harnessing of dedicated action must be for a common good of man and society."

"Hypocrisy, pride, conceit about one's caste and class are unacceptable. Disapproved also is the displaying of wrath by throwing one's weight around, and rudeness when seeking to self-honour. Long-lasting anger and speaking cruel words are born of ignorance and oblivion about consideration, *Arjuna*. These are belongings of those born with demoniac qualities. This character is born with them and they appear spontaneously."

"What is it that binds such a one to such tendencies? How does he free himself?"

"Godlike assets are qualities for deliverance to emancipation. The demoniac intrinsic values lead to suffocating bondage. Filling the mind with attachments makes him a guardian of the materialism he desired. However, grieve not, O son of *Pandu,* for you are born with godlike personality assets."

"How so?"

"Even good qualities change over time. Perfection is only single. Man changes both individual and social life by developing divine qualities. One needs to construct on fundamentals that are previously laid down. The struggle is about evolution of life principles. Self-consciousness is provoked and motivated towards soul-unfoldment. The desire for liberation and soul-consciousness has the ability to change the destiny of Man."

The blind king *Dhritarashtra* asks *Sanjaya* how the self-conscious individualist has the aptitude to change his life's course.

Sanjaya replies, "*Krishna* has asked us to develop divine or *daivic* tendencies and avoid the demonic or *asuric* ones. The essence of all demonic qualities is cooperatively chasing after power, culture and wealth. To the *asuric* these three are necessary. Through pedigree, Man tries to prove his own greatness in all matters. He prefers to be the richest, the noblest and the most powerful. He finds no happiness in it because his unfulfilled needs make him angry and greedy for more of the same. When desperation overwhelms him, he seeks spiritual action. A *yogi* leads him to an understanding of self-control. He learns to break away from desire, anger and greed and control the senses."

"After realising his mortality, Man connects with his own unchangeable centre. He connects with God. At first he develops his own ideas of God, conditioned by his mind's likes-and-dislikes. Once securely embedded in this understanding, the *yogi* finds security in God's friendship and presence. Even this God-image is a delusion. It is a silhouette of God. It is the *yogi's* shadow-image projected from his innate knowledge and concept of God. But, God is the all-knowing eternal link with the collective Love of Creation, and caters to the needs of his devotees of varying personalities and different needs," *Sanjaya* adds.

Krishna tells *Arjuna* that every word, thought and deed has the power of expression and in spiritual endeavours, every desire becomes possible by harnessing the power of the will. Accepting Him as the power behind all activity is the first step of self-awareness to soul-awareness. The next step is to realise Him within and without himself. The third step is to allow for spontaneous friendship with Infinity and to raise self above all prescribed spiritual action.

"*Krishna,* describe to me divine souls who are awake and those who are yet not fully awake. What of those who are under a spell of delusion and have no intellectual capacity to judge their faulty ideas and confused conclusions?"

"There are two kinds of created beings in this world - the divine and the demoniac. I have already described the godlike at great length. Hear now from me, O *Arjuna,* about the demoniac who do not reflect or meditate because their minds are on other matters."

"People of demoniac nature know neither inclination for withdrawal nor disinclination for engagement. They do not care for purity, or good conduct. In their words, there is no Truth at all. The demoniac does not know the right path of action; also, he does not refrain from incorrect action. He lacks purity, truth, and proper conduct."

"Why does this happen, *Krishna*?"

Predetermined falsehood exists in the world. The deluded, say the universe is devoid of Truth, or lacking in guiding principles. He or she states there is no God or sovereign. They feel all is assembled by the union of one another from sexual lust, and nothing else."

The blind king asks, "What happens to the world that is ambushed by the deluded? Is it wrong to desire? And why do thwarted wishes trigger such wrong pastimes?"

Sanjaya replied, "O King, it is not wrong to want. Every passion reveals as an accomplishment because every thought of longing approves an atomic unit of life. If the mind can be reprogrammed to practice a philosophy of rightful craving, the thought will congeal into the object of desire."

Miscarriage of a craving and unrequited prayer are because of multiple distractions from too many wishes, many of them illogical, depraved and egotistic. The demonic say the world has no righteous foundation, no lasting truth, and is without God. They thus contradict their wish and produce inefficient causal commands written for the mind of the Cosmic Deity."

"These individuals rely on impermanent camaraderie. The result is hostility. They suffer pain, separation, and want self-reliance to solve life's struggles. They bring in remoteness between the self and the soul and live a conflict-ridden life, giving reality to double-dealings by the ego. With their tattered intellects, these bankrupt deluded men stick to their misguided philosophy and commit many a mayhem. They are enemies of progress of the world," *Sanjaya* said.

"What happens to the world when such men proliferate, *Krishna*?" *Arjuna* asks.

"Those who do not continue contemplating, they are incapable of steadying their mind and intellect on anything in life. They spread mischievousness and devastation among men. They are enemies of the world and are born for destroying the universe. They cherish lustful wishes that are insatiable. Endowed with hypocrisy and a conceited mind, their recklessness allows them to adopt false notions. Swallowed by delusion they engage in unholy practices with polluted purposes."

The blind king questions *Sanjaya* but also displays his exasperation with the counsel given to *Arjuna*, "Is Man not entitled to make choices in life? Is God the only Being with the privilege to assemble and disassemble expressions of desires? Why must there be separation between Man and God because of wants?"

Sanjaya replies, "There is a deficiency of reverence for the underlying principles of materialisation of desires. This is also the basis of disconnection between Man and God. Overpowered by unquenchable wants, pride and insolence, and immoral ideas during deception, all Man's actions are defiled and erroneously motivated. Man fails to understand that every atom in the revealed universe is God. Unless such an ignorant one has a mental picture of God, he cannot love *Brahman*. Knowledge is necessary to understand the atom as the foundation of every name and form. Schools do not teach this knowledge. This information is personally understood, realised and experienced. When a *yogi* experiences the atom also as an expression of God, the distance between Man and God disappears."

"Life's requirements and choices must be made in harmony with the Collective Choices for the Universe. The experience of this Omniscient enlivening energy creates a loving understanding of God. The seeker sees the common thread in every name and form and wishes for a Collective Good."

"What happens to a deluded man who enters the cycle of birth and death because of a self-created separation between Man and God?" asked *Arjuna*.

Krishna replies in detail.

"Cherishing such never-ending feelings they live for the pleasures of lust, restricted only by their total termination in death. They are certain that fulfilment is the perfect endowment of wants. They want this proposition as their highest objective. They indoctrinate all conditions for wish fulfillment. For them, this is a fundamental field of interest. They feel certain nothing else is of much value."

"Bound by so many expectations, they see no wrong in carnage also. Fettered by these hundreds of ties and snares of hope, habituated to lust and wrath, they covet to earn wealth today, even if unlawfully, for enjoyment of lustful pleasures."

"At that moment he thinks he has gained enough wealth. Later, thinking I can pick up even more of the same, he hopes additional prosperity will be his also. Reconciled that he has killed a foe today, he later plans to slay even others. He persuades himself he is the Lord and the only vindicated enjoyer. Successful and powerful materialistically, he feels happy that he is rich, perfected, realised and noble of birth."

'You have spoken of how he feels about his attachments, but what then is this person's character, *Krishna*?"

"He is deluded by his lack of knowledge, and convinced there is nobody equal to him because he is wealthy and powerful. He asks himself, who else is there that is like me and surrounds himself with comparable minds and people? He decides he will make sacrifices to gods and he makes these offerings to false gods to make merry."

"What are the underpinnings of such behaviour?"

"Because he is screened within a network of dishonesty, this deluded one who is afflicted by ignorance suffers ruthlessly in the mind of his *chitta*. While enveloped in this trap of delusion his intellect tosses about with many thoughts. Attached and hooked to enjoyment of lustful objects of desire, he sinks deeper into a ghastly anguish of licentious pleasures. He lives in misery but outwardly displays arrogance."

"What then is the basis of his arrogance, *Krishna*?"

"Because he boasts about whatever he owns, his vanity and conceit make him obstinate. Filled with self-importance and intoxication of wealth he swaggers. To reduce his mental suffering, he performs sacrifices for egotistical reasons and self-proclamation. He performs *yagnas* in which he has no faith. Two-facedness dictates rites, which neglect prearranged regulation and scriptural rulings."

"Why then would he perform rites he has no belief in?"

"Because he is wedded to vanity, control, self-importance, covetousness and rage, he secretly reproaches himself because he is resentful of others happier than himself. By performing them, he wishes he too could feel such inner happiness. However, he hates the Lord in these fortunate ones and in the bodies of others."

The blind king asks one more time, "Why is it so wrong to want? If causal desires have been exhausted and fulfilled, why must I stop wanting? Will the human race die when all wants fulfill themselves? They say the earth is excessively hot and others say it is getting colder all the time. Will all creatures die? Will the world perish once all desiring is done? What if they do not possess this knowledge? What happens to those that are not spiritually awake? How do they perish?"

Sanjaya replies.

"As long as there is one man devoted to duty or *dharma* and lives an ordered life, even if he is in the throes of final dissolution of the universe, there is no fear of his discontinuation. Those who believe that fulfillment of bodily desires is Man's highest aim, treat this world as if all is for their pleasure. These people will remain engrossed only in their wants even until the moment of death. Such ambitions are fettered by selfish hopes and expectations. Enslaved by wrath and passion these tendencies are soul-destructive. These individuals strive to provide for physical enjoyments by amassing wealth even if by unlawful means. Ever dissatisfied, they continue to aspire for more now and in the future."

"We have been planned to perform four roles for life, *dharma, kama, artha, moksha* [duty, desire, wealth, liberation]. Is it not my duty to aspire for material wealth?" asks the visionless monarch.

"There is nothing incorrect with having goals, desires, wealth, and success. While claiming to be enjoyer and ruler among men, think to share your possessions. Led astray by lack of wisdom, he harbours bewildering and fanciful thoughts and becomes addicted to sensual delights. Vain, stubborn, and intoxicated by pride of wealth, he performs actions, which renounce self-righteousness. Without following scriptural commandments, spiteful men look down on the divinity that lives within them. They therefore enter the wombs of transmigration," *Sanjaya* replied.

Krishna continues speaking to *Arjuna* and says, "Those haters of *Brahman* are subhuman. They are unkind and vilest among men. They are hurled repetitively into demoniac wombs. They are incapable of living in the *kutastha.*"

"Why are such individuals incapable of existing in the *kutastha*?"

"Because they live and stay in the *tamasic* domains of cravings, antagonism and insatiability. By coming into demoniac wombs, they are deluded birth after birth. They, O son of *Kunti,* without reaching *Brahman,* go downwards and stay behind in the vilest state along the path of fall. The cruel ones, who are perpetrators of wickedness, are the worst among men. They launch repeatedly into spheres of transmigration. Entering places of the demoniac *asuras,* they remain deluded birth after birth and fail to arrive at the Self. O *Arjuna,* they in consequence descend to their lowest depths of despair."

"Is there no salvation for such individuals who are trapped in ignorance and live in lust, anger and greed?" asks the stone-blind king.

Sanjaya answers, "The mere use of the mind and intellect is not enough to create an idea of God. Routine book learning is incapable of harnessing True Knowledge about Matter and Spirit. That becomes available only through intuitive knowing. Unless a *yogi* understands the Science of

Creation, even he will remain preoccupied with a need for immortality through desire, anger and greed. His individualistic self-will searches for this knowledge, which he does not grasp. However, he swaggers with pretension that it is his personal discovery."

"Speak to me about the *tamasic* characteristics of *kama, krodha* and *lobha* or lust, wrath and greed. How does Man get trapped in this cycle?" asks *Arjuna.*

Krishna explains this human tendency propelled by Matter's supremacy by *tamas* and *rajas.*

"Threefold is the way to misery that is harmful to Man. Lust, wrath and greed destroy access to the Self. By staying at these three sites, Man is incapable of lasting in the *kutastha.* Therefore, these three paths are for renunciation by action without aspiration for fruit of achievement."

"Once free of this vicious cycle of three, dwell in the *kutastha* by contemplation. Renounce these three gates of obscurity. Man naturally first works out his own welfare, but then looks after his highest goal – liberation. When Man abandons ordinance of scriptures, he or she acts only under the impulses of desire or *kama.* They never reach perfection of true happiness, as the highest goal. He who practices meditation gains this place of Stillness and Tranquillity."

Sanjaya elaborates on this discussion even further because he sees that even though the blind king believes what is alleged, he lacks the capacity to put it into deed.

"Detachment between Man and God needs abridgement. After that, this dividing wall must disappear. By contemplation, it is possible to support such a beginning. Disappearance of time and space makes such consideration fulfilled."

Man acts for his excellence by turning away from these three passages of obscurity. He intuitively realises that all he desires is mere thought-energy condensed into matter. When a *yogi* realises this, he reduces his distance from wants. Material object is energy. He knows synthesis of matter and spirit enlivens and sustains. He experiences and revels in this information. He wants no more of the worldly gifts. Cravings for real happiness dawn on him. He experiences and desires happiness for the sake of the Cosmic Whole. The *yogi* becomes part of the whole and there is no distance between Man and God. He is fulfilled."

"How does one put together matter and energy?"

Sanjaya replies, "Firstly, hold fast to the principles of self-control for such understanding. Live an ordered life in creation, constantly controlling the senses and avoiding involuntary impulses. Desire has no enduring numerical value. Thought-desire crystallises as energy-infused objects. However, it ends up eating Man. Become free of anger and greed by attenuating unfulfilled expectations. Avoid the stresses of separation causing sites between self and soul. Make physical and physiological corrections of the physique. Energise and enliven the essence of the astral body. Make active *Vishnu* in the *Kutastha* for permanent causal rejuvenation. Transform all units and charge all atoms of cells from the nail to the core in the spinal pathway with spirituality. All of this has already been discussed, O King."

Krishna then offers some concluding advice to *Arjuna*.

"Therefore, the scriptures should be your authority in deciding what should be done and what should not be done. It is better to do work here having found out what ordinances declare. This is the only way to gain perfection in your destiny. Whatever work you embark on, do it flawlessly and without wish for its fruit. This is the path to true happiness, which has the character of Stillness."

"O *Arjuna* perform all dutiful actions as unwaveringly declared in the scriptures. Become Still in the centre of Supreme Intelligence. Perform dutiful actions in tranquillity. It is described as contemplation and meditation, for Oneness."

Like a lotus leaf, Man is asked to let the worldly stream roll off his or her back to discover how trivial its true worth is.

19. Guidance

Arjuna wants more details, knowing that an explanation of the science of life is already given. He wants *Krishna* to explain how the reflection of war raging inside him has succeeded in appearing in their friendship. Are the qualities of integrity, ingenuity and obscurity inborn in all matter, influencing them? Are these qualities touching these soldiers to make choices about who they must fight with? If the goal in life is faith-specific and inborn, then one's inclination patterns must also be personality specific. Are the foods they like, sacrifices they perform and the degree of self-control they exercise, determined by their dominant quality trait? Is Man's daily action programmed by these compulsions? If Man wishes to be happy and free, while still under the influence of these compulsions, what must he do?

Arjuna therefore asked, "What is it that is experienced in the goings-on of the body? What is the state, O *Krishna,* of those who do not stay in the *kutastha*? What can happen by abandoning the ordinance of the scriptures? What about performing sacrifices established with inborn faith for results of their actions? For those who have rejected Stillness, how are the effects of *sattva, rajas* and *tamas* different in the different types of actions? Is their faith one of goodness, or passion, or darkness?"

And the blessed Lord *Krishna* said, "Even the inborn *faith* of embodied creatures is of three kinds. Because Man is also born propelled by their individual natures, this is experienced through the *kutastha* because, in there also are three types of embodied beings – *sattvic, rajasic,* and *tamasic.*"

After a moment's silence, he continues, "Man accepts

some rules and organises his life with whereabouts of the Sun, the Moon and all of Nature. They are self-governing, sovereign and consistent. However, if they were not, Man would choke in the chaos. Man must find a way to adjust life within the limits of truth and consistency. Unless there is faith in self-organisation, there will be misconceptions of truths about *Purushottama.*"

"What then is the true explanation about action? What dictates the temperament of individuals involved in action? What motivates Man to adore in a particular way?" asked *Arjuna.*

"Man is sophisticated, obsessive, and sinister by design. Now hear this, O descendent of the *Bharata* dynasty – *Arjuna.* When faith and reverence go with his own character, his disposition is of goodness. If this person is fully confident and esteems the molecule of *Brahman* in the *kutastha,* the *Purushottama,* this veneration is for the form of God who lives there. Whatever is one's faith, he is that, born of *sattva.*"

Arjuna was listening carefully when *Krishna* explains further.

"The natural conviction of the embodied is of three varieties - *sattvic* people are awarded with the righteousness of gods, *rajasic* people are obsessive selfish villains, and *tamasic* ones are delusive spirits ruled by lack of knowledge. Hear more about this now, *Arjuna.* They that are of the quality of goodness or *sattva,* worship the gods in the *kutastha.* They that are of the quality of enthusiasm or *rajasic,* worship wealth and worldly enjoyment – they induct *yakshas and rakshasas.* Others that are of the quality of gloom worship the five elements as spirits and hosts of *bhutas.*"

The blind king asked, "*Sanjaya,* what is inherent loyalty and faith? Are these instincts impelling us to act under our conditioned inclinations? Are these qualities nurtured by the worth of our wants? Alternatively, does fantasy motivate us?"

"Faith is each man's belief in him to act according to his

inborn quality-impelled nature. Whatever his faith is, it shows in his habits awarded from past lives. The effects of these habits become obvious in the present life, as wants. He will be what he needs," *Sanjaya* answered.

"As *Krishna* just explained, personalities having the quality of goodness are *sattvic.* They pay homage to *devas* and gods. *Rajasic* characters are like *yakshas,* they pay homage to the guardians of wealth. But *rajasic* persons who have *rakshasa* dispositions, become giants of power and aggression. *Tamasic* individuals pay homage to the *pretas* or dead spirits and hosts of *bhutas* who live as nature spirits in natural elements."

"What do you mean by dispositions, *Sanjaya*?"

"Dispositions and presenting circumstances decide one's attitudes, quality of actions, and inborn beliefs. These are motivated and regulated by cosmic forces and contribute to one's radiance, restiveness, or belief in the deceased spirits," *Sanjaya* replied.

Krishna goes on to explain the types of personalities that motivate actions and their reactions, "Those who do not reflect and who practice severe ascetic *austerities* not ordained by the scriptures are given to double standards, self-importance and arrogance. They are not only contracted with aspiration and attachment for the present, but have forceful longings for the future. They aspire for it with fury, whether under the hot sun or amid fires burning on all sides."

"These people have no insight. They torture and inflict their bodies with pain. Dehydration makes their senses cataleptic. They are unaware the Lord is seated within their physiques. These are practices causing afflictions and originate from impious designs."

The blind monarch was lost in thought. He marvelled that *Krishna* could counsel *Arjuna* in the middle of a battlefield with both sides ready to slaughter each other. He surprised *Sanjaya* when he asked, "How does one identify a true ascetic and teacher guiding a seeker?"

Sanjaya answered, "Spiritually inclined beings may not have the Knowledge about God, but they attract towards them holy beings and forces of Nature. They can begin relying on this real or imagined saint for health and salvation. He may be helpful but, in the end, the self-conscious seeker must rely on his own efforts and endeavours. He may only reach intermediate levels of understanding but this is progression nonetheless."

"How does such a person react to real or imagined saints?" asked the king to whom *Sanjaya* answered, "The self-centered perform terrible austerities not approved by ordinance. Impelled by strong wants, they undergo the senseless and irrational torture of all of their body. They imagine angels with special powers grant them blessings. Some deluded ones call on deceased friends and relatives. They propitiate cooperation for their wants."

After a pause he continued, "O King, all invoke the mentor their personality needs. All need to be encouraged to grow physically, mentally, and intellectually. Those physically inclined must learn to energise their bodily cells. The emotionally inclined self must learn to surrender individuality. The intellectual must have the humility to learn the Knowledge of Nature and Spirit and agree to their influence. *Krishna* has contrived these ways for seeking and finding God."

Now *Krishna* goes on to describe how different personalities choose their daily activities. He started with diet, "*Food* that is esteemed by all is of three kinds. Some sacrifice it in *yagna,* others in penance or *tapas,* and many in gifts or *danam.* Listen *Arjuna* about their distinction."

"Longevity, coolness, calmness, steadiness and affection comes from *sattvic* diet of milk, rice and clarified butter. Strength comes from milk. Bitter foods heighten immunity. Happiness comes from honey. Mixture of rice, honey and especially sunned rice strengthens it with a loving natural world. These kinds of foods extend life, energise, strengthen, and promote health, well being and joy. Their juices smoothen and improve peacefulness in the heart. These are *sattvic* foods and bring about goodness."

"There are also three types of sacrifice, austerity and almsgiving. A spiritual seeker is expected to provide his body with ideal nourishment, just enough to promote health. There are of course preferred tastes that are tendency-driven but a seeker is encouraged to make a wise move towards choosing. Seekers were advised caution lest indulgence produce pain, sorrow and disease."

Krishna describes tendency-driven choices for foods in greater detail, "Those kinds of food which are sour, salted, over-hot, sharply pungent, excessively dry and fiery, which produce pain, grief, and disease, are labelled *rajasic* and are necessary by the passionate. Savoury and alkaline foods may increase enjoyment, but God likes nutritive and good, foods like moong. Oleaginous, deserts and rock candy damage the heart."

"How do you categorize *tamasic* foods, *Krishna*?" asks *Arjuna*.

"Inert food that is cold, overcooked and without fragrance, is stale, malodorous and unclean, which is rejected as despoiled, is dear to the *tamasic* drawn to darkness", he replies.

It is also an accepted practice to outline religious observances and spiritual practices for ancestors to reinforce their soul qualities towards self-awakening. *Arjuna* therefore intuitively understood the slow but sure evolution of the *sattvic, rajasic* and *tamasic* personalities and of their actions just described by *Krishna*.

"A *sacrifice* is superior if it is prescribed by ordinance and is performed by people, without any longing for the fruit of the act. The effort is *sattvic* because it brings the mind to calmness. They concentrate, reflect and meditate with a stilled mind, knowing it is a dutiful *sattvic* action and seek no results."

"Many do perform actions with sincere passion, do they not?"

"Action which is performed with expectation of fruit and for the sake of show, pride and arrogance, know that sacrifice, to have *rajasic* quality," *Krishna* says.

"What then of the ritualistic?"

"Sacrifice which is against ordinance, in which no food is offered, which is lacking of *mantras* and sacred verses, in which no price is paid to the priestly *Brahmins* are born for obscurity. When an act is performed without faith, it is said to be of the quality of vulgarity or *tamas.* Not stilling the mind while contemplating on *Omkar* as trained by a teacher is meaningless action," *Krishna* says.

Just as religious observances have a role in spiritual exercises, worship too has a place in developing harmony with the cosmic forces and universal actions. *Arjuna* understood *Krishna* throughout the discussions on every aspect of spiritual practice. *Krishna* detailed all the steps that are indispensable for self-unfoldment and soul-consciousness.

"The worship and reverence of gods and saints, preceptors and men of knowledge, are wholesome and worthy. They are the practices of a *brahmachari* who is uncorrupted. Such practices and nonparticipation with injury confirm *bodily austerities.*"

Cultivation of *speech* was also discussed and fundamentals listed by *Krishna.* It is universally understood speech reveals mental and intellectual constitution of a speaker. Regulating thoughts by controlling moods is a means for precise, knowledgeable, and focused speaking. Disorganised thoughts from an emotionally disturbed personality originate from a confused, disruptive personality. Speech of this type is unproductive. *Arjuna* and *Sanjaya* both know that thinking before speaking or not speaking at all could regulate such thoughts.

Krishna now goes on to describe the regulations of speaking.

"Speech which causes no agitation, which is true and loving, which is agreeable and useful, and follows the diligent study of the *Vedas,* is said to be *austerity of speech.* Even truthful speech should cause no offense, *Arjuna.*"

Arjuna understood the reparations made on the mind are an evolution from self-awareness to soul-awareness. Through wilful cultivation of harmlessness and self-transformation it is possible to still all bodily agitation and silence the mind. *Arjuna* recognises that through control of sense indulgences these exercises could lessen all extrovert mental tendencies and impulses. In meditation, they reach states of higher awareness.

Arjuna therefore understands when *Krishna* says, "Serenity of the mind, calmness and tranquillity, gentleness, self-restraint, and purity of disposition in thought and feeling: these are said to be the *austerities of the mind.* They bring about sanctified happiness and contentment. This is what follows when enduring in the *kutastha* where there is Bliss, Stillness and Silence."

Tradition understands that those who practice austerities of action, devotion and speech control are trait-endowed personalities. *Krishna* described them individually.

'*Reverence* is also of three types. Faith infused reverence, by men without desire for fruit but united in devotion is said to be of the quality of goodness or *sattva, Arjuna.*"

"Reverence and austerities performed with arrogance for the sake of gaining respect, honour and flattery for doing charitable works is hypocrisy. Such reverence is unstable and transient and is of the quality of passion or *rajas.*"

"But reverence through self-punishment which is performed under a deluded conviction that torturing oneself and rituals are for the good or destruction of another, is said to be of the quality of darkness or *tamas.*"

Even from old times, tradition of *giving* is treated as an investment. *Krishna* wants giving to be an opportunity for service. It should stand for an offering of genuine love of sharing life's resources with those who need love, tenderness and help. *Krishna* taught *Arjuna* about giving also.

"A gift of *charity* is because it ought to be given. Give even to one who is incapable of returning anything. Gifting is righteous when issued at an appropriate time to a suitable person. Such charity has the quality of *sattva, Arjuna.*"

"But charities given reluctantly with the expectation of receiving in return – that gift is said to be of the quality of passion or *rajas.*"

"*Arjuna,* when donations are given to an inappropriate individual or to one with immoral purpose, at an improper time, it is *tamasic.* Giving to dishonest and unworthy people, without deference, and with condescension, is of the quality of darkness or *tamas.*"

"*Krishna* described three sets of duties we are tutored to perform. He spoke about sacrifice, charity and austerities, or *yagna, dana* and *tapas.* How does one fulfill all the three?" asked the visionless monarch.

"The three duties in life are collectively executed in every action, Sire. This is the only way to give meaning for this body, as it relates to Nature and society. In a spirit of *yagna* Man restores Nature's wounds and purifies what we contaminate. Mitigating our debt to Nature and society is assured by serving and giving in charity. Austerities empower by removing bodily deficiencies. Together, the three duties become harnessed to actions of life and living."

"But *Krishna* has earmarked them as separate entities, *Sanjaya.*"

"They are not distinct entities, Sire. Society is not outside Nature or an individual being. They are many units of one creation. Whether in sacrifice, charity or austerity, these three come together in a single structure. Whether eating, surrendering in devotion, or sleeping – make it all pure or *sattvic,* inside and outside. Surrender the act to the Lord, and avoid expectation of its fruit."

"*Sanjaya,* noble actions do produce noble reactions," said the king.

"Noble reactions go the way of transparency. Man must espouse distance from action and reaction. Only the Lord of Actions has the ability to infuse reaction with beauty and love, Sire. In so doing, there emerges the highest cooperation between individual and society."

"Who is this Lord and how is He invoked?" the monarch asks.

"This has already been discussed, Sire."

Further clarification of the Supreme Reality with and without appearance is called for, once more. Having agreed that life is a *yagna,* Man needs dedicating life to the Lord also. *Krishna* elaborates on worship and surrender of all actions to the Lord. Scriptures describe this but to understand one must realise and experience the harmony of sound with the Lord's name in *mantras.* It is a personal knowing through devotion and surrender. Uniting Man with Creation is the first step towards merging with *Brahman,* the Lord.

Sanjaya was pensive. He has been unsuccessful at convincing the sightless king to abandon the fight. Perhaps a discussion about the Lord of Actions will help. "The *Vedas* describe ***AUM*** as the first action-reaction of the Lord. Materialisation of Creation is from the Word of God who exists today and continues into tomorrow. He alone will be. ***Om*** enters Man's being to enliven it for works waiting to be done. ***Tat*** is that which is unattached to Creation and detached from Matter. It is separate from Man's body, as witness. ***Sat*** is reaction of Truth, which is immersed in and transcendent in God's Cosmic Dream, which purifies all to enjoy Creation."

In addition, *Krishna* interrupted by saying, "The title *Om Tat Sat,* is offered in three types of work and rituals dedicated to *Brahman, the Purushotama.* By performing sacrifices, *Brahma* the Creator appoints *sattvic Brahmins* to speak of it. It is uttered as a surrendering of all acts of oneself. This is in accordance with ordinance of the *Vedas.* Its origin is with Creation and ordained from old. *Om Tat Sat* is the three houses of God. *Om* is the form of the body; *tat* is the *kutastha;* and *sat* is *Brahman* - the one who stays there. The act of meditation is *yagna.* Offering the mind and intellect in meditation for Stillness is charity. The knowing that occurs from enduring in the *kutastha* is a true *Brahmin.* He or she knows the *Vedas* through the experience of Stillness."

"Therefore, reflecting with the body, one is able to see oneself spontaneously in complete Stillness. When surrendering to *Brahman,* Man offers oneself to the Form of the Self in the *Kutastha.* Having been there, such a one is constantly in the Form in all his actions. The uttering of the syllable ***Om*** in *yagna* during sacrifice, charity or *danam,* in penances or *tapas* and in meditation is proper. *Om* is offered as prescribed by the ordinance of the scriptures and is uttered by seers in all beginnings."

"Those who utter and concentrate on ***Tat*** at various rites of sacrifice, penance, and charity with expectation of fruit are desirous of deliverance from re-emergence."

"Those who enter the *Kutastha* in meditation without desire for fruits of action are able to perform all types of actions. He also does not hanker for liberation with such acts."

"***Sat*** is employed to mark existence and goodness. O *Arjuna,* the word *Sat* is used in a special acts of goodness."

"The essence of **Truth** remains locked in *Brahman* where Man lives eternally. Man remains merged from there where no action remains to be done except to nurture in peace and surrender."

Sanjaya adds for the benefit of the blind king: "*Sat* is

used to give the *yogi* a name of the Supreme Reality beyond creation and for goodness which emanates from It into all of creation. *Sat* also refers to the higher forms of spiritual action, on which the seeker focuses for illumination. Sire, the aspiring spiritual practitioner must restrain from indulgences and adhere to his practices of restraint through constant practice. Stilling of the body and silencing the mind is the next step. Withdrawal from the senses, objects of the senses and the mind follows naturally. Breath-control and lifting life force *prana* to the centre of the Cosmic Vision leads the seeker to hear *Om*. In That *[Tat]* awareness, the seeker looks at the Cosmic Deity as well as at the transcendent Truth *[Sat]* from which both *Om and Tat* emerge."

Krishna next went on to describe the assimilation of a *yogi* while reflecting on *Om* and his realisation of *Tat* and the experience of *Sat*.

"Constancy in sacrifices, in austerity and in charity, is for reaching the *Om* Substance. It is also called *Sat*, and It acts also for the sake of That which is called *Sat*. Man realises there is nothing else to be done except aiming to reach *Brahman*, enduring in the *kutastha*, and giving oneself up into it. Man, stable in this Stillness, knows he remains in *Brahman* and keeps himself in Supreme Intelligence."

"Whatever oblation is offered to the fire, whatever is given away, whatever penance is performed, whatever is done without faith is, O *Arjuna*, is said to be the opposite of *Sat*. It *is asat* and that is worthless both here and in the hereafter. Performing oblations with *Omkar* without enduring in *Brahman* is performing sacrifice in nontruth. There is no benefit for such a one in this world or in the next."

Sanjaya added in conclusion for the benefit of the blind king: "The use of the *mantra Om Tat Sat* cures all shortages of actions to which they are applied, Sire."

20. Grace

In this realm of coincidence, transformation, confusion and execution of any pledge depends on the decree of the Lord, *Brahman*. The path of self-denial or *sannyasa* is the highest technique by which one can realise the individuality of the self and uncover God. It is said to be the only way known to carry out Life's responsibility. The process of blending with everything, whether creature or being, needs restoration of body, mind and intellect. This ensures a state of compatibility to acknowledge God. *Krishna* has told *Arjuna* that he needs to indoctrinate in himself the routine of seeking God with every breath and constantly in all things.

Until *Arjuna* and seekers like him find God, *Arjuna* must remain flexible in accepting the Truth in the various stages of changes he experiences while on the path of a spiritual journey. When he finds God within and without him, the true vision of Matter or *prakriti* and Spirit or *purusha* is cleared by the eternal presence of *Om* that is intuitively seen, heard and understood. Man realises the vibration-less *Brahman* or God. He delights he is at home in Creation of the many Universes of *Brahman's* Cosmic Dream.

Arjuna understands action is alienated by three tendencies – *sattva* celebrates when action is harmonious and superior; when *rajasic* it is ingeniously obsessive and fanatical while *tamasic* act is unaware it evokes detrimental obscurity. He has learned that although dedicated actions are encouraged, they must be in the service of society and Mother Nature. Intentional action must integrate service, charity and austerity. By enshrining over and over again the *mantra Om Tat Sat,* Man of *sattvic* intent will bear in mind that *Om* stands for faithfulness to idealism, *Tat* for detachment from self and *Sat* for the pure *sattvic* nature of his doings in action.

Activity and actions are not renounced *Krishna* cautions. Renunciation must be for the fruits of action. Understandably *Arjuna* is confused. If every action's consequence must be renounced, what then of dutiful actions? Are they to be renounced as unworthy? Is it the action or the results of action that need rejection?

Krishna was always clear with the advice. Action is for all time to be performed. The end result of action whether beneficial or otherwise should be shorn off agency. Giving up fruit of action has universal application. Renunciation of action in *tyaga* and *sannyasa* is applicable to all three types of actions, whether of the quality of goodness, passion or ignorance. Renunciation allows the results of relinquished fruit to gather its own thrust. Either renunciation or relinquishment dies at completion of the act or both terminate together. If a worthy act is performed without desire whether *sattvic* or *rajasic,* positive consequence of action multiplies itself. If the fruit is goodness, it blesses the person, the society and Nature also.

Here, amid the two opposing warrior divisions on the battlefields of *Kurukshetra, Arjuna* is ready to fight the war against unrighteousness. But *Arjuna's* spiritual journey is not yet completed. His self-unfoldment has only reached the stage of intellectual understanding. He still needs to realise the effect of this gained Knowledge. He craves to surrender his mind, intellect and destiny at the feet of Supreme Intelligence. He intuitively knows that *Krishna* is the *guru* as well as the path. The appearance of Self from the self by the Self is both of Matter or *prakriti* and Spirit or *purusha.* He craves the experience of Oneness in *Brahman. Arjuna* understands that both *rajasic and tamasic* tendencies should be worn judiciously. *Sattvic* actions have inherent deficiencies and must await dedication for a greater good. What is he to do in these situations?

Arjuna said to *Krishna,* "O Mighty-armed one, my beloved *Krishna,* I want to know the true meaning *of sannyasa* which you say is renunciation and *tyaga* which you call relinquishment. Explain to me the distinction between them. Please elaborate renunciation and relinquishment in the different facets of life."

Krishna replied, "Whatever I speak of, is experienced at the *kutastha.* Obliterating instantaneous gratification in a current action is renunciation or *sannyasa* and rejection of fruit of action in the future is relinquishment or *tyaga.* The learned sages call *sannyasa* the denial and rejection of all activities motivated by desire. The wise declare that *tyaga* is the denial and surrender of fruits of all activities."

"I understand that life advances by progressive understanding. Dodging action does not provide any resource for anyone. In truth, Man constantly thinks of ways to free himself from action. But work has a blueprint for multiplying itself," *Arjuna* continued, "Some philosophers say that all devotional work like concentrating and enduring in the *kutastha,* should be completed. Otherwise the act of abandoning this action pollutes by corruption. It causes suffering through the cycles of cause and effect. Others declare that self-giving actions like *yagna or* sacrificial fire rites, *dana* or charity, and *tapas* or penance with austerities, should never be abandoned until soul – realisation is reached."

"There is concern with tapering action within the domains of goodness, *Krishna.* Such acts also constrict a Man's soul."

Krishna in his compassion replies, "You have raised an important point. Therefore understand from me about the final correct revelation about *sannyasa* for renunciation. O best of the *Bharata* dynasty *Arjuna,* a *sannyasi* is also a *tyagi.* He who surrenders like a powerful tiger and devours all unworthy wants is one nobody dare approach. His proximity to the present and future is renounced also. A surrendering *tyagi's* action is spoken of as being of three kinds, O best among men."

Krishna continues, "Acts such as in *yagnas* for committed sacrifice, *dana* for unselfish charity and *tapas* for intelligent austerities should be performed. They should not be abandoned, because sacrifice, charity and austerity direct and sanitise the body and decontaminate the mind even in the wise. *Arjuna,* these should be performed without self-conscious or egoistic attachment to them and without wish for their fruit and outcome."

Arjuna interjected and asked, "*Krishna* why is soul awareness disturbed by self-awareness in action and also in reaction?"

And *Krishna* answers, "A *sannyasi* ends all wants through steadfast abandonment while in the present. If a *sannyasi* renounces through delusion, the self-sense shifts its attention towards the world and the mind identifies with his innate egocentric personality. World awareness triggers unsettled emotions and disordered thought of *rajasic-tamasic* type. Causal impulses and tendencies reveal and cloud the intellect and the individual forgets all about soul-awareness."

Arjuna asked: "What then of renunciation of obligatory action?"

Krishna replies, "It is improper to renounce compulsory actions prescribed by the scriptures. Being immersed in concentration, contemplation, meditation and becoming spontaneously desire-free is *sannyasa.* Yielding to a necessary action through a delusion of painful experience is spoken of as renunciation having the quality of gloom. It is therefore evil or *tamasic.*"

"He who relinquishes action because he thinks it is difficult, or it will cause him bodily pain is carrying out *rajasic* renunciation. His deed has the quality of passion. He cannot reach the consequence of such renunciation."

Arjuna asked, "All action comes with a reaction. How

can this be prevented? How does one live life skillfully so all Man's dutiful binding actions are fulfilled? If there is a defect in all actions why should we not give them up altogether? But how does one give up these countless actions? *Rajasic* and *tamasic* actions have a deficiency and no merit and *sattvic* actions have merit with only a modest defect."

Krishna's reply describes renunciation with discrimination.

"Actions appointed, as dutifully necessary by the Laws of Nature, must be performed even while on a numinous path. Once there is physical, emotional, and intellectual reformation through restorative spiritual practices, blindness resolves. Such a one who then performs action without judgment and craving for fruit does so as a *sattvic tyagi.*"

Every expression is answerable to the triggering cause of materialization. Circumstances and preordained conditions must be attended to with the understanding that all is for experiencing inner growth.

Arjuna asks, "There seems to be much difference between renouncing *rajasic, tamasic* and *sattvic* actions. *Krishna,* do unwise actions not cause confusion and restlessness?"

Krishna explains how actions based on correct understanding do not interfere with spiritual growth, "*Arjuna,* when binding action is to be performed, and the *sattvic tyagi* has no dislike for bad work and no want for good works. Work is done intelligently only because it should be done. Free of doubt and abandoning attachment to it and its fruit, this renunciation is considered to be pure, good, and *sattvic,* because it is commanded by mandate."

"The *sattvic tyagi* or renunciant is absorbed in goodness and acts out what the scriptures prescribe by abandoning attachment to the act and the fruit of his action. Possessed of clear intelligence and with calm understanding, he dispels all doubts. Granted with the quality of goodness or *sattva,* he neither despises unpleasant action nor delights in a pleasant one."

Arjuna asked, "Is it possible for Man to abandon and renounce all actions? Many of us entrenched in the self perform dutiful compulsory actions and forget soul-awareness. Such unwise actions have a habit of producing confusing results. Even little sacrifices produce contradictory results. How then does one perform *sattvic* actions?"

Krishna replies, "It is impossible for an embodied being to abandon or renounce actions completely. But he who performs *sattvic* actions and surrenders the fruit of action is called a *tyagi* who does it with a stilled mind. Others who do not renounce even with a stilled mind, have a restive character and take up those actions previously renounced."

Arjuna wants more information about *sattvic* actions. "Must the act as well as the fruit of action be rooted out? Should *sattvic* action be considered inauspicious if embedded in cravings for fruit? If the fruit is unfavourable does the *sattvic* act become tarnished? Must *sattvic* action always result in untainted fruit?"

"There are three types of fruits of action – good or desirable, harmful or undesirable and of mixed quality. These three types of fruits of action can be renounced in its present condition as well as in the future. Renunciations of all three types of fruits happen to one who relinquishes or is a *tyagi*. But it never happens to a *sannyasi* that aspires for liberation in the future and is unable to renounce the fruit of action."

Arjuna continues to speak with *Krishna,* "Even if man renounces the fruit of his actions because he is in tune with Nature and becomes Her agent, is there a good and a best way to end the act in action itself?"

Krishna answered, "All action done by individuals has five causes for their happening. Because of these causes, all action unfolds to arrive at its fulfilment. When you align your will with the Total Will, you not only see an unfolding of the innate knowledge existing in you, but you experience

Nature's pulses acknowledge the coalition with your own soul impulse. You will realise directing your life is for spiritual growth and soul understanding. Once you have understood why you are where you are and are expected to do what you must, you will act with constant motivation. As stated, according to the faithful, there are five reasons for reaching perfection."

Arjuna answers, "If my *karmic* impressions of past lives compel my nature to act in a particular direction, will I continue to confront these propelling cosmic forces? My present spiritual activities, although uplifting, still drag me towards selfhood. *Krishna,* please tell me how I can be freed from my self-motivated attachments, habits, fantasies, and likes-and dislikes."

Krishna replies, "O mighty-armed *Arjuna,* learn from me all the five groups of agents performing all actions – the place of action, the doer, the action, the many efforts and the deities involved. It is recorded in the highest wisdom of the *Sankhyan* philosophy. It speaks of how all actions can be ended in annulment, when these facts are properly understood and realized."

"They are, **first** the mind that is placed in the body which is the seat of all action where the doer fixes himself on a foundation of all actions in all three worlds. Here he begins with many types of efforts. **Next**, the agent of action or doer is being propelled by the forces or *gunas* of Nature, so whatever is to happen, occurs because of subtle forces. The inherent organs involved in performing action are the mind, intellect, ego, the five senses, and the organs of actions – these are the **causes** of *karma*. **Fourth**, the diverse kinds of *prana* or life forces, which include the breath and physiological works, support the expression. This happens through interaction between physical, mental, intellectual, causal sheaths. Subtle forces of the mind and intellect dictate them. If they are stilled in contemplation they do not impel action for desire of fruit. **Finally**, providence has assigned to you diverse deities entrusted with your spiritual destiny – these agents also support all your life-enhancing actions."

Arjuna states "If these five groups of agents are the cause of all actions, whether they are right or wrong, I do not execute any action myself. Is that true?"

Krishna replied, "These are the five causes of all that Man does, whether related to the body, mind, or speech. The cause for all is the mind, which fixes its attention in different directions on various things. On hearing about anything this attention wants it without discrimination. Whether gained by naturalness or by annoyance, actions are put into motion for takeover. Therefore right actions support life's processes and wrong actions are disorderly, self-serving, and individualistic, but all are because of these five agents."

And he continues, "The Lord of the Self is the soul in the *kutastha* who is able to see this absurdity. This being the case, those of perverted and unrefined awareness, view their individualistic self as the sole agent of action. That is because Man is incapable of seeing beyond his attachment-filled mind and intellect."

"He who is freed from the obsession of egotism, whose mind and intellect are not enmeshed in *karma,* even when engaged, he neither acts nor destroys. Fully awake in the *kutastha,* the soul sees through the illusionary cloud and cannot be fettered by any action."

Arjuna is optimistic he will grow away from action propelled by his ingrained habits, tendencies, opinions, and likes-and-dislikes. Armed with Knowledge of the scriptures, he hopes he can unravel the forces of nature enforcing the texture of his feelings, thoughts, emotions, and actions. Understanding that self should lead him to gradual soul-unfoldment and through will and his innate intellect, he should be able to adjust his life-style through adherence to restraints and constant practice at refraining from indulgences.

His newfound satisfaction with himself allows him to spend more time sitting at meditation in concentration. Energising his body parts should ensure there is both physical and astral transformation. He is able to withdraw his attentiveness into the spinal pathway and away from the senses.

Arjuna has thus discovered there is a difference between action or *karma* and activity or *kriya.* With progressive inward purity, actions gradually decrease. To perform acts, activity must become obvious in pure reaction. A sage may not perform any activity but his mere presence can have the power to confer reactions of assistance to those around. *Arjuna* understands that the subtler the activity, the greater the energy of action. The purer the mind and soul, the more spontaneously does activity reach Infinity. He therefore assumes that all externally visible actions leave behind reactions. Performing actions with faith regardless of fruit, as though put into motion by a power within, is true actionlessness.

Krishna reads *Arjuna's* thoughts. He therefore outlines how the three entities, the knower, the knowledge and the known come together. "Beyond Knowledge and the Knowing is the Knower. These three are the triple types of causes or doers of action. The act of knowing Knowledge by the knower constitutes the threefold impulses of action. Knowing the Knowledge to be known is *Brahman* alone. The one who will know is the soul who by concentrating, reflecting, and meditating arrives at the supreme Knowledge. The work of self becoming the Self is true work. It is an act of going to the *kutastha* where the Self becomes known as the *Brahman* himself."

"Knowledge, act of knowing, and the knower are agents. They are acknowledged in the *Sankhyan* philosophy to be of three distinctions or quality temperaments."

"*Arjuna,* understand that by which one sees the One Indestructible Essence in all beings and things, undivided in the divided, know that Knowledge to have the quality of goodness - it is pure and therefore *sattvic.* Such knowledge is experienced in meditation."

"But that knowledge, which sees all beings as diverse essences with varied distinctions from one another, is *rajasic.* He is taught to see the One *Brahman* and understands that knowledge. But because of *rajasic* sense of separateness, he sees with qualities of passion and aggression."

"And that knowledge, which concentrates on a worthless single effect as if it were the whole, which is without reason and without truth, which discounts motive and lacks conformance with the principles of integrity and regards all as trivial and narrow, possesses the quality of darkness. This knowledge is said to be *tamasic* and dulled with error."

Krishna recognizes that *Arjuna* is finding it difficult to understand fully the knower-knowing-knowledge agents of action. *Krishna* who was teaching the truth that all expression is nothing but condensation of thought energy, made *Arjuna* mindful of what was being said to him. To make easy his spiritual growth, *Arjuna* mentally accepted what was being taught until his understanding improved in that personal realization.

Krishna now goes on to speak of motives of action. "That action which is divinely directed by the ordinances, which is performed in complete nonattachment, and is performed by one without want or dislike, who longs not the fruits of action, is said to be of the quality of goodness. This action of concentration, contemplation, meditation performed without want is *sattvic.*"

"But action that is inspired by longing for satisfying desires or performed with egoism or with large effort is said to be of the quality of passion. This action is *rajasic.*"

"That action which is undertaken through and from delusion, without regard to outcomes, bound to destruction, loss and injury to others is considered ignorant. Neglect of our skill to do action, which causes loss of health, wealth and influence and resulting in harm to others is said to be of the quality of delusion – this action is *tamasic.*"

Krishna is aware that *Arjuna's* life and actions are harmless and cover up no self-motivated gains. Governed by restraint, his actions are for self-evolution. Increasingly consumed with soul-awareness, *Arjuna* has been living instinctively, his actions impelled by soul impulses. His life forces and energy are inwardly productive. *Krishna* therefore describes the three types of doers.

"That agent who is free from attachment is one who never speaks of himself. He is endowed with constancy and energy and is unmoved by success and defeat. He is without desire and remains in *Kutastha* saying work is being done by *Brahman*. He is said to be of the quality of goodness – he is a *sattvic* doer."

"The agent who is full of affections, who longs for the fruit of actions, who is covetous, awarded with cruelty, and impure, who feels joy and sorrow, is declared to be of the quality of passion. Caught up in want and fruits of action, he performs with impure motives and is a *rajasic* doer."

"An agent who is devoid of application in meditation, without insight, stubborn, deceitful, malicious, slothful, despondent, and procrastinating, is said to be of the quality of darkness. Not mentally engaged and uncaringly silent, he cheats himself with laziness and brings sorrow to others. Although his mind is full of regrets, he aspires for *dharma* and good works at a later time. He performs slothfully and is a *tamasic* doer."

Arjuna comments, "*Krishna,* it is not always easy to remain focused away from ingrained thoughts, moods and behaviours. How does one overcome such influences?"

Krishna understands the problems facing a shifting seeker of the Truth and thus describes the threefold distinctions of understanding so that he resolves to remain on the spiritual path.

"*Arjuna,* I will explain next, separately and exhaustively, the threefold distinctions of the intellect or *buddhi* and courage of resolution or *dhriti,* according to qualities or *guna.* Please listen. The intellect which knows action from inaction, what ought to be done and what is not to be done, understands fear from fearlessness, bondage from deliverance is, *Arjuna,* of the quality of goodness or *sattva.* The one who remains in his still intellect in the *kutastha* and is fearless, free of all bondage and released because he is able to remain in the *sushumna.*"

"The intellect by which one imperfectly detects right from wrong, as to what ought to be done and that which ought not to be done is, O *Arjuna,* of the quality of passion or *rajasic.* The meaning of dutiful action in meditation is unknown to this intellect."

"That intellect which when shrouded by darkness regards wrong as right and all things as contrarily reversed and obscured by darkness is O *Arjuna,* of the quality of darkness or *tamas.* Such an intellect thinks that not practicing contemplation is *dharma.*"

Arjuna asks again, 'If *sattvic* action comes to Man naturally, even though defective, you say they should be performed but with their fruit renounced? Is it true that only dutiful actions in accordance with one's *svadharma* have the ability of being *sattvic?*"

Krishna therefore decides to describe the *dharma* or behaviour to be aspired for self-improvement until new behaviours become a habit in sympathetic of meditative practices. Experiencing states of super-consciousness through repetitive practices *Arjuna* has gradually transformed his physical, astral and causal atoms. *Krishna* therefore outlines qualities of steadfastness for skill over unconscious impulses.

"The determined and those of unswerving constancy by which one regulates the works of the mind, *pranic* life breath and the senses through devotion and the practice of *yoga,* is *sattvic.* Such fortitude and steadfastness *or dhriti* is of the quality of *sattvic* goodness, O *Arjuna.* When *dharana* or concentration is constant, the mind, the *prana,* the senses, the organs of action all retreat into Stillness during *pratyahara* of withdrawal. Contemplation or *dharana* and meditation or *dhyana* result into oneness of *samadhi.* Here there is no attachment in any other direction. Such a *dharana* or concentration is *sattvic.*"

"But that steadfastness of *dharana,* by which one holds to religious *dharma* or duty, for want of profit gained through attachment of wished fruit, that resolve is of the quality of obsession or *rajas.*"

"And that by which an unintelligent man will not give up oversleep, fear, grief, arrogance, conceit, and depression, is *tamasic.* O *Arjuna,* his fidelity and tenacity is judged to be of the quality of darkness and therefore *tamasic.*"

Arjuna always enjoyed life and took pleasure in working for his requirements. He felt grateful for the material comforts made accessible to him through wealth. *Arjuna* therefore asked, "*Krishna,* are you asking me to withdraw from life and existing? Is there not a way to do one's duty and exist properly? I have never been obsessed by wants that consume me. Can I not regulate my lifestyle to adhere to the teachings you have just given me? What is it that which interferes with enjoying life for direct worldly happiness?"

Krishna had just finished telling *Arjuna* to pay special attention to his duties, to remain watchful, and to disallow all issues that interfere with effective living through emotional detachment and intellectual reasoning. Successful living, *Arjuna* was educated, needs perfect understanding of the purpose of life. By adjusting attitudes and refining the self about the principles of restraints, *Arjuna* can ensure he grows psychologically and outgrows ego-centeredness.

Krishna proceeded to respond to *Arjuna's* questions about seeking enjoyment for happiness. He firstly describes transcendent happiness of supreme bliss, gained by repetitively practicing contemplation until amity is achieved. He then talks of happiness that appears at first like nectar but in the end is like poison.

Happiness, *Krishna* says is in the mind. He explains this further. To become aware that worldly gratification is not the purpose of life, is the first step. Not giving in to aggravations of unconscious inclinations is the next step. Then rising above emotional tendencies is to transcend immaturity and self-absorption. Intellectual reasoning to self-educate is the step that *Arjuna* must take to adjust into a healthy lifestyle for spiritual living. He should then definitely be able to work and live in the service of the Cosmic Whole.

Krishna highlights this even further, "Happiness, I insist is to experience the end of all pain born of self-centeredness. O best of the *Bharata* race *Arjuna,* hear from me on how this is possible. There are three kinds of happiness and pleasure." He stoops down towards the seated *Arjuna* in the chariot.

"That by which one finds pleasure from repetition of enjoyment, which brings an end to pain, which is like poison at first and resembles nectar in the end, that happiness born of serenity produced by a knowledge of Self, is said to be of the quality of goodness."

"The mind is at peace with its inner unfoldment. It is not dependent on external circumstances for inner serenity. Progressive and deepening inwardness leads to nectar-like soul awareness, born of a clear perceptive discrimination of Self-realization. That is *sattvic* pleasure arrived at by the Lord's grace."

"That happiness which springs from contact of the senses and their matter objects which resembles nectar at first but is poison in the end, that happiness is said to be of the quality of passion. It is happiness dependent on a relationship with external circumstances and therefore *rajasic.*"

"When right from the beginning, such objective is already doomed; he seeks for any little pleasure because this mind is deluded. That happiness which, from the first and in its outcome, infatuates and deludes the soul, and springs from oversleep, slothfulness, idleness, and miscomprehension is of the quality of darkness. Such a one lives and behaves submissively as a pawn of physical, emotional and intellectual circumstances. Depending on the degree of soul awareness, he lives life propelled by need for *tamasic* pleasures."

Krishna now goes on to describe how Man lives in self-centredness as well as during soul awakening. He reminds *Arjuna* that all expressions, whether physical, astral, or causal are governed by the Laws of Matter. He also speaks of societal lifestyles chosen by humankind, conditioned by personal and inherent inclinations and the opportunities offered by society for satisfying duties and wants.

And *Krishna* continues, "There is no being on earth, or among deities in the astral heavens, who is free from these three qualities of *gunas*. They are born of *Prakriti* – of Cosmic Nature as Matter. O *Arjuna,* make note of duties of scholarly *Brahmins,* guiding *Kshatriyas,* methodical *Vaishyas,* and also of the struggling *Shudras.* They are also renowned by their three *gunas* or qualities, that spring from their own inherent distinguished nature for work and action."

Krishna then discusses the idealistic way of discovering and gaining experience from life opportunities by skilful self application. He explains that in the past and even in the present, children adopt the profession of their fathers. *Krishna* argues that children be allowed to discover their own abilities to take on life's opportunities. *Krishna* goes on to describe citizens with varying physical, psychological, and intellectual tendencies. The professions they choose and enjoy are determined by instinctive guidance whispered to them by their personality type. Their moral fibre also decides inclination of life style.

Krishna elaborates, "Serenity, sense control, self-discipline and austerities, purity, forgiveness, honesty, wisdom, knowledge and experience, and belief in the existence of the hereafter create duties of the *Brahmins,* springing from their own accurate nature as scribes. They cultivate much intrinsic worth, but remain free of arrogance. Soul unfoldment liberated from superiority is the secret for such a person. He overcomes the six senses, remains in the *kutastha,* refrains from action with desire for fruit, sees Stillness in *yonimudra,* and remains in it. Here there is no day or night nor anything except *Kutastha.* Here he sees the self becoming the Self in the Self."

"Valour, radiance, firm endurance, skilfulness and dexterity, courage, generosity, are the dignities of leadership. These are the natural duties of the *Kshatriyas,* born of his own nature as warriors and rulers. You *Arjuna,* are expected by all, to live such a lifestyle. To overcome your soul-destructive mental tendencies and habits, you must practice self-discipline and also gain expertise in meditation. Through the teachings of a *guru,* move towards the *kutastha* and fix yourself in the heart of Stillness."

Arjuna is embarrassed and *Krishna* continues anyway, "And there are those in agriculture, tending and rearing cattle, and successfully trading with money as these are natural duties of the *Vaishyas.* They have innate tendencies for organization which also allow them to skilfully apply their lifestyles to meet other needs of self-unfoldment and application for noble activities. By performing the *kechrimudra* as taught by the *guru,* such temperaments should role the tongue back and perform all duties without fruit of action as the motive. This enables them to remain in the *kutastha.*"

"One always keeps his attention on his work of the self. Gradually such a one gains perfection in all things, including contemplation. Actions that are of service to others are the natural duties of the *Shudras.* Effective living happens when one applies one's body, mind, and intellect skilfully for effective work in accordance with inborn tendencies. The peaceful mind then is able to connect with the needs of the Infinite Mother of the Universe."

Krishna reminds *Arjuna* that Man must be at peace with himself and all his circumstances. Searches for Knowledge and soul unfoldment need a firm foundation of remaining true to this innate nature.

And *Krishna* says to *Arjuna,* "When each one is devoted to his own inborn tendency and duty, Man gains the highest success by enduring in the *kutastha.* There he triumphs in perfection supported by teachings of a *guru.* Having reached there which he wants most; he neither wishes nor craves for fruits of action. Now hear from me how one gains perfection by application to his duties."

"Man gets faultlessness by worshipping with his innate natural gifts. Him from whom are all movements of all beings evolved, and by whom this entire world is permeated and pervaded, worshipping Him in contemplation is performing one's highest duty, for he gains perfection."

"To remain in one's inferior path in which the mind sometimes slips away from the *kutastha* is better than performing actions of another's path. There is no sin in performing even flawed dutiful actions natural to one. Desires gradually stop and he experiences Stillness even just before death."

Krishna is intent on discussing efficiency and skilful activity when supported by innate tendencies. He tells *Arjuna* Man is born to learn a competent career first for self-satisfaction and then to dutifully serve. The more dexterous the Man, the more accomplished and successful he becomes. Success is now actually obvious through the viewpoint of his prosperity. He is emotionally and intellectually able to detect his own inner growth. Insight allows him to detach towards inwardness and innate knowledge.

Krishna speaks of that to *Arjuna. Sanjaya* and *Dhritarashtra* listen fully engrossed in these discussions also, "Better is one's own duty at contemplation and meditation, though performing faulty, than the duty of another, even if well-performed. He who concentrates, reflects and meditates as decreed by his own inborn nature incurs no sin."

"O son of *Kunti – Arjuna,* one should not abandon one's inborn duty especially when revealed by his teacher. Even though it has a flaw, it is like the eye-irritating smoke which comes before fire. Are not all undertakings marred by some blemish – in the fumes is there not a fire brewing for satisfaction, in its stacks?"

"That individual whose mind and intellect is unattached, who has subdued his self, who is ever detached from worldly ties and passions, has renounced fruits of action. Such a person has arrived at supreme perfection and has freedom from action and reaction. He is a *sannyasi* who is encouraged to persistently take his self to the Self to discover the Oneness in Self in his own *kutastha.* He gains everything in receiving the Supreme and although he acts, he discovers he is the non-doer. Such condition is experienced here in the Silence of Universal Intelligence."

Arjuna asks, "*Krishna,* what is the use of such lifestyles? Isn't all what you have taught me wishful thinking? Compelled and impelled by Nature can man awaken to soul-knowledge?"

Krishna replies, "O son of *Kunti,* hear and learn from me in brief, how one who has arrived at such perfect lives. By reaching *Brahman* in Stillness, which is that Supreme end of Knowledge, this seeker remains there because he has gained the Self through devotion to Wisdom. Absorbed in a purified mind and intellect he subdues the self by concentrated constancy. Renouncing the senses by determined patience he abandons as much as possible sound and all other objects of sense entanglements. He surrenders attachment and repulsion and he takes sanctuary. Here in profound Stillness he discovers Silence and remains there with the soul enraptured and ignoring wants and their fruits."

"Speak to me of this one who has arrived at perfection, *Krishna.*"

"Such a person prefers remaining in a sequestered place

for solitude, eats lightly, with body, speech and mind subdued, he is ever absorbed in concentration and divine meditation with soul-uniting *yoga.* He succeeds by taking refuge in extreme dispassion. His detachment is born of performance of *pranayama* all the time. As a result, the mind and the senses remain subdued. He, who is peaceful, renounces egotism, power, vanity, lust, anger and possessions, he is freed from notions of selfishness of me and mine. He has arrived at Peace. With such tranquillity he is qualified to win stillness and silence in the *kutastha* and become one with *Brahman.*"

They have all realised that *Krishna* guarantees soul-realization to Man who uses his will for self-control and adherence to restraint through constant and repetitive practice until the self withdraws from sense objects automatically. *Arjuna* is told he should prefer places of solitude. "Expect to remain engrossed in spiritual practices that disclose your unique self. With physical, mental, and intellectual understanding of life's higher purposes expect to unfold. Life flows towards inwardness," *Krishna* says. *Arjuna* realizes he has reached the doorsteps of dispassion. Steadfastness should lead him to attenuate ego through selflessness and service. *Krishna* promises soul contentment.

Krishna pledges insight and intuitive experience of his soul. "By becoming engrossed and one with *Brahman,* this calm-souled and serene one, neither grieves nor wants anything. The enchanted soul, by beholding sameness and equality in all beings, gains supreme devotion or *bhakti* toward the Lord. With faith in the teachings of the *guru,* such a one takes his self into the Self, realizing he has gained the highest fortune in the form of Wisdom. By that supreme devotion he realizes God in Essence – what and who I am. After knowing the *Brahman* Substance, he quickly makes his entry into the Supreme *Kutastha* with the realization that 'Me' is the real 'I Am', the Self."

Arjuna is told, "When self-awareness changes to soul-awareness, expect to become one with the Cosmic Soul. By living increasingly within the divine cave, you will experience a personal knowledge of God. The changes within the spine in areas you previously found difficult to feel, will awaken. The centre of intuitiveness enters life and soaks up humility, even-mindedness, and patience."

Arjuna realizes that pain and pleasure are mere expansion and contraction of body parts experienced on the platform of touch – also a power of God. He experiences even-mindedness on the stage of revelations. He understands attachments to likes-and-dislikes and to attraction-aversions as illusions viewed through the prism of Matter.

Arjuna's practices at even-mindedness on a framework of controlled senses – touch, taste, and smells, sound and sight, made all spiritual practices easier. Through this discussion with his mentor, *Arjuna* progressed from physical to astral application until he saw the reflection of Creation in the *kutastha.*

Arjuna always experienced universality of all religions. His understanding of One Truth began during his training in material and spiritual warfare in angelic worlds with astral beings. All his brothers saw this changing state continually. His life was always directed towards the Truth of Changelessness. On reaching the pulpit of Changelessness, he became a *devotee of Krishna.*

Krishna in many previous discussions described this status of a devotee such as *Arjuna.* "Doing all actions while taking refuge in *Brahman,* Man realizes it is by the Lord's grace that a devotee gets the Eternal Indestructible State, which is the seat of eternal Peace and imperishable house of Stillness. Know that by mentally dedicating all actions to the Self in the *kutastha,* all action is realized as done by *Brahman.* From the depths of your heart, think of the Self in concentration as the Doer and the Supreme Goal also. Through Intelligence and uniting with Stilled consciousness through discriminative wisdom, continuously absorb your heart in the Self."

Meditation, *Krishna* said, is the path for outgrowing distaste and attachments. *Arjuna* is told to enter the centre of his own *kutastha* where he will see his soul as the nucleus of his own expression. Once the body is transformed, he will once more see the nucleus of the Cosmos, the Cosmic Deity – *Jagadishwara*.

Krishna reminds *Arjuna* that, in all meditative techniques, he must watch the mind without judging. *Sanjaya* attentively listens to this discussion. The blind king remains absorbed in his anxiety for success. *Arjuna* is preoccupied with the advice being given. Should he approach the war as a meditative exercise in action?

And *Krishna* replies, "With your mind absorbed in the *kutastha*, and by my grace as your teacher, you shall overcome all situational obstacles of the mind and intellect. But if your ego does not heed me, you will meet with your own destruction through many births and deaths. If, by clinging to the ego, you think that you will challenge the teachings of the *guru*, your flawed decision not to meditate will take you to the fruit of action. *Prakriti*, your inborn Nature, will compel you towards devotion for such results."

Arjuna is gently warned that even if he refuses to listen to his own soul-urges, his innate inclinations will compel him to act.

He will relate himself in his duties as well as in the cycles of his destiny over and over again. He must remain involved in life's circumstances.

All participants in this discussion already know he has no choice but to fight unrighteousness. "O son of *Kunti* - *Arjuna*, you are shackled by your own *karma* and worth of past achievements. They are accepted and expected from your own nature. Even if you refuse to do them because of this inborn deception, you will be compelled to act. Act you will as if helplessly and involuntarily in this or the next birth. After experiencing birth, death and suffering you will helplessly seek for peace. You will then realize that Peace and Stillness is not in worldly action. It is gained only by enduring in the *kutastha.*"

"Why?" asks *Arjuna.*

"*Arjuna,* the Lord lives in the hearts of all creatures, and it is His Cosmic Illusive power of *maya* that compels all beings, to revolve, as if mounted on mechanical clockwork. Man who contemplates has the Lord established in his heart, in all circumstance whether mobile or immobile. There is no escape from inbred duties in life. Remember Man experiences through the three embedded nerve paths - *ida, pingala and* the *sushumna* are entrenched in illusion and quality compulsions. Attachment-filled attention overpowers Man."

Krishna tells *Arjuna* there is no escape from the compulsions of Nature who has programmed Herself to enforce Her will on each creature. She is unconscious at first but Her own creativity desires to become neutral in *sattva.* Only then can She dissolve Her separateness to merge into the Cosmic Being. This happens only when Man secures both stillness and silence in the *kutastha.* . This is the Grace She shares when connecting with each individual soul within Her own Being. This is the mystery of life. It can only be earned through Knowledge. And even when understood insight is only possible through contemplation until Nature Herself unfolds Her secrets.

Krishna therefore, says, "O descendent of *Bharata* race – *Arjuna,* take shelter in *Brahman* with all your being. By His grace, you will earn the Supreme Peace and the Eternal Shelter. Man realizes that even the *gunas* are born of *Brahman.* He knows that by enduring in the *kutastha* the Supreme Intelligence will lead him to the path of both Peace and Stillness. *Arjuna,* I have given you this Wisdom because you are my beloved friend. There is no greater mystery or secrets to tell you about. After reflecting on this exhaustively, you may act as you wish."

"I still wish to know in simple words, what is the most priceless way to arrive at the goal of life, *Krishna*?"

"Renouncing fruit of action shows Man the bounds within which to act," *Krishna* replies. "That is the state of mind Man must reach for the noblest outcome of life, liberation."

Dhritarashtra, who had been listening to the conversation between *Krishna* and *Arjuna,* now intervened with a question. He asked *Sanjaya,* "*Arjuna* found himself a teacher in the instructive *Krishna.* What of other seekers on the spiritual pathway?"

Sanjaya replies, "The Love of God attracts beings to seekers who sincerely need a true teacher. He is exposed to circumstances and influences that are expressions of grace. All you must do, O King is to accept and surrender to this divine grace. That is the secret of a spiritual journey. To agree to every opportunity to serve the Cosmic Whole is perfected action."

Krishna enlightens *Arjuna* with some final comments.

"Again listen to my definitive words. I will tell you even more about this secret, because you are dearly beloved to me. Therefore, I will tell you what is helpful to you. Absorb your mind in me within the *kutastha* in contemplation. Be devoted to the words of the *guru* in me. Resign all to me. Because you are dear to me I promise, you will surely reach Me. Abandoning all other *dharmas* of duties of body, mind and intellect remember Me alone. I will free you from all sins gathered from the non-performance of lesser duties. Therefore do not grieve."

Spiritual practices are not for everyone. Many show no interest in them while others do not wish to use effort in them. Those who have an interest in the philosophy of living begin by listening. Only those who are interested in learning after listening are awakened into the path of spiritual endeavours.

Sanjaya reminds himself that the blind king was introduced to *Vedanta* and spirituality as a child while studying with his family *Pandu* and *Vidura.* Books on *Vedic* Knowledge were provided to the three sincere seekers for self-motivated learning. Personal learning and evolution was encouraged and made compulsory before embarking on spiritual practices. In time, however, this lustful son *Duryodhana* led the blind king astray. However, he has endured the conversation between *Krishna* and *Arjuna*. The right to hear spiritual truths is what *Krishna* speaks of next.

"Renounce all other duties and surrender directly to the *Kutastha*. Never voice these truths to one who is without self-control, nor to one who performs no service or austerities. Do not recite this to one who does not care to hear about Me, nor to one who speaks ill of Me."

"Whoever shall teach My devotees, this supreme secret knowledge, with the utmost of devotion to Me, that person shall, without doubt, come to Me. There is nobody among men, who performs more priceless, a service to Me than such a one. In the entire world there is none dearer to Me than he who teaches this Knowledge. And he who will study this sacred discussion of ours, and knows it intuitively worships Me by the sacrifice or *yagna* of knowledge. Such is My holy utterance."

The blind king who had been following the discussion asks, "Does this mean that *Arjuna* will automatically reach Selfhood? Does spiritual advancement arrive at worlds of superconsciousness only? Does the devotee benefit from intuitive revelations or does he need further liberation?"

Krishna addressed *Arjuna* and *Sanjaya* repeats this conversation to the blind king.

"Even that individual, full of devotion and lacking of scorn, who merely listens to and heeds this sacred dialogue, he, too, freed from earthly *karma,* shall arrive at the blessed worlds of virtuous deeds. O *Arjuna,* have you heeded this wisdom with a focused feeling? O mighty armed one, has your delusion born of ignorance been wiped out?"

Arjuna replied, "By your grace my delusion is now destroyed and I have regained my recollection about the knowledge of my soul. O matchless *Krishna,* I am now firmly fixed. I am tranquil and my doubts have vanished. I will act by your word and bidding."

Sanjaya said to the blind king *Dhritarashtra,* "I have listened to this wonderful dialogue between *Krishna* and the high souled *Arjuna.* It has caused my bodily hair to stand on end thrilling with joy. Through the grace of *Vyasa's* knowledge and wisdom, this supreme and most secretive of all *yogas* has also been given to me. It was clearly projected into my consciousness through the *kutastha. Krishna* directly declares it Himself, this Lord of Yoga Meditation."

"O king *Dhritarashtra,* as I remember this extraordinary and secret exchange between *Krishna* and *Arjuna,* I am overjoyed again and feel contented. And Sire, I am enraptured and filled with wonder as I remember that astounding vision of the Lord's Cosmic Expression."

And then *Sanjaya* in ending adds, "Such is my faith. Wherever there is within the *kutastha,* a display of a *Krishna,* and wherever there is a true disciple like *Arjuna* who is an expert wielder of the bow of self-control, there shall be success and victory over unrighteousness. There will be attainment of powers and an unfailing law of discipline that leads to liberation. This is my deepest conviction."

21. The War of Mahabharat

When Man reaches the furthest confines of a pilgrimage, contentment stands there in expectancy with folded hands seeking deliverance. He understands that if he remains in position here, he may not reach his objective. Therefore he begins walking again towards the *kutastha* until the Lord himself suddenly confronts him.

Sanjaya and *Arjuna* both have the faith that whatever controversies trouble them, they will get clarification when they are ready. When the operations are completed, the answers will be there also. Step-by-step they advance slowly seeking answers. Unless the pilgrimage is completed how can there be a destination? How can there be an answer unless a defined path is followed? How can a discovery be made unless the searching is completed?

Sanjaya suddenly says, "I see *Arjuna* take up his bow and arrows once again. The mighty *Pandava* warriors utter an enormous roar and those who follow him are filled with joy. They blow their sea horns and conches. Drums and cow horns are beaten and blown together, and the clamour is tumultuous."

"And then, look O King, here come the gods and hosts from heaven wishing to see this sight. And the *rishis* are blessing them. I see the two armies, which look like oceans, preparing for the battle and moving constantly."

The visionless monarch is overcome with fear and anticipation. Skirmish will soon follow. Whatever happens he has no other thought except a wish that his children the *Kauravas,* win this battle between his contemptible descendants and the fitting heirs of his brother *Pandu*.

Sanjaya interrupts his thoughts. "I see the heroic and just King *Yudhishthira,* your oldest nephew and son of your late brother *Pandu,* take off his coat and screen shield. He has shed his weapons. He hastily descends his chariot and with folded hand advances on foot. With his eyes fixed on the grandsire he approaches *Bhishma.* With a trembling tone of voice he greets him. He faces the east where the spiteful forces led by your son *Duryodhana* are standing. Seeing the dauntless young king advance, the remaining *Pandava* family has speedily alighted from their chariots led by *Arjuna.* All his family now escort King *Yudhishtra. Krishna* is now following, also."

Sanjaya reports that *Arjuna* has questioned the actions of their normally clear-sighted eldest *Pandu* brother, *Yudhishthira. Bheema* wonders if the just King *Yudhishthira* is abandoning his comrades in this war between virtue and unrighteousness. For their part the twins *Nakula* and *Sahadev* fear for the safety of their wise and perceptive oldest brother who is now walking towards the unfriendly detachment of appalling and countless foes. Would they have the guts to hurt him? *Yudhishthira* ignores the sibling concerns, and says nothing but continues eastwards.

The high-souled *Krishna* of great understanding smiled and said to the *Pandu* family, "His objective is known to me. In all wars, you must pay respect to those preferred seniors who have helped and taught you. This is about ordinances that for aeons have revered the lineage of preceptors. Only then can one be sure of victory in battle."

Suddenly, a loud angry disturbance arises from the ranks of the blind king's sons but the righteous *Pandu* army remains still. The eldest of the *Dhritarashtra's* sons points at *Yudhishthira* and says,

"This one is the most infamous wretch of his race. Obviously he is coming in terror over to *Bhishma's* side. *Yudhishthira,* with his family must be seeking asylum from our unconquerable distinctive grandsire, *Bhishma.* But, with

Krishna as his protector, why does this oldest, most celebrated *Pandu* of perceptive astuteness come here in fear?" The *Kauravas* started to yell and protest against the just King *Yudhishthira*. Then both armies became still, prying to hear what *Yudhishthira* has to say.

Sanjaya said, "O king, your sons' hostile armies are bristling with darts and arrows. Your eldest son *Duryodhana* of many lusts and needs quickly goes towards the grandsire, as if to protect the proud *Bhishma*."

Yudhishthira reaches *Bhishma's* chariot, and while surrounded by his family and *Krishna,* seizes *Bhishma's* feet with his two hands, and addresses him: "Salutation, O unassailable reclusive one. With you we will unquestionably do warfare. Grant us permission in that declaration. Give us also your presumed endorsement."

Bhishma replies, "If, O peer of the realm of the earth, you had not come to me thus, I would have made you disaster-prone and brought you defeat. I am appreciative, of you my son. Do battle and achieve triumph, O son of *Pandu*. Seek also a stroke of luck, which you need to have from us. Defeat will not be yours, but ask for a boon. A man can be a slave of wealth, but wealth is no one's slave. I am bound to the *Kauravas* in the company of their wealth. It is for this reason that I say that apart from victory over me in battle, what else can you want from me?"

Yudhishthira said, "O grandsire of great understanding. Do battle only for the *Kauravas*. Sire, tell us how can we in battle conquer you who is invincible?"

Bhishma replies, "I do not see the person who, even if he were a celestial himself, can defeat me in battle. The time of my death is not yet come."

Yudhishthira salutes *Bhishma* once more and goes towards his mentor and teacher, *Drona*. He walks in the midst of guards and around the invincible warrior of many routines and ingrained background. He asks him for authorization to fight and take home conquest against him. *Drona,* pleased with his most talented student's act, blesses him with victory but tells *Yudhishthira* that unlike the taught, the teacher fights for materialistic gains. *Yudhishthira* then asks for support. *Drona* answers, "Victory for righteousness is assured for you, O just King, who has *Krishna* for counsellor. Where *Krishna* is, goodness is certain to triumph."

"How then do I kill you O preceptor?" asks *Yudhishthira.*

"I see no one who can to slay me. Slaughtering me is impossible while I stand in battle, while I am angry and excited, and while dispersing my arrows. I see that one of you will kill me only if I lay down my arms and have withdrawn away from all sights. I will be killed when withdrawn from the battle," *Drona* replies.

Yudhishthira respectfully venerates his preceptor *Drona,* the son of *Bharadwaja,* the *rishi* of the *Atharva Veda.* He then advances to the emotional and kindly but non-discriminative *Kripa* who is also his preceptor. Members of the *Pandu* family genuflect and give homage to all the other leaders of the *Kaurava* army, seeking their permission to fight and gain victory. *Kripa* apologizes for the entire *Kuru* band, stating they were fighting for the sake of wealth, possessions and need for pleasure. But he wished *Yudhishthira* and the *Pandu* family success. *Yudhishthira* and the brothers return to their chariots on the *Pandava* side where he puts on his shining coat of golden radiance.

The battle rages over many days, and the *Kauravas* are crushed. The blind King *Dhritarashtra* is alarmed and says to *Sanjaya,* "I regard providence to be superior to exertion. Because of destiny my sons' army is being continually slaughtered by the *Pandava* army. *Sanjaya,* you speak of my children as dispossessed of endurance. The conquered are falling. Although they battle to the best of their powers and strive hard for victory, I am constantly hearing culpability from countless cases of unbearable and poignant bereavements because of *Duryodhana's* actions."

"I hear of acrobatic agility in the sons of *Pandu*. My heart is filled with fear and doubt. My sons are humiliated in every way. I am filled with apprehension about the outcome of this war. These high-souled *Pandu* sons have performed ascetic penances. They are therefore gifted with many blessings. Perhaps they are masters of sciences only known to them and like stars in the heavens suffer no decline. I cannot bear to hear that my army is repeatedly massacred. In what way and why are my sons destroyed? Why are the *Pandu* sons impossible to kill?"

Sanjaya said: "This mighty evil originates from you, O King. Listen now with patience and with attention and having listened, let it go to your heart. Nothing happening now on the battlefields is the result of any magic formula. The kings helping the *Pandu* family are not uninformed and have no misimpression about right and wrong. The sons of *Pandu* have not created any new fears. They are granted with efficacy and are ready to fight by fair means in this battle. The *Pandus* weigh every act, including those that support their mundane life's needs, and perform under the laws of morality. They are granted with abundance and possess great moral strength. They never exhibit inconsistency and keep their eyes on righteousness. Victory is where virtue is. They are unslayable and will always be triumphant."

"Your sons, the *Kauravas* are evil souls who are addicted to wickedness. They are barbarous and linked to contemptible acts. It is for this that they are being demoralized in battle. Your sons, O King, have on many occasions embarrassed the *Pandavas*. Let them now reap the regrettable fruit, which should really be experienced by you, your sons and relatives. Your well wishers did not succeed in counselling you. Your wise brother *Vidura* repeatedly forbade you to fight the righteous *Pandu* sons," *Sanjaya* adds.

"You even rejected the counsel of that extremely gifted and self-absorbed grandsire *Bhishma* who has contributed to the *Bharata* dynasty for generations. The lofty souled

Drona, the meritorious preceptor of your sons and nephews, also tried to persuade you not to fight for the crown that rightfully belongs to *Yudhishtra,* but you did not identify with any of them. I, too, tried hard to stop this war but you have rejected all wise actions that are intended for your own good and are worthy of acceptance. Instead you have accepted the views of your sons and estimated the *Pandavas* as already overthrown."

Sanjaya continues, "Often have I harangued you, O King, but you do not do what I have voiced. Let peace be made with the *Pandavas.* Although I have cried myself hoarse, O Sire, you refuse to listen to me. There is not, was not, and will not be a being in all the worlds that would or will be able to defeat the sons of *Pandu,* your brother. The conduct manipulators of truth and morality protect them. All the souls of sages and celestials are united and wait reverentially on the mountains nearby to serve these *Pandavas* who are experts in meditation, have restrained hearts, are delighted within, and offer greetings to the highest Divine Being. Friendly with *Brahma,* the Creator of the Universe, they are enlightened with the highest morality. They seek refuge in Him who is the heart and soul of *Yoga.* They seek victory for the good of the worlds."

Sanjaya, who is gifted with perceptive eyes by *Vyasa,* sees *Duryodhana,* the eldest son of the blind king approach the grandsire and general of the *Kaurava* army. He is heard to question *Bhishma,* "O blessed one, you are born of ascetic austerities and your strength is born of obedience to your words, morality, and religious rites. Your energy is like fire, and you control the wind with your breath. You direct the flow of waters and have the goddess of speech sitting on your tongue. Your knowledge of the *Vedas* is so extensive that even *yogis* and *yoginis* consult you. You, who are able to consult with the celestials, please tell me about the celebrated *Krishna.*"

Bhishma replied, "That distinguished deity with *Arjuna* is the Lord of the three worlds. Through *yoga* of meditation,

I experience him. He is called *Tat* who is supreme and existent and who will be for all-time. He is the soul of all beings and is known through detachment from worldly pleasures. He is the Self, the Lord of the Universe and was called for by me for the good of the Universe. He is here for the slaying of the unrighteous and has taken birth among men. He is worthy of your adoration. Granted with great energy, he bears with him a conch of *Om* and the discus of Time. He is without decay and unmanifest except as the Supreme Energy. He, from whose Self, I have sprung as my individualistic self, is worthy of your adoration. Only people of foolish understanding, out of slight, speak of *Krishna* as Man. They labour under darkness that discounts *Krishna.* He is the Father who begot the Son and the Son who begot the Father."

"You and your family were warned by sages and cultured souls never to go to war with *Krishna.* This, from some foolish impression, you could not comprehend. I regard you therefore, as forsaken and enveloped in anonymity. *Arjuna* is full of goodness and stripped of all qualities of foolhardiness and infatuation. Where *Krishna* is, is where virtue stays. And, there is victory where goodness is. It is by the *Yoga* of this ultimate distinction, and the *Yoga* of the self, that the sons of *Pandu* are supported. Victory, therefore, is surely theirs."

Bhishma continues, "*Krishna* who has always made known to the *Pandavas* the understanding that when skilful in uprightness, strength to battle is always protected from danger. He with whom *Krishna* is satisfied wins bountiful regions. Those men who get *Krishna* are never seduced. He delivers those who are overwhelmed by great fear. Knowing this to be true, *Yudhishthira* with his whole being has sought the shelter of the eminently divine *Krishna,* the Lord of *Yoga,* and the Lord of the Earth. O *Duryodhana,* hearing this consecrated story, turn your heart in love for *Krishna.*"

Sanjaya now again turns to the blind king, "You have heard about the object for which *Krishna* has taken birth among men. You have also heard why the *Pandava* heroes are invincible. O king the sons of your brother *Pandu* are incapable of being slain in battle by anybody. This is why O King of kings, I say, 'let peace be made with the *Pandavas'*. By restraining passions enjoy the earth with all those around you. By discounting the goal of the divine *Krishna,* you shall be wiped out."

Hearing these words, the king became silent but also mentally dismissed *Sanjaya.* He entered his tent and passed the night in sleep. The next morning, the sun rose and the two armies approached each other in battle for the tenth day. Each rushed towards the other eager with frenzy and desirous of victory. Both fought fiercely. The battle that took place between the *Kauravas* and the *Pandavas* was appalling to the highest degree and many great heroes fell.

In the morning, the blind king turned to *Sanjaya* and said, "That our army should yet again be slaughtered in battle is because of destiny, *Sanjaya.* That such a large army, congregated according to science and devoted to us because of our wealth, why should they be slaughtered? Is the result of this battle not predetermined by fate?"

Sanjaya replied, "Sire, because of your own fault, you are overtaken by this misfortune. *Duryodhana,* your passionate son, does not see the faults, underlying the unrighteous course of conduct taken towards the *Pandavas.* It is your fault also that this battle has taken place. Having committed offense, you must now reap the fruit of this assault. One must harvest the fruit of acts perpetrated by one's own self. Therefore, prepare yourself to suffer the outcomes of your own actions both here and later."

The blind King replied, "Many and wonderful were the battles I heard you speak of between the *Pandavas* and my warriors. Before, you never spoke crudely about my sons' heroism. But now you speak of mine as miserable, disadvantaged, powerless, and relentlessly conquered in battle. All this you say is without doubt, my destiny?"

Sanjaya replied, "Your men, O King, wield themselves according to the measure of their might and courage. They display their valour to the utmost extent of their strength. This destruction of the world is swelling the population of the domains of the dead. It arises from your misconduct and that of your sons. It is important that you do not grieve for what has arisen from your own fault. Kings do not always protect the world with their lives. But some rulers of Earth, winning by battle the regions of the righteous; they fight daily, penetrating hostile divisions, with paradise as their only endeavour."

Meanwhile, *Duryodhana,* is overwhelmed with grief. He goes to the grandsire *Bhishma,* and there overcome with sorrow, began to lament, saying, "My heroic family is slain in battle by one of the *Pandavas, Bheema.* Although our troops are fighting bravely, they are falling. You grandsire neglect us, behaving like an indifferent spectator. Alas, what direction have I taken? Note my unfortunate inevitability."

Hearing these cruel words of *Duryodhana, Bhishma's* eyes were filled with tears as he replied, "Even this was predicted what you have just said to me. I was warned about your statement also by *Drona* your preceptor. The realized *Vidura* your uncle and your distinguished mother *Gandhari,* who foresaw the effects of all your past evil actions against your *Pandava* cousins, warned you not to embark on this unrighteous war. Son, you did not understand the advice given to you. O great barrier of foes, the outcome of this war was recognized even before *Drona* and I decided to join forces with you. We are with you for fear of material scarcity. Neither *Drona* nor I will escape from this battle alive. I tell you, that those on whom *Bheema* casts his eyes in the battle, he will surely kill. Therefore, call on all your patience. Make a firm resolve to contest with the sons of *Pandu.* Make heaven on earth your goal. The *Pandavas* are incapable of being defeated even by gods. Therefore, surround your heart courageously with the inspiration of battle and fight."

Suddenly, the war crushes all the contestants. The kings emerge slain. Horses and horse-riders are chopped down in thousands. Seeing the *Kaurava* troops fleeing towards their tents, *Drona* and *Bhishma* cry out at the top of their voices, saying, "Fight! Do not retreat from the battlefield. All this is a misimpression conjured up by the *Pandava* sons."

The *Kauravas* were struck with panic and ignored these words. Seeing them flee, the *Pandavas* regarded victory as theirs and filled the air with their joyful shouts, mingled with the blare of conches and the beat of their drums.

The blind king sighed once more in dismay and said to *Sanjaya,* "The *Pandus* relied on *Krishna.* I started a fierce war with the *Pandavas.* Though armed to the hilt, I and mine are defeated in battle. It is this that devours my limbs like fire consumes a dry tree."

"Listen, O King, to these words of mine. I will tell you about the way in which you should always behave. In all worldly matters one's own personality should be sheltered from stifling character foes. In battling the *Pandavas* following one's duty toward divine sovereign comes first, before attending to oneself," *Sanjaya* said.

The blind *Dhritarashtra* said: "Without doubt, that high souled wise brother of mine *Vidura* foresaw this destruction of the *Kauravas* by the *Pandavas.* It was for this that he forbade battle. In this encounter, many heroes from both sides have been slain. O *Sanjaya,* for the sake of possessions, contemptible acts are done. Disgraceful is such prosperity for the sake of which bloodshed of loved ones is perpetrated. For those who obtain such assets, even death is better than winning through slaughter of relatives. I condemn myself. As one belonging to the warrior *Kshatriya* race, I have shamed them."

Fierce clashes restarted. It was terrible to watch. The competence of *Kunti* and *Pandu's* sons was astounding. *Drona* held the *Pandus* in check, but they still killed the blind king's sons. Meanwhile, *Ganga's* son *Bhishma* began resisting *Arjuna.* Warriors headed by *Dhrishtadyumna* battled with the

Kaurava troops. The armies faced one another in skirmishes and crushed each other. Dark night set in, and the battle could no longer be seen. Both armies withdrew and rested for the night.

That night, *Duryodhana* consulted with his generals. He said, "I am becoming weaker in strength and my weapons are squashed or destroyed. The *Pandavas* have cheated me with their heroic deeds. They are incapable of being overthrown by even the gods that protect them. How indeed shall I succeed in pummelling them in battle?"

The brave but self-interested *Karna* then offered *Duryodhana* unscrupulous advice: "Do not grieve, O chief of the *Kauravas*. Even I shall do whatever is acceptable to you. Let *Santanu's* son *Bhishma* quit from this enormous battle. After *Ganga's* son has withdrawn from the fight and laid aside his weapons, I will slay *Arjuna* and all his army. Remove *Arjuna* from the range of *Bhishma's* vision. I pledge my integrity, O friend. Definitely I have noted *Bhishma* show compassion towards the *Pandavas*."

Duryodhana suddenly feels elated with hope. *Karna* continues, "The grandsire is incapable of overpowering those mighty *Pandu* warriors. *Bhishma* is proud and he only wishes to show his adeptness in battle. He is self-indulgent towards a good prolonged fight. Why, will he therefore subdue the assembled *Pandavas*? Would not then the battle be over? Therefore persuade the old and reverend senior to lay aside his weapons. Once he has done this, think of the *Pandavas* as already slain."

Duryodhana sent for his brother *Dussasana*. A letter asking the mighty chief of the Kauravas to withdraw was scripted and sent. The high souled *Bhishma* was deeply hurt by the message. Overwhelmed by sorrow he did not say a single disagreeable word in reply. He sighed in anguish and bottled fury. He reflected in silence for a long while.

Then addressing *Dussasana* he said, "I have always endeavoured to do my highest to toil for your good. Indeed, in doing what is agreeable to you, I have cast away my life in engagement for your covetousness. The *Pandavas* are invincible. Who can defeat in battle the son of *Pandu* for he has as his champion, the Protector of the Universe armed with the conch of *Om,* the discus of Time, and the mace of Action? *Krishna* is possessed of infinite power and is the obliterator of the Universe. Because of your folly, you know not what should be understood and what should not be said," *Bhishma* said.

"Man at the point of death sees all trees to be made of gold. You see everything inverted. Having provoked hostilities, you must fight them in battle. Act like a man. About myself, I will slay all those who are assembled avoiding *Sikhandi* alone. *Sikhandi* was born in *Drupada's* palace as a female first. She is born this time with a male physique because of a boon. In truth he is she, *Sikhandini.* He I will not slay, even at the cost of my own my life."

Filled with great grief and reduced now to the status of servitude, *Santanu's* son *Bhishma* reflected for a long time. *Ganga's* son at last made his decision to depart this life. *Duryodhana* sensed *Bhishma's* thinking and ordered his army to protect *Bhishma* from *Sikhandi* in battle.

Seeing *Bhishma* surrounded by many chariots, *Arjuna* addressed the self-controlled chief of the *Pandu* army, *Dhrishtadyumna* and said: "O prince, place that tiger among men, *Sikhandi,* today in front of *Bhishma.* I will be his protector."

Then the oldest P*andu, Yudhishthira* ordered all the family armies to take position in a battle array at the head of their troops. Death dealing arrows were fired up. The *Pandus* subdued all troops. The *Kaurava* warriors were incapable of slaying their foes. Like insects impelled by fate they could not hold up under the blazing fire. By confounding *Kripa* the spiritual preceptor, and *Drona* the worldly preceptor, the *Pandus* haunted the enemy troops.

Bhishma, the son of *Santanu* and *Ganga,* seeing his own troops routed exposed *Arjuna* to a thick shower of arrows.

Then ailing like a moon eclipse approaching the sun, *Bhishma* rushed towards *Arjuna* and fought him with angst. It is then that *Dhrishtadyumna, Sikhandi, Virata* and *Drupada* fell on *Bhishma* and struck the mighty warrior with many arrows. *Sikhandi* pierced the grandsire with many shafts, but *Bhishma,* regarding his foe as female, did not strike back.

Deeply wounded by many missiles from the *Pandu* forces, *Bhishma* became covered with blood, and appeared like a beautiful red *Ashoka* covered with flowers. The *Kshatriya* warriors seeing the carnage *Sanjaya* exclaimed in utter despair, "Alas, through *Duryodhana's* carelessness the *Kshatriyas* race is being exterminated. Why O undiscerning King deluded by greed, did you harbour jealousy for the sons of your brother *Pandu*? They are graced with the virtues of restraint, adherence to constraint, goodwill for humankind, control over life's forces, and are awarded with insight. They fought for society without self-importance, and their army has routed all forces in this battle."

Duryodhana, now filled with grief, runs to protect the afflicted *Bhishma.* The *Kaurava* army suddenly seemed to be in a stupor and cried in consternation, "*Bhishma* is slain, *Bhishma* is slain. He is on his back covered with piercing arrows. He bleeds profusely." *Arjuna's* chariot, commandeered by *Krishna,* chased after *Bhishma.* The sight was an eagle-eyed vision of a mass of clouds charged with lightning precipitously rushing towards the noble *Bhishma.*

Bhishma saw *Krishna* approaching and said to him: "Come, draw near. Come great charioteer whose eyes are like the blue lotus petals. O Lord of gods, I bow to you. O best of your tribe. I am not sorry losing today in this great battle of goodness against unrighteousness. O God, if slain by you in battle by the sinless one, great will be the good done to me. In the three worlds, no greater honour can be given to me today in this combat. Strike me as you please, for I am your captive."

As *Bhishma* lay on his back perched uncomfortably on a

bed of piercing arrows, *Yudhishthira,* the eldest *Pandu,* reflected for a long time, and moved away from where the grandsire lay wounded. He said these words to *Krishna:* "*Bhishma* is incapable of being conquered in battle, even if he is wounded and afflicted with arrows. I regard his life to be of high value, even this life that now seems difficult to save."

Krishna, with compassion, said these words to comfort *Yudhishthira,* "O son of *dharmic* virtue, you who are firm in truth, do not indulge in sorrow. You have invincible heroes for associates. They are true slayers of foes. Look at *Bheema,* granted with the energy of the Wind and Fire. The twin sons of *Madri* are more heroic than the chief of the celestials, *Indra.* Your brother *Arjuna* is my friend, relative, and disciple. I would cut off my own flesh and give it away for the sake of *Arjuna.* This young tiger among men would also lay down his life for Truth and for my sake, his teacher."

Then *Krishna* continued, "Once granted with pure intensity, *Bhishma,* the son of *Santanu* and *Ganga,* is now fogged up by a perverted judgment, decayed intelligence, and has little reason left for living. He does not know what he should now do. Let us all return to *Bhishma* and ask him for the way to his own death. He who practices harsh vows will give us counsel."

Bhishma addressed them saying, "Welcome *Krishna* of the *Vrishni* race. You too are welcome, O *Arjuna,* the mighty archer. Welcome also O King *Yudhishthira* the just, and you, *Bheema.* Welcome also to you twins. What can I do for you to reinforce your pleasure? Even if it is difficult, I will do it with all my soul."

"How and when would you like to leave this body which is sure to happen?" asks *Yudhishtra.*

"Not just yet, my son," replied the grandsire. "Congratulations you are now the king. While we wait for that moment of departure, speak what you wish."

Yudhishthira said, "Tell us the method of your own death. O great conqueror, injured as you are, how will we be battling you in this hour also?"

Hearing these words, *Santanu's* son said to the eldest *Pandu* sons: "As long as I the individualist am alive, O son of *Kunti,* victory cannot be yours in battle. After I am subdued, you may have your victory in battle. Therefore pummel me down without delay. After I am slain, all the rest will also be slain. Therefore do as I say. Only a woman was able to wound me. And only *Krishna* can comfort me to leave my body. *Ganga's* son must prepare to go to the otherworld."

Bhishma then became as an island sinking into the fathomless waters. The son of the oceangoing *Ganga* did not strike again and even as he lay wounded, *Bhishma* was able to ward off the god of death *Yama* and the god of life force *Varuna.* But, though pierced in every part, *Bhishma* elicited no signs of pain. He then began to reflect.

"Even now, with only one blow I could slay all the *Pandavas,* if the mighty *Vishnu* himself had not been their protector. Formerly, when my father *Santanu* wedded my stepmother *Satyavati,* he gave me two boons. First that I would be incapable of being slain by man in battle and second that my time of death should be of my own choice. I, the free spirit, now wish for my own death. Today however is not the proper time for departure."

Having discovered *Bhishma's* resolve, the *rishis* and the gods in the heavens stationed themselves where the individualistic *Bhishma* lay and said, "That, which he resolves, is approved by us also. O son of *Ganga,* act according to your resolution. Withdraw your heart from this battle."

With these words, a fragrant and special breeze charged with particles of water began to blow in *Bhishma's* direction. Heavenly cymbals of loud vigorous music began to beat. A flowery shower fell on *Bhishma.* Different vibrations of *Om* were not heard by anyone save *Bhishma* himself.

There was not on *Bhishm's* body space of even two fingers breath that was not pierced with arrows. He had fallen with his head to the east, a little before sunset. Felled, he looked like an uprooted emblem of *Indra,* making the earth tremble. While falling *Bhishma* had noted the Sun was in the southern solstice. He would not allow his senses to leave yet, thinking it inauspicious.

Ganga, his mother, heard of her son's resolve to leave his body and sent *Bhishma* the great *rishis* in a swanlike form, to the spot where *Bhishma,* the first among men, was lying on his bed of arrows. The swans walked around him and decided that he need not pass out of this world during the southern solstice. Having discussed this, they silently left.

Bhishma said to himself: "While waiting for the northern solstice I will cleave to my life. I will hold the spirit, and expect death during the northern declension. This boon granted to me by my distinguished father *Santanu,* should make my wish possible."

Bhishma lay on his bed of arrows without touching the earth with his body. The Earth also uttered loud shrieks when the son of *Santanu* lay slain and seemed to say, "This one is the most important of those familiar with the *Vedas.* Did not creatures long ago speak of this bull among men who now lies on his bed of arrows? This one, having found out that *Kama* or Desire afflicted his father, resolved to draw up his own ascent. Look at all his laughable *Kaurava* descendants stand here in shame, hanging down their heads. The virtuous *Pandavas* stand at his feet and swoon at the sight of their fallen warrior."

Santanu's son addressed the *Pandavas* and the *Kauravas,* "Welcome to all, you blessed ones. Gratified am I with your panoramic picture. You are equals in divinity." *Bhishma* addressed them while his head was hanging down. He said to them, "Let a pillow be given to me!"

The warriors fetched excellent pillows that were soft and made of delicate fabrics, but *Bhishma* needed them not.

The tiger among men then said, "*Arjuna,* O you mighty armed son of *Pandu,* my head hangs down, give me a pillow such as you regard fit"

Reverentially saluting *Bhishma, Arjuna* with tears said, "Command me, O invincible one, for I am your slave. What shall I do, O grandsire?"

"Get me a pillow! Indeed give me one without delay, that which befits my bed of arrows. You are the first of all the wielders of bows. You are familiar with the duties of warriors and are granted with intelligence and goodness."

Wishing to do *Bhishma's* bidding, *Arjuna* took up his bow and straight shafts. He inspired them with *mantras* and with great force pierced the earth. A cross of two arrows now support *Bhishma's* head. Seeing *Arjuna* divining his thoughts, *Bhishma* felt grateful and applauded *Arjuna,* "You have given me, O son of *Pandu,* a pillow that is well-situated and convenient as I lie on this bed of arrows. I will nod off on this bed till the Sun turns to the northern solstice. When the Sun on his chariot comes yoked by seven steeds of great speed, I will go towards the direction of *Vaishvanara,* the Cosmic Being."

As they all waited around, *Krishna* prompted *Yudhishtra* towards the grandsire. He must seek from him the wisdom of ruling not only himself, the family, the society and also the nation.

"O grandsire, who is a proverbial household name about everything, how shall we take home success and how do we bring in independence of all within sovereignty? How can the desolation of creatures be blocked?

"Sharing through input by each, righteousness and self-determination are the wellsprings of life. The story of the *Mahabharata* and its history will someday augment human intrinsic worth and virtues in both the readers and listeners. This sacred history will amplify resolves made for idealistic aims. Vow-observing scribes of many nations will bring about justice for mankind. It will improve and transform their devotion towards order and protection by rulers. It will grant attention and fairness for justice, equality and freedom in the subjects of the world. It will instil reverence for all workforce in every nation."

The blind king's eyes, *Sanjaya,* had seen the whole story unfold. He now viewed the battlefield of *Kurukshetra* where the *Pandu* army of virtue again faces the crushed *Kaurava* army of unrighteousness. *Sanjaya* reflects on the previous day's happenings. The blind king is secluded and in his own thoughts.

The blind king knew success in this battle could have given him opportunities for fame and greatness while in his earthly existence. The anguish he now suffers needs a makeover for secular and spiritual growth. He suddenly understands the significance of *Krishna* by which *Arjuna* had achieved understanding of the philosophy of living and about his duty to life. To correct his despondency-causing understanding *Arjuna* needed *Krishna* by his side.

The night passed away as if in suspense. The wounded were nursed and the dead were given final burial rites. The chaste approached *Bhishma* by the thousands. Like creatures of other worlds beholding the Sun, they covered him reverentially with medicinal and powdered sandalwood. Garlands of flowers adorned his majestic build. *Bhishma* cast his eyes on the assembled kings and asked for water to drink. They returned with gleaming vessels of cold water.

Santanu's son said, "I cannot, O sires, use any article holding the water used for human enjoyment. I am removed from the pale of humanity. I am laying on a bed of arrows, waiting for the return of the Moon and the Sun. Send for *Arjuna,* the great archer. Only he can provide me with water."

The heroic *Arjuna* who was also among the kings said, "So be it." He then mounted his chariot and lifted his bow with force and removed one arrow from the quiver on his back.

Arjuna forcefully stretched the string of the bow. The shrill twang of his bow and the slap of his palms resembled the roar of the thunder. The troops and kings shook from their apathy and roused with fear. *Arjuna* respectfully circled around the horizontally placed chief of the *Bharata* race – on this vertical forest of piercing arrows. He geared up a blazing arrow and inspired it with *mantras.* He branded it as *Krishna's* weapon, and in the sight of the entire army, he pierced the Earth a little to the south of where *Bhishma* lay. Then there arose a jet of water that was pure and special and cool. That water resembling nectar itself was of celestial scent and taste. It poured directly from the earth and into the grandsire's mouth. And with that cool jet of water *Arjuna* pleased *Bhishma.* All the rulers of the earth were filled with astonishment.

Santanu's son, his thirst quenched, then said praising *Arjuna* in the presence of all those kings: "O *Arjuna* of mighty arms, even the heavenly *guru, Narada* spoke well of you to the old *rishis.* We were told by many – with *Krishna* as your ally, you will achieve many mighty feats. They who have knowledge of such things know you to be the destroyer of evil. You are the foremost among men."

In the meantime, the eldest *Pandu* had returned to the palace. Accompanied by priests, *Yudhishthira* took with him a large quantity of clarified butter, floral garlands, scents, silken clothes, and excellent sandalwood for cremating the body of *Bhishma.* Placing the close family on chariots, he led his uncle *Dhritarashtra* and his queen *Gandhari* to where the old man of celebrated virtues lay. Those chariots, which followed, carried his mother *Kunti* and all his family. *Yudhishthira* with *Krishna* and *Vidura* of great wisdom went with a long trail of followers to the place where *Bhishma* lay on his bed of arrows. Eulogists and bards sang hymns of praise. The sacrificial fires of *Bhishma* were also borne in the procession.

Soon they all came on the spot where the son of *Santanu*

lay. *Vyasa* the author of this story, the heavenly guru *Narada, Devala* who later spread the story of *Mahabharata* and *Asita* who in time explained philosophy of rebirth, arrived. The miscellany of still living kings from various parts of the country were there waiting with reverence on *Bhishma. Yudhishthira* was attentive that his high-souled grandsire, as he lay on his heroic bed, was guarded on all sides.

Yudhishthira ordered all to alight from their chariot and with his family; they saluted their grandsire, the one who forever disciplined all foes. He approached that spot where *Bhishma* lay surrounded by reverential *rishis*. Then he addressed that first one of the *Kuru* race, the son of the River *Ganga,* as he lay on that bed, saying, "I am *Yudhishthira.* We salute you, O son of *Ganga.* If you hear me still, tell me what I am to do for you. I bear with me the sacrificial fires. We have come here, O King, and wait on you for this signalled hour. Preceptors of all branches of learning, priests, all my family, and your son *Dhritarashtra* are all here with my counsellors. *Krishna* is also here. Open your eyes, O chief of the *Kuru* race, and behold them."

Thus addressed, *Bhishma* opened his eyes. Taking the strong hand of *Yudhishthira,* he addressed him in a voice as deep as that of the clouds. "By good luck, O son of *Kunti,* you have come here with all your counsellors. The holy Sun has begun its northward course. I have been lying here on my bed for fifty-eight nights. I have felt this period to be as long as if it were a century. The lunar month has come. The lit fortnight is over."

Bhishma then addressed the blind king, "O King *Dhritarashtra,* you are well-conversant with duties. All your doubts about the science of wealth have been solved during your discussions with *Sanjaya* as I lay on my bed of arrows. You have waited on many scribes of learning. The subtle sciences connected with the *Vedas,* all duties of religion, and all the four *Vedas* are all well known to you. You should not grieve, therefore, O son of *Kuru.* That which was preordained has happened. You have heard the mysteries about duties from the lips of *Vyasa* himself. *Yudhishthira* and his family are morally as much your sons as they are the sons of *Pandu.* Observe duties to religion, cherish and protect them. In their turn, they will always remain devoted to their seniors. *Yudhishthira* the just is pure-souled. He will always remain obedient to you. Your own sons were depraved and wedded to wrath and lust. Overwhelmed by jealousy, they picked up wickedness. Do not grieve for them, they who have been slain."

Bhishma then turned to *Krishna* and said: "O holy one, O God of all gods, greetings to you. O wielder of the conch, discus, and mace, you are the planner of the universe and are of vast parts. You are the total Soul and the individual soul. Rescue me and give me permission to go from this world. Virtue is where *Krishna* is. I counselled the *Kaurava* family to make peace with the *Pandavas.* The foolish *Duryodhana* did not do my bidding and caused havoc on the earth, and lay down his life. The heavenly preceptor *Narada* told me that you and *Arjuna* are old *rishis* born among men. O *Krishna,* grant me leave, I shall cast off my body. Sanctioned by you, I shall arrive to the highest end."

Krishna said: "I give you permission to leave. Do what must be done and grasp the status of angelic *Vasus.* You have not been guilty of a single misdeed in this world. O royal sage, you remained devoted to your father. It is therefore that death awaits your pleasure."

Bhishma once more addressed the *Pandavas* headed by the blind *Dhritarashtra* and other well wishers and said: "I want to cast off my life-breath."

Having said this, *Bhishma,* the son of *Santanu* became silent. He connected with and then withdrew the *pranic* life-breath consecutively from different parts of the body as pointed out in *Yoga.* The enlivening *prana,* now restrained then rose towards the cranium. Within a short time, the entire body of *Bhishma* became limp and senseless. Those who watched were filled with wonder. The life-breath, restrained and unable to escape through any of the outlets, pierced the crown of *Bhishma's* head and rose to heaven.

Heavenly drums began to play and floral showers rained down. Evolved souls and *rishis* filled with delight exclaimed, "Excellent! Excellent! The life breath of *Bhishma* piercing through the crown shot up through the skull like a meteor and became invisible. This is how *Santanu's* son, that pillar of the *Bharata* race, united himself with Eternity."

Then the high-souled *Pandavas* and their uncle *Vidura* took large quantities of wood, diverse kinds of fragrant scents, and made a funeral pyre. *Yudhishthira* wrapped *Bhishma's* body with silken cloth and floral garlands. The *Pandava* family held an umbrella, and fanned the body with pure white yak tails. The twins *of Madri, Nakula* and *Sahadev* held two headgears. *Yudhishthira* and the blind king *Dhritarashtra* stood at the feet of the lord of the *Kurus.* The *Pitri* sacrifice for ancestors was performed. Libations were poured on the sacred fire. The singers sang many *Samans,* or *mantras* about the highest Reality. Then, covering the body of *Ganga's* son with sandalwood, black aloe, bark wood, and fragrant fuel, they set fire to the body, standing to the right of the funeral pyre.

Having cremated the first one of the *Kuru* race, they gathered the ashes of the *Ganga's* son and advanced to the sacred *Bhagirathi,* the river *Ganga. Vyasa, Narada, Krishna,* the women of the *Bharata* race, and the citizens of *Hastinapur* followed them. When they arrived at the sacred river they offered oblations of water to the son of *Ganga.*

With this, *Ganga* rose from the stream, weeping and distracted by sorrow. Amid her lamentations, she addressed the *Kurus,* O sinless ones, listen to me as I tell you what happened to my son. Possessed of royal conduct and disposition, and granted with wisdom and high birth, my son was the beneficiary of all the elders of his race. He was devoted to his father and his vows. He could not be conquered with celestial weapons of great energy. A woman, *Sikhandi,* whom he would never strike, defeated him. It breaks my heart to see my son dead. There was no one on earth that equalled him in might. My heart breaks on hearing about the slaughter of my son by *Sikhandi*!"

Krishna hearing the goddess of the great river indulging in lamentations consoled her with soothing words, "O amiable one, be comforted. Do not yield to grief. Without doubt, your son has gone to the highest region of bliss. He was one of the angelic *Vasus* of great energy. Through a curse, he had to take birth among men. You must not grieve for him. In accordance with warrior-like *Kshatriya* duties, your son was slain by the mighty warrior *Dhananjaya – Arjuna,* while engaged in battle. He was not slain by *Sikhandi,* O goddess. O you of beautiful face, your son, with pleasure has gone to heaven. Let the malady of your heart be dispelled. Remember he was one of the *Vasus,* O goddess!"

Thus addressed by *Krishna, Ganga* was restored to composure. All the kings present, headed by *Krishna,* honoured that goddess *Ganga,* and received permission to go from her banks.

Aum Tat Sat

Glossary of Sanskrit Terms

A

Abhayam	fearlessness
Abhyas	repetition/practice
Achala	fixed
Achintya	unthinkable
Achetana	unconscious
Achit	inanimate matter
Achyuta	indestructible
Adbhuta	wonderful
Adharma	degraded or lowly
Adhibhuta	primordial form of matter
Adhyatma	spiritual science
Adrishta	unseen principal
Advaita	monism or non-dualism
Advaita Vedanta	non-dual philosophy that Reality is the only existence
Agati	stability
Agni	fire
Agni vidya	meditating on Fire as symbolizing Brahman or God
Aguna	without quality or guna
Aham	I the ego
Ahamkara	"I-am" – ness
Ahamkara-rajasic	dynamic egoism
Ahamkara-tamasic	inert or ignorant egoism
Ahamkara-sattvic	virtuous egoism

Ahamkara tyaga	renunciation of ego
Aham karta	I am the doer
Ahimsa	non-injury in thought words or deed
Aishvarya	materialistic or spiritual wealth
Ajapa	mantra 'soham' for 'I am He' produced by the breath itself
Ajapa-gayatri	hamsaa-soham
Agyana	ignorance
Akarma	inaction
Akarta	non-doer
Akhanda	indivisible
Akshara	syllable of imperishable Brahman
Alinga	without mark
Amrita	nectar
Anadi	beginningless
Anahata	fourth chakra opposite the heart
Ananta	infinite
Annam	matter or food
Annamaya kosha	food sheath
Antaratma	indwelling soul
Anu	atom
Anubhava	perception or direct experience
Apah	water
Apana	nerve current for excretory functions of the abdominal region
Apunya	sinful
Artha	object of desire or wealth
Asat	that which is not
Asteya	non-stealing
Asthira	wavering
Ashubha	inauspicious
Asura	evil tendencies of man

Ashvata	peepal or banyan tree
Atyanta	too much
Avatara	incarnation of divinity on the human plane
Avidya	ignorance; Shakti – the illusive power of Brahman also called Maya
Ayukta	lacking concentration or one who is not a yogi
Abhasa	not true
Aditya	sun-god
Ahara	any food for the senses
Ahuti	oblation
Akasha	ether
Ananda	happiness
Aradhana	worship
Arati	divine service at the altar
Asana	posture
Ashrama	hermitage
Atma	Self or soul

B

Bandha	bondage
Bhagavan	Lord
Bhajana	worshipping Lord
Bhakti	devotion
Bhavana	attitude
Bhaya	fear
Bhiksha	alms
Bhuh	earth plane
Bhuvah	astral world
Bija	seed
Bindu	point or dot
Brahma	God the Creator

Brahmachari	celibate
Brahman	Reality or God or Supreme reality or Spirit & Matter Or Consciousness or combined purusha and prakriti Or Purushottama
Brahmanda	macrocosm
Buddhi	intellect

C

Chaitanya	consciousness that knows itself
Chakra	plexus or center of psychic energy
Chinmaya	full of consciousness
Chit	universal intelligence
Chitta	mind-intellect-ego or subconscious mind or feeling or personality

D

Daitya	giants
Daiva	controllers of destiny
Dana	charity
Daivi	divine
Daya	mercy
Deha	physical body
Devata	deity
Dhana	wealth, dharana concentration
Dharma	righteous living or duty
Dhyana	contemplation
Divya	heavenly

E

Eka	one

G

Gayatri — mantra Vedic
Gotra — family
Guna — quality born of nature
Guru — preceptor

H

Hamsaa yoga — mantra involuntarily uttered with each breath
Hari — Krishna

I

Ida — psychic nerve current flowing through the left nostril
Indra — lord of the senses or chief of celestials or rain-god

J

Jagat — changing world
Jiva — individual soul with ego

K

Kama — desire or passion or lust
Karma — action – 3 types: sanchita of previous births; prarabhda being worked out in this life; agami operating presently
Kaya — physical body
Kosha — sheath
Kriya — particular action
Krodha — anger
Kripa — mercy
Kshara — perishable
Kshatriya dharma — code of conduct of the warrior class

Kshetra	field
Kundalini	primordial cosmic energy located in the spinal cord
Kusha	grass used for ritualistic purposes
Kutastha	center of changelessness found without exception in all creatures who shines as the Self and remains as the witness of the mind and intellect; rock-seated; unchanging, another name for Brahman
Kutastha chaitanya	individual inner consciousness

L

Lila	sport or play
Linga	sign or symbol
Lobha	greed
Loka	world of names and forms

M

Mada	pride
Maharishi	great sage
Mahat	first product of creation as intellect
Mahatma	great soul
Mahatattva	great principle of intelligence
Maheshvara	great lord or Shiva
Mala	rosary
Manana	reflection
Manas	mind
Mantra	sacred syllable
Mantra-shakti	power of mantra
Matsarya	jealousy
Mauna	silence
Maya	veiling power of Brahman projecting the universe

Mithya	false
Moha	deluded attachment
Moksha	release or liberation
Mrityu	death
Mudra	exercises during worship
Mukta	liberated one
Muni	sage
Murti	image

N

Nadi	nerve channel or psychic channel
Narayana	name for God meaning Being that supports all things
Nidra	sleep
Nirvana	final emancipation
Niyama	internal and external purification

O

Ojas	spiritual energy
Om	syllable symbolizing Brahman
Omkar	same as Om
Om Tat Sat	designation of Brahman used for benediction

P

Padma	lotus
Phala	fruit
Pingala	psychic current terminating at the right nostril
Pitr	deceased progenitors of ancestors
Pitra-yagna	sacrificial rites of all householders gratifying the manes
Pradakshina	circumambulating

Prakriti	causal matter
Pralaya	dissolution of cosmos
Prana	life force
Pranayama	regulation of breath
Pranava	syllable Om
Puja	adoration
Punya	merit
Purusha	best of purushas in the heart of all being as Spirit or Self
Purushottama	lord of the universe

R

Rajas	dynamism, dynamic in nature
Rishi	seer of truth

S

Sa	she
Shabda	sound of Om
Sah	he
Saham	she I am
Shakti	divine power or energy
Samadhi	superconsciousness
Samsara	worldly life through repeated births and deaths
Sannyasa	renunciation
Sat	existence
Satya	truth
Sneha	friendship
Shudhra	servant class
Sushumna	psychic current piercing all chakras in the spinal cord
Svadharma	one's duty in accordance with eternal law

T

Tamas	inertia, ignorance, perishability, darkness
Taijas	subtle
Tapas	austerity
Tattva	element
Tejas	brilliant as fire
Tyaga	renunciation

V

Vairagya	indifference, detachment
Vaasana	subtle desires
Vayu	wind-god
Veda	highest scriptural authority
Vedanta	end of Vedas containing Upanishads upholding Hindu thought
Vishva-rupa	Cosmic Form containing multiforms

Y

Yagna	sacrifice
Yama	death-god dispensing justice
Yoga	union
Yogi	one who practices yoga
Yoni	womb
Yonimudra	Mudra that enables one to hear the Om sounds

Bibliography

The Holy Geeta by Swami Chinmayananda

Bhagavad Geeta by Swami Hari Har Ananda

Srimad Bhagavad Gita by Mahasaya Lahiri and Swami Yukteshwar

Talks on the Gita by Vinoba Bhave

God Talks with Arjuna: The Bhagavad Gita by Paramahansa Yogananda

The Mahabharata translated by Kesari Mohan Ganguli

Light on the Yoga Sutras by B K S Iyengar